T0129433

America in the
United States
—— and the ——
United States
in America

GABRIEL MORAN

America in the United States —— and the —— United States in America

A Philosophical Essay

iUniverse®

AMERICA IN THE UNITED STATES AND THE UNITED STATES IN AMERICA
A PHILOSOPHICAL ESSAY

iUniverse books may be ordered through booksellers or by contacting:

iUniverse
1663 Liberty Drive
Bloomington, IN 47403
www.iuniverse.com
1-800-Authors (1-800-288-4677)

Because of the dynamic nature of the internet, any web addresses or links contained in this book may have changed since publication and may no longer be valid. The views expressed in this work are solely those of the author and do not necessarily reflect the views of the publisher, and the publisher hereby disclaims any responsibility for them.

Any people depicted in stock imagery provided by Getty Images are models, and such images are being used for illustrative purposes only.
Certain stock imagery © Getty Images.

ISBN: 978-1-5320-4447-2 (sc)
ISBN: 978-1-5320-4448-9 (hc)
ISBN: 978-1-5320-4446-5 (e)

Library of Congress Control Number: 2018905224

Print information available on the last page.

iUniverse rev. date: 08/27/2018

Contents

Preface

I have been waiting for half a century for someone to write this book. Since to my knowledge no one has, I am taking up the challenge. It was during the war in Vietnam that I was struck by what seemed to be a peculiar confusion in the United States about how to talk about the country and its history. A slogan at that time warned dissenters: "America. Love it or Leave it." I wondered why that was the choice. Why was it "anti-American" to oppose the war? I did not think I had a problem with "America," but I was opposed to what the United States, through its government, was doing in another country. Why did it seem impossible to state that disagreement and have it be heard? Both the proponents of the war and the critics of the war seemed locked into a language that did not get us anywhere.

Whatever was the problem at that time, it obviously did not start in the 1960s. And the war's end did not clear up the problem. In fact, as I followed the issue through the following decades, the linguistic confusion got worse. Unfortunately, evidence suggests that the 2016 election may have brought the problem to a terrible crisis point. The country has become so divided that it is difficult to see how a unity can be reestablished.

There cannot be a solution for the disunity of the country without grasping the problem of how "America" is used in the United States, but there seems little awareness on any side that there is a problem at all. This problem, which runs throughout the entire history of the United States and has roots that go back to the sixteenth-century origin of "America," cannot be solved by introducing some clever new word or by calling for a definition of terms.

The only way to understand the problem and to suggest a way to address it is by showing its presence and its effects throughout American and US histories. There is no lack of material. On the contrary, the material is nearly endless. This book is a very selective use of the evidence, but I hope that my chosen examples will provoke the reader to examine the language of America as it is spoken in the United States.

This book is not an attack on America. Left-wing critics who attack America, either from within or from outside the nation, have little persuasive power with the citizenry. The most realistic and effective criticism of this country is found in documents that say little to nothing about "America" but deal with facts about the United States and its government. This book is an attempt to join that criticism by clarifying the relation of the United States to America.

Despite what may appear to be a historical study, this book is mainly a philosophical study of language. Our ways of speaking affect the ways we think. The first chapter is an invitation to the reader to consider the possibility that the language we use when speaking about the country underlies almost every political, cultural, and economic problem. The reason many badly needed reforms are not carried out is that it is nearly impossible to talk about the actual country. Even more serious, the foreign policy of the United States is enveloped in mythical language that leads the nation into disastrous involvements in other nations. This book examines the 500-year history of "America" and its relation to the 230-year history of the United States.

1

The United States and America

The premise of this book can be simply stated: the most basic problem in the United States is confusion between itself—an existing nation-state—and a mythical idea termed "America." The solution to this problem can also be simply stated: people, especially world leaders, should speak in a way that eliminates, or at least mitigates, this confusion. This book advocates a distinction that everyone knows and that everyone knows is correct, yet the distinction is constantly violated in practice. The violations are so common that there is only a dim awareness that there is any problem at all. That is why it is the most basic problem in the United States—a problem that influences US foreign policy and every aspect of its domestic life.

A consistent distinction between the United States and America would not solve all the domestic problems of the United States or eliminate the intense hatred of the country found in many countries. The distinction would simply make possible a more helpful discussion of what is good and what is bad about the intentions, influence, and policies of the United States.[1]

---

1   Kurt Andersen's *Fantasyland: How America Went Haywire: A 500 Year History* (New York: Random House, 2017) is an engaging history of the myth of America since the first English American settlements. The author makes no attempt to sort out the conflicting meanings in the term "America." The result is a lack of context for understanding the bizarre aspects of "America" in relation to the emergence of the United States as a world power. He is right that "America was the dream world creation of fantasists" (426), but that seems to make impossible

This book fits neither on the political left nor on the political right. It is an attempt to step back from the radical split in today's politics. Its aim is to open a conversation that is impossible to have so long as both the left and the right offer up their contrasting versions of America. The problem is more obvious in the language of the political right, but the left does little to provide an alternative.

"America" from the first use of the term, has referred both to an ideal world and to a continent. When the United States calls itself "America," it does two things: it confuses the country with a mythical idea, and it also obscures the existence of other American nations. The distinction advocated in this book is thus a struggle on two fronts. First, the distinction is an insistence that the United States is a nation, not a mythical idea. Second, the distinction recognizes that the United States is one of the nations on the American continent. Consequently, if the distinction between "the United States" and "America" were consistently put into practice, it would have two effects: It would restrain the United States in its missionary impulse toward the rest of the world, and it would encourage bilateral relations with other American nations.

The title of this book, *America in the United States and the United States in America,* indicates a priority for the problem of "America" as a mythical idea. Periodically, someone points out that there are other nation-states on the American continent—a geographical fact that is obvious. But there is usually an obliviousness of the much more fundamental problem with "America"—that is, the mythical meaning of "America" that prevents a realistic discussion of the strengths and weaknesses of the United States.

Elizabeth Cobbs Hoffman, in the first footnote of her book *American Umpire,* dismisses any significance to the distinction between "United States" and "America." She asks, "What's in a name?" and answers, "Not much, except a handy identifier generally associated with the first group to use it."[2] Her view is not uncommon, but it is nonetheless shockingly innocent regarding the importance of language. The purpose of this book is to show that there is much in a name.

---

his claim that "it will require a struggle to make America reality-based again" (439).

2   Elizabeth Cobbs Hoffman, *American Umpire* (Cambridge, MA: Harvard University Press, 2013), footnote 1.

The Philosophical Question of Language

In making my case, I begin with a general reflection on the relations between speech, thought, and action. This book is a philosophical essay that attempts to get at a problem of language. It is not an attempt to write a new history of the United States. Even less is it an "untold history" of the country in the manner of people who are attracted to conspiracy theories.[3] I depend on the work of reputable historians. I am not searching for hidden documents; I am looking at what is right on the surface of known facts. "The aspect of things that are most important for us are hidden because of their simplicity and familiarity. One is unable to notice something because it is always before one's eyes."[4]

Meaning and Context

In the statement that the focus of this book is the study of the United States in relation to "America," the quotation marks indicate that the meaning of the *term* "America" is the issue. I will have to remind the reader periodically that I am referring not to America but to "America." One of the most dominant themes in philosophy throughout the last century has been the importance of language. Perhaps the most important point in that concern is the recognition that language not only expresses thinking but that language in turn is formative of thinking. Hardly anyone would deny that the way we think is important in determining the way we speak. But it is less often realized that the way we speak influences the way we think.

An emphasis on language is often taken to mean that people should define their terms before the start of a discussion. When there is

---

3   Oliver Stone and Peter Kuznick did a ten-part series on Showtime called "The Untold History of the United States" based on their book by the same name (New York: Gallery Books, 2012). Many people were surprised that the series was not as extreme as Stone's films have often been. An encouraging sign was that it was an attempt to tell the history of the United States, not the history of America. But as many historians pointed out, it was not an "untold" history. It was an interpretation of events that have been recounted many times. The interpretation itself, for the most part, leaned only a little left from academic interpretations that have become common.

4   Ludwig Wittgenstein, *Philosophical Investigations* (New York: Macmillan, 1953), 129.

disagreement about how to define an ambiguous word, people regularly go to a dictionary to find out the true or the real meaning of a word. A dictionary that defines one word simply by equating it with several other words is not much help.

A more helpful dictionary provides contexts in which the word has been used. The *Oxford English Dictionary* (OED) does not provide the definition of a word; it provides meanings of a word in use. Any good dictionary today does a mini version of the OED's gigantic project. It is always helpful to know the etymology of a word, why someone thought a new word was needed, who first used the word, and the word's subsequent history. The English language is a crazy quilt that is derived from many other languages. Knowing where a word came from and what has been its evolution of meaning are particularly helpful in the examination of English words.

Some books list multiple definitions of terms that have long histories. For example, there are numerous books that provide a half dozen definitions of "nature," one of the most ambiguous words in the English language. One work claimed to find sixty-six definitions of "nature."[5] But six or sixty-six definitions do not help much in understanding how to use a term. One needs to know the original meaning of the word and a history of its important shifts in meaning. Many words have one dramatic change of meaning, almost to the point of a reversal in meaning. A few words (such as "nature") have several major shifts in their histories. In using a term today, one has to control the ambiguity of the term by considering each main context in which it has been used.

It is not convincing when a speaker says that a word has three meanings and then says he or she is going to *stipulate* a chosen meaning. What a speaker *intends* to mean by a word has a limited effect upon the meaning that is conveyed. The word still carries the two, three, or more meanings that were first identified. For a word that has recently been coined or is used for an esoteric purpose, the speaker may be able to control most of the meaning of the word. But any word that has been around for a while already carries more than one meaning, which both the speaker and the

---

5   Arthur Lovejoy and Franz Boas, *Primitivism and Related Ideas in Antiquity* (New York: Octagon, 1965).

listener encounter either consciously or subconsciously. Nietzsche's dictum that any word that has a history cannot be defined applies to nearly all words.[6]

An individual word abstracted from its use does not have a meaning. A person who says "Uh oh" can mean a half dozen things depending upon the literary and social context or the tone of voice when it is used. The meaning of a word is determined by examining its history (past uses) and its geography (present uses). Neither source can be exhaustively examined. In trying to convince someone of the meaning or meanings of a term, one can only present a series of examples of the word in its contexts until one's interlocutor says, "Now I see"—that is, "I recognize the meanings."

Human language is such an ordinary reality that people are barely aware of it until they are brought up short when they find themselves surrounded by people who speak a different language. It is not just that some people happen to have other names for rocks, rivers, and rain. Anyone who tries to learn another language by memorizing words from that language discovers that such an approach does not work. If one does not know the language of the country that one is in, it helps to memorize words for "toilet," "train station," or "price"; nevertheless, learning the language is not a matter of just adding words to the list.

A person might manage to read a language by studying it, but one can only learn to speak a second language similarly to the way one learned one's native language—namely, by living among people who speak the language. Humans begin life by acting to survive. The child watches carefully the activities of people in the vicinity—especially the people who are providing food, warmth, and protection. The child tries to imitate the activities of those people, including their flow of speech. The activities of eating breakfast and going to bed are associated with strings of sounds. A small child cannot put together a proper sentence with subject, predicate, and modifiers. The most that the child may be able to manage is a few words, or even one word, but "hungry" and "no" can be used as sentences of desire or rejection.

---

6   Friedrich Nietzsche, *Genealogy of Morals*, vol. 2 (New York: Oxford University Press, 2009), 13.

People who study children, and those who care for small children, are well aware of this process.[7] But most of us become oblivious to the mysteries of language and some elementary truths about language. An adult cannot duplicate a child's openness and lack of fear at making embarrassing mistakes. Some adults come close to that attitude; they have a childlike approach of letting themselves be immersed in the language rather than trying to remember a grammatical rule or the meaning of a word.

A scandal in the history of philosophy is that most philosophers have given little attention to how infants and young children learn a language. With few exceptions, modern philosophers examine knowledge by looking into the mind of a middle-aged man.[8] As a result, most philosophical theories about knowledge do not reflect how children first learn through immersion in adult conversation and how people continue to learn by using the language that is available to them.

In the ready-made language provided to a person, there are words for each thing that one wishes to name. Occasionally one notices that the name of something is confusing or illogical, but so long as other people use the word in the same way, there is no problem in making oneself understood. A speaker is surprised when he or she says something that seems obvious, only to have other people misunderstand. An individual's limited control of the meaning of his or her words is painfully brought home when the speaker is accused of racial, religious, ethnic, or some other kind of prejudice. The speaker's inevitable line of defense is "That is not what I meant" or "I did not intend to insult anyone." Sometimes, indeed, the speaker may not be at fault; an individual or a small group of individuals may take umbrage at all kinds of perceived slights.

---

7   Alison Gopnik, *The Philosophical Baby: What Children's Minds Tell Us about Truth, Love, and the Meaning of Life* (New York: Farrar, Straus and Giroux, 2009).

8   There are exceptions to this indictment. Augustine of Hippo and Jean-Jacques Rousseau were keenly aware of the importance of infancy and early childhood for philosophy. Most striking is the work of Ludwig Wittgenstein's *Philosophical Investigations*, which concentrates on how language is originally learned and the place of language in all knowledge. Sigmund Freud led the twentieth-century interest in infants and young children, but the work has been mainly carried out by psychologists, not philosophers.

In many cases, however, a speaker offends a whole race or a religion without intending to do so. Saying "I did not intend to offend anyone" may gain some forgiveness for the individual, but it actually worsens the seriousness of the case. It means that the problem is deeply buried in the words that were used.[9] If someone says something with the intention of offending a group of people, the remedy is clear: stop saying that and apologize. But if someone is not conscious of offending a group, then the remedy may require a change of life on the part of a group that speaks that way.

For example, the emergence of the Christian church from Judaism included using language that had an anti-Jewish bias. That kind of thing is typical, if not universal, in religious reform movements. The bias can fade away with time as the reform group goes its own way. But if the two groups regularly interact, the biased language can worsen. As the second group defines itself more clearly, it uses the first group as a foil, and the first group may push back. Even though there is considerable overlap in the language they use, the people in each group wish to clearly differentiate themselves from the other group.

The long history of Jewish-Christian relations is a sad and tragic story. Over the last half-century, Christian scholars and church officials have made admirable efforts to root out anti-Jewish bias in their religion.[10] Most Christians and many theologians still do not grasp how deep the problem is buried. Only with much more conversation between Christians and Jews—including that between ordinary people as well as scholars—will each group learn how to profess its religious belief in a way that fully accepts the existence of the other and makes possible an extensive cooperation between them.

---

9   Friedrich Nietzsche, *Beyond Good and Evil* (New York Penguin Books, 1973), 45: "The suspicion has arisen that the decisive value of an action resides in precisely that which is *not intentional* in it."

10 A recent effort of the Roman Catholic Church is a 2015 document from the Vatican entitled *The Gifts and Calling of God are Irrevocable*. The intention is praiseworthy, but the Church has a long way to go in rethinking its doctrine in relation to Judaism. Jewish efforts in response can be found in *Between Jerusalem and Rome*, the first official declaration on Christianity by rabbinical organizations, described by the German bishops as "a milestone in Christian-Jewish relations." the *Tablet* (London), September 9, 2017, 30.

Meaning and Form

The context of a word's meaning refers not just to the surrounding words but also to the form of speech in which the word is used. Examples of forms of speech are telling, asking, asserting, doubting, celebrating, mourning, and praying. The form of speech and the meaning of a word depend on what kind of action a person is performing. I will comment on differences of meaning when one is speaking politically or artistically.

Political Speech

Politics is a form of speech that has its own purpose by which it is measured. No one gets elected to an office and nobody exercises political power by just stating factual truths. But politics should not be a matter of telling lies. The issue of political speech is how to shape language so it reaches into people's lives, memories, and convictions. Political speakers try to change people's minds and hearts by means that go beyond stating facts and making scientific deductions. Politicians are embarrassed to admit that their form of speech is a kind of preaching. Their embarrassment at admitting the form of their speech is one reason that so many of them do it poorly.

Today's political speech in the United States may show the triumph of the policy enunciated by John Mitchell, US attorney general under Richard Nixon. Mitchell said, "Watch what we do, not what we say." The trouble with that policy is that speaking is the main thing politicians do. Barack Obama was less cynical but equally dismissive of political speech when, commenting on the lack of indictment of a police officer in the killing of an unarmed black man, he said, "I am not interested in talk; I'm interested in action." There is a terrible irony in Obama dismissing talk in the middle of a talk. Like Mitchell's statement, the words undermine the value of political speech.[11] The separation of words and *other* actions reduces the value of political speech to simply another instrument of raw power.

---

11 William Safire defended Mitchell at the time of his death by claiming that Mitchell's slogan was an assurance to blacks in the South about what the Nixon administration would do for them. Safire is no doubt accurate, but that strategy meant that the Nixon administration had to constantly use falsehood to mask what it was doing. William Safire, "Watch What We Do," *New York Times,*

Many people today dismiss the criticism of political speech as not worth bothering about because no one takes the words of politicians seriously. In his 2002 State of the Union address, George W. Bush used the phrase "axis of evil." He was surprised when his remarks set off student protests the next day in Tehran. The young people seemed to take Bush's words more seriously than he did. They knew that such phrases, casually tossed out, can have serious consequences.

Political skill can produce its own profound truths that are distinct from factual assertions. "To assert that 'Freedom is better than slavery' or 'All men are of equal worth' is not to state a fact but to choose a side."[12] The statements are not, or at least need not be, empty platitudes or mere rhetoric. They can be part of establishing the basis of realizing freedom or equality in practice. The political speaker is expressing a willingness to be on the side of the movement in which these statements are true. One could conceivably use the term "America" as a way to urge US citizens to create a country of greater justice. There has, in fact, been some remarkable writing and speaking on "America" by US blacks who, while keenly aware that their country is not America, have retained a hope for "the land that never has been yet—And yet must be—the land where every man is free."[13]

Artistic Speech

Another area of human life in which speech is used with a distinct form and particular purpose is art. The reader or listener may find a meaning in the work of art that the artist did not intend to put there. Sometimes that result is a gross misreading of the art. But it is true for the artist, as for everyone else, that the meaning of what is said is not confined to what the speaker intended.

November 14, 1988. Barack Obama's comment was about the Eric Garner case in New York City when the grand jury announced a decision not to indict. "President Obama on the Eric Garner Decision," *Newsweek*, February 22, 2014.

12 Dwight Macdonald, *The Responsibility of Peoples and other Essays in Political Criticism* (London: Gallancz, 1957), 55.

13 Langston Hughes, "Let America Be America Again" in *Selected Poems of Langston Hughes* (New York: Random House, 1974), 291-97.

In literary art, the main story is how the words are put together. A poet uses language for a different purpose than a novelist does, although the distinction is not airtight. The poet tries to express some truth about life—a truth most of us are likely to miss. The poet, having experienced something profound, uses the frail medium of words to provide a response. The words may fail to be adequate for their task, or the listener may not be ready to hear a truth that is painful, frightening, or mysterious. Great works of literature are likely to require time to be appreciated, both by the individual who encounters a work of art and by the human race, which is slow to grasp greatness.

A poet or a composer is rightly said to have license to use language in unusual ways. My criticism of the use of "America" might suggest to the reader that I have no appreciation of poetic speech. I claim no special talent in that area, but I do know the difference between a president making a foreign policy statement and someone writing a poem or a song about "America." Poetry is not history or philosophy or political science.

The danger lies in poetic myth being so omnipresent as to obscure or eliminate a grasp of the events that historians are intent on describing. "America" lends itself to poetry, music, and myth-making better than does the name of a nation-state. No one felt inspired to write a song called "United States the Beautiful." Who could oppose the sentiments of "God Bless America," although someone might wonder about its place in the seventh-inning stretch of US baseball games. If people in Brazil or Mexico sang "God Bless America" or "America the Beautiful" about their respective countries, the land and the myth would seem to have a fruitful relation. However, the lyrics of "America the Beautiful" and "God Bless America" are not directed at Brazil, Mexico, or any American nation except the United States.

Meaning and Exclusion

Language intrinsically includes and excludes. If a speaker were to attempt to speak without excluding anyone, his or her language would consist of empty generalities. But there is a legitimate concern regarding a use of language with a particular reference that unfairly excludes some groups. If $x = a + b$ and yet a common way of speaking is $x = a$, then b will lose out on political and economic power or even recognition of its existence. The most obvious case, but one that was not at all obvious to most people fifty years ago, was a bias against women in the English language. "Man" and "he" were routinely used to refer to all humans as well as only to males. When some women and men pointed out this fact, they were at first ridiculed. The standard responses were "You can't change language; anyway, that is just a way of speaking," "Everyone knows what is meant," and "That's too silly to be worth discussing." These days, however, there is not a male politician or a businessman who does not watch his gender-inclusive language. The revolution is not over, because the English language needs more elegant solutions, for example, in referring to "he and she." But going back to using "he" in the sense of "he and she" is clearly not an option. Once you have seen the problem, you cannot unsee it.

This particular problem of the English language was not a case of discovering that "my goodness, women have been accidentally excluded." The language in use reflected the social, political, and economic reality of what English-speaking nations had constructed in modern centuries. Language eventually began to change when the social and political realities had begun to change; then the language, in turn, opened up more changes. When only 2 percent of physicians were women, it may have seemed unnecessary or even silly to say "he or she" in reference to a physician. But that use of language was a needed step toward medical schools becoming 50 percent women. The recent awkward changes to the English language were an indispensable part of improving women's lives.

The fact that US citizens so often refer to their country as "America" and that they have succeeded in getting most of the world to speak that way is reflective of how they understand their country and how people in other countries perceive the United States. Similar to gender relations, this illogical use of language reflects social, political, and economic relations. To the extent that "America" carries social, political, and economic significance, those other nations tend to lose out or become almost invisible in the United States.

The language spoken in the United States shapes the worldview of US Americans. When this issue surfaces in the United States, it is usually dismissed with a bit of humor. In a column entitled "In Search of the Real Namericans," William Safire wrote that "other residents of the Americas were taking umbrage at this linguistic imperialism. Our persnickety good neighbors to the south are Americans, too." Safire ridiculed any proposed neologism for people of the United States and concluded that it would be wiser to stick with "American." "Our diplomats can point out it is short for United States of Americans, which is a mouthful."[14] Safire did not even notice the underlying problem of equating the United States and America. The whole issue was reduced to a joke.

A more serious example can be found in a document from the Clinton library. Responding to a letter by Wendy Gray that asked about President Clinton's use of "America" and "American," David Halperin wrote, "The basic rule, as I perceive it (no one ever explained), is we use 'Americans' a heck of a lot because POTUS likes it, it's shorter, it has an easier possessive, it sounds great – except when we address Latin America." Halperin admits that "using 'Americans' is not only misleading, it is also considered insulting by the Latins and all who love them (not to mention Canadians). But hey (Wendy!), it's our century – the American century."[15] Halperin's lame attempt at humor cannot cover over the arrogance of asserting that we—the superior country—can insult anyone we care to insult. The deeper problem that both Halperin and Safire show in their use of ridicule is obliviousness to the fact that their "America" is a myth and not a nation-state.

Examining US Language

In this book, I try to look at the United States from the perspective of an impartial observer, which, I admit, may be impossible for anyone immersed since birth in the glories of America. If one revolts against the smothering patriotic rhetoric in the country, the result very often is a cynical antipatriotism. But if one's focus is language, one need not become disillusioned on discovering that, in contrast to the shiny American history that is celebrated in schoolbooks, US history is a mixture of the good, the bad, and the downright awful.

---

14   William Safire, "In Search of the Real Namericans," *New York Times Magazine*, June 29, 1986.

15   David Halperin's letter in the Clinton library is from July 13, 1998. Document 350E064 FIN, released in July 2014.

To my claim that this distinction is the most basic problem affecting the country, a dismissive reaction takes one of two forms. Some people object that the distinction is trivial and that it is one everyone already knows. A different reaction is from people who think that my claim is somewhere between absurd and preposterous. I have a better chance of my argument convincing this second group. When someone says that a statement is absurd, it sometimes is. Another possibility is that the apparently absurd statement is from a different context of language.

I agree with those people who say that the distinction between "United States" and "America" is already known. Unfortunately, people do not speak that way. The distinction is violated not only in popular speech every minute of the day but also in scholarly writing and in the speech of politicians. Some writers make an effort in this direction, but they do not do so consistently. The reason that they do not follow through is that to do so requires a stubborn resistance to customary ways of speaking. To carry out the distinction in practice requires that one seem to be either silly or a bit mad.[16]

It is not actually difficult to always say "United States" when one is referring to that nation-state. "United States" can even function as an adjective as well as a noun. No convoluted phrases or neologisms are necessary for accuracy in referring to the country. However, a perplexing issue is the lack of a name for the people of the United States. In the appendix, I discuss names that have been tried, especially in countries to the north and south of the United States, but "the Americans" dominates. One can say "US people" or "US citizens," although that sounds overly formal. I sometimes refer to "US Americans" which is admittedly awkward but accurate.

This absence of a word for the people of the United States is significant. The lack of an important word usually indicates a different framework for looking at the world. Simply trying to invent a word almost never works;

---

16   Juan Enriquez, *The Untied States of America* (New York: Crown, 2002) is fairly consistent in using "United States" when referring to the country. In a few key places (for example, in the chapter on Canada) he slips back into a contrast between Canada and America. He does not raise the issue of an existing linguistic problem in discussing the relation between the US and other American nations.

language evolves as a worldview changes. But when a profound problem exists, the use of a clumsy phrase (for example, "he or she") can be a way of pointing to the need not only for a new word but also for a fundamental change of worldview. In any case, the fact that there is no simple and accurate term for referring to people of the United States is not an excuse for simply dismissing the need to distinguish between the United States and America.

A clear distinction between the American nation of the United States and the mythical idea about that country would make possible a better politics. However, the possibility should be acknowledged that if this distinction were ever to be consistently made, the country might literally fall apart. Many US people believe in America but do not accept the nation-state of the United States and its government.[17] Presidential elections since 2008 have shown that it is no exaggeration to say that the existence of a United States has become an issue.

The unity and stability of the United States may be more tenuous than is usually recognized. A poll in 2014 found that almost one-fourth of the people in the United States "strongly support or tended to support" the secession of their state from the union.[18] As the example of the Soviet Union shows, the dissolution of a fragile union can be rapid. If US people were to stop believing in America, the many people who "hate America" might get more than they have wished for. The celebrants of America in the sovereign states of South Carolina or Texas might have a chance to discover what life would be like without the help of the United States.

At least for the present, the United States is "too big to fail." What the United States has and what the Soviet Union lacked is a world of codependents. The fall of the Soviet empire caused tremors around the world, but the breakup of the United States would set off a tidal wave of uncontrollable effects. The world might eventually be better off without the United States, but a preferable course would be that the United States

---

17 Practically no one in the country rejects the Declaration of Independence, at least the part about self-evident truths. Acceptance of the US Constitution is more qualified. What is celebrated by many people is the Bill of Rights, or at least a select few of its ten amendments.

18 The poll by Reuters/Ipsos was conducted in August and September 2014. It found 23.9% of people in support of secession; only 53.3% opposed to secession.

move toward becoming a political unit that can realistically look at its strengths and its failures, and become one nation within a community of nations.

I have called "United States" the name of a nation-state, even though from its beginning the United States did not exactly fit that category in the way that France or England or China did. What was true to some extent at its beginning, and has become increasingly the case, is that the United States is a nation of nations, or the first international nation. It is quite possible that the United States, under the idea of America, is evolving into some new kind of political and social entity that will eventually leave behind the concept of nation-state. But there is still the present. A peaceful evolution cannot occur if there is confusion about the name of what is evolving.

There have occasionally been calls for a "United States of Europe" that would be modeled on the United States of America. Victor Hugo, in 1851, was probably the first one to use the phrase; similarly, French prime minister Édouard Herriot spoke in 1926 of the need for a United States of Europe. Winston Churchill, in 1946, said, "if we are to form the United States of Europe, or whatever name it may take, we must begin now." Europe chose the "whatever" name for its union, although a comparison to the United States of America has never died out.[19] Churchill and more recent proponents of a United States of Europe have not seemed to notice that the country that has the name "United States of America" is not the United States of Argentina, Brazil, Canada, and the rest. Joseph Stiglitz called it a "fatal decision" for the European Union "to adopt a single currency without providing for the institutions that would make it work."[20] The European Union is more like the United Nations than the

---

19   T. R. Reid, *The United States of Europe: The New Superpower and the End of American Supremacy* (New York: Penguin Books, 2004), 35. Lionel Sosa, in *The Americano Dream* (New York: Plume, 1999), 209, turns the question around to suggest that the United States and Latin America might someday form "an American Union based on the model of the European Union."

20   Joseph Stiglitz, *The Euro: How a Common Currency Threatens the Future of Europe* (New York: W. W. Norton, 1992; reissued in 2016).

United States of America.[21] The United Nations wisely avoids issuing its own currency.

The misleading comparison of a United States of Europe to the United States of America has recently caused misunderstanding in the opposite direction. The rebellion of European nations against the controls of the European Union, which was dramatically shown in the United Kingdom's Brexit vote, led to claims that a similar phenomenon was occurring in the United States. The cry in several nations of Europe has been to take back control of their nation from the European Union. But the cry to "take back America" is not comparable. Take it back from whom? A slogan such as "Make America Great Again" is about taking back an idea or a myth. There would be some logic to a cry to "Make the United States Great Again," but no one has been saying that.

A union of the states of America or a union of the states of Europe might be steps in the direction of world unity. The danger in both Europe and America is the unequal power of the states that would form such a union. But Europe does not have the problem that one state already calls itself the United States of Europe.

The Twofold Meaning of "America"

There is abundant writing in the United States on the theme of two Americas. The contrast is used to refer to two parts of the United States. For example, some US politicians and writers have used the language of two Americas to draw a contrast between the rich and the poor within the United States.[22] Recently, the two Americas theme has been used as a contrast between what have been named blue states and red states. This book addresses not the question of two Americas but the twofold meaning of "America" as continent and as mythical idea.

---

21 The United Nations is itself misnamed in that it is a union of states, not nations. The organization should logically have been called the United States (of the World), but that name would no doubt have been opposed by the United States of America.

22 For referring to the rich and poor, the two Americas theme was made prominent in Michael Harrington's influential book *The Other America: Poverty in the United States* (New York: Scribner, 1997); two Americas was the central theme of John Edwards in the 2004 presidential campaign.

America as a Continent

"America" as the name of a continent might seem unproblematic. No one denies that the word has carried this meaning since it was first put on a map at the beginning of the sixteenth century. As European nations established outposts on this land, one could speak of Spanish America, Portuguese America, French America, Dutch America, or English America. Each of these settlements carried the name "America" in reference to the land they shared.

"America" retained a continental meaning even when it became customary to speak of two continents. The tendency to split America into two continents became pronounced in the nineteenth century. The movement to speak of two continents signified a split that was mainly cultural rather than geographic. The use of "North" and "South" before "America" puts Mexico in an uncertain location. Canada also has a problem of trying to be in North America but not America. There is no logic in referring to "the Americas" in the sense of continents while one nation calls itself "America."

Throughout the nineteenth and twentieth centuries, there was plenty of writing, most of it in Spanish, on America as the continent and Americans as inhabitants of the continent. The Chilean writer José Victorino Lastarria wrote in *La America*, "We must use European science and get all we can from it, but we must adapt it to our own needs and must never forget we are first and foremost Americans, that is to say, democrats."[23] David Walker, in his 1829 *Appeal to the Colored People of the World*, several times refers to "Americans of the United States."[24]

Spanish-language writers who insisted that they were Americans living in America were not unmindful of the nation to the north, where people spoke as if they were the only Americans. People in the southern part of America were aware that the use of "America" by United States people was a sign of the US intention to control the continent.

---

23 Quoted in Arthur Whitaker, *The Western Hemisphere Idea: Its Rise and Decline* (Ithaca, NY: Cornell University Press, 1954), 65.
24 David Walker, *Appeal to the Colored People of the World* (New York: Hill and Wang, 1995).

There were two southern strategies for resisting the increasing power of the United States in relation to continental America. The first was to negotiate with the US in the hope of achieving some benefits through mutually binding agreements. The imbalance of power all but guaranteed that this strategy would fail.

In reaction, there was employed an illogical strategy of declaring that the United States was not a part of America. A union of American nations was sought that would exclude the United States. Starting with a conference in 1826, the term "inter-American" was an appeal to the American nations to form a cooperative bond for political and cultural purposes. Simón Bolivar, who was the force behind the meeting, resisted inviting the United States; he said it would be "like inviting the cat to the mice's party."[25] He relented in his opposition, but the US did not attend the meeting; its representatives were approved too late to participate. A nation that imagined itself to *be* America was not much interested in talking to *other* American nations.

In a similar move to exclude the history of the United States from America, Jaimé Delgado's history of America says that "the history of the United States has no place in American history since its colonial period is a part of English history and its later times a part of universal history."[26] Delgado was drawing upon that nineteenth-century language of "inter-American" as being exclusive of the United States. Even in 2010, Mexico tried to establish a hemispheric entity that excluded the United States and Canada.[27]

America as Mythical Idea

Although at its origin "America" was the name of a continent—a large land-mass separated from other land-masses—that historical fact already

---

25   L. Ronald Scheman, *Greater America: A New Partnership for the Americas* (New York: New York University Press, 2003), 44.

26   Jaimé Delgado, *Introducción à la historia de América*, cited in Lewis Hanke, *Do the Americas Have a Common History?* (New York: Knopf, 1964), 41.

27   Stephen Clarkson and Matto Mildenberger, *Dependent America? How Canada and Mexico Construct U.S. Power* (Toronto: University of Toronto Press, 2011), 277.

hides something about this particular place and its name. "America" did not just name a continent; it was the basis for the invention of the modern meaning of continent that almost reversed the previous meaning of "continent."[28] But more than a continent, "America" was said to be a *new world*. That claim implied a reality that could not be captured in the everyday language of this ordinary world. From its beginning to this day, "America" has had a mythical quality. "America" as a *new world* refers to a world before this world or after this world or outside this world. By not being of this world, "America" has functioned as an ideal or standard. It has been a religious idea about the end of history and a secular idea about the bounties of the future. In both cases, it has connoted liberation from the confines of present reality.

The myth of America was centuries in gestation before it was born at the beginning of the sixteenth century. That is, the idea that there was an exotic land in Europe's western sea long fascinated explorers, historians, and geographers. Several European explorers made contact with land by sailing west, but an overall picture of the earth's lands and oceans only emerged from a concentration of voyages toward the end of the fifteenth century. What was "discovered" was new to Europeans, even though it had been previously imagined. Economic and religious considerations joined in inventing "America."

"America" was coined to name this "new world." A claim to be new could take one of two forms: what extends and completes the old can be called new; what breaks free and rejects the old is also a way to be new. For people in the middle of efforts at trying to be something new, the two ways to be new can blur together.

"America" as a claim to novelty often carried an explicit repudiation of an *old* world of Europe. But people who claim to leave the old behind are usually unaware of how much of the old they carry with them in themselves. Language and rituals embody past attitudes and beliefs.

---

28 "Continent" was an ancient word that referred to large bodies of land that are contiguous. Starting in the fifteenth century, "continent" has referred to a large body of land that is separate from other large bodies of land. While that change of meaning worked fine for America; it made the relation between European and Asian continents problematic.

In both northern and southern parts of America, there was continuing dependence on European languages, arts, and cultural practices.

Both newness as completion of the old and newness as destruction of the old were included in the Christian idea of history. History can be imagined as having its end within the historical process itself, and thus history would reach its fullness in an immanent goal. This idea of historical progress was implied in one version of Christianity. However, a theory of progress based on this kind of movement did not fully blossom until the advent of new knowledge and the discovery of new lands.[29]

In a nearly opposite meaning of "end," the end-time can be imagined as a conclusion to history and a destruction of everything historical. The book of Revelation says, "Then I saw a new heaven and a new earth" (21:1). For several centuries before the sixteenth century, Christians had believed that the end of the world was near. The "discovery of America" was interpreted as a sign of the final stage of history. The Greek word for "revelation" is "apocalypse"—a word that simply means "to unveil or bring to light." But "apocalypse," early in the Common Era, acquired connotations of a fiery end. Apocalypse is good news for those who are saved but bad news for all those who are left behind. "America" and "apocalypse" have retained a close association.

The image of history's end as completion is likely to motivate believers to work hard at perfecting history. The image of history as time waiting to be replaced by eternity can induce believers to withdraw from history. Unfortunately, both images can lead to violence. Believers anxious to achieve the end of history as perfection can get impatient with anyone resisting their mandate. And believers waiting for the end of time to appear may imagine that violence is the necessary divine preparation for the final separation of good and evil.

"America" could also function as a secular name for the future. In addition to "America" as an idea that attracted religious people by holding out the possibility of spiritual freedom, "America" was also a name for the dream of fabulous material wealth. The two ideas were often mixed together in the European colonization of America. A *New Yorker* cartoon showed two pilgrims on a ship bound for America. In the cartoon, one

---

29   Gabriel Moran, *Both Sides: The Story of Revelation* (New York: Paulist Press, 2002).

man is saying to the other: "My first interest is religious liberty; then I want to get into real estate."

"America" was imagined as being so fantastic that it helped to give birth to the term "utopia," which means "no place." The utopia described by Thomas More in 1516 and located out in the Atlantic Ocean was a (no) place of human happiness, justice, and goodness.[30] Ever since then, the term "utopia" has most often referred to a fulfillment of human desires beyond the conflicts of history. But some people concluded that a state beyond the conflicts of human history might be a mind-numbing destruction of what is humanly valuable. The twentieth century was especially productive of novels called "dystopian"; these novels most often located the technological nightmare in the general area of the United States.[31]

America and European Nations

Thomas Jefferson, in an 1813 letter, said in reference to the nations in America that "in whatever governments they end they will be American governments."[32] An observer might have thought, "Of course they will be American governments; what else could they be?" But in using the term "American governments," Jefferson had in mind that other nations would be adopting the US government's way of doing things. The same letter of Jefferson's says, "America has a hemisphere to itself." Shouldn't he have written "America *is* a hemisphere to itself?" Given the language already present in 1813, "America has a hemisphere to itself" implied the United States' ownership of the continent.

The new nation-state in the eighteenth century called itself "The United States of America." It was almost inevitable that in practice it would shorten its name. There were two obvious ways that "United States of America" could be shortened. First, one could simply refer to the United States. These days there is little ambiguity in what that name refers to, even though an observer from another planet might be puzzled that one of

---

30   Thomas More, *Utopia* (New York: Harmony Books, 1978).

31   A flood of dystopian novels began with Aldous Huxley's *Brave New World* (New York: Harper Perennial, 1931) and George Orwell's *1984* (New York: New American Library, 1948).

32   Whitaker, *The Western Hemisphere*, 29.

the places on earth is called *the* United States. Are there not many places, including places in America, that claim to be a union of states, such as Estados Unidos Mexicanos? "United States" is no more logical a name today than it was in 1790, but it is a way to shorten the full name of the United States of America without causing significant linguistic confusion or oppressing any other country.

The second way to conveniently shorten the name was to use the last of the four words, "America." Although that choice might seem a parallel to using the first two words of the official name, this shortened version of "United States of America" conveys something entirely different. "America" was a term that already had a history of 280 years (longer than the current history of the United States). The third word in the official name, "of," suggests that this new nation encompasses America.

The founders of this nation could have made a credible claim that they were forming a United States *in* America. Of course they would then have had to come up with a name for this particular United States *in* America (as did other American nations). The new nation could have coined a name, similar to what now regularly happens when marketing specialists invent "Exxon," "Verizon," or "Xerox." If the country had called itself the United States of Verica, or the United States of Xenco, there would be no problem in referring to the country as Verica or Xenco. But "America" was not available as a name for a new nation. It was already a term with a complex meaning that included a continent and a myth.

The nation of the United States, by regularly calling itself "America," laid claim to being a utopia. Within the United States, there is no word more positive in meaning than "America." There is a minority of un-American Americans who see the nation as a dystopia. These un-American Americans have numerous allies around the world. While "America" is an attraction for some people, it can generate extraordinary contempt and hatred. US citizens are mostly bewildered by this widespread attitude.

George W. Bush seemed to be genuinely puzzled when he asked, "Why do they hate us?"[33] Bush, like most citizens, attributed the hatred to misinformation or envy, postulating that "they" must hate us because either they do not really know us or they wish that they had what we have:

---

33 Address to Congress on September 9, 2001.

"They hate our freedoms: our freedom of religion, our freedom of speech, our freedom to vote and assemble and disagree with each other."

Perhaps the United States is neither a utopia nor a dystopia but instead is one of the nations of the world. Where are the voices that would say to the United States and its people, "As nations go, yours is not so bad. That simple fact would be clear if you would just stop shouting that you ["America"] are the best nation that has ever existed." It might be expected that European voices would shoulder this task of reminding Europe's offspring that it has both good and bad features, that it is an interesting experiment that must be cautiously appraised, and that it needs some friendly criticism from a concerned parent. But it has never been easy to find such an attitude among prominent writers in England, France, Germany, and other European nations.

The critics on the other side of the Atlantic might know little about the United States, but they are sure they know America. Some of them do not bother to visit the United States before they issue their judgment on America. America is an idea that has been around for five hundred years. One simply has to gather easily available evidence to prove that the country that calls itself America falls far short of its claim. The German writer Heinrich Heine begins his poem on America by seeming to be attracted: "Sometimes it comes in my mind / To sail to America." But then he proceeds to describe America as "that big pig pen of freedom / Inhabited by boors living in equality."[34]

Some of the severe critics of America do come to visit the United States for a day or a few weeks, or even a year. The influential Arab theorist Sayyid Qutb, spent a year in the United States and then wrote a book, *The America I Have Seen*.[35] Similar to European writers, Qutb found America to be "technologically advanced but spiritually primitive." He wrote that it "reminds one of the days when man lived in jungles and caves." However, America was not there for Qutb to see. He did see Greeley, Colorado, where he studied at Colorado State Teachers College. Conclusions he drew from that experience might indeed be accurate about the city of Greeley,

---

34 Quoted in James Caesar, *Reconstructing America: The Symbol of America in Modern Thought* (New Haven, CT: Yale University Press, 1997), 171.

35 Sayyid Qutb, *The America I Have Seen* (1951): see *Milestones* (New York: Kazi Publications, 2003).

the state of Colorado, and—in part—about the United States, but drawing up a portrait of America is a different kind of project.

A European visitor who made an attempt to get an adequate sample of life in the United States was Alexis de Tocqueville. He came to study the prison system of the country, and he managed to get around to several parts of the country. Despite the title of his book, *Democracy in America*, Tocqueville realized that he was touring "one of the American nations"— that is, a nation, not an ideal, and a nation that is only one of the nations in America.[36] He went home and wrote a book that has insights into the US political system as well as helpful cautions about the fragility of "democracy in America."

Another example of a visitor who was fascinated by what he discovered when he spent some time in the United States is the English writer G. K. Chesterton. His book *What I Saw in America* is intended to give his readers some insight into the strange country across the ocean. As his title indicates, Chesterton never fully sorted out the relation between the country and the idea of America. He writes that "America is the only nation in the world that is founded on a creed. That creed is set forth with dogmatic and even theological lucidity in the Declaration of Independence."[37] Chesterton here perceived something important about the country. His statement would have been even more perceptive if he had been able to see that it is the United States that is the nation founded on a creed and that the creed is its belief in America.[38]

---

36 Alexis de Tocqueville, *Democracy in America* (New York: Schocken Books, 1961).

37 G. K. Chesterton, *What I Saw in America* (New York: Dodd, Mead and Company, 1922), 7.

38 Susan Mary Grant, *A Concise History of the United States of America* (Cambridge, MA: Cambridge University Press, 2012). The author launches into her history with this announcement: "Why go looking for America? Surely it is everywhere. And yet America is also nowhere. America is vanishing.... It is already slipping away into an Atlantic paradigm, that of the 'Americas,' in which the very invocation of America as the name of the United States is deemed potentially offensive to those who live proximate to the nation-state that has selfishly seized that signifier"(pg. 2). Whatever the author is trying to say in those confused assertions, it does not seem to influence the next 450 pages of text. "America" is casually used throughout the book as the name of the United States, despite

European immigrants in the nineteenth century who were desperate to get a new start in life understandably put great hope in America. They were captured by the public relations and advertising gimmicks that the United States had already developed. It was said of the immigrants that they came to the country thinking that the streets were paved with gold. They quickly discovered three things: First, the streets were not paved with gold; second, the streets were not paved; third, they were expected to do the paving.

Immigrants who had thought that they were coming to America were shocked to find themselves in the United States. Some of them got off the boat and kept running until they reached the open fields of the Midwestern United States—land that had some resemblance to their imagined America. Other immigrants—those who were too tired to run any farther—accepted horrible conditions in the tenements of a few big cities. They still believed in America, which meant that they now clung to the mantra "Life will be better for my grandchildren." For millions of those immigrants, their belief was realized; their grandchildren had much better living conditions than they did.

What is not highlighted in US history books is that about half of the immigrants, realizing they had not arrived in America, promptly got on ships and went back home. Between 1908 and 1925, 50 percent of Romanian, Magyar, Italian, and Russian immigrants re-emigrated. Only one group, the Jews, had 90 percent of its population stay. They did not have a home to go back to. Jews understandably became great supporters of America; for them, their freedom in the United States seemed almost like the imagined place America.[39]

At the other end of the spectrum was the forced immigration of African slaves, for whom "America" was the opposite of liberty. Although the international slave trade stopped in the nineteenth century, the effects of this horrific side of United States history continue to reverberate in the lives of US blacks. The country has yet to accept its "original sin" and

---

its having "selfishly seized that signifier." Nowhere in the book does the author reflect on her statement that America is both everywhere and nowhere; nor does she withdraw her announcement that "America is vanishing."

39   Walter Karp, *Politics of War: The Story of Two Wars which Altered Forever the Political Life of the American Republic* (New York: Franklin Square, 1979), 15.

to face the sometimes hard truths of United States history instead of its reciting the myths of American history.

The United States has been an apocalyptic nation, declaring itself to be the ideal toward which human history moves. The end of the world will restore the innocence and goodness of the original humans. But the restoration of paradise will not come without a struggle. Those who are called Americans have to lead the way, which sometimes involves giving a coercive push to recalcitrant nations. US Secretary of State Madeleine Albright said, "If we have to use force it is because we are America. We are the indispensable nation."[40] Hillary Clinton, at the beginning of *Hard Choices*, echoes Albright's claim: "Everything that I have done and seen has convinced me that America remains the 'indispensable nation.'"[41]

Because the United States identifies itself with an idea, the people who accept this idea tend to think alike on many issues. Belief in America creates an ideology—a closed worldview. Richard Hofstadter got it nearly right when he said that "it has been our fate as a nation not to have ideologies but to be one."[42] One of the common criticisms by European intellectuals is that all Americans think alike. Freedom of speech has not produced a rich diversity of opinions; on the contrary, there is little variety. The political parties shout slogans at each other, but they actually accept the same American pieties. For many people, Heinrich Heine's poem accurately describes a country "where the most extensive of all tyrannies, that of the masses, exercises its crude authority."

It would take sustained attention to language over many years, together with some key political and economic changes, for this linguistic change of "America" and "American" to occur.[43] The change almost certainly is

---

40   Interview on the *Today* show, February 19, 1998.

41   Hillary Clinton, *Hard Choices* (New York: Simon and Schuster, 2014), author's note.

42   Richard Hofstadter, *Anti-intellectualism in American Life* (New York: Vintage Books, 1963). I think it is more accurate to say not that the nation is an ideology but that the ideology, America, is used to refer to the nation.

43   Barry Rubin and Judith Cole Rubin, in *Hating America* (New York: Oxford University Press, 2004), 256, write in the first footnote of a chapter on Latin America, "Of course, it is possible to say that the use of the term 'America' for the United States is in itself an example of an arrogant expropriation of the type that could produce anti-Americanism. But since it is commonly accepted, this term

not going to happen until the United States ends its current status, which, depending on one's outlook, is either that of the guardian of the world's freedom or that of the world's biggest bully. For the present, there could at least be awareness that there is a semantic problem. Some effort can and should be made to mitigate the effects of the dominance of mythical or religious language in place of factual and historical language in discussions of United States culture, United States history, and the foreign policy of the United States government.

An Exceptional Nation?

Is there an "American exceptionalism"? People who give a positive answer to this question intend to make a claim about the United States. But because they conflate the United States and America, their use of "American" in the phrase "American exceptionalism" has to be untangled before any historical data can be used to answer the question. For example, the question of American exceptionalism can refer to Canada as well as to the United States. The political right wing in the United States celebrates American exceptionalism as obviously true.[44] Most historians dismiss the idea as demonstrably false on the basis of historical data, but they do so without understanding what is wrong with the question. America is an exceptional idea, but "America" is not the name of a nation.

In 2009, President Obama, at an overseas press conference on NATO, was asked if he "still clung to belief" in American exceptionalism. He began by saying, "I believe in American exceptionalism," and then he immediately qualified his belief as being similar to the British believing in British exceptionalism and the Greeks in Greek exceptionalism. James Fallows said that Obama "went on to give so balanced a response that no

---

will be used in this book, while the names South America or Latin America will be applied for that part of the New World." The authors' dismissal of the basic linguistic problem leads into a confused and confusing discussion of America in Latin America.

44 The tenor of Ben Carson's popular book *One Nation: What We Can Do to Save America's Future* (New York: Sentinel, 2014), 211, is captured in the statement "If we are not an exceptional nation, we can quietly continue our slide into insignificance."

one, Yank or otherwise, could fail to be satisfied."[45] Fallows surely knows
that for the political right wing in the United States, a "balanced response"
to the question is equivalent to denial. Commenting on Obama's answer,
Dinesh D'Souza referred to "Obama's ignorance" and said, "In the spirit of
presidential education I venture to prove him wrong." D'Souza proceeded to
recite lines from the Declaration of Independence.[46] Barack Obama's attempt
to affirm both sides, far from doing what Fallows said, satisfied almost no one.

Besides the ambiguity of the adjective "American" there is a complexity
in the term "exceptionalism." The starting point for understanding
"exceptionalism" is that individuals and nations can be exceptional but
it has to be specified in which direction and to what degree the nation or
individual is exceptional. A person or a nation can have exceptionally good
qualities or exceptionally bad qualities.

The United States is exceptional in both positive and negative ways.
To the extent that the United States identifies itself as already America,
it is an exceptionally violent country. Gun ownership is only part of
the story, but easy access to guns plays a big part in the high rates of
murder and suicide in the United States. The National Commission on
Causes and Prevention of Violence said that "Americans have been given
to a kind of historical amnesia that masks much of their turbulent past."
Every time there is a mass shooting, the local people inevitably say, "How
could this happen in our peaceful town?" The commission concluded that
"Americans have probably magnified the process of selective recollection
owing to our historic vision of ourselves as a latter-day chosen people, a
New Jerusalem."[47]

In relation to other countries, the United States is more belligerent
than it imagines itself to be. Eric Hobsbawm notes that in contrast to
Europe, where a nation's enemies tend to be its neighbors, "America has
only ideologically defined enemies who reject the American way of life."[48]

45 James Fallows, "Obama on Exceptionalism," the *Atlantic*, April 4, 2009.
46 Dinesh D'Souza, *America: Imagine the World Without Her* (Chicago: Regnery,
    2014), chapter 3.
47 *Violence in America: Historical and Comparative Perspectives,* Report of the
    National Commission on Causes and Prevention of Violence (Washington:
    Supt. Documents, US government, 1969).
48 Eric Hobsbawm, *On Empire, America, War and Global Supremacy* (New York:
    New Press, 2008), 80.

Especially during the past century, the United States has repeatedly sent its young men to fight against some enemy because it disrespected America, even though the United States was under no threat of attack. The result is a United States that is almost constantly at war and in need of a military budget to prepare for war anywhere and everywhere.

The United States, to the extent that it realizes it is not America, can be an exceptional nation in a positive direction. It is a nation that, despite its flaws, attempts to live up to ambitious moral ideals. Its citizens can appeal to principles of justice with some hope that leaders will listen. In its openness to future possibilities, the nation is always in danger of neglecting the past, but it is also free of some of the baggage of the past. It has been a place that allows for the creation of new things, as well as for people to try creating themselves anew.

The United States has been exceptional in creating a nation out of many nations. Most nation-states today contain more than one nation. African and Asian countries often had their state borders drawn by outsiders who did not understand ethnic and tribal loyalties. Many European nations are struggling with immigrant populations that are not easily assimilated into a French, German, Dutch, or Swedish people. The United States could help other nations if it realized that it is still a work in progress for a new kind of nation-state, or possibly a successor to the nation-state.

When Zhou Enlai was asked if the French Revolution had been a success, he is said to have answered, "It is too early to say."[49] The same can be said of the United States in relation to American and world history. The United States is an experiment in humanity that can be exceptional according to opposite forms of exceptionalism. The United States undoubtedly has some exceptional qualities. But which form of its American exceptionalism will triumph remains an open question.

---

49 There is a dispute as to whether Zhou Enlai was referring to the French Revolution or to the revolution of 1968. John Dewey, in responding to a question regarding what is wrong with the United States, wrote, "Be the evils what they may, the experiment is not yet played out. The United States are not yet made; they are not a finished fact to be categorically assessed." See "The Public and its Problems," in *Later Works*, vol. 2 (Carbondale, IL: Southern Illinois University Press, 1927), 350.

2

The Invention
of America

I attended an educational conference a few years ago at which there were four speakers. The first speaker wished to demonstrate how history should be taught. He chose what he assumed to be an obvious historical truth—namely, that Columbus discovered America. He showed how to lead students to see that "Columbus discovered America" is a fact of history. The second speaker criticized the first speaker, pointing out that the Vikings, led by Leif Erikson, were the real discoverers of America. The third speaker said that both of the previous speakers were wrong. America, he said, had been discovered by people who came across the Bering Strait many thousands of years ago. The fourth speaker said that the view of the third speaker was offensive to American natives. According to the legends of North American peoples, they had always been on this land.

If the four speakers had planned this sequence of views as a demonstration of the difficulty of reaching historical truth, the exercise might have been encouraging. Unfortunately, each of the four speakers was serious about asserting that his statement was *the* truth. The only thing clear after these successive refutations of an answer to the question was that there was something peculiar about the question.

Perhaps "Who discovered America?" is not answerable with a historical fact or the name of somebody. The philosophical question would be "Is 'who discovered America?' an intelligible question?" The question of who discovered America assumes that there was a place called America that was unknown and that at a certain moment it became known to one person or a group of people. Each speaker at the conference was claiming to identify when the discovery was made and who the person was that made the discovery. Critical-minded scholars today say that America did not need discovery; there was a native population who were doing fine before the European invaders showed up. That criticism might leave intact the question of who was the first European to discover America. But was there an America waiting to be discovered by Europeans?

In this chapter, my questions are as follows: (1) When was "America" invented? (2) Who invented "America"? and (3) What did "America" mean at that time? There are clear historical answers to these questions.

The Invention: Who and When

It should be noted that at the beginning of the sixteenth century, the words "invent" and "discover" were close in meaning. An invention was not something that had never existed and that found its beginning in human creativity. But since that century, an endless stream of inventions has been credited to human skill and entrepreneurship. As a result, our meaning of "invention" is sharply opposed to the meaning of "discover." There is some anachronism in attributing our meaning of "invention" to people in the early sixteenth century. But there were some people in the sixteenth century who had a sense that the human understanding of the world was being drastically changed. The moment when "America" was invented was revolutionary not just for Europe but also for the whole earth (which at that time was called "the world").

In 1982, a proposal came before the United Nations to prepare for the observance in ten years' time of the five hundredth anniversary of the discovery of America. The proposal set off a contentious debate. The US press treated the incident as a hilarious joke. Critics of the United Nations said that the organization was so inept that it could not agree on the most obvious of historical facts. Every schoolchild in America knows that Columbus discovered America.[50] The United Nations could not readily agree. When the year 1992 arrived, it passed with very little fanfare over Columbus. That lack of response for the five hundredth anniversary was

---

50 "For Columbus in U.N., a Stormy Passage," *New York Times*, December 22, 1982, A3.

very different from the elaborate observances of the fourth centennial in 1892.

The main change during the twentieth century was not the discovery of new historical facts. True, there was added confirmation of the second speaker's view at the conference referred to above—namely, that a number of individuals made contact with the land in Europe's western sea long before Columbus did. But that fact had been known for centuries, and yet those explorers had not been credited with discovering America. The change in the twentieth-century thinking on this question is the perspective from which the question is asked. The objection to celebrating "Columbus's discovery" reflects a conviction that native people on the "American continent" did not need discovery by Europeans, and that what Columbus initiated was a long history of oppression and destruction.

The story of America is very different when viewed from the side of the people that Columbus is said to have discovered. Howard Zinn, in *A People's History of the United States*, writes, "I prefer to tell the story of the discovery of America from the standpoint of the Arawaks ..."[51] That perspective provides a valuable corrective to most US history books. But it is still a little puzzling why Zinn's history of the United States should begin with the "discovery of America" from any perspective.

Many textbooks that used to be called "American history" are now called "US history." That change of title sometimes indicates a change of outlook, but often it does not. If the field is US history, the beginning of that story would be the late eighteenth century. Of course, a good case can be made for introducing material from before the nation's founding. The establishment of the English colonies in the early seventeenth century might be a logical place to begin the prehistory of the United States. If one wishes to include more of what shaped the beginnings of the country, perhaps one has to go back to Greek and Roman conceptions of a republic. But starting from 1492 seems to indicate a wish to continue writing "American history" but leaving out whole centuries and several dozen countries that are part of American history.

I think the reason why the United States is presumed to begin in 1492 is that, for most people who call themselves "the Americans," the

---

51 Howard Zinn, *A Patriot's History of the United* States (New York: Harper, 2001), 10.

discovery of America is the founding myth of their world. Howard Zinn's history book is an admirable effort to penetrate the myth of America and provide a more accurate account of United States history, especially as seen through the eyes of conquered and oppressed people who were in the way of the United States' march through history. But simply trying to "demythologize" the history of the United States leaves out the driving force of the myth of America, which is a significant part of US history. By simply reversing the perspective of the encounter between Columbus and the natives, Zinn leaves undisturbed the discovery of America as the assumed beginning of US history. *A People's History of the United States* has the subtitle *1492-Present.*

There is less mystery about those history books that begin with Columbus if their aim is to solidify the mythical meaning of America that envelops the United States. For example, *A Patriot's History of the United States*, by Larry Schweiker and Michael Allen, was written to counteract Zinn's history. The subtitle of their book is *From Columbus's Great Discovery to the War on Terror.*" Columbus's discovery of America begins a smooth narrative in which "America" and "United States" are used interchangeably. The authors assert in the introduction, "That is what American history is truly about – ideas. Ideas such as 'All men are created equal'; the United States is the 'last best hope of earth'; and America 'is great because it is good.'"[52] Those statements do not seem to be "ideas" but instead (puzzling) articles of faith. They represent a peculiar premise from which to begin a book that is dedicated to correcting the historical record.

The authors never question throughout the book the interchangeability of "United States" and "America." That use of language gives them more justification than Howard Zinn has for beginning a history of the United States with Columbus. However, it would be awkward for the authors to make explicit the linguistically implied claim that Columbus discovered the United States.

The one thing clear from this discussion is that "Columbus discovered America" is neither a statement of a historical fact nor a misstatement of fact. Insofar as Columbus never grasped what he had stumbled upon in his

---

52   Larry Schweikart and Michael Allen, *A Patriot's History of the United States: From Columbus's Great Discovery to the War on Terror* (New York: Penguin Books, 2004).

attempted journey to the Indies, he accomplished less than the discovery of a previously unknown continent. But insofar as Columbus's voyages were central to a transformation of consciousness, he accomplished more than uncovering a hitherto unknown land. Columbus, together with other explorers at the end of the fifteenth and the beginning of the sixteenth centuries, invented "America" and changed the meaning of "world."

In the last few years, the problem with "Columbus discovered America" has spread to groups who have been protesting the celebration of past heroes despite these men being slaveholders or otherwise less-than-admirable characters. Christopher Columbus has joined the parade. Why is Columbus Day a US holiday? Why are there hundreds of statues of Columbus throughout the United States? Why are there towns and cities named for Columbus?

If groups wish to protest the myth around Christopher Columbus, are they willing to examine the myth of America that has surrounded the entire history of the United States? Would they be willing to give back US land—or at least, say, Virginia, Carolina, Massachusetts, and Manhattan Island—to the (native) Americans?

Christopher Columbus might be said to have discovered a landmass that was later to be America. But he died in 1506, before "America" was invented. Columbus and other explorers at the time invented or discovered a "new world" that Columbus thought might be the entrance to paradise and that other Europeans thought might be a sign of the end of history. What was finally agreed upon was that this exotic place would be called America.

Before America

To understand the significance of the invention of America, it is necessary to consider how the world looked to Europeans before the late fifteenth century. Our knowledge of how people imagined what they called "the world"—that is, the place of human habitation—is mainly based on religious stories and philosophical speculation.

We do know that the myth that people once thought the world was flat is not accurate. That idea seems to have originated in the nineteenth century, but it became a commonplace belief that people once thought that if you sailed far out on the ocean, you were in danger of falling off the edge of the world. Jeffrey Burton Russell, who has studied this myth, traces its beginning to Washington Irving's *Life and Voyages of Christopher Columbus* in 1828. Russell surmises that the myth took hold, especially in the United States, as a way to contrast Columbus's great discovery with the ignorance and superstition of previous ages.[53]

Although educated people in the fifteenth century knew that the earth was spherical, there was a lack of understanding about distances on the earth. There was no direct way to measure the size of the globe. Ancient authorities in Europe provided conflicting theories of how distant were places in Asia. Travelers in the early Middle Ages filled in some data on overland travel. Sea travel was harder to measure.

There was little inclination to travel far out on the sea. The human world was the island of Earth. The ocean was not part of that world but was instead the limit of the world. The Latin word for "island" was "*insula*," which referred to a house available for rent. The humans were tenants of the landlord (*dominus*) and received what they needed for life on the island.

One element in the Christian story would eventually prove important when joined to the rise of modern science and technology. Although humans had indeed been given everything they needed in the garden of paradise, they had rebelled against the Creator and had been banished from the garden. Henceforth, a man would have to earn his living by the sweat of his brow. That meant human beings were now called upon to master their environment.

For many centuries, the limits of the world seemed to be the single landmass that had emerged from the receding waters. This single landmass, in the European view, was thought to be divided into several parts. The division probably began with a Greek contrast between Greeks and "barbarians"—people whose language was unintelligible to the Greeks. The original division was between Europe and Asia, but the line did not follow a logical pattern of natural contours.

---

53 Jeffrey Burton Russell, *Inventing the Flat Earth: Columbus and Modern Historians* (New York: Praeger, 1991).

By the time of Herodotus in the fifth century BCE, a third part to the world was recognized; it was called Libya or Africa.[54] The threefold division of the world took hold among classical authors. Pliny's *Natural History* says that "the whole circuit of the earth is divided into three parts: Europe, Asia and Africa." The classification was taken over by Isidore of Seville (560-636), who was an important authority for the Middle Ages. He describes in detail the world's three parts: Europe, Asia and Africa.[55]

One of the most important writings on the geography of the world was Claudius Ptolemy's *Geography*, published in the second century CE. The work was unknown in Europe until it was discovered in 1295 by the monk Maximus Planudes in Constantinople.[56] Ptolemy's name is generally recognized in the context of astronomy. The Ptolemaic image of the sun circling the earth is contrasted to the Copernican image of the earth revolving about the sun. Many people are unaware that Ptolemy was equally important to geography, where he was a more trustworthy guide than in his astronomy.

Ptolemy's description of the earth was the basis for maps even into the sixteenth century. Any new discoveries were an adjustment to the map that Ptolemy had provided. It was not until Gerardus Mercator produced a new kind of map toward the end of the sixteenth century that Ptolemy was retired as the main authority for the earth's geography.

The link that Ptolemy had made between geography and astronomy was significant. Humans could not change their image of the earth's place in the universe without also changing their image of the earth. Copernicus's *On the Revolution of Heavenly Spheres* was published in 1543, but he had developed the ideas within the work several decades earlier.[57]

---

54 Herodotus, *The Persian Wars* in *The Greek Historians*, vol. 1 (New York: Random House, 1942),
IV, sec. 36-44, 240-41.

55 Isidore of Seville, "The Earth and its Parts," in *The Etymologies of Isidore of Seville* (Cambridge, MA: Cambridge University Press, 2006), 285.

56 Oswald Dilke and Margaret Dilke, "Ptolemy's Geography and the New World," in *Early Images of the Americas*, ed. Jerry Williams and Robert Lewis (Tucson, AZ: University of Arizona Press, 1993), 265.

57 Nicolaus Copernicus, *On the Revolution of Heavenly Spheres* (New York: Prometheus, 1995).

Copernicus was influenced by what the explorers were finding in their journeys during the late fifteenth and early sixteenth centuries.

The meaning of "world" made two jumps of meaning in the sixteenth century. The world as a place of human habitation was expanded from the island Earth to a "new world" where humans also live. A discovery of a new world meant a reconception of the whole world. But this meaning of "world" still equated "world" and "Earth"; even today this equivalence is still commonly made in the way people speak. A second and bigger jump in meaning was to move from "world" as a place of human habitation to "world" as a universe of stars and planets. The earth became a small part of this new meaning of "world." Many people found it difficult to accept what seemed to be a devaluation of human existence. They might be consoled by the thought that, however big and old the world is, human beings can still be imagined as the center of all *meaning* in the world (at least until a superior being makes an appearance).[58]

What was called the discovery of America was indeed part of finding a "new world," but it was a mistake to call this new land the "new world." The new world was both the reconception of the earth as well as the world that Copernicus was discovering or inventing. The continued use of "new world" to refer to America indicates a lack of comprehension of what happened in the sixteenth century. A new piece of Earth had come to light, but that was not the new world. Instead, the new world was the way Europeans, and eventually everybody, perceived the whole earth and its relation to the universe.

Ptolemy used the standard threefold division of the inhabited earth: Europe, Asia, and Africa. Humans could live only where it was neither too hot nor too cold. That conviction limited the possibilities of habitation to places that were above the equator and below the frigid zone to the north. Concerning the size of the world, Ptolemy's guidance was not precise, but he was much closer to the mark than other ancient authors, including

---

58 Fredrick Turner, "Escape from Modernism," in David Ray Griffin, ed., *Sacred Interconnections: Postmodern Spirituality, Political Economy and Art* (Albany, NY: State University of New York Press, 1990), 147: "Measured in terms of space and time, human kind is indeed, as scientists traditionally remind us, a tiny speck in the vastness of the cosmos. Measured in a more fundamental way, by density and complexity of information, we are already the largest objects in the universe."

Aristotle, who said that "small is the sea that separates Europe from India." The Latin writer Seneca speculated that "the distance may be traversed in a few days if the wind is favorable."

Favorable wind was indeed a concern in the age of sailing vessels. Any mariner who ventured into open waters had to consider the difficulty of the return trip. Sailors generally went against the wind on their outgoing journeys so that they would have the wind to their back on the return. The wind currents in Europe's western sea were especially treacherous and hard to predict.

Sailing west to reach the Indies and China was less inviting than staying close to the shore of island Earth and finding an eastern sea route to Asia. Europeans had made the journey by land for many centuries, crossing through the Ottoman and Persian Empires. Travelers had brought back stories of wealth and exotic products. The most famous of those travelers was Marco Polo (1254-1324), who had supposedly traveled to China while still a boy and eventually returned to Europe with detailed information about China, the superpower of that time.

Europe in the fifteenth century was poor. In retrospect, its poverty can be seen as an advantage. If they had not been so much in need, Europeans probably would not have been motivated to travel to distant places and explore the best routes for getting there. Europeans did not have many goods to barter, so they had to buy goods with silver. That was a severe limitation until silver rose in value and made Asian goods more affordable. China, for its part, had no impulse to travel to Europe or set out on the sea to the east.

Europe's exploration of new lands was one part of European advances in knowledge and the "practical arts" (technology). Modern science and technology have their roots in the eleventh and twelfth centuries, when there arose an interest in the natural. It is important to recognize that at that time, the "natural" rose in contrast to the "supernatural."[59] By the fourteenth and fifteenth centuries, the Christian attitude to nature and human nature had undergone a major shift. The world was no longer

---

59   M. D. Chenu, *Nature, Man and Society in the Twelfth Century* (Toronto: University of Toronto Press, 1995); Charles Radding, *A World Made by Man: Cognition and Society 400-1200* (Chapel Hill, NC: University of North Carolina Press, 1985).

presented to men ready-made, needing only its preservation. Humans were called to a mastery of the world and the development of new resources for human well-being.

Instead of only a fair distribution of the earth's goods, it was seen as possible to increase the amounts of those goods by the application of human ingenuity. Pico della Mirandola, in the fourteenth century, attributed to God this instruction to Adam: "It is given to him to have that which he chooses and to be that which he wills."[60] Pico may have thought that he was stating a traditional belief, but the idea that man can be anything he chooses to be was a novelty.

The new daring on the part of Europeans found expression in the search for a sea route to Asia that went around Africa. Portugal led the way in exploring the eastward route to China and India. Portuguese mariners made their way down the coast of Africa under the prodding of Henry the Navigator. Portugal's ultimate success in this project was a motivating factor in Spain's willingness to face west and engage in its own exploration of an Asian route.[61]

After several Portuguese journeys along the African coast, Bartolomeu Diaz, in 1487, succeeded in rounding the southern tip of Africa. He called it the Cape of Storms, indicative of the adverse currents he met. The king of Portugal changed the name to the Cape of Good Hope as a kind of promotional pitch.[62] It was still unclear, until Vasco de Gama's journey in 1498, whether the Indian Ocean was landlocked as Ptolemy's *Geography* seemed to suggest.

Christopher Columbus

By 1487, Christopher Columbus had already proposed to the Spanish sovereigns, Ferdinand and Isabella, that he find a passageway to Asia via the western sea. It took courage, along with some miscalculation of distances, for Columbus to venture westward. For many centuries before Columbus, there had been speculation about a different world at the other

---

60 Pico della Mirandola, *Oration on the Dignity of Man* (New York: Gateway, 1971).
61 Bailey Diffe and George Winnius, *Foundations of the Portuguese Empire, 1415-1580* (Minneapolis, MN: University of Minnesota Press, 1977).
62 Felipe Fernandez-Armesto, *1492* (New York: Harper Collins, 2009), 256.

end of the earth. Secular fiction joined biblical belief in a paradise with exotic plants and animals. On his third voyage, Columbus touched upon the mainland of what was later called America, but even then he did not know what he had found. What he was hoping to find, a route to Asia, he never did find.

Columbus did play an important part in the reconception of the human world, although Charles Mann's description of him seems extreme: "Of all the members of humankind who ever walked the earth, he alone inaugurated a new era in the history of life."[63] Columbus's voyages have to be placed within the change in European consciousness that began Europe's ascent to world hegemony. The change was philosophical, theological, astronomical, political, artistic, and economic. "The generation that lived in the late fifteenth and early sixteenth centuries – the generation of Erasmus, Copernicus, Machiavelli and Leonardo da Vinci – witnessed the most transformation in geographical knowledge and experience that the world has ever known."[64]

The voyages of Columbus produced reflection and new data that led up to the invention of America. Columbus made four voyages, starting with his most celebrated journey in 1492. He kept a log of that first journey so that we know what Columbus himself thought. At least we know from the fragments that survived and were used in biographies of Columbus by his son Ferdinand and by Bartolomé de Las Casas. We also have letters in Columbus's hand that he wrote as he made his case for what he had accomplished on his first mission and why financial backing was needed for further exploration.[65] After all four of his voyages, it was still unclear to Columbus and his contemporaries what he had discovered. It took a long advocacy by his son Ferdinand and other people who followed, to establish the proposition that "Columbus discovered America."[66]

---

63 Charles Mann, *1493: Uncovering the New World that Columbus Created* (New York: Knopf, 2011), 4.

64 Charles Gibson, *Spain in America* (New York: Harper, 1966), 22.

65 Bartolomé de Las Casas, *The Log of Christopher Columbus' First Voyage to America in 1492* (New York: William Scott Publisher, 1938).

66 Ferdinand Columbus, *Life of the Admiral Christopher Columbus* (London: Folio Society, 1960).

Thomas Bender places the "discovery" by Columbus in global perspective: "The actual 'discovery' was greater in significance than the exploration of a landmass unknown to Europeans or even the beginnings of the United States. The real discovery was of the ocean, which entered history, creating a new world."[67] No longer was the ocean the limit of the world; now oceans were the connecting link of continents within the world.

From the way Columbus annotated Pierre D'Ailly's *Imago Mundi*, it can be deduced that he relied on that author for the calculation of the distance to Asia. D'Ailly restated Aristotle's belief that only a narrow body of water separated Europe and Asia. Columbus disregarded or misinterpreted the much more accurate estimate of Arab geographers. Columbus thought the distance from Portugal to Japan to be 2,760 miles; actually it is about 12,000 miles.[68]

There has been much debate over Columbus's purpose in making the voyages. Felipe Fernandez-Armesto suggests that the answer to this "mystery" is that Columbus kept changing his mind. In the 1480s, the young Columbus did not manifest any special religiosity. But he underwent a conversion during the time he spent with the spiritual Franciscans, the apocalyptically inclined wing of the Franciscan Friars.[69] As one reads Columbus's own words, it is startling to find a constant use of religious language and allusions to the Bible. Columbus took seriously the meaning of his name, "Christopher," meaning "Christ bearer."

Columbus began his first voyage on August 3, 1492, proceeding from Spain to the Canary Islands. The Canaries had the port that was most conducive for travel westward. Columbus left the Canary Islands on September 6 and reached the "Indies" on October 12. His main evidence that he had reached Asia was simply that the land was inhabited.

The sighting of land on October 12 was hardly as dramatic as biographies of Columbus and celebrations of "America" would later make

---

67 Thomas Bender, *A Nation among Nations: America's Place in World History* (New York: Hill and Wang, 2006), 16.

68 Introduction to *Four Voyages of Christopher Columbus*, ed. J. M. Cohen (New York: Penguin Books, 1969), 13; Tzvetan Todorov, *The Conquest of America* (Norman, OK: University of Oklahoma Press, 1999), 29-30.

69 Fernandez-Armesto, *1492*, 183.

it out to be. Samuel Morrison, Columbus's chief hagiographer, lyrically described the moment: "Never again may mortal man hope to recapture the amazement, the wonder, the delight of those October days when the New World gracefully yielded her virginity to the conquering Castilians."[70] The end of that passage ominously foreshadows the interaction of conquering Castilians and the "New World's virginity."

What Columbus wrote in his logbook for October 12, 1492, was a description of the natives: "They should be good servants and very intelligent, for I have observed that they soon repeat anything that is said to them, and I believe they would easily be made Christians for they appeared to have no religion."[71] These first "Indians" that Columbus met on the island of Hispaniola were the Arawaks, a peace-loving people. In the eyes of Europeans, they were lazy, but the Arawaks were apparently content in a simple way of life.

Since Columbus found "no human monstrosities" among the islanders, there was a presumption in favor of their humanity. Columbus judged the Arawaks to be "the best people in the world and the most peaceable." The Arawaks would be subjected to a kind of slavery, against which they rebelled. They were not very successful at defending themselves against the guns and diseases of the invaders. Within a few decades, most of the tribe had disappeared.

Columbus saw the Indians as fertile ground for conversion to the Catholic religion. In a letter dated November 6, he wrote to Ferdinand and Isabella: "I hope in Our Lord that Your Highnesses will determine to send [priests] in great diligence in order to unite to the Church such great populations and to convert them, just as Your Highnesses have destroyed those who were unwilling to confess the Father, the Son, and the Holy Ghost."[72]

The last phrase refers to the expulsion of the Jews and Moors (Muslims) from Spain in 1492. The timing is more than coincidental. The sending of Columbus was part of the Spanish sovereigns' project of enforced religious conformity. The grand inquisitor, Tomas de Torquemada, made his first

---

70   Samuel Morrison, *Admiral of the Ocean Sea*, vol. 1(Boston: Little, Brown and Co., 1942), 308.
71   Columbus, *Four Voyages*, 56.
72   Todorov, *Conquest of America*, 50.

draft of the decree expelling Jews in March 1492. Jews were suspected of being a fifth column and were often labeled as heretics. Jews were forced to convert to Christianity or to leave the country. That might have been a big loss for Spain, except that "the decree of expulsion created more converts than expulses." Many Jews simply pretended to be converted. These *conversos* played an important part in the life of the nation.[73]

Ferdinand and Isabella were also intent on rolling back the Muslim advance in Europe. A conflict with rebellious elements in Granada and Alpujarras dragged on for ten years, at which time the Muslims were given two months to convert or to leave. Fernandez de Oviedo refers to the subduing of "all the Moors in Spain who had insulted and maltreated Christians since the year 720."[74]

Ironically, the period of Spanish history that Oviedo refers to has often been cited as an example of ecumenical tolerance. It is true that in recent years historians have cautioned that this *convivencia* was not a model of religious peace and understanding.[75] Under Muslim rule, Christians and Jews were "protected peoples" whose rights were restricted. Oviedo is right that Christians were maltreated. Nonetheless, in the grand sweep of religious history, Muslim treatment of Christians in medieval Spain would be among the better examples of tolerance.

Columbus's journeys as a spillover of Spain's conquest of the Moors had unfortunate repercussions. Images of Christian-Muslim conflict were imposed on the European-Indian encounter. Even though the native religion bore little resemblance to Islam, the natives were imagined to be

---

73 Fernandez-Armesto, *1492*, 94-99.

74 Columbus, *Four Voyages*, 36 (Oviedo's image of the Indians showed the same attitude: "… naturally lazy and vicious, melancholic, cowardly and in general a lying and shiftless people. Their chief desire is to eat, drink, worship heathen idols, and commit bestial obscenities"); Louis Hanke, *The Spanish Struggle for Justice in the Conquest of America* (Philadelphia, PA: University of Pennsylvania Press, 1949), 11.

75 Jonathan Riley-Smith, *The Crusades: Christianity and Islam* (New York: Columbia University Press, 2008); Sidney Griffith, *The Church in the Shadow of the Mosque: Christians and Muslims in the World of Islam* (Princeton, NJ: Princeton University Press, 2008).

Moors, and their place of worship was called a mosque.[76] The natives had to be pushed out of the land that had been divinely destined for Christian dwelling.

As a result of Columbus's first voyage, Spain immediately petitioned the papacy for confirmation that its discoveries were outside the jurisdiction previously given to Portugal. In May 1493, Pope Alexander VI issued the bull *Inter Caetera Divinae*, which drew a line from north to south giving the "islands and firm lands" in the western sea to Spain. The pope wrote that "just as some kings of Portugal discovered and acquired the regions of Africa, Guinea, El Mina on the Gold Coast, and other islands, we concede to you and your heirs and successors the islands and lands discovered by you ... with the same rights, privileges, liberties, faculties and immunities."[77]

Portugal was unhappy at this gift to Spain made by a pope who had family and political connections to the Spanish sovereigns. By employing some aggressive diplomacy, Portugal succeeded within a year in getting the "division of the ocean" moved farther westward. To the west of the line, all the islands would be Spanish; to the east, all the land—with the exception of the Canary Islands—would be Portuguese. A substantial part of latter-day Brazil became a Portuguese possession. This agreement, known as the Treaty of Tordesillas, was later confirmed by the pope.

In 1493, Peter Martyr's account of Columbus's first voyage calls Columbus the "novi orbis reportor" (discoverer of a new world). In his second voyage, Columbus referred to an "otro mundo." These phrases did not have the radical connotations that would soon be attached to the idea of a new or different world. Martyr was only pointing out that Columbus had discovered a group of islands that Ptolemy had not described. It was "another world from that in which the Romans and Alexander and the Greeks labored to gain dominion."[78]

---

76 Hugh Honour, *The European Vision of America* (Kent, OH: Kent State University, 1975).

77 Hugh Thomas, *Rivers of Gold: The Rise of the Spanish Empire* (New York: Random House, 2005), 105-6.

78 John Archer, *Old Worlds: Egypt, Southwest Asia, India, and Russia in Early Modern English Writing* (Stanford, CT: Stanford University Press, 2001), 1.

Columbus's second voyage, beginning in 1493, was an ambitious undertaking of seventeen ships and more than a thousand men. He also introduced horses and cattle to the islands that he visited. He had planned to return to the settlement at Navidad on Hispaniola. He finally did arrive there after traveling by way of Dominica, the Virgin Islands, and Puerto Rico. What he found on reaching Navidad was that the settlement of forty men had been wiped out in a conflict with the natives. The bloody history of the encounter between white men and natives had begun. Columbus established a new settlement on Hispaniola that he called Isabela, in a location that proved to be inhospitable.

Columbus also reached Cuba on this second trip in April 1494. The exploration of the island was a difficult undertaking, and some of Columbus's crew complained and rebelled. Columbus was convinced that Cuba was a peninsula, not an island. To support his belief, Columbus had the men sign an oath that Cuba was part of the mainland. As Tzvetan Todorov notes, Columbus was trusting a religious belief over his own experience.[79] Throughout 1495-96 Columbus governed his little colony as a sovereign. He was a poor administrator, and his reign was not popular. Many of the fifteen hundred colonists grumbled at not finding the gold that had been promised. As supplies were running short, Columbus returned to Spain in 1496.

The process of colonization had begun. The Europeans' bifurcated image of the natives was set for the future: innocent, peace-loving, and childlike on the one side; fierce, savage, and violent on the other side. "How can Columbus be associated with these two apparently contradictory myths? It is because both rest on a common basis, which is the failure to recognize the Indians and the refusal to admit them as a subject having the same rights as oneself, but different."[80] They could not be trusted until they were civilized and Christianized.

Columbus left Spain on his third voyage in May 1498 with six ships. Three went directly to Hispaniola; the other three, commanded by Columbus, sought a more southerly route. He visited an island that he called Trinidad. From the southern coast of Trinidad, he had a view of the Gulf of Paria, which separates Trinidad from present-day Venezuela. For

---

79   Todorov, *Conquest of America*, 22.
80   Todorov, *Conquest of America*, 49.

three days in August, Columbus traveled along the coast of the mainland. At the mouth of the Orinoco River, he rightly concluded that such a large freshwater river could not originate on a small island.

The significance of what Columbus achieved was swept up into his increasing religiosity. Guided by Pierre D'Ailly's *Imago Mundi*, Columbus was certain that the Orinoco was connected to the four rivers of paradise. Columbus thought that he had found the entrance into the earthly paradise. Columbus imagined the world as pear shaped, with paradise located at the stalk of the pear. That is, paradise was not in the heavens; nor was it on level earth. Instead, as he wrote in the narrative of his third voyage, "by gradually approaching it one begins, while still at a great distance, to climb toward it." One can therefore get close to paradise, but "no one can enter except by God's leave."[81]

For the location of paradise, Columbus cites Genesis 2:8: "The Lord God planted a garden eastward in Eden." More important than references to Genesis, Columbus's new world refers to the "new heaven and new earth" described in the book of Revelation. A discovery of the original Eden would not have signified for Columbus a return to the past but rather an approach to the end-time. Like numerous thinkers before him, Columbus had worked out a precise system of measuring the years until the end of the world. Starting with 5,343 years between Adam and Christ, Columbus calculated that from the year 1500 there were 150 years "for the completion of the seven thousand years that would be the end of the world."[82]

After Columbus's ecstatic moment at the Gulf of Paria, he returned to Hispaniola, where he faced open rebellion against his governance. He hanged a few of the rebels, but that did not stabilize the situation, and he asked for assistance from Spain. In 1500, the sovereigns sent Francisco Bobadilla, who promptly put Columbus and his brothers in chains.[83] They were returned to Spain as prisoners. Although Columbus was able to talk his way out of prison, the experience was humiliating for the admiral of

---

81 Christopher Columbus, "Narrative of the Third Voyage of Christopher Columbus to the Indies," *Four Voyages*, 221.
82 Toby Lester, *The Fourth Part of the World* (New York: Free Press, 2009), 297.
83 Thomas, *Rivers of Gold* 163-78.

the seas. His titles of governor and viceroy were stripped from him, as were any rights and privileges for his heirs.

Columbus's fourth and final journey with four ships and 140 men set off from Cadiz on May 11, 1502. "The most adventurous of the Admiral's four voyages, it was also the most disappointing."[84] Columbus was accompanied by his brother Bartholomew and his thirteen-year-old son, Ferdinand. His purpose was to find the strait linking the Indies with the Indian Ocean. Marco Polo had described the strait on his way back from China, but Columbus was looking for it in Panama. Actually, Columbus came very close to discovering that Panama is a thin strip of land separating two oceans. Despite native testimony of a great sea not far to the west, Columbus "missed by a few miles the most important geographical discovery he could have made on the High Voyage."[85] The whole voyage was marked by bad weather that damaged his small fleet. The ships were trapped for weeks in a bay at Jamaica. They were finally rescued in June 1504, and they set sail for home.

Although Columbus by 1504 was a sick and dying man, he was still talking about the great quantities of gold that could be found and used for a crusade. In a letter after the fourth voyage, he wrote that "Jerusalem and Mt. Sion shall be rebuilt by Christian hands; whose they are to be said by David in Psalm 14. Abbot Joachim said this builder would come from Spain."[86] Neither the Spanish sovereigns nor the pope, to whom Columbus also wrote, were moved by his plea.

Columbus's only consolation was a voice that he heard on his return trip: "O fool, slow to believe and serve thy God, the God of All. What more did he do for Moses or David his servant than he has done for thee? He gave thee the Indies which are so rich a part of the world, for thy own, and then has divided them at thy pleasure. He gave thee the keys of the barriers of the ocean seas which were closed with such mighty chains."[87]

---

84 Samuel Morrison, *Christopher Columbus, Mariner* (Boston: Little, Brown and Co., 1955), 192.

85 Morrison, *Christopher Columbus*, 178.

86 Christopher Columbus, "Letter to the Sovereigns of Spain," in *The Four Voyages of Christopher Columbus*. The Abbot Joachim whom Columbus refers to is Joachim of Fiore, the most influential thinker of the Middle Ages for prophesying the third age of the Spirit as the last stage of history.

87 Columbus, "Letters to the Sovereigns of Spain," in *Four Voyages*, 293.

Columbus thus consoled himself with the belief that he had "gained an honorable fame throughout Christendom." In fact, his reputation was at a low point. "Columbus had the ill fortune to die at the moment when his discoveries were little valued and his personal fortunes and expectations were at their lowest ebb."[88] It is not especially surprising that when the new world was named in 1507, Columbus was passed over.

Amerigo Vespucci

The name of Amerigo Vespucci is not as well known today as that of Christopher Columbus. Much of what is known of him may be fiction—partly the result of his own self-promotion. He imagined himself competing for fame with Columbus, and in one very impressive way he won the competition. Felipe Fernandez-Armesto, in his book *Amerigo*, writes that "the lesser mariner's self-confidence, lies, luck and salesmanship ensured that his reputation outshone Columbus'." The result is that we are left with "the extraordinary accident or error that bestowed his name on the western hemisphere."[89]

The attack on Vespucci's reputation began with the work of Bartolomé de las Casas, the famous defender of the Indians. Especially in the United States, Columbus achieved heroic and saintly stature, and Vespucci has been disdained. Ralph Waldo Emerson, who is sometimes described as the quintessential American, wrote, "Strange that all America should wear the name of a thief. Amerigo Vespucci, the pickler from Seville, whose highest naval rank was boatswain's mate in an expedition that never sailed, managed in this lying world to supplant Columbus and baptize the earth with his own dishonest name."[90] However, a comprehensive study of Vespucci's life by Germán Arciniegas considerably softens the bad reputation that Vespucci acquired.[91]

---

88 Samuel Morrison, *Christopher Columbus*, 198.
89 Felipe Fernandez-Armesto, *Amerigo* (New York: Random House, 2007).
90 Germán Arciniegas, *America in Europe: History of the New World in Reverse* (San Diego, CA: Harcourt, 1986), 268.
91 Germán Arciniegas, *Why America? 500 Years of a Name: The Life and Times of Amerigo Vespucci*, 2nd ed. (Bogota, Columbia: Villegas Editores, 2002).

The name of "America" (Amerigo) was associated with the document called *Mundus Novus* published in 1503. The title of that pamphlet was created by a Venetian editor rather than by the author, Amerigo Vespucci. Nonetheless, the document's contents helped to establish the mythical meaning that "America" has had ever since then. "Its crafted idealism prevailed over the much more realistic and singular depiction of other texts."[92] These other texts would include not only the narratives of Columbus but also the letters of Vespucci himself.

There are three so-called "familiar letters" of Vespucci from 1500, 1501, and 1502. The letters announce not a new world but an exploration of Asia. The first voyage of Vespucci was supposedly in 1497-98, which would place him at the Gulf of Paria before Columbus reached that area on his third voyage of May 1498. Vespucci claimed to have made four voyages, perhaps so as to equal Columbus's journeys. It is possible he made two voyages and was not commander of the fleet in either case.

Mundus Novus was developed from a letter that Vespucci sent to his Medici patron in Florence. Some of the errors in the letter may be the result of translators and editors. The letter did not lack in self-promotion: "Through the teaching of the marine chart for navigators I was more skilled than all the ship-masters of the whole world. For those have no knowledge except of those waters which they have often sailed."[93] It takes chutzpah to claim to be more skillful than all the shipmasters of the world because one has studied a navigation chart.

In detailing the discoveries of the journey, Vespucci moves between first-person singular and first-person plural: "In those southern parts I have found a continent more densely populated and abounding in animals than our Europe or Asia or Africa."[94] The basis for such a generalization was shaky, but he was intent on establishing the novelty of this world. By drawing a comparison to "Europe or Asia or Africa," he was claiming that

---

92 Angel Delgado-Gomez, "The Earliest European Views of the New World Natives," in *Early Images of the Americas* (Tucson, AZ: University of Arizona Press, 1993), 16.

93 Amerigo Vespucci, *Mundus Novus*, trans. George Tyler Northrop (Princeton, NJ: Princeton University Press, 1916), 4.

94 Vespucci, *Mundus Novus*, 1.

he had found a "fourth part to the world"—a phrase he used in his first letter.[95]

A reference to the land being a continent might suggest that Vespucci had a clear picture of a continent sitting between the Atlantic and Pacific Oceans. But like Columbus, he never reached the Pacific Ocean; nor could he project from his travels how this continent was related to the Indian Ocean and the mainland of Asia. He confidently claimed that "we knew that land to be a continent and not an island both because it stretches forth in the form of a very long and unbending coast, and because it is replete with infinite inhabitants."[96]

The term "continent" was in the process of changing its meaning. Etymologically, "continent" means "to be contiguous." Europe, Asia, and Africa were called continents because they touch one another. The distinctions between Europe and Asia and Africa were based more on race, language, and culture than on geography. Geographically, "continent" was never a very helpful category. The line dividing the continents of Asia and Europe is quite arbitrary in running through the country of Russia and the city of Constantinople.[97]

The invention of America gave a new, even if illogical, meaning to "continent." From this time onward, a continent was a large body of land that was *separated* from other continents. The movement from an island of earth (with three continents) to a world of four continents connected by oceans was a tremendous change that neither Columbus nor Vespucci could grasp. "Both of them missed the revolutionary transformation of the ocean from a barrier into a connector of continents, a medium for the global movement of people, money, goods and ideas."[98]

Amerigo Vespucci was therefore saying less than we might assume when he wrote, "The Most High was pleased to display before us a continent, new lands, and an unknown world."[99] The religious references here and elsewhere indicate that Vespucci, like Columbus, never abandoned a

---

95 Arcinegas, *Why America*, 354.
96 Vespucci, *Mundus Novus*, 3.
97 Martin Lewis and Karen Wigen, *The Myth of Continents* (Berkeley, CA: University of California Press, 1997), 30, 219-20.
98 Bender, *Nation among Nations*, 18.
99 Vespucci, *Mundus Novus*, 2.

religious—or, more exactly, biblical—context for his explorations. Like Columbus, Vespucci thought when he reached the Gulf of Paria that he was approaching the world as it was when it was first created. "Surely if the terrestrial paradise be in any part of this earth, I esteem that it is not far from these parts."[100]

Vespucci was struck by finding "in those parts such a multitude as nobody could enumerate." He obviously had not taken a census or based his judgment on travel across the continent. Instead he refers to what "we read in the Apocalypse."[101] This reference to the Apocalypse (the book of Revelation) might seem to come from out of nowhere, but it is part of the thought world in which he lived. The end of the world, according to the Apocalypse, will be a great city of God. The multitude of people Vespucci saw was a sign of a new world not far from where the present world began and also a portent of a new heaven and a new earth that would transform the present world. Henceforth, "America" and "Apocalypse" would never be far apart.

The Map

On April 30, 2007, a press release from the Library of Congress announced the purchase of a map from Germany by the United States; the map dates to 1507. The price tag was $10 million. Obviously, the map was not of the kind that used to be free at the local Shell station or one that can be downloaded from Google. The press release described the map as "America's birth certificate." The US public showed little interest in the acquisition of this extraordinary document. Perhaps the claim did not make sense to them. Each year, the press and television, politicians and advertisers, herald the Fourth of July as the "birthday of America." If that is true—and it would be considered unpatriotic and un-American to think otherwise—then how could the birth certificate have been issued 269 years before the birth?

The Library of Congress had good reason to call the map the birth certificate of America. Written across the southern part of the continent was "America"—the first time the word was used. For anyone who takes

---

100 Vespucci, *Mundus Novus*, 9.
101 Vespucci, *Mundus Novus*, 5.

language seriously, the first use of a term is significant. In this case, "America" would acquire in subsequent centuries a powerful emotional content that would be the basis for disputes, loyalties, and hatred. The Spanish resisted the term "America" for a long while, preferring "Indies." But "America" would eventually triumph everywhere.

The mapmakers in 1507 had little doubt about how they were using "America." They had considered carefully how to name the continent, and they recognized that the picture they were putting forth had revolutionary implications. There was now a fourth continent (or second half) of the world. America now ranked with Asia, Africa, and Europe as a continent. And America being a second half of the world meant that Africa/Asia/Europe was altered in meaning. A "new world" meant that, for the first time, Africa/Asia/Europe constituted an old world. The year 2007 was the five hundredth anniversary of America. One might have expected a gala celebration of this event in the United States and elsewhere. However, the year passed with barely a nod from an op-ed essay.

The map was put on permanent display at the Library of Congress in December 2007. The title given to the exhibition was "Exploring the Early Americas." That description is anachronistic. No one in the sixteenth century was exploring the "Americas." Splitting the continent into "Americas" came much later. It was part of a blurring process in which people talk of "the Americas" even though one nation calls itself America.

The reason why the display refers to "the early Americas" may be to soften the disappointment of US Americans when they look at the map. "America" is written across what later became Brazil and Venezuela. It was logical to write "America" there because that was the part of America that had been explored and for which fairly accurate measurements were available. Despite voyages over the centuries to the north, including that of John Cabot's landing in 1497 in Newfoundland, the contours of northern America remained sketchy.

Many copies of the map were made in 1507, but all of them were thought to have been lost until the discovery of a copy in 1901. The discovery was a great find for cartographers, but it took a while for historians to appreciate the map's significance. Gradually, the story of the map's origin was pieced together.

A team of mapmakers had gathered in 1505 at the Abbey of Saint-Die to begin the project of updating Ptolemy's map of the world. Matthias Ringmann, a key figure in the group, composed a poem in 1505 addressed to Ptolemy. It included the claim that *Vespucci* had discovered "a world not known in your pictures." A version of the poem was included in the handbook *Introduction to Cosmography*, which accompanied the map in 1507. All or most of the handbook was composed by Ringmann and Martin Waldseemüller. The map itself is usually credited to Waldseemüller.

The most striking thing about the map is that its makers, unlike Columbus and Vespucci, clearly visualized the new continent as separated from Asia by a great ocean. This was a decade before Balboa is credited with being the first European to view the Pacific Ocean. Waldseemüller and Ringmann "discovered" the Pacific Ocean by a leap of imagination. Looking back from today, it may seem like an obvious conclusion that anyone could draw from the fact that Columbus and Vespucci reported the existence of a large continent. However, the existence of that other large ocean had to be imagined. In a new version of his poem in the *Cosmography*, Ringmann changed the words "a land far under the Antarctic Pole" to "a land encircled by the vast ocean."[102]

Having conceived this fourth part of the world, Ringmann and Waldseemüller had the opportunity to provide it a name. Ringmann wrote, "I do not see why anyone should rightly prevent this being called Amerigen – the land of Amerigo, as it were – or America, after its discoverer, a man of perceptive character."[103] Ringmann here plays with variations on Vespucci's name: Amerigen, Amerigo, Americus, America. While Vespucci is known to history as Amerigo or Americus, "America" won out for purposes of symmetry with the feminine names of Europa, Asia, and Africa. The contentious issue, of course, was not the choice to use the feminine ending but the choice to use the name of the person who was called the discoverer of the land.

To later supporters of Columbus as the one who had discovered the land, the bestowal of the honor on Amerigo Vespucci is bewildering. For contemporaries it was a reasonable choice. Copernicus, in the opening pages of *On the Revolution of Heavenly Spheres*, says, "we now know that

---

102 Lester, *The Fourth Part of the World*, 366-67.
103 Lester, *The Fourth Part of the World*, 356.

the earth is inhabited in greater proportion than is left to the ocean." The reason we know this is because of the discovery of "that place known as America, a land so named by the captain who discovered it."[104]

The 1507 map (accompanied by a globe), together with Copernicus's treatise, finally placed "man" on the earth and in the universe. The controversy between Galileo and the Church in 1615 was in some ways an aftershock to what had occurred a century earlier.

The invention of America was a central symbol of the transformation of human consciousness. Toby Lester concludes his thorough study of the 1507 map with an appropriate lyricism: "It's the world viewed as a whole from above, a godlike vision of the earth suddenly accessible to all … It's a record of the past, a commentary on the present, and a dream of the future; a world at once ancient and medieval and modern."[105]

Embodiments of America

From its beginning, "America" was an idea embodied in a particular land. The land was a continent, and the word "America" has never lost its continental meaning. But various European nations established an embodiment of the American idea and created diverse versions of America. Edmund Burke, in 1770, wrote, "All America is in the hands of four nations. The Spaniards, who as they first discovered it, have the largest and richest share."[106] Burke seems to have undercounted the number of nations involved, or else he dismissed the importance of some nations, but he was certainly right in singling out Spanish America as the largest and richest version of America. But by 1770, Spanish America had begun to suffer serious setbacks and British America was emerging as a powerful competitor. Part of the British settlement was soon to assert its independence. After this time, the versions of America have often been reduced to "Anglo America" and "Latin America."

---

104 Arciniegas, *America in Europe,* 79; Copernicus, *On the Revolutions of Heavenly Spheres* (New York: Prometheus, 1995).
105 Lester, *Fourth Part of the World,* 397.
106 Edmund Burke, *An Account of the European Settlements in America* (London: J. Dodsley, 1770), 208; *Three American Empires,* ed. John TePaske (New York: Harper and Row, 1967), 13.

Latin America

Histories in the English-speaking world often paint the Spanish version of America as the bad side of the picture compared to English settlements. Some of the dark picture (the black legend) is drawn from prophetic criticism in Spanish American literature. Those judgments have often been unfair in criticism of the Spanish treatment of native peoples.

A more radical kind of English-language history is simply oblivious to there being a Spanish America at all. Samuel Huntington, in *Who Are We? The Challenges to America's National Identity*, writes: "Before immigrants could come to America, settlers had to found America ... Before there could be founding fathers, there were founding settlers. America did not begin in 1775, 1776 or 1787. It began with the first settler communities of 1607, 1620 and 1630."[107] In this history of America, nothing much happened from 1507 until 1607.

Both Anglo and Latin versions contain a sizable amount of material on the scandalous treatment of the native peoples. A comprehensive and evenhanded moral judgment as to which intervention was worse may not be possible. Where the two versions of America can usefully be compared is in their respective understandings of America as the "new world."

The English settlements can serve as a contrast to the Latin south in how they represented newness. For the English colonies, newness meant keeping the Indians at a distance so that the English could establish the model Christian society. The races and religions were not allowed to commingle in the north. The new world would be independent of the old by not mixing Indian and European peoples.

In southern America, the new world was a mixture both of races and of religions. In Spanish America, the new man might be a mixture of white, Indian, and negro. That does not mean that racial equality was immediately achieved and that class differences disappeared. But racial intermixing was simply a fact of life and not something illegal or shameful.

The newness in the south was not premised on a break from Europe or on anti-European sentiment. Spain imagined setting up colonies (or "kingdoms") to which the blessings of Spanish culture would be brought.

---

107 Samuel Huntington, *Who Are We? The Challenge to America's National Identity* (New York: Simon and Schuster, 2005), 40.

The fate of Spanish America was closely tied, for better and for worse, to what happened to Spain. Even when political independence was asserted by American nations in the nineteenth century, Spanish philosophy, art, and science continued to be appreciated in Latin American countries.

During the first half of the sixteenth century, the news in Spanish America was of constant victories. Spanish explorers staked out territory from Chile to the northern border of Mexico. Hernán Cortes, with a small army, after several setbacks, brought down the Aztec empire in 1521. The Aztecs were a powerful nation that had built an impressive world, albeit with some violent underpinnings. A Spanish soldier, on first viewing the capital city Tenochtitlan, was quoted as saying, "Some of the soldiers among us who had been in many parts of the world, in Constantinople, and all over Italy, and in Rome, said that so large a market place and so full of people, and so well regulated and arranged, they had never beheld before."[108] On the site of the Aztec capital, the Spanish built Mexico City, one of the first grand American cities.

Francisco Pizarro, in 1532, led a small army in conquering the Incas, a people that originated in the Cuzco Valley; by the sixteenth century, "Inca" referred to an elite group that stretched from Ecuador to Central Chile. The Incas were the largest and richest of the Indian empires. The Incas were weakened, however, by civil war and disease. Pizarro, with only 170 soldiers but backed by horses, swords, and firepower, was able to overcome the Inca people. It took several decades for the Spanish to pacify the country, and the Incas went into precipitous decline in numbers.[109]

After midcentury, Spain suffered serious economic and political setbacks. Most spectacular was the defeat of their armada in 1588. The problems in the mother country hampered development throughout Spanish America.

The other main story of Latin America was Portugal. The papal bull of 1493 that drew a line in the ocean had been more favorable to Spain

---

108 Bernal Diaz del Castillo, *The Conquest of New Spain* (New York: Penguin Books, 1963), 219; Miguel Leon Portilla, *The Broken Spears: Aztec Account of the Conquest of Mexico* (Boston: Beacon Press, 2006).

109 William Prescott, *History of the Conquest of Peru* (New York: Cooper Square, 2000); Kim MacQuarrie, *The Last Days of the Incas* (New York: Simon and Schuster, 2007).

than Portugal. But the Treaty of Tordesillas in 1494 gave Portugal legal claim to much of Brazil. Portugal, until the end of the fifteenth century, was preoccupied with journeying eastward to the Indies. Vasco de Gama, in 1497-98, had brought back spices and precious stones from the East. In 1500, Portugal sent a fleet of thirteen ships and twelve hundred men west under the command of Pedro Alavares Cabral. The quest was for a western route to India. However, Cabral's fleet was blown off course and thus made first contact with Brazil.

After claiming Brazil and sending back word to Portugal, Cabral continued his journey by going east around Africa and laying the foundation for a Portuguese worldwide empire. With Portugal's attention still mainly on Asia, its American possession progressed slowly. After 1510, trade with India declined and the demand for spices became limited. At the same time, the value of Brazil wood was recognized (the country was named for the wood; not vice versa), and in later times, sugar became a valuable commodity.

Portugal feared the power of Spain in the new world and was made a subject of Spain from 1580 to 1640. English, French, and especially Dutch explorers influenced Brazil's early development. The Dutch occupied twelve hundred miles of coastline in the early seventeenth century. The mother country, Portugal, sent its nonconformists, including many Jews, to Brazil.

Portugal's rule of Brazil was more lax than Spain's control of its colonies. Government was largely in the hands of plantation owners and local councils. Church organization in Brazil also lagged behind the Spanish colonies. In 1549, six Jesuit missionaries arrived and began a distinguished Jesuit mission in the country. They tried to protect the natives while helping to civilize the country. They made enemies in doing so and were eventually expelled in the eighteenth century.

The Original Americans

For centuries or millennia, there were tribes that dwelt in the land that became America. They can properly be called Native Americans (or simply "the Americans") because they were there when America was invented. The Europeans should logically be called Foreign Americans. From today's vantage point, it is difficult to view the Europeans as anything other than oppressors, ready to use all means of violence to satisfy their greed and rapaciousness. In contrast, the Spanish, Portuguese, French, Dutch, and English of that era saw themselves as bearers of advanced civilization.

While European practices were laced with violence and the destruction of the native people, we know of the cruelties from historians who were among the invaders. The best of the histories were written by Bernardino de Sahagún and Diego Durán. Much better known is the writing of Bartolomé de las Casas.

What these historians and other European thinkers struggled with was how the American native was to be accepted as part of the human family, and in turn, what light was cast upon the origin and nature of man by the Indian. The Renaissance view of human nature had been optimistic about the goodness and peace-loving qualities of man. But the emphasis on the sinfulness of man in medieval Christianity carried over into Reformation and Counter-Reformation churches.[110] Both Catholic and Protestant versions of Christianity portrayed the human being as incapable of doing good on its own. In secular literature, too, a pessimistic view of the humans as greedy and violent was evident. Thomas Hobbes, in the early seventeenth century, exemplified that view. Hobbes's influential writing described each man as being at war with every other man.[111]

The European view of the Indian was a kaleidoscope of these images of human nature. The images from European thought were imposed on the Indian; secondarily, the American natives helped to shape and reshape European images of primitive man.

The most fundamental question was whether the Indian was human. Or, as it was phrased in a question that was metaphysically equivalent but experientially different, "Did the Indians have souls?" A concern for the existence of the soul focused on the religious state of the natives, not necessarily their physical, political, and economic well-being. The logical connection should not have been difficult to make; the person with a human soul is a member of the human family with the dignity, rights, and

---

110 John Elliot, "The Discovery of America and the Discovery of Man," in *Spain and its World, 1500*-1700 (New Haven, CT: Yale University Press, 1989), 50.

111 Thomas Hobbes, *The Elements of Law Natural and Politic* (New York: Oxford University Press, 1994).

privileges of human beings. However, from at least the time of Aristotle, it had been held that some people were born to be slaves.

The Spanish sovereigns, as early as 1495, had disallowed enslavement of the native population. But Columbus returned from his first voyage with five hundred slaves on board, two hundred of whom died in transit. The Portuguese in Africa had already used slaves as a substitute for the promised but missing gold.[112]

It was necessary in 1537 for Pope Paul to publish a bull that stated as follows: "... the Indians are truly men and they are not only capable of understanding the Catholic faith but, according to our information, they desire exceedingly to receive it."[113] The history of Negro slavery in the south lacked some of the brutality of the north. But the longstanding incapacity of Christians to see the radical conflict between slavery and the profession of their religion is baffling.

There were Christian voices, especially from within the religious orders, who were staunch defenders of the natives.[114] The Dominicans and the Franciscans, and later the Jesuits, were critics of Spanish policy, although how exactly they were to view the Indians, with their good and bad qualities, was not clear. The Dominicans tended to have a "separate but equal" attitude. They were intent on maintaining orthodox Catholic practice and required a total conversion of the natives. The Franciscans were open to some creative mixing of Indian religion and Catholic liturgy. Although Columbus had first judged the Indians to have no religion, they had a rich set of religious practices that bore similarity to the sacramental practices of Catholicism.

The most famous critic of Spain's policies was Batholomé de las Casas, who provided a bleak picture of Spanish oppression that was red meat for anti-Spanish propaganda. Even today, Las Casas's *Very Brief Recital of the Destruction of the Indies* (1552) is, for many people, the chief source of

---

112 Thomas, *Rivers of Gold*, 121.

113 Henry Steele Commager, ed., *Documents of American History* (New York: Appleton, Century, Croft, 1963), 3.

114 Lewis Hanke, *The Spanish Struggle for Justice in the Conquest of America* (Philadelphia, PA: University of Pennsylvania Press, 1949).

their view of Spanish America in the sixteenth century.[115] The work was translated into many languages and went through numerous editions. This work unfortunately contained exaggerations and inflated numbers. For example, he writes that "we give as a real and true reckoning that in the said forty years more than twelve million persons, men, women and children, have perished unjustly by the infernal deeds and tyranny of the Christians."[116] It is too bad that Las Casas is not better known for his other writings that are also critical of Spanish policies but more balanced.

Las Casas followed an unusual path to becoming "Protector of the Indians." Born in Seville in 1476, he became a soldier of fortune and did well financially in Hispaniola and Cuba. At the age of forty, he suddenly awoke to the cruelty of the Spanish treatment of the natives. For the following fifty years, he was a tireless spokesperson for the cause of the natives. He presented a plan to Charles I for reorganizing villages so as to remove some of the burden from the natives, who were virtual slaves. His plan included bringing Negro slaves from Africa, which was not a new practice, but his proposal was something that he was later ashamed of. He retired to a monastery in Santo Domingo during the 1520s to write his great work, *History of the Indies*.

Las Casas returned to active life in Guatemala and later, as a bishop, wrote *The Only Method of Attracting Men to the True Religion*. Like many other defenders of the Indians, Las Casas was not opposed to colonialism and Spanish expansionism. What he opposed was enslavement as the means to spread the "true faith." Las Casas thought that Christian missionaries should preach the gospel for the Indians "to fulfill their natural purposes – a gentle, coaxing, gracious way."[117] Las Casas's theory was given a test in the Vera Paz experiment in Guatemala from 1537-50. Oppression of the native was replaced by an attitude of respect. Christian missionaries did not try to force their religion on the natives. In time the experiment was eclipsed, but its example remained important for future missionary efforts.

---

115 Bartolomé de Las Casas, *The Devastation of the Indies* (Baltimore, MD: Johns Hopkins, 1992).

116 Bartolomé de Las Casas, *Witness: Writings of Bartolomé De Las Casas* (New York: Orbis Books, 1992), 145.

117 John Noonan, *A Church that Can and Cannot Change* (Notre Dame, IN: University of Notre Dame, 2005), 72.

One of the most important debates of the sixteenth century took place in Valladolid in 1550-51 between Bartolomé de Las Casas and the scholar Juan Gines de Sepulveda.[118] Las Casas had succeeded in preventing the publication of Sepulveda's book, which followed Aristotle in saying that some human beings are by nature destined to be slaves. It is a shame that Francis de Vittoria, who has since become famous in the history of the development of human rights, died in 1546 and was barely mentioned by either Las Casas or Sepulveda.

Las Casas did not take on Aristotle directly, but he defended the full humanity of the American natives. Sepulveda claimed the validity of "just war" theory as it applied to the natives. The panel that was supposed to judge never came to a conclusion of who was the winner. But the failure of Sepulveda to triumph was important for the future.

Perhaps the most competent historian of the period was Bernardino de Sahagún (1499-1590), a Franciscan missionary to Mexico. His monumental study, *General History of the Things of New Spain*, is also known as the *Florentine Codex*.[119] Sahagún learned Nahuatl, the native language of the Aztecs. He conducted what might be the first ethnographic study by interviewing native people and gathering a massive amount of material with the help of the natives. He documented Nahuatl language and literature in twelve volumes, and produced a grammar and a dictionary of Nahuatl.

In the prologue to the *Florentine Codex*, Sahagun writes, "What is certain is that all these people are our brothers … they are our neighbors whom we must love as ourselves." He wrote his history "to assay the worth of the Mexican people which has remained unknown up to now." Sahagun said that because of ignorance and bias, the Mexicans "are held to be barbarians and of very little worth; in truth, however, in matters of culture and refinement, they are a step ahead of other nations that presume to be quite politic."[120]

---

118 Todorov, *Conquest*, 151-67.

119 Miguel Leon-Portilla, *Bernardino de Sahagun: First Anthropologist* (Norman, OK: University of Oklahoma, 1999).

120 Bernardino Sahagun, *Florentine Codex: Part I: Introduction and Indices*, ed. Arthur Anderson and Charles Dibble (Salt Lake City, UT: University of Utah, 1982), 47-49.

Even in this "objective" history, Sahagun is unsure of how to judge the native people. Like Las Casas, Sahagun tended to excuse native defects, such as drunkenness and infant sacrifice. He placed the blame on "the most cruel hatred of our ancient enemy Satan, who with the most malign cunning, persuaded them to engage in such infernal acts."[121]

The Catholic Church was losing large numbers of people in Europe by way of the Protestant Reformation, which began in 1517. At the same time, it was gaining millions of converts in America. Early America was almost entirely Catholic. And by means of new trade routes opened up by Spanish and Portuguese explorers, Catholic Christianity achieved global status. The Portuguese brought their religion to Eastern outposts in Siam and Burma. The Spanish acquired the Philippines in 1565. A Catholic mission in China that began in 1582 might have had success, but it was early aborted.[122]

In the twentieth century, a number of Jesuit priests and Catholic nuns in Latin America lost their lives in opposing right-wing military government and the oppression of the poor. The Vatican worried about the ferment in a land that was thought to be safely and quietly Catholic. Books on American Catholicism are usually about the United States. But the fortunes of worldwide Catholicism are tied to the Spanish and Brazilian missions of the sixteenth century.

---

121 Sahagun, *Florentine Codex*, vol. 1, 142.
122 David Mungello, *The Great Encounter of China and the West* (Lanham, MD: Rowman and Littlefield, 2005).

3

Constructing the United States: Part 1

This chapter reflects on the emergence of the United States and its relation to both the continent and the idea of America. The previous chapter used the metaphor of invention to describe the origin of America. The same metaphor could be used for the beginning of the United States but I think construction is a more appropriate metaphor.

"Invention" has been used in a number of histories that recount the founding of the United States.[123] The strange thing is that authors use the title or subtitle "The Invention of America" in describing 1776 and the period that led up to the Declaration of Independence. The logic of this use of language is peculiar. Surely everyone acknowledges that America existed from the beginning of the sixteenth century. How can anyone say that America was invented in 1776? The answer seems to be that authors assume that no matter what "America" may have meant for the preceding two and a half centuries, it was now a name for the new nation (which actually did not come into existence in 1776).

The metaphor of constructing the United States of America means that there were states that had to be assembled into a union of states. The formal title of the Declaration of Independence is "The unanimous Declaration of the thirteen united States of America."[124] The lowercase treatment of

---

123 Jack Rakove, *Revolutionaries: A New History of the Invention of America* (Boston: Houghton Mifflin, 2010); Garry Wills, *Inventing America* (New York: Doubleday, 1978).

124 The name "United States of America" had earlier been proposed in a 1774 letter to a newspaper: Pauline Maier, *American Scripture: Making the Declaration of*

"united" was accurate. There was no entity that was called "the United States of America." There were thirteen British American colonies that were declaring themselves to be thirteen free and independent states.

The components of a "United States" remained largely independent until at least the 1780s, when there was approval of a federal constitution. Even then, "these united states" was a work in progress. Given the tension inherent to a federal union of states, the unity has always been precarious. The idea of America has been a powerful force to hold the nation together, especially during foreign wars. But the idea of America has also been used to avoid the realistic problem of uniting not the states of America but the states of Massachusetts, New York, South Carolina, Arizona, and the rest. It is a job of construction that is not finished.

The focus of this chapter is the period from the late sixteenth to the late eighteenth centuries. I will highlight the origin of the English colonies in America, the period leading up to the Declaration of Independence, and the Declaration of Independence itself. This chapter makes no claim to offer new historical facts. My intention is to trace the meanings of "America" and "American," starting with how the terms were used in England and by the English colonists to refer to themselves. Although "America" had a meaning long before the English began to plant colonies, the English contributed a distinctive twist to that meaning

The Spanish, French, Portuguese, Dutch, and English agreed that America was a new world. It represented almost limitless possibilities, but each nation took a distinctive approach to this new world. The newness of this world, as I have pointed out, could be taken as an attempt to sever all relations with the old. But it could also mean an extension or completion in relation to the old. In practice, the attempt at discontinuity could not be entirely successful, and conversely, attempts at continuity inevitably introduced unforeseen novelties.

One therefore has to break down the question of continuity into categories such as cultural, political, educational, and religious elements. The continuity of language guaranteed considerable continuity of culture. The colonists brought about an impressive pattern of education, starting with the family and continuing in the school. But subtle changes began almost immediately as they tried to adjust to a new environment. American

Jurisprudence (New York: Knopf, 1997), 44.

education would take on its own distinctive character; in practice, it has struggled to keep pace with ambitious claims.[125]

However, religion, which is a central element of culture, was in a period of conflict between European countries—and sometimes within individual countries. The question of religious tolerance was an inevitable issue in the life of each American colony. The structure of political life was also in flux during the sixteenth and early seventeenth centuries. The new political instruments that were tried out in the colonies originated more from trial and error than as a result of political theory.

Spanish America remained closely tied to the Roman Catholic Church and to the Crown in Spain. A similar pattern was present in French America. While France was coping with Protestants (Huguenots), New France kept out the disorder that would result from mixing in Protestants with Catholics. The English colonies embodied religious dissent but not a rejection of England's political tradition. The Dutch, among all the European nations, had achieved a high degree of religious diversity and toleration. New Netherland carried that spirit into the new world.

England laid claim to a long stretch of coastline on the American continent. The English colonies had the French to their north and the Spanish to their south. In the middle of the English claim was New Netherland, part of which was New Amsterdam, the island of Manhattan. Most of the earliest settlers of New Amsterdam were not Dutch; they came from a dozen different European nations.[126] The English never accepted the legitimacy of this settlement.

The Dutch quickly recognized that their colony could be an invaluable commercial property with its great harbor on the East River. Toleration of differences was not based on any theory of religious freedom. Rather, whoever could make it financially in New Amsterdam was welcome. When the local government was not welcoming to Jews, Lutherans, and

---

125 Bernard Bailyn, *Education in the Forming of American Society* (New York: Vintage, 1960). For reflection on this comprehensive meaning of education, see Gabriel Moran, "Educational Model," *Education toward Adulthood* (New York: Paulist Press, 1979), 37-55.

126 Jaap Jacobs, *The Colony of New Netherland: A Dutch Settlement in Seventeenth-Century America* (Ithaca, NY: Cornell University Press, 2010); Russell Shorto, *The Island at the Center of the World: The Epic Story of Dutch Manhattan and the Forgotten Colony that Shaped America* (New York: Vintage Books, 2005).

Quakers, the population protested in a document known as the Flushing Remonstrance. The people's successful assertion of tolerance against a sometimes too rigid leader, Peter Stuyvesant, helped to establish an attitude of political dissent.

The Dutch were well aware that the English found unacceptable the presence of another nation's colony separating the English colonies. The Dutch built a wall in 1653 to defend themselves against an attack from the English. The wall was situated where the famous Wall Street now stands. The wall was intended to defend against an attack from the north. But when the English launched a blockade of New Amsterdam's harbor in 1664, the Dutch surrendered without a fight.

The English were generous in victory, allowing the continuance of the Dutch language and many of the cultural and political differences in New York that had flourished in New Amsterdam. About 90 percent of the population decided to stay at the time of capitulation to the English. The arrival of the first printer in the 1690s was a key to a shift in the language of the colony. To this day, however, the Dutch imprint on Manhattan is evident. In its place names, architecture, street pattern, and attitude of tolerating diversity, New York bears more resemblance to Amsterdam in the Netherlands than to York in England.

Liberty and Freedom

The history of the United States in relation to America is tied to a distinction between "liberty" and "freedom." As is often the case in the English language, the two words seem to have the same meaning. Sometimes when English has two terms for the same thing, there is a class bias; the educated class prefers words derived from Latin and French, while a word with Anglo-Saxon origin is judged to be vulgar. That simple class bias does not apply to "freedom" and "liberty," although the Germanic *"Freiheit,"* which gave us "freedom," has connotations that differ from the Latin *"libertas,"* from which "liberty" is derived.

In the Germanic languages, the concept of freedom has a philosophical meaning related to the nature of human beings. Freedom is a birthright of free people who are equal before the law and can rule themselves. The Latin language's *"libertas"* was derived from the Greek and Roman experience of a republic in which a superior class possessed political liberty and provided it in varying degrees to other classes. In a republic, therefore, liberty and slavery were not incompatible. After the Norman conquest of England in 1066, these meanings of "freedom" and "liberty" became mixed together. The freedom of the Anglo-Saxon was in tension with liberties sought from the monarchy. The British came to speak of the liberties of their common law as the rights of every Englishman.[127]

In 1989, the French threw a big party in Paris to commemorate the two hundredth anniversary of the *Declaration of the Rights of Man and of the Citizen*. During the festivities, Margaret Thatcher struck a discordant note by saying that the British did not owe anything about rights and liberty to the French Revolution.[128] Thatcher had considerable historical backing for her assertion about the origin of English rights and their relation to liberty. The English claim to liberties goes back as far as the twelfth century and found expression in a thirteenth-century document known as the Magna Carta. Its full Latin title is Magna Carta Libertatum (the great charter of liberties). The English translations refer in the text to "liberties."

When the colonists emigrated to America, they were promised "to have and enjoy all liberties and immunities of free and natural subjects." However, there was a difference between freedom and liberty that was eventually reflected in differences between southern and northern colonies. New England's freedom meant a place of self-governing towns based on the equality of all citizens, although citizenship was not extended to African slaves. Virginia's liberty implied hierarchy; the assertion of political liberties was compatible with indenture and slavery for some of the population. Out of that Virginia setting came many of the individuals (Washington, Jefferson, Madison) who gave an emphasis to liberty in the founding documents of the United States.

The meaning of liberty in the United States was filtered through the protections of English common law and the Glorious Revolution of 1688.

---

127 Colin Woodard, *American Nations: A History of the Eleven Regional Cultures of North America* (New York: Viking Books, 2011), 54-55.

128 Ian Buruma, *Taming the Gods: Religion and Democracy on Three Continents* (Princeton, NJ: Princeton University Press, 2010), 31; Conor Cruise O'Brien, "The Decline and Fall of the French Revolution," *New York Review of Books*, February 15, 1990.

Liberty meant freedom from intrusion by the government into particular areas of personal life. The French Revolution gave a more radical twist to *liberté*, which has affected the United States' meaning of "liberty." A word whose essential meaning is negative—that is, liberty as a *freedom from* oppression—came to be used as an equivalent to "freedom." But freedom is not restricted to political liberty; it can be a psychological, social, or religious description of personal life.

A cry for liberty or liberation usually means resistance to an oppressor. Freedom comes later, when the oppression ceases. When Sarah Grimké said in the nineteenth century, "all that I ask of our brethren is that they will take their feet from off our necks," she was not describing the freedom of women but rather an indispensable step before women could explore their own freedom.[129] When Abraham Lincoln proclaimed an emancipation from slavery, he provided liberty from the condition that the slaves had experienced. Unfortunately, neither the North nor the South was prepared to guarantee that freedom would actually be experienced as a result of liberation. Such freedom would include food, shelter, health care, and employment. Liberty was instantaneous; freedom was a long road.[130]

What was remarkable about the British American colonies was the close link they sensed between asserting liberty from oppression and the constituting of an instrument for working toward freedom. That is, the colonies in 1776 declared their independence because their liberties had been violated. After a decade of experience with the liberty of independence, they decided to follow their declaration of liberty with a constitution of their freedom. John Adams said that "neither morals, nor riches, nor discipline of armies, nor all these together will do without a constitution."[131]

The authors of the US Constitution sought to balance liberty from government with a freedom that requires governmental authority. There is a big difference between the usual pious picture of the nation's founders and what many historians find regarding class and race biases in those founders. The debate is helped if one recognizes that the Declaration of

---

129 Sarah Grimké, *Letters on the Equality of the Sexes* (New Haven, CT: Yale University Press, 1988).
130 For the devastating condition of the "freedmen" during and after the war, see Jim Downs, *Sick from Freedom* (New York: Oxford University Press, 2012).
131 Hannah Arendt, *On Revolution* (New York: Viking Press, 1963), 140.

Independence and the US Constitution are about different topics. A tension between liberty and freedom is a more helpful subject for discussion than democratic versus antidemocratic.

The British American and French Revolutions began the attempt to universalize rights. The meaning of "liberty" was altered by being made part of the declarations of rights inherent to "man." The first article of the *Declaration of the Rights of Man and of the Citizen* declares that humans are born free. That seems like a strange claim given that human babies are so completely dependent on others at birth. Perhaps one can refer to a birthright of freedom, but people might still need *liberating* from their present condition. Article four of the French declaration says that "liberty consists in the freedom to do everything which injures no one else." So defined, liberty becomes a desirable ideal for individual human beings, but the place of government is left unclear.

If one could count the uses of "freedom" and "liberty" in the history of the United States, "liberty" would be the clear winner. Certainly, the idea of liberty as a freedom from restriction was enthusiastically embraced by people of the United States. The revolution was fought in the name of the "sacred cause of liberty." The Bill of Rights to the United States Constitution includes a series of rights as liberties. The rights are not guaranteed by the ten amendments; instead, they are promises that the federal government will not interfere. For most US citizens, the right to be left alone ranks near the top of the rights that they cherish. Unfortunately, an overemphasis on liberty in the United States is detrimental to the existence of good government.

New York magazine once did a series of interviews with recent immigrants to the United States. One of them said, "What a marvelous country this is; you can say anything you want and nobody cares." The statement captures an exhilarating feeling of being free but also the danger of equating freedom and liberty. If you are running from the secret police back home, the fact that no one cares what you say is a wonderful experience. If you are a widow with three children begging for help, the fact that no one cares about your plea is no help to feeding your family; nor is it an experience of human freedom.

British America

John Adams said that the American colonists began declaring independence "upon taking ship in European ports to find a land of their own in America."[132] They left their homes to make a precarious trip to a "wilderness" that was thousands of miles away. Why would any seventeenth-century European do that? Although individual motives are difficult to ascertain, the people who wrote accounts of colonial life consistently cited two reasons for colonization—namely, economics and religion.

The two given reasons were almost always intertwined in promotional advertising for the colonies. America has always been imagined as a place of wealth, both spiritual and material. The Christian gospel and profitable business have been close allies throughout the history of the British American colonies and the United States of America. What was said of the Mormons in Utah also applies to many other religious groups: they came to do good, and they did well.

The first attempt at colonization by the English was at Roanoke in 1585. Not much is known about the hundred men, women, and children who formed the colony. The settlers had the misfortune to be trying this precarious mission at a time when England was distracted by war with Spain. A request for supplies was not answered for three years, and when a ship did arrive, there was no trace of the settlers. A study of the evidence concludes that some of the settlers were killed; others intermarried with the native population.[133]

Jamestown

In 1606, a charter was granted to a company to settle in Virginia. The charter states the purpose of the plantation as "the propagating of Christian religion to such people, as yet in darkness and miserable ignorance of the true knowledge and worship of God."[134] There is no reason to think that

---

132 Quoted in Germán Arciniegas, "The Four Americas," in Lewis Hanke, ed., *Do the Americas Have a Common History?* (New York: Knopf, 1964), 240.
133 James Horn, *A Kingdom Strange: The Brief and Tragic History of Roanoke* (New York: Basic Books, 2010).
134 Perry Miller, *Errand into the Wilderness* (New York: Harper, 1956), 101.

this ostensible purpose of converting the natives was a lie. An intention to spread the Christian gospel was a regular part of the invitation to migrate to America. However, the economic motive, which is usually stated as secondary, was no doubt the primary reason for many individuals.

Captain John Smith, in a 1608 promotional pitch, begins with the statement that "the eyes of all Europe are looking upon our endeavors to spread the gospel among the heathen people of Virginia …" But he concludes the same sentence with "… to the end we may thereby be secured from being eaten out of all profit of trade by our more industrious neighbors."[135] America was the land of opportunity for individuals and a potential source of wealth for the mother country.

The importance of this economic motive seems to be confirmed by the individuals who went to Virginia. The demographics of Jamestown contrast sharply with those of the later settlers in New England. Most of the original settlers in Virginia were young, single males of ages fifteen to twenty-four. They were unskilled laborers drawn from the lower strata of society. They went to America as indentured workers for four to seven years.[136] America seemed like a chance worth taking compared to what they were leaving. There was a new world possible and little to lose. By 1625, 74 percent of the colony members were adult males, and only 10 percent were adult women. That imbalance led to slow population growth.

The Virginia settlers were not in rebellion against the Church of England. The mission had the blessing of the church back home. On the other hand, the settlers were not ardent preachers of the Christian gospel. Thomas Dale complained that "not many give testimonie beside their names that they are Christians."[137] The judgment of a historian a century later was that Virginia was founded not by God but by hucksters and swindlers.[138]

In the course of a dozen years, a new political phenomenon emerged; it was an elective council modeled on the British House of Commons. The

---

135 John Smith, *A True Relation of Virginia* (New York: Nabu Press, 2010).

136 Susan Hardman Moore, *Pilgrims: New World Settlers and the Call of Home* (New Haven, CT: Yale University Press, 2007), 21.

137 Miller, *Errand into the Wilderness,* 131.

138 Robert Beverley, *The History and Present State of Virginia* (Charlottesville, VA: University of Virginia Press, 1968).

assembly in Virginia was called the House of Burgesses. When Virginia was made a royal colony in 1624, its local rule was severely restricted. Nonetheless, the House of Burgesses was a seed for later independence movements and the source of some leading statesmen in the new nation, including George Washington and Thomas Jefferson.

By 1620, the Virginia Company had relinquished sole ownership of the land, hoping to attract new investors. The company was still promoting its settlement as a place where riches were easily available. "The rich Furres, Caviary and Cordage, which we draw from Russia with so great difficulty, are to be had in Virginia and the parts adioyning with ease and plenty."[139] The actual economic condition was bad and getting worse. The introduction of tobacco in 1617 was the one big success. The death rate among the colonists was staggering.

History books in the United States tell the story of Virginia from the perspective of the white European settlers. America represented liberation from the old world and old ways. Unfortunately, one man's liberty is often another man's oppression. In the case of Virginia and in later colonies, the white man's liberty came at the expense of American natives and imported Africans.

Until the second half of the twentieth century, historians of the conflict between the Europeans and the native population paid little attention to the perspective and the rights of the natives. The Indians were presented as the barbarous enemy of European progress. Today's historians do their best to recount a clash of civilizations in which neither side was innocent of barbarity.[140] Still, it was the "Americans" who were simply trying to defend their homeland and the Europeans who were the invaders. And it is not clear how much of this rebalanced history has penetrated the popular

---

139 Nick Bunker, *Making Haste from Babylon: The Mayflower Pilgrims and their World* (New York: Knopf, 2010), 248.

140 Bernard Bailyn, *The Barbarous Years: The Peopling of British North America: The Conflict of Civilizations, 1600-1675* (New York: Knopf, 2012); for a more radical attempt to view the history from the native side, see Francis Jennings, *The Invasion of America: Indians, Colonialism, and the Cant of Conquest* (Chapel Hill, NC: University of North Carolina, 1975); Daniel Richter, *Facing East from Indian Country: A Native History from Early America* (Cambridge, MA: Harvard University Press, 2003).

understanding in which "American history" is still imagined as beginning with the arrival of the English.

The arrival of Africans in 1619 probably seemed at the time a minor event. Laborers were needed to work the tobacco crop. An African American writer of recent times puts the event in proper perspective: "The flag she flew was Dutch; her crew a motley. Her port of call, an English settlement, Jamestown, in the colony of Virginia. She came, she traded, and shortly afterwards was gone. Probably no ship in modern history has carried a more portentous freight. Her cargo? Twenty slaves."[141] These first Africans were the beginning of a system of slavery; their condition of indentured servitude in these alien surroundings produced the terrible practice of slavery, the source of unending conflict.

It is difficult to understand how the colonists failed to see that the importing of slaves in great numbers was an untenable basis on which to build an economy. The threat of a slave rebellion was an ever present source of anxiety for the white population. And there were indeed regular uprisings throughout English (and, later, British) American colonial history, although most of them were localized and do not show up in history books. Even after the founding of the United States of America, the country continued on a self-destructive path of enslaving millions of people while proclaiming liberty.

As for the native people, they could not be subdued for work. They could be bargained with, as occasionally happened, or they could be subdued with firepower. The two disparate cultures lacked a common language, which generated fear on both sides and outbursts of violence. The Europeans looked on the Indians as savages ignorant of civilization. From their perspective, if the Indians could not be converted, they would have to be eliminated.

Captain John Smith's writings are a good index of the colonists' paradoxical attitude toward the people for whom they supposedly came to bring truth and civility. Smith describes the colony waiting for its first supplies in January 1608: "Each hour we were expecting the fury of the savages, when God, the patron of good endeavors in that desperate

---

141 J. Saunders Redding, *They Came in Chains* (Philadelphia, PA: Lippincott, 1973), quoted in Howard Zinn, *A People's History of the United States* (New York: Harper and Row, 1980), 23.

extremity, so changed the hearts of the savages that they brought such plenty of fruits and provisions that no man wanted."[142] This extraordinary generosity of the natives and cooperation is attributed by Smith to God alone; the Indians get no credit.

Smith had recommended that the Indians be treated firmly but not brutally. But after a massacre in 1622, Smith and other leaders changed their attitudes about a nonviolent strategy of converting the Indians. Smith quotes a letter to the council from a minister, James Stockam: "I confess you say well to have converted them by fair means, but they scorn it … and till their priests and ancients have their throats cut there is no hope to bring them to conversion."[143] Smith agreed with this strategy, saying "… it is more easy to civilize them by conquest than fair means, for the one may be made at once but their civilizing will require a long time and much industry."[144]

Plymouth

The myth that envelops the United States' origin is centered on the 1620 settlement at Plymouth. For a great many US Americans, the Puritans fled the religious oppression of Europe and founded America (read: United States) as the land of freedom. The holiday of Thanksgiving, with Puritan paraphernalia, ranks with the Fourth of July as a celebration of the religion of America. "Other Renaissance explorers and emigrants discovered America as a geographical entity; they put it on the European map of the world. The Puritans discovered America in Scripture … and they proceeded to put it on the map of sacred history."[145]

There is no doubt that Plymouth Plantation contributed significantly to the religious meaning of America and the politics of the United States. The story, however, is more complicated than their journey to America as the land of freedom. The Puritans were intent on liberty for themselves,

---

142 Captain John Smith, *History of Virginia: A Selection,* ed. David Freeman Hawke (Indianapolis, IN: Bobbs-Merrill, 1970), 27-28.
143 Smith, *History of Virginia,* 150.
144 Smith, *History of Virginia,* 159.
145 Sacvan Bercovitch, in David Segal, *Puritans, Indians and Manifest Destiny* (New York: Putnam, 1977), 16.

but that did not entail religious liberty for others. (Roman Catholics were especially unwelcome.). Like other immigrant groups, the Puritans came with a mixture of motives. They contributed to the economic, political, and religious origins of the United States, but for religious tolerance one would have had to look to Pennsylvania, Rhode Island, or Delaware.

The relation of Plymouth Plantation to the United States could use some demythologizing. Presumably that is the intention of Nick Bunker in his carefully researched book, *Making Haste from Babylon: The Mayflower Pilgrims and their World*. But his formulation of the problem worsens the confusion. After saying that "as for the Pilgrims themselves, we discover that they were not quite the people we thought they were," Bunker says, "'America' did not exist in 1620 and the Pilgrims were never Americans but neither were they English in any simple, modern definition of the word."[146]

It is bizarre to say that America did not exist in 1620; clearly it had existed for more than a century. The Puritans were English who became Americans once they had settled into America. The evidence for their being (English) Americans in America is not only the language they used at the time but also the fact that Bunker uses this language throughout his book. There is indeed confusion in today's meaning of "America" and "American," but denying that America existed in 1620 is not the solution.

In sixteenth-century England, the Puritans were unhappy that the Church of England had not purified itself of Catholic remnants. They were constantly on guard against any tendencies toward a recatholicizing of their churches. In reaction to their rebellion, the government put some restrictions on the Puritans' way of worship that centered on preaching, or "prophesying." The battle lines were clear for the Puritans: Protestantism and liberty versus popery and authoritarianism.[147]

Under King James I, the Puritans had finally seen the need to separate from the church and from England itself. In 1608, after receiving permission to leave, they removed themselves to Amsterdam. But as often happens with radical dissenters, the group almost immediately faced dissent within its own ranks. A controversy over infant baptism in 1609 led to a large part

---

146 Bunker, *Making Haste from Babylon*, 20.
147 Nathan Hatch, *The Sacred Cause of Liberty: Republican Thought and the Millennium in Revolutionary New England* (New Haven, CT: Yale University Press, 1977), 73.

of the group moving to Leiden. The Netherlands, and Leiden in particular, were experiencing economic growth and welcomed new laborers. However, for the laborers, conditions were hard. When a new theological controversy broke out in 1617, some of the group considered another move.

Economic conditions in England at that time were bad. The Leiden group and its supporters in England sought "a spacious land, the way to which is through the sea."[148] After many complications and false moves, the *Mayflower* set sail with 102 passengers. Most of the four hundred members of the Leiden community had backed out for one reason or another so that as a result they made up only half the passenger list.[149]

William Bradford, in his history of Plymouth, says little about economic conditions that led to the founding of the colony. The main motive, he says, was "a great hope and inward zeal … for the propagating and advancing the gospel of the kingdom of Christ in these remote parts of the world."[150] It could be added that what was especially attractive in these remote parts of the world was the beaver. The French had already shown the wealth to be had from the trade in furs. At the same time, the English were being overwhelmed by the Dutch in fur trading with the East. During the 1620s, the value of other commodities from the East Indies (e.g., pepper, indigo, and silk) fell precipitously. England turned its attention westward.

The Virginia Company had been given the right to colonize up to the forty-first degree of latitude. The aim of the *Mayflower's* journey in 1620 was "to find some place about the Hudson's river for their habitation."[151] They missed, of course, by about 250 miles and planted "the first colony in the northern parts of Virginia" at Plymouth.

Since they were technically beyond where the patent of the Virginia Company applied, the group on board were required "to Covenant and Combine ourselves into a Civil Body Politic." The one-paragraph document known as the Mayflower Compact has been highlighted in the myth that the Puritans were establishing the United States and its

148 Bunker, *Making Haste from Babylon*, 268.
149 Nathaniel Philbrick, *Mayflower: A Story of Courage, Community, and War* (New York: Penguin, 2007), 50.
150 William Bradford, *Of Plymouth Plantation* (New York: Knopf, 1952), 25.
151 Bradford, *Of Plymouth Plantation*, 60.

government. This covenant, the first of many in New England, does deserve credit for its contribution to evolving notions of government. John Quincy Adams would later describe the Mayflower Compact as "perhaps the only instance in human history of that positive, original social compact, which speculative philosophers have imagined as the only legitimate source of government."[152]

The Mayflower Compact had both symbolic and real, if indirect, effect on the body politic of the United States. The forty-one signers of the pact promised "all due submission and obedience to the constitution and offices as shall be thought most meet and convenient for the general good of the Colony."[153] The due form of government in Plymouth would exercise civil power to suppress heresy. The church would be modeled on what "church" means in the New Testament—the communities of people who are followers of the Christ. The New England way would be known as congregationalism; each local gathering was the church.

The rocky soil that the pilgrims found on disembarking was not the land of plenty that they had hoped for. In a 1622 pamphlet promoting the colony, Bradford calls it "a godly land." His more candid assessment is found a decade later, when he admits that it was "a hideous and desolate place full of wild beasts and wild men." There was nothing to sustain them, Bradford says, "but the Spirit of God and His grace."[154] The *Mayflower* made its return voyage empty, a sign of things to come. The fur trade was the one profitable business, but it took eight years before the demand for beaver hats enabled the colony to turn the corner economically.

When the prosperity of Plymouth did improve, it attracted new groups of people, not all of whom were committed to a strict Puritan covenant. Bradford would complain that people were being sent by their friends with the hope of bettering them but, when free of the shame those people might have experienced at home, they followed a dissolute course in the colony. Bestiality seems to have been a particular concern. The Puritans enjoyed a healthy sex life in marriage, but a man having sex with cows, goats, or turkeys went well beyond the pale. Bradford was stunned by this

---

152 "An Oration Delivered at Plymouth," December 1802, quoted in Edmund Morgan, *Inventing a People* (New York: W. W. Norton, 1988), 123.

153 Bradford, *Of Plymouth Plantation*, 75.

154 Bradford, *Of Plymouth Plantation*, 63.

"wickedness." The influx of immigrants had changed the composition of the colony. "And thus by one means or another, in twenty years' time it is a question whether the greater part be not grown the worser."[155]

A subtler change than sudden outbursts of wickedness was that the improving of economic conditions led to a kind of "suburbanization." The church and the town welcomed new settlements made possible by grants of land. They did not foresee that the solidarity of Plymouth and its church would be undermined. Describing the condition of Plymouth in 1644, Bradford has one of his most poignant passages: "And thus was this poor church left, like an ancient mother grown old and, forsaken by her children, though not in their affections yet in their bodily presence and personal helpfulness."[156]

As in Virginia, the Indians were the other side of the story of God leading his people across the sea to conquer a wilderness. Commentators who were otherwise humane seemed oblivious of the native people having a right to defend their homes and their way of life. The settlers assumed that if God was on the side of the settlers, then their enemy was the enemy of God. Just as the Spanish imposed the imagery of the Moors on the natives, the English imposed their image of the Irish. "Unable to comprehend the Brehon laws, the English simply decided that the wild Irish were savages. Unable to understand Indian polity, they reached a like conclusion. Used to savagery in one place they looked for it, provoked it, in the other."[157]

In a war with the Pequot in 1637, William Bradford describes the killing of four hundred Indians: "It was a fearful sight to see them frying in the fire and the streams of blood quenching the same, and horrible was the stink and scent thereof." These horrible sights, sounds, and stench do not generate sympathy for the Indians' loss of life. On the contrary, Bradford says, "the victory seemed a sweet sacrifice [referring to Leviticus 2:1-2] and they gave praise thereof to God who had wrought wonderfully for them to enclose their enemies in their hands and give them so speedy a victory over so proud and insulting an enemy."[158] Relations between the

155 Bradford, *Of Plymouth Plantation*, 322.
156 Bradford, *Of Plymouth Plantation*, 334.
157 Howard Mumford Jones, "The Colonial Idea in England," in *Three American Empires*, ed. John TePaske (New York: Harper and Row, 1967), 41.
158 Bradford, *Of Plymouth Plantation*, 286.

settlers and the Indians remained precarious and intermittently bloody. A brief but especially destructive war in 1675-76 ended chances of permanent reconciliation.

Massachusetts Bay

In tracing the origin of the revolution in British America, the settlement in Massachusetts Bay rightly gets center stage. The Sons of Liberty and like-minded rebels would emerge from this colony. The Massachusetts Bay colony was not composed of separatists, as was Plymouth, but their church life was similar. Life was built around a covenant that brought the religious and the civic into close association.[159]

In England, king and parliament were at a standoff. When the king dissolved parliament and could not raise taxes, the war with France came to a quick end. Ships became available for a westward voyage, and the company obtained the *Arbella*. The passengers on the *Arbella* did not sign a covenant before disembarking, but they were admonished by their leader, John Winthrop, to "knit together" as a community. In his speech "A Model of Christian Charity," he said, "We must delight in each other, make others' concerns our own, rejoice together, mourn together, labor and suffer together."[160] He warned that getting rich could not be the aim of the settlers. He used the image of a city on a hill that had the eyes of the world on it—a favorite of Ronald Reagan and right-wing speakers. Reagan seemed to be suggesting that Winthrop was referring to the United States and that the world has ever since looked up to the country in admiration.[161]

A less often quoted part of Winthrop's sermon reminded people that they should know their place and stay in it. He was unwittingly setting the stage for rebellion against the assumptions of social roles and hierarchical

---

159 Edmund Morgan, *Visible Saints: The History of a Puritan Idea* (Ithaca, NY: Cornell University Press, 1965), 64.

160 John Winthrop, "A Model of Christian Charity" in Winthrop Hudson, *Nationalism and Religion* (New York: Harper and Row, 1970), 21-24.

161 Larry Schweikart and Michael Allen, *A Patriot's History of the United States* (New York: Penguin, 2004), xii: "We think that an honest evaluation of the history of the United States must begin and end with the recognition that, compared to any other nation, America's past is a bright and shining light. America was and is the city on the hill, the fountain of hope, the beacon of liberty."

authority that were brought from the old world. Winthrop told his hearers that "God almighty in his holy and wise providence hath so disposed the condition of mankind as in all times some must be rich, some poor, some high and eminent in power and duty, others mean in subjection." It may be that there will always be rich people and poor people, but even God-fearing Calvinists did not necessarily accept that the present arrangement of rich and poor was God's disposition.

As in other American colonies, there was an economic motivation as well as a religious one. People might not become rich, but they were in search of a better life for themselves, their children, and their grandchildren. When the residents of Marblehead were asked to join their Boston colleagues in resisting the English government's interference in religious matters, they replied: "It may be that your fathers came because of religion; ours settled here to catch fish."[162] Massachusetts was eventually a successful colony, but it took a few years to establish stability. Of the thousand people who arrived in 1630, two hundred left in the first year, and eventually about half of the group followed suit.[163]

The religious life of the colony relied upon a strict orthodoxy and included some distinctive characteristics. The most striking feature was the place of religious experience and a public testimony of having been touched by God's grace. These narratives provide an extraordinary window into the inner lives of the believers, their exhilaration, and their anxieties.[164] For church membership, a person had to give testimony of having had a religious experience. And church membership was required for political participation. The church was guaranteed to be composed of vitally involved adults (no hangers-on in the last pew). Each family was to be transformed from a mere biological unit to a "Christian family," in which father, mother, and children had their proper places. The civic society was to be the family unit writ large.

This plan to set up a model church and a holy commonwealth had one big drawback: the child, as an extension of the parents, could be baptized

---

162 Lewis Hanke, *Do the Americas Have a Common History?* (New York: Knopf, 1964), 257.

163 Moore, *Pilgrims*, 35–36.

164 Patricia Caldwell, *The Puritan Conversion Narratives: The Beginning of American Expression* (Cambridge, MA: Cambridge University Press, 1985).

only if the parents had experienced religious conversion. By the second and third generations, this restriction was a problem. What was the status of a child of the unbaptized? In 1662, a compromise was reached in what was called "the half-way covenant," a partial church membership that Puritan theology had had no place for. "The Puritan transformation of the family remained incomplete; so long as children were born, instead of appearing voluntarily like colonists in a new country, the family could not become a purely political society."[165]

The differences among the Puritans surfaced in 1636 with a controversy over "free grace." Roger Williams was banished to what became Rhode Island and the home of the Baptists. The most intense controversy in 1637 centered on a woman named Anne Hutchinson, who apparently knew more theology than many of the divines and was not averse to saying so. She was charged with breaking the fifth commandment, playing the part of "a husband [rather] than a wife, and a preacher [rather] than a hearer, and a magistrate [rather] than a subject."[166] In Cotton Mather's description, she was "a gentlewoman of an haughty carriage, busie spirit, competent wit, and a voluble tongue."[167]

At her trial, Hutchinson might have avoided a judgment of heresy except, swept up in the drama of the moment, she launched into a speech claiming that the Holy Spirit spoke directly to her. Her judges finally had their conviction. "No item stood higher in the Puritan list of heresies than the claim that God revealed himself directly to men … Every respected minister in Christendom agreed on at least this one point, that the age of revelation was over."[168]

The leaders of Massachusetts Bay got rid of Anne Hutchinson, but they could not eliminate the tension between religious experience and scriptural authority. Preachers encouraged their listeners to attend to the Spirit, but the leaders came down hard when the hearer's experience did

---

165 Michael Walzer, *The Revolution of the Saints: A Study in the Origins of Radical Politics* (Cambridge, MA: Harvard University Press, 1982), 196.

166 Morgan, *Puritan Family*, 19.

167 Cotton Mather, *Magnalia Christi Americana* (Cambridge, MA: Harvard University Press, 1976), 130; Edmund Morgan, *American Heroes* (New York: W. W. Norton, 2009), 90-101.

168 Kai Erikson, *Wayward Pilgrims: A Study in the Sociology of Deviance* (New York: Macmillan, 1966), 98.

not align with the accepted scriptural interpretation. The Quakers, a gentle and peaceful group, were especially feared and hated. Mather called them "the sink of all heresies, the ground of all errors."[169] What was so terrible about them? They wore hats in the presence of the magistrate, they said "thou" and "thee," and they gathered for private religious services. In short, they were a threat to the control of scriptural interpretation.

In this setting with its new opportunities, the tighter the reins were pulled, the more likely were the children to rebel. The people of the first generation, who were mostly middle class and urban, did not adapt very well to the wilderness. That kind of reaction is a frequent happening with immigrant groups. As the children adapt to their surroundings, the adults are likely to feel that the world is falling apart.[170]

By the 1660s, everything seemed to have crashed. A synod in 1679 published a document with the title "The Necessity of Reformation." It describes the dire condition of a colony "destitute of civic spirit." In the middle of the document is the lament that family government has decayed; the result is that fathers are not keeping their sons and daughters from prowling the streets at night. Signs of decay are obvious: Laborers are making unreasonable demands, salesmen are telling lies, taverns are crowded, the Sabbath is wantonly violated, and lawyers are thriving.[171]

For the older generation of civic leaders, the problem was not a few individuals but the society. Speaking in the 1660s, John Wilson said, "I have known New England about thirty-six years and I never knew such a time as this that we live in."[172] A few decades later, Cotton Mather would conclude that "the old spirit of New-England hath been sensibly going out of the world, as the old saints in whom it was have gone."[173] From a longer-range perspective, we can see that the colony had survived bad times and was preparing the way for the beginning of a new nation. But perhaps Governor Winthrop's original hope to establish a society that would be the

---

169 Mather, *Magnalia Christi Americana*, 134.

170 Darrett Rutman, *Winthrop's Boston: Portrait of a Puritan Town, 1630-1649* (Chapel Hill, NC: University of North Carolina Press, 1965), 96: "The land with its opportunities was proving disruptive of the communal spirit."

171 For the full document, see Miller, *Errand into the Wilderness*, 7-8.

172 Emory Elliot, *Power and the Pulpit in Puritan New England* (Princeton, NJ: Princeton University Press, 1975), 90.

173 Mather, *Magnalia Christi Americana*, 113.

marvel of the whole world had been overly ambitious. "Having failed to rivet the eyes of the world upon their city on the hill, they were left alone with America."[174]

Liberty and Revolution

As the previous section explains, the English settlers did give their own distinctive twist to the theme of liberty. Furthermore, the eighteenth-century British Americans provided an interpretation of the previous century, in which liberty—religious and civil—became the one central concern. Children in the United States would later read the history of seventeenth-century New England through the myths elaborated in the eighteenth and nineteenth centuries.

The lead up to 1776 involved a slow evolution of attitudes regarding political instruments of liberty and then a quick shift of attitudes regarding the king and parliament. The idea of liberty took shape beginning in the 1730s, drawing together separate strands of the preceding century. Alexis de Tocqueville was puzzled in the 1830s that "the Americans combine the notions of Christianity and liberty so intimately in their minds that it is impossible to make them conceive the one without the other."[175] Tocqueville almost gets it right, but his surprise that the Americans combined Christianity and "liberty" results from an inaccurate formulation of what they related.

The colonists did not join the Christian Church to liberty; what they understood to be united were two kinds of liberty: civil and religious. Liberty was a central concept of Protestant Christianity. And the overarching idea that held together the two ideas of liberty was "America." For many Americans, both then and now, America is another name for liberty. Both the Christian Church and the United States government are taken to be legitimate insofar as each of them is an instrument of liberty.

The increasing emphasis on political liberty was influenced by an opposition between power and liberty. Thomas Hobbes, the seventeenth-century political philosopher, provided the intellectual context that led to

---

174 Miller, *Errand into the Wilderness*, 15.
175 Alexis de Tocqueville, *Democracy in America*, vol. 1, ed. Henry Reeve, (New York: Bantam, 1959), 355.

a distrust of power, which was understood as a lust for dominating others. Hobbes's solution for the danger and destructiveness of power was an authoritarian system—a sovereign power to restrain individuals.[176] The British American colonists agreed with Hobbes that power is evil and the opposite of liberty. But almost by accident, they came up with a solution different from Hobbes's, involving interacting powers and the liberty of individuals who are educated to use liberty with virtuous restraint.[177]

Bernard Bailyn traced the history of the eighteenth-century meaning of "faction" as an index of political change.[178] At the beginning of the eighteenth century, "faction" (or "party") was wholly negative in meaning; factions were the disruptions of minorities who had only their own interests at heart. At the end of the eighteenth century, James Madison, in "Federalist No. 10," was still distrustful of factions: "… but because the cause of faction cannot be removed, relief is only to be sought in the means of controlling its effects."[179] The common good was to be sought through "a shifting sea of interest groups that can be constrained to observe the minimal rules of procedural justice."[180]

Bailyn identified a shift in "faction" starting in 1733 with the recognition that "a free government cannot but be subject to parties, cabals and intrigues."[181] Parties or factions could conceivably have at least a neutral meaning for political participation. The widespread involvement of the population was bound to include conflicts of interest. Until the revolution, voting and other political participation in the colonies was limited to white men who owned property. Today that seems a severe restriction, but the availability of land spread the franchise more widely

---

176 Thomas Hobbes, *Leviathan* (Cambridge, MA: Cambridge University Press, 1996).

177 Stanley Elkins and Eric McCitrick, *The Age of Federalism* (New York: Oxford University Press, 1993), 28-29.

178 Bernard Bailyn, *The Ideological Origins of the American Revolution* (Cambridge, MA: Harvard University Press, 1967).

179 *The Federalist Papers* (New York: Bantam Books, 1982), 51-52.

180 William Johnson Everett, *God's Federal Republic: Reconstructing Our Governing Symbol* (New York: Paulist Press, 1988), 81.

181 Bernard Bailyn, *Ideological Origins*, 125, citing the *New York Gazette*.

than in Europe.[182] On the eve of the revolution, two-thirds of the white males were voters compared to one out of six in England.

In the early eighteenth century, the colonists were still convinced that England was the world's leader in liberty. The constitutional monarchy established at the end of the seventeenth century guaranteed the rights of Englishmen. During England's Seven Years' War with France, there was little doubt that liberty was on the side of the English. At the same time, however, egalitarianism and rebelliousness in the colonies were growing. Pamphlets and newspapers spread political ideas; the existence of a lively press was itself a sign of rebelliousness in the name of liberty.[183]

The corner was perhaps turned in 1753, when it was suggested that the Crown itself could be "factious."[184] Instead of the king as a paternal presence presiding over political order, politics came to be seen as a search for order out of competing factions that included the king. The colonists had to struggle to separate the king from the paternal role he had played. As late as 1774, they addressed the king as "our dear father." In 1776, one of the things that Thomas Paine's *Common Sense* did was to sever the bond of a parent-child relation between king and colonies.[185] Later that year, Thomas Jefferson, in the Declaration of Independence, made a list of twenty-nine accusations directed at the king.

On the religious side, there were movements from the 1730s that might seem coincidentally parallel to political unrest, but under the aegis of "America," they were integral to a movement toward political independence. Historians today often give some credit to the religious revival of the 1740s, the Great Awakening, for helping to create a "national consciousness." But the religious factor is often thought to stop there. The revival had subsided in the colonies by the end of the 1740s. The religious

---

182 Bailyn, *Ideological Origins*, 86: Governor Thomas Hutchinson of Massachusetts said that "it seemed that anything with the appearance of a man" was allowed to vote.

183 Bernard Bailyn, *Pamphlets of the American Revolution, 1750-1776* (Cambridge, MA: Harvard University Press, 1965).

184 Bailyn, *Ideological Origins*, 127.

185 Winthrop Jordan, "Familial Politics and the Killing of the King, 1776," *Journal of American History* 60, no. 2 (September 1973), 294-308; Thomas Gustafson, *Representative Words: Politics, Literature, and the American Language, 1776-1865* (Cambridge, MA: Cambridge University Press, 1992), 241-52.

influence on the declaring of independence might therefore seem distant and minimal. Nathan Hatch, in his book *The Sacred Cause of Liberty*, tracked the theme of liberty in the New England sermons of the 1750s, 1760s, and beyond.[186] Equally important were demands for liberty among Baptists in the 1760s. Civic and religious liberty were inseparable.

The first "national" revival in the 1740s was the work of independent preachers who appealed for individual conversions.[187] The best known revivalist of the 1740s is Jonathan Edwards, who unfortunately is mainly remembered for one scary sermon about God dangling souls over hell fire.[188] Edwards was in fact one of the greatest theological minds in American history. His preaching was based on scholarly and intellectual reflections on scripture. He was surprised that his preaching generated an outpouring of emotion.

Other preachers, such as George Whitefield and Gilbert Tennant, became with Edwards "household names" across the colonies.[189] Revivals then and now tend to burn brightly by the western campfire and attract individuals who have been dislocated geographically, psychologically, and economically. Revivals, including the Great Awakening, do not generate new church membership. If anything, they tend to undermine the authority of the minister and his congregation.[190]

Hatch contrasts Edwards's call for liberty by means of prayer and piety with the New England preachers of the 1750s and 1760s, who hailed

186 Nathan Hatch, *The Sacred Cause of Liberty* (New Haven, CT: Yale University Press, 1977).

187 The style did not change much in US history until the advent of television, which could spread the word more widely but could feed the danger of egoism among preachers.

188 Jonathan Edwards, *Sinners in the Hands of an Angry God* (New York: Dover Books, 2005).

189 Winthrop Hudson, *Nationalism and Religion in America* (New York: Harper and Row, 1970), xxv.

190 Gordon Wood, *The Radicalism of the American Revolution* (New York: Vintage Books, 1991), 332; on the disrupting effect of the Great Awakening on the churches of New England, see Patricia Bonomi, *Under the Cope of Heaven: Religion, Society, and Politics in Colonial America* (New York: Oxford University Press, 1986), 131-60.

resistance to tyranny in God's name by the "new American Israel."[191] Edwards had thought that the millennium was soon to begin and that the most likely starting place was Massachusetts.[192] While the later preachers also saw the millennium beginning in America, they thought it would be by America embodying the sacred cause of liberty. The term "millennium" had shifted from representing a fearful, apocalyptic end of a sinful world to representing a march toward freedom led by America. "The last step in human progress is to be made in America."[193]

The year 1763 represented a dramatic change in the colonial perception of who was the enemy of their liberty. The war between France and England was over; the colonists had sided with England as the seat of liberty; the forces of liberty had triumphed. The end of the war meant the opening of new lands and the development of new instruments of local government. Uneasy with the colonists going their own way, the British tried to rein in the colonies. A series of "coercive acts," including the Sugar Act of 1764 and the Stamp Act of 1765, proved to be a disastrous strategy for controlling the increasingly rebellious colonies. The colonists suddenly saw themselves as Carthage being assaulted by Rome.[194]

This claim that England was treating the colonists as slaves was ironic, given that colonial leaders were slaveholders. One of the events that led to the colonial rebellion of 1776 was a 1772 ruling by Lord Mansfield in London, freeing an American slave who was about to be taken to Jamaica to be sold. The ruling was the beginning of an abolitionist movement that would end slavery throughout the British Empire. The American colonies recognized that their huge slave population would be inclined to side with England in a conflict with the colonies.

---

191 Hatch, *The Sacred Cause of Liberty*, 24-25.

192 Jonathan Edwards, "The Latter-Day Glory is Probably to Begin in America," in *God's New Israel: Religious Interpretations of American* Destiny, ed. Conrad Cherry (Englewood Cliffs, NJ: Prentice Hall, 1971), 55-59.

193 Richard Price, "On the Love of our Country," 1789, quoted in Henry Steele Commager, *The Empire of Reason* (New York: Phoenix Press, 2001), 223; for the changing meaning of "millennium," see Ernest Tuveson, *Millennium and Utopia* (New York: Harper and Row, 1964).

194 Eran Shalev, *Rome Reborn on Western Shores: Historical Imagination and the Creation of the American Republic* (Charlottesville, VA: University of Virginia Press, 2009), 50-62.

A second event that added to colonial fears was an edict by Lord Dunmore in 1775 in which he offered to free and arm Africans to quash a colonial revolt. That ruling from within the colonies was greeted with denunciation by such people as Patrick Henry, the great champion of liberty. If one looks at the 1770s from the perspective of the slaves, then the rebellion of 1776 was a "counterrevolution" in defense of a society based on slavery.[195]

By 1770, parliament had become a "foreign jurisdiction" and a "pretended power." The colonists were not represented in parliament, so they claimed that the imposition of taxes was tyrannical. By rejecting the legitimacy of parliament's power and appealing to their position as subjects of the king, the colonists were vulnerable to the criticism that they were reactionary rebels who would destroy popular liberty by restoring the king's power, which had been limited by parliament.

Several British statesmen, most prominently Edmund Burke, warned that repression was the wrong policy for distant colonies who had become accustomed to self-rule and where the literacy rate was higher than in England. In several places, starting in 1774, Burke protested British policy in the colonies. In a speech before parliament on March 22, 1775, Burke listed six ingredients of American liberty, including the fact that the Americans had emigrated from England. "They are therefore not only devoted to liberty, but to liberty according to English ideas and on English principles."[196]

The shooting war is usually dated from the skirmishes at Lexington and Concord in April 1775. The other colonies did not immediately jump to the defense of Massachusetts. The army that was eventually put together was a ragtag collection of farmers and artisans under the direction of George Washington. Britain suffered the embarrassment that would in the future happen to the United States; that is, the greatest army in the world could not put down this ill-clad bunch of rebels who used "unfair tactics" and absorbed one defeat after another. A celebrated battle at Bunker Hill

195 Gerald Horne, *The Counter-Revolution of 1776: Slave Resistance and the Origin of the United States of America* (New York: New York University Press, 2014), 209-34.

196 Clinton Rossiter, *The First American Revolution: The American Colonies on the Eve of Independence* (New York: Harcourt Brace, 1964), 5.

overlooking Boston was won by the British but with severe losses on their part.[197] Washington's retreat to Long Island and Brooklyn did not stop the advance of the British. Only a brilliant surprise raid on Trenton at the end of the year gave the rebels some hope.[198]

Later in the war, the British accurately perceived that some of the southern colonies were highly vulnerable. The British were successful in one respect; their campaign "marked the greatest slave rebellion in American history."[199] In March 1779, Congress wanted Georgia and South Carolina to arm three thousand Negroes to fight the British. South Carolina, whose population was 60 percent slaves, was resistant to arming slaves. Even George Washington feared that the slaves might start getting ideas about liberty. Some Negroes did take up the invitation to join the British side, but most stayed where they were.

The war that lasted from 1775 to 1781 is usually called the American Revolution. From one perspective, the war was a *consequence* of the revolution that had occurred in the 1760s. In another respect, the war was a first step to the completion of the United States' revolution in the 1780s and beyond. The first of these two perspectives was expressed by John Adams in an 1818 letter to Hezekiah Niles: "The revolution was effected before the war commenced. The Revolution was in the minds and hearts of the people ... This radical change in the principles, opinions, sentiments and affections of the people, was the real American Revolution"[200]

Adams was accurate in pointing to the change in minds and hearts that swept across the colonies in the 1760s and early 1770s. But in political terms, a more important point was made in 1787 by Benjamin Rush: "The American war is over; but this is far from being the case with the American revolution. On the contrary, nothing but the first act of the great drama is closed. It remains yet to establish and perfect our new forms of

---

197 Nathaniel Philbrick, *Bunker Hill: A City, A Siege, A Revolution* (New York: Viking, 2013).

198 David McCullough, *1776* (New York: Simon and Schuster, 2005), tells an engaging story of that year leading up to crossing of the Delaware and the surprise attack on the British at Trenton.

199 Gary Nash, *The Unknown American Revolution* (New York: Viking Press, 2005).

200 John Adams, *The Works of John Adams*, vol. x (Boston: Little, Brown and Co., 1956), 180.

government."[201] The "new forms of government" did emerge after the war, although they were far from perfect.

Someone might object that both authors are just using a metaphor of "revolution." Actually they were recovering an earlier meaning of "revolution." After the French Revolution, the term "revolution" came to mean a violent uprising; "revolution" became the name for one form of warfare. However, there is some hope in the twenty-first century for revolutions that are nonviolent, and the wars that are consequent upon revolution can be perceived as counterrevolutionary.[202] The attempt to return to a nonviolent meaning of "revolution" goes back not only to Adams's reference to minds and hearts but also to the etymology and history of "revolution." The word has always referred to a turning, returning, or circling back. Its first prominent use in English was in the translation of the fifteenth-century work of Copernicus entitled *De Revolutionibus Orbium Coelestium*, which refers to revolution as the regular, lawful motion of the stars. In both Latin and English, the word "revolution" implied neither complete newness nor violence.[203]

The political use of "revolution" in the seventeenth century drew upon this astronomical meaning. The English reform of 1688, called "the glorious revolution," was to *restore* the monarchy and rights that had been lost or suppressed. The revolution looked back to the Magna Carta and the rights of Englishmen guaranteed by the unwritten constitution of four centuries. The eighteenth-century colonists in America looked to this revolution as the model for their own when they claimed their rights as Englishmen. In 1775, they appealed to the British people, acting as "descendants of Britons" and acting in defense of "the glorious privileges" for which their ancestors had fought.[204]

---

201 Benjamin Rush, "An Address to the People of the United States"; see Hannah Arendt, *On Revolution* (New York: Viking Press, 1963), 301.
202 George Lawson, *Negotiated Revolutions: The Czech Republic, South Africa and Chile* (Burlington, VT: Ashgate, 2005); Timothy Garton Ash, "Velvet Revolution: The Prospects," *New York Review of Books*, December 3, 2009, 20-23.
203 Arendt, *On Revolution*, 35.
204 Maier, *American Scripture*, 20.

The Declaration of Independence

In the rebellious colonies, the declaring of independence on July 2, 1776, brought to a close that phase of revolution seeking to restore the rights of English citizens. The political revolution, however, was just beginning. A war of liberation cannot succeed unless it is followed by a constitution of freedom.[205] Unlike so many attempted revolutions during the last two centuries, the British American revolution was based on local constitutions and functioning governments. Thirteen self-governing colonies was a blessing, but it would also be a challenge to forming a national union.

The document declaring independence was signed by representatives of twelve colonies on July 4, 1776 (New York came in a week later). There are innumerable points of debate concerning the sources and the interpretation of the text. The standard reading for many years was Carl Becker's 1932 book *The Declaration of Independence*. In 1978, Garry Wills's new interpretation in *Inventing America* drew immediate praise and then some strong criticism.[206] Critics complained that Wills had imposed his own liberal ideology on the text, although most critics seemed to bring to the document their own ideologies, which often tilted to the political right.

Wills played down the influence of John Locke on Jefferson and emphasized Scottish thinkers. This interpretive move was from an individualism in which government exists primarily for the protection of private property, to a communal orientation in which moral "sentiments" are the ground of reason. Wills introduced many helpful concerns but perhaps overplayed his hand. There are many interesting points of interpretation that I will not pursue. For my purposes, there is one overriding concern that the Declaration of Independence raised regarding liberty and freedom.

---

205 Arendt, *On Revolution*, 140-41.

206 Carl Becker, *The Declaration of Independence: A Study in the History of Political Ideas* (New York: Create Space, 2010); Wills, *Inventing America*. For some of the severest criticism of Wills's book, see Ronald Hamowy, "Jefferson and the Scottish Enlightenment: A Critique of Garry Wills' *Inventing America*," *William and Mary Quarterly* XXXVI (1979), 503-23; for a balance of criticism, see Ralph Luker, "Garry Wills and the New Debate over the Declaration of Independence," *The Virginia Quarterly Review* (spring 1980), 244-61.

The Continental Congress was intent on achieving cooperative action by the thirteen separate colonies. The declaration's heading reads, "The unanimous Declaration of the thirteen united States of America." In the text itself, the last paragraph says, "We therefore, the Representatives of the united States of America, in General Congress assembled ... do in the name of these *colonies* [Jefferson's draft used "states"], solemnly publish and declare, that these united colonies are and of right ought to be free."

Garry Wills writes that "all thirteen original colonies subscribed to the Declaration with instructions to the delegates that this was *not* to imply formation of a single nation."[207] If "nation" connotes a real or mythical kinship, then a nation could not be formed by a vote. The declaration asserts that the former colonies are now states that are associated with other states.

The authors did not innocently or carelessly use "state." They precisely list the powers of a state: "To levy war, conclude peace, contract alliances, establish commerce and do all other acts and things which independent states may of right do." If each state could do these things, how could there be one state made up of thirteen states? When the Articles of Confederation were approved, they included in Article II that "each state retains its sovereignty, freedom and independence." A United States of America was still in the future.

These independent states immediately began setting up or revising constitutions for governing the people of their respective states. A federation of these states was feasible for the purpose of fighting a war for independence. But the Declaration of Independence did not establish a United States government. Even when the British abandoned the fight and recognized the independence of the states, the future was not promising for a United States.

Looking back now at 1776, it seems clear that the purpose of the Declaration of Independence was to do what its title stated: declare independence or separation from England. Its main concern was political liberty rather than human freedom. The heart of the document is the series of accusations leveled against King George III that made separation "necessary." That is the way the document was received domestically. Consequent upon this claim to have "separate and equal status among the

---

207 Wills, *Inventing America*, xvi.

other powers of the earth," this new federation of states could negotiate for help with other international players.

The move was most successful in gaining military aid from France. Such a realignment of former enemies in a mere two decades was surprising. France entered the war on the colonists' side out of rivalry with England, not from philosophical agreement about the rights of all men. As Pauline Maier points out, a declaration of universal rights would not have received enthusiastic embrace from King Louis XVI.[208]

Jefferson's preamble on equality, rights, and the purpose of government did have a later influence on French political thinking. And after the War of 1812, the Declaration's meaning shifted from being understood primarily as asserting liberty to being a theory of human freedom. Jefferson himself toward the end of his life encouraged this interpretation of the document. In the United States of today, especially among people deemed conservative, the Declaration of Independence is referred to as if it provides the legal structure of the United States and a model of government for the world.

David Armitage makes the paradoxical statement that the Declaration of Independence was a declaration of interdependence.[209] He means that the delegates, by addressing themselves to a "candid world," were signaling that they wanted to join the international order rather than overthrow it. Their revolution was thus "unrevolutionary" in relation to the regulatory pattern of political arrangements. The claims of universal rights and the equality of all men would not have had much effect without the success of the new republic.

The glaring failure of these united states was their retention of slavery. The declaration makes no effort to address this contradiction of liberty. Actually, Jefferson, in his draft of the declaration, did take on the question of slavery in a way that is breathtaking in its arrogance. Among his accusations against the king, Jefferson stated, "He has waged cruel war against human nature itself, violating its most sacred rights of life and liberty in the person of a distant people." And Jefferson expressed disdain at this "warfare of the *Christian* king of Great Britain, determined to keep

---

208 Maier, *American Scripture*, 40.
209 David Armitage, *The Declaration of Independence: A Global History* (Cambridge, MA: Harvard University Press, 2007), 30, 64.

open a market where men should be bought and sold."[210] The convention delegates, showing a modicum of prudence or wisdom, excised the whole paragraph. (Jefferson's notes say it was done "in complaisance to South Carolina and Georgia.") They replaced the paragraph with an accusation that the king had "excited domestic insurrections."

The declaration was thus spared even greater mockery by British critics, who focused on the contradiction between the right to liberty and the practice of slaveholding by Jefferson and other signers of the Declaration. Thomas Day, an English abolitionist, said, "They signed the resolution of independence with one hand, the whip over slaves with the other."[211] Jeremy Bentham, in his "Short Review of the Declaration," provided the most extensive criticism of what the Declaration says about universal rights.[212] Bentham notes, "… rather surprising it must certainly appear that they should advance maxims so incompatible with their own present conduct."[213]

This painful disparity was not just a topic for philosophical debate. The slaves had the most accurate and long-suffering view of the hypocrisy in the declaration's philosophical claims. Slavery was a key issue as to whether there was a *united* states immediately after the Declaration and even after the compromises of the US Constitution. Economic considerations pushed together a group of southern states to defend slavery. The cry of "states' rights" would have surfaced without slavery, but slavery became the leading edge in controversies over the rights of states and the power of the federal government. States' rights were often a cover story for the defense of slavery.

The commonly used term "American Revolution" hides the fact that it was also a civil war—the first of several wars for the control of "America." As the Loyalist Claims Commission archives show, "civil war" was regularly

---

210 The full statement of Jefferson is found in Maier, *American Scripture*, 239.

211 Quoted in Armitage, *The Declaration of Independence*, 77.

212 Jeremy Bentham, "Short Review of the Declaration (1776)," in Armitage, *Declaration of Independence*, 173-86.

213 Bentham, "Short Review of the Declaration (1776)," 175. A *New York Times* editorial on July 3, 2013, says that "if Jefferson's 'cruel war' passage had stood, the founders' endorsement of liberty wouldn't need an asterisk." That seems to miss the point entirely, which is the contradiction between their words and their deeds.

used on both sides of the Atlantic.[214] The war involved conflicts among and within whites, blacks, and Indians. Everyone in the north of America was forced to choose sides between the stability of the British Empire and the precarious path of thirteen disparate colonies who wished to separate from the empire.

The whites who cast their lot with the British are called loyalists. They were not necessarily the most conservative people in the colonies. "Many of the loyalists were among the most radical proponents of a transformed American society, people who sought a place in the body politic for ordinary people and an overhauled legal system where those in the lower classes could obtain simple justice."[215] Even among the whites who stayed, there were severe conflicts that at times bordered on chaos. The end of the war did not end the rebellion of the poor against the upper class.[216] The poor had legitimate fears of how liberty would be limited in the newly liberated united states. "The century and a half after the revolution saw wealth and power concentrated to such an extent that it would make the revolutionaries of 1776 shudder."[217]

About sixty thousand loyalists were forced to flee to other parts of the empire; a large portion of them went to colonies that collectively retained the name British North America. The maritime provinces of Nova Scotia and New Brunswick were havens for the loyalists fleeing from the south. The creation of Upper Canada (Ontario) provided new land for emigrants from the rebellious colonies; a small number came during the revolution, and a larger number of "late loyalists" made the journey in the years following. Black slaves usually went with their owners, although about ten thousand black loyalists joined in the emigration to Nova Scotia and other

---

214 Keith Mason, "The American Loyalist Problem of Identity in the Revolutionary Atlantic World," in *The Loyal Atlantic: Remaking the British Atlantic in the Revolutionary Era* (Toronto: University of Toronto Press, 2012), 45.

215 Nash, *The Unknown American Revolution*, 239.

216 There is now an extensive literature on this underside to the revolution; examples are Garry Nash, *The Unknown American Revolution* (New York: Viking Press, 2005), Terry Bouton, *Taming Democracy* (New York: Oxford University Press, 2007), Woody Holton, *Unruly Americans and the Origin of the Constitution* (New York: Hill and Wang, 2007); and William Hogeland, *Inventing American History* (Cambridge, MA: MIT Press, 2009).

217 Bouton, *Taming Democracy*, 263.

parts of the empire.[218] The whole region was unstable for the three decades that followed until the civil war was renewed in 1812.

Most of the native tribes believed that the British provided them more protection than the colonists. In the long run, none of the tribes was safe. An attempt to recruit native people on the side of the patriots was not helped by Jefferson's claim in the Declaration of Independence that the king had "endeavored to bring on the inhabitants of our frontiers the merciless Indian savage, whose known rule of warfare is the undistinguished destruction of all ages, sexes and conditions." Some individual Indians joined the patriot cause, but the tribes "knew all too well that the rebelling Americans rising up to secure their liberty in the East were equally desirous of establishing an empire in the West."[219]

---

218 Mason, "The American Loyalist Problem," 42.
219 Nash, *The Unknown American Revolution*, 249.

4

Constructing the United States: Part 2

This chapter examines some of the strengths and weaknesses of the United States in the use of America to unify "the people." The process begins with the writing of a constitution and a bill of rights. An entity with the name United States of America did not realistically exist until at least 1788, but it came into existence with big ideas about itself. It announced that it was something new on the face of the earth and ready to spread its message of liberty to the whole world.

This chapter also looks at Canada, the nation to the north of the United States, which has from the time of the revolution in British North America been a counterpoint in its attitude to liberty and order.[220] The revolution of 1776 was the beginning of a civil war, which simmered until there was a full eruption in 1812. The last section of this chapter describes the rapid expansion of the United States westward and the effect on the native people, who suffered the worst as the result of the war.

Constitution

The term "declaration," as noted in the previous chapter, has a double meaning: the act of declaring and the document that records the declaring.

---

220 Eric Hobsbawn, *On Empire: America, War, and Global Supremacy* (New York: New Press, 2008), 78: "The heroes of the U.S. Wild West are gunmen who make their own law of the John Wayne kind in lawless territory. The heroes of the Canadian West are the Mounties, an armed federal police force (founded in 1873) maintaining the state's law."

The first declaration of independence occurred on July 2, 1776; the second declaration, on July 4, 1776. Aside from raising a question about whether the holiday in celebration of liberty should perhaps fall on July 2, the ambiguity does not create serious problems.[221]

The same is not true of the double meaning of "constitution." In the 1780s, the people's agreement *constituted* a government; the Constitution as a legal code was then set up by the government. "The people should endow the government with a constitution not vice versa."[222] As the case of Great Britain shows, a second constitution is not necessary for the existence of a first. The Constitution of the United States government by the people was to establish freedom; the power over that Constitution remains with the people. The written Constitution was the product of a particular time.

In the early 1780s, eleven of the states wrote new constitutions; nine of them held conventions that were separate from their existing legislatures.[223] These constitutional conventions were typically a broad representation of the people; state conventions tended to create free-wheeling democratic structures. The right to vote was extended beyond property owners in all the states except Virginia and Delaware. Most states, following Pennsylvania's lead, enfranchised all taxpayers. Vermont admitted all males. For a short while, New Jersey included women as voters.[224] These developments worried the upper-class gentlemen who thought of democracy as mob rule.

The great strength of the US Constitution is that it emerged from and built upon the local constitutions of villages, townships, and states. The Declaration of Independence had not thrown the colonists into "the state of nature" because they had previously developed self-governing bodies with their own constitutions.[225] However, the fear of many delegates to the convention in 1787 was that because of a distrust of executive power, most of the state constitutions made the government practically equivalent to capricious popular assemblies. Edmund Randolph said in his opening

---

221 John Adams thought that July 2 would be celebrated as the date for the declaration of independence.

222 Hannah Arendt, *On Revolution* (New York: Viking Press, 1963), 144.

223 Gary Nash, *The Unknown American Revolution* (New York: Viking Press, 2005), 268.

224 Nash, *the Unknown American Revolution*, 279; on New Jersey's enfranchising of women, 289.

225 Arendt, *On Revolution*, 164.

remarks at the convention that there was a need to redress "insufficient checks against the democracy."[226]

The gentlemen who came together in Philadelphia in 1787 did not arrive with the intention of creating a new form of government. Their instructions were to improve the Articles of Confederation of 1781, which had obvious weaknesses as an instrument for uniting the thirteen states. The most obvious problem was that Congress had no power to levy taxes; it could therefore pass resolutions but not make laws or enforce the terms of treaties. The first article of the US Constitution gives to Congress the power to tax. It also assumed the war debts that were held by the states. That might seem a generous move. However, it was a way to burden the taxpayers to "fund" the war debts, which were now in the hands of a small group of rich men.

The soldiers in the war had been paid in paper money that decreased in value. To survive, the soldiers exchanged the paper at a discounted rate. After the war, the rich who had acquired the paper were paid at face value. It was the first scandalous example of the US government trampling on the rights of the poor.[227] Whether an effective national government is desirable can be distinguished from the biases of rich gentlemen. A strong national government is not incompatible with democratic protections and can benefit those citizens who are in economic need.

The fact that the US Constitution was the work of one group of gentlemen meeting in Philadelphia in the 1780s does not mean that it should be discarded for something more up to date. But even if William Gladstone was right in describing the US Constitution as "the most wonderful work ever struck off at a given time from the brain and purposes of man," it is nonetheless an eighteenth-century document.[228] It should not be expected to give answers to twenty-first-century questions that were unimaginable at the time it was written.

---

226 William Hogeland, *Inventing American History* (Cambridge, MA: MIT Press, 2009), 115.

227 Terry Bouton, *Taming Democracy* (New York: Oxford University Press, 2007), 177.

228 James Beck, *The Constitution of the United States* (London: Hodder and Stoughton, 1922).

The writers of the US Constitution did not base their hopes for a republican form of government on virtue. They did not have an exalted notion of human nature. "The well-being of the Republic required promotion of learning and intellect, infused with a spirit of public service in order to develop an expanding class of responsible social leaders."[229] A class of hereditary privilege was to be excluded; a class of disinterested gentlemen (what was then called a natural aristocracy) was to be cultivated. Unfortunately, now, as then, this natural aristocracy tends to confuse wealth and virtue.

For some people, the Constitution is a pulling back from equality, universal rights, and the sacred cause of liberty. The complaint is not entirely fair. "The basic misunderstanding lies in the failure to distinguish between liberation and freedom; there is nothing more futile than rebellion and liberation unless they are followed by the constitution of the newly won freedom."[230] A social order necessarily puts some restrictions on individual liberties. Nonetheless, an enlightened social order can exist and even embrace the give-and-take of disagreements among individuals and "factions."

James Madison had the insight that the Constitution should protect liberty not only from the oppression of rulers but also against the tyranny of majorities. One part of society can oppress another part. The Constitution was to save "the rights of the individuals or of the minority ... from interested combinations of the majority."[231] However, some of those checks and balances that were thought to be effective then are now of questionable value.

The critics of the newly written constitution were called by the name "anti-federalists," which made no logical sense; they were in fact criticizing one form of federalism and defending another. Until 1787 the states were a federation united by the Articles of Confederation. The convention in that year was intended to revise this federal form of government.

---

229 William Sullivan, *Work and Integrity: Crisis and Promise of Professionalism in America* (San Francisco, CA: Jossey Bass, 2005), 72.

230 Arendt, *On Revolution*, 140-41.

231 "Federalist No. 51" in *The Federalist Papers*. The theme was picked up and developed by John Stuart Mill in *On Liberty* (New York: W. W. Norton, 1975), 5-6.

Instead the convention produced a US Constitution in order to "produce a greater union." But it was still a federal form of government. There was a widespread opposition to the proposed Constitution that was based on a desire for a more democratic form of government. David Robertson describes the debate in the convention as one between "broad nationalism" and "narrow nationalism." The debate might also be described as one between two forms of federalism.[232]

The name "anti-federalist" was, not surprisingly, coined by the people who called themselves "federalists." With that dichotomy in place, defenders of the proposed Constitution undercut the opposition.[233] The terms of the debate implied that federalists were in favor of a federal government, while anti-federalists were just against everything. A collection of essays by proponents of the Constitution was called *The Federalist Papers*. These essays are often assumed to be a candid and comprehensive view of the Constitution. Instead, *The Federalist Papers* was a promotional document to get New York's approval of the Constitution. It smoothed over the intense debates and the compromises that produced the final document.

The terms of debate excluded what the real debate should have been about—namely, the nature, value, and extent of a national government. Should a national government have the power to tax, to charter a national bank, to establish health standards for all citizens, and to prevent racial discrimination in the country? Madison, Hamilton and many other founders thought that at least some of these powers should belong to the government that they were forming. A debate conceived as federalists versus anti-federalists buried these questions.

The failure to have an effective debate at the time of the Constitution's ratification has haunted the country ever since. After a horrendous civil war in the nineteenth century, a partial remedy was found in several amendments to the Constitution. But up to the present, every move by

---

232 David Robertson, *The Original Compromise: What the Constitution's Framers Were Really Thinking* (New York: Oxford University Press, 2013).

233 Pauline Maier, *Ratification: The People Debate the Constitution* (New York: Simon and Schuster, 2010), 94: "The terms 'Federalist' and 'Anti-federalist' which were mainly by 'Federalists,' oversimplify the debate over the Constitution by suggesting there were only two sides." The terms were misleading as to any sides of the debate.

the government in Washington has been suspected of encroaching on the liberty of the individual and the rights of the states. Of course, there are often good grounds for doubting the effectiveness and fairness of the federal government. But the problem is not that the government is too big; for some national problems, such as repairing the country's infrastructure or responding to national crises, the federal government is too small or at least too starved of resources.

Suspicion of the government is an integral part of United States history. The best government, Jefferson thought, would be the least government and, when people were ready, no government at all. That would be America. In his Declaration of Independence of the thirteen united states of America, Jefferson had written "that to secure these rights [life, liberty and the pursuit of happiness] governments are instituted among men, deriving their just power from the consent of the governed." He was not stating a historical fact; he was advocating an ideal. Governments throughout history were not constituted to secure the rights of people. Governments were usually imposed on the rest of the population by the most powerful group without much regard for the poor and the vulnerable. Jefferson and others hoped that the history of the United States would be different. He thought a revolution every twenty years would be needed to remind rulers of the source of their power.

Effective government depends upon local political structures and the participation of well-informed citizens. Unfortunately, most state governments today are ineffective at representing the local concerns of people. Newspapers can no longer do the job of educating the citizens, and the replacement of newspapers by electronic media has not been a smooth transition. The power of giant, rich corporations, unplanned for by the Constitution, threatens to overwhelm the voices of individuals and the fragile protections of minorities. James Madison recognized that "a nation without a national government is ... an awful spectacle."[234]

Similar to what had happened in England in the 1640s, when the House of Commons invented a "sovereign people" to overcome a sovereign king, a US Constitution had to rely on a fiction of its own creation. The possibility of national government depended on the authority of "the people." Madison realized that for a "United States" to exist, the national

---

234 James Madison, "Federalist No. 85."

government had to have veto power over its component states, which he considered "subordinately useful."[235] The complicated mechanisms of the Constitution were a set of compromises intended to balance local interests and national unity.

The Constitution, which starts with the words "We the people of the United States," could just as well have begun with "We the states of the united states." The great concern to balance local and national interests was undermined by the fact that representation was not of people in their local interests but based on states, which were not truly local and in many ways were resistant to a national government. Even the House of Representatives, which was supposed to represent ordinary people in their ordinary lives, was based on regions of thirty thousand people within each state. In the end, Madison was not optimistic about the resulting document, which would "neither effectually answer its national object nor prevent the local mischiefs which everywhere excite disgust against the state governments."[236]

The US Constitution divided Congress into two parts. The House of Representatives was to represent local concerns. The Senate equalized the power of the states. The Senate was to exercise thoughtful deliberation on important matters. However, for many people at that time, the Senate seemed too much like the House of Lords. That perception was not far off; eventually the Senate became composed of rich white men.

An executive and a judicial branch were intended to restrain impulsive acts of Congress and create a balance of powers. The idea was not "separation of powers," as is usually said, but an interaction of powers. The indirect elections of the president and the senate were further restraints on what were thought to be dangers of a democracy. The federal government would establish a unity of interests among the several states while it was regulated by a complicated set of interactions. The result was a "harmonious system of mutual frustration."[237]

---

235 Maier, *Ratification*, 24.

236 James Madison, September 6, 1787, in *The Papers of James Madison*, vol. 10 (Charlottesville, VA: University of Virginia Press, 1984-92), 163-65.

237 Atlee Kouwenhoven, *The Beer Can by the Highway: Essays on What's American about America* (Baltimore, MD: Johns Hopkins University Press, 1988), 54.

Germán Arciniegas writes that when the constitutional convention's delegates met, "they did not think of giving the new state a name of its own, and thus the United States is the only country in the world that does not have one. To say United States is like saying federation, republic or monarchy."[238] That is not quite accurate. The Constitutional Convention took over the Declaration of Independence's "united States of America" and simply capitalized the first word. The United States of America became the name by which the country is known throughout the world. Admittedly, it was an illogical name and a dangerous name in what it implied.

It is also inaccurate to say that the founders did not consider other names. Arciniegas acknowledges that at one point they planned to call the country Columbia. Another possibility they discussed was Freedonia. That name, derived from the Greek word for liberty, would have been a logical name but not one with popular backing. In the end, they let "United States of America" stand or stand in for a name.

From the seventeenth century onward, the English had casually referred to England and America. The British did not radically change their way of speaking after they recognized the "said United States to be free, sovereign and independent States." When referring to the United States, they continued to use the term "America," and they still do. Europeans generally follow the same custom of referring to the United States as America. For a comparison, (the united states of) Australia is accurately called Australia because the continent and country are coextensive. "United States of America" suggests an equivalence of continent and nation-state.

This linguistic equivalence of "nation" and "continent" indicated political aspirations that even preceded the Declaration of Independence. The British American colonists in the 1770s seem to have had affection for the term "continental." The meeting of delegates to a conference in 1774 was called the First Continental Congress; and the Second Continental Conference issued the Declaration of Independence. When the defense of the colonies was called for, they raised a continental army. And the currency they created was called the continental.

One could say that the two problematic claims by the new nation—that the states were united and that the states were continental

---

238 Germán Arciniegas, "The Four Americas," in Lewis Hanke, *Do the Americas Have a Common History?* (New York: Knopf, 1964), 237-38.

America—represented hopes rather than hard facts. That may be true, but while the aspiration to be united was their own business, and one that had to be resolved by internal efforts, the aspiration to be continental America was tied to illusions at home and violence for anyone who stood in the way.

The claim to be America might not have seemed a major problem in the eighteenth century, but it grew in importance throughout the nineteenth and twentieth centuries. Other American countries, including the United States of Brazil, the United States of Venezuela, the United States of Mexico, and the United Provinces of the Rio de la Plata (Argentina) are hindered from finding linguistic, economic, and political space by the claim that there is a United States of America.

The native peoples in the northern part of America were keenly aware that continental America was a direct threat to their existence. The glory of westward expansion by the United States of America meant a brutal and relentless war on the people who had been on the same land for centuries or millennia. Jefferson, Adams, and other founders thought it was inevitable that the United States of America would fulfill its name and spread across America.[239]

In the debates that followed the convention, the document was subjected to criticism from all sides. One of the earliest supporters of a national government, James Mason, opposed ratification. Some people thought the document went too far in revising the existing government. Other supporters of a purer form of democracy opposed the new Constitution as regressive. Why not a system in which one vote would count as one? How about a system not controlled by the moneyed interests on the East Coast? If there was going to be a powerful central government, where was the "bill of rights" that would protect the liberties of the individual?

---

239 John Adams said that the country was "destined to spread over the northern part of that whole quarter of the globe"; Thomas Jefferson thought "it is impossible not to look forward" to a time when our multiplication will "cover the whole northern, if not the southern continent, with a people speaking the same language, governed in similar forms, and by similar laws." Thomas Jefferson, Letter to James Monroe, November 24, 1801, in *The Works of Thomas Jefferson*, ed. Paul Leicester Ford (New York: Knickerbocker, 1905), X: 315-19.

Bill of Rights

From the perspective of the Constitution's proponents, a government by the people and for the people did not need protection against itself. James Wilson said at the convention, "Unlike the Magna Carta or the British Declaration of Rights, which were concessions from kings, the Constitution was the work of the sovereign people." That fact, said Wilson, "could ease the mind of those who heard much about the necessity of a bill of rights."[240] However, to get the Constitution ratified, Madison and other proponents agreed to what seemed to them redundant: a listing of the rights of citizens.

This statement of liberties has regularly been celebrated as one of the great achievements of the United States of America. For many US citizens, the Bill of Rights is more important than the Constitution itself. In their view, the Constitution represents the US government while the Bill of Rights represents the people, who must constantly be on guard against the government's encroachment on their God-given rights. "It is a remarkable but rarely noted irony that Americans owe their most cherished rights … not to the authors of the Constitution but to its inveterate enemies."[241]

The Bill of Rights was intended to be protection for an individual against an overly intrusive arm of government. When the process works, the result can be a wonderful support for people to be free in the "pursuit of happiness." However, once these rights had been carved in stone, it became difficult to get a consensus that some of these statements from the eighteenth century make little sense today or are obstacles to desperately needed reforms.

The effort to discover the intentions of eighteenth-century authors is a valuable exercise for understanding the text. But a claim that even a perfect reconstruction of their intentions could resolve contemporary debates is a bizarre assumption. Speaking of the Constitution, James Madison in the 1790s said that searching for the intention of the writers was not the way to interpret the document. Madison advised looking to the state conventions

240 Maier, *Ratification*, 107.
241 Woody Holton, *Unruly Americans and the Origin of the Constitution* (New York: Hill and Wang, 2007), 253.

that accepted and ratified the Constitution.[242] The meaning of any text is not confined to what the author intended; the meaning includes how a text is understood. That principle is especially important for a legal document that has a long history of commentary and applications. Today one would have to examine how the Constitution and its Bill of Rights have been accepted and understood by generations of people since the 1780s. That would seem to be the meaning of "conservative."

Akhil Reed Amar, in his book *America's Unwritten Constitution: The Precedents and Principles We Live By*, acknowledges what is seldom admitted by constitutional lawyers: the theories on both the left and the right for interpreting the Constitution must rely on principles outside the Constitution and outside the law.[243] Amar raises many interesting questions in his survey of difficult cases. However, his title is somewhat unnerving. If it is the United States that has a Constitution, shouldn't it be the United States, not America, that has an unwritten constitution? Furthermore, the concerns that are expressed in his subtitle might be better captured by the concept of tradition rather than that of an unwritten constitution. A tradition includes written documents while going beyond them. Tradition necessarily includes disagreements of interpretation but also includes rules for how to argue and how to set borders of the tradition.

"Tradition" does not have positive connotations in United States history. America began as a seeming rejection of Europe's traditions, although, as I pointed out earlier, a "new world" that had no continuity with an old world was impossible. Of all the American nations, the United States made the loudest claim to be "starting the world all over again." When Thomas Paine proposed that idea, he was obviously exaggerating but he was making a point about the emerging new republic. When Ronald Reagan several times quoted this line from Paine, it was a weird rejection of two centuries of United States history. Even a tradition of opposing tradition still becomes a tradition. And clearly the United States has built

---

242 *Records of the Federal Convention of 1787* (New Haven, CT: Yale University Press, 1937), III, 374; cited in Jack Rakove, "The Perils of Originalism," in *What Did the Constitution Mean to Early Americans*, ed. Edward Countryman (Boston: Bedford, 1999), 156.

243 Akhil Reed Amar, *America's Unwritten Constitution: The Precedents and Principles We Live By* (New York: Basic Books, 2012).

up an extraordinarily complicated legal tradition that includes original documents and layer upon layer of interpretation. But because of a bias against the idea of tradition, courts often work from a fiction that they are finding particular rights in the text of the Constitution.

For example, there are few rights more highly valued in the United States than a right to privacy. But one looks in vain for a statement of that right in the Bill of Rights. The authors of the Constitution undoubtedly valued privacy. But privacy underlies the idea of a person having rights rather than privacy itself being a right. There are no movements in the country to do away with privacy; on the contrary, there are intense debates about how to preserve privacy, and there are obvious differences about what people mean by privacy. The question can be raised whether "privacy"—a word that was undergoing a radical shift in meaning in the eighteenth century—is helpful in a discussion of rights today?[244]

In 1890, when big corporations and large governments were becoming a threat to individual autonomy, Samuel Warren and Louis Brandeis wrote an essay titled "The Right to Privacy."[245] They argued that it should be possible for an individual to be left alone if he or she wishes and that the government should not intrude into areas of life's intimate decisions. This invention or discovery of such a right could be helpful, but only within a tradition of relating the private and the public. Brandeis later said that he should have written a companion piece called "The Duty of Publicity."[246]

Two notable cases of Supreme Court decisions based on the right to privacy concerned the purchase and use of contraceptives by unmarried and married people, and the right to an abortion. In the first case, *Griswold v. Connecticut*, the country was ready to accept such a right.[247] In the decision, however, the court claimed that the right was found in "penumbras formed by emanation" from other constitutional guarantees. Amar understandably calls that language "sloppy" and "breezy." A more

---

244 In previous eras, privacy was mainly negative in meaning; privation was the shadow of public life. The United States was a main player in creating a positive meaning for "privacy," with consequences both good and bad.

245 Samuel Warren and Louis Brandeis, "The Right to Privacy," *Harvard Law Review* 4 (1890), 183-200.

246 Mary Ann Glendon, *Rights Talk: The Impoverishment of Political Discourse* (New York: Free Press, 1993), 50.

247 *Griswold v. Connecticut*, 381 US 479 (1965).

truthful admission by the Court would have been that the law had been far in the rear of an evolution in sexual attitudes. A moral tradition now existed to support the ruling. There were still voices of protest, but getting the government out of the business of monitoring bedrooms allowed for a continuing debate within the tradition.[248]

The decision of *Roe v. Wade* in 1973 is much better known to the public, but many people would not know that it was based on an extension of the right to privacy.[249] A large segment of the public still believes that the decision on a "right to abortion" was at least procedurally wrong. Justice Harry Blackmun, in his majority opinion, found the right in the Fourteenth Amendment. In subsequent decisions upholding *Roe v. Wade,* the Supreme Court shifted the basis of the right, though it did so without a thorough rethinking of the issue.[250] The conflict settled into two passionate lobbies without any serious debate about the philosophical, moral, scientific, and religious elements involved. The political far right considers abortion to be murder—a term that is not helpful to thoughtful discussions or political compromises. The liberal view is that "abortion rights" simply protect "a woman's right to choose." The reduction of abortion to a question of privacy has the effect of limiting the availability of abortion, because clinics that provide safe and affordable abortions are a public matter, regardless of how the services are funded.

Perhaps time will solve the conflict over abortion, but time by itself is no guarantee of a solution. Certainly, better contraceptives and better sexual education would reduce the need for abortions. At this point, criticizing the reasoning behind *Roe v. Wade* or trying to overturn the decision are not likely to be effective strategies. At some point, the "silent majority" has to emerge at the center of an evolving tradition that views abortion not first as a right but as a serious decision that is sometimes compelling but comes with moral reverberations. When good medical

---

248 The question of gay marriage did not surface as a legal issue until recent years. The court said that the Constitution gives them that right. *Obergefell v. Hodges,* 576 US (2015).

249 *Roe v. Wade,* 410 US 113 (1973).

250 *Planned Parenthood v. Casey* 1992 said that a woman's decision to terminate a pregnancy was within the "realm of personal liberty which the government may not enter."

and moral reasons exist for an abortion, the government's job is mainly to get out of the way. But government services are crucial for reducing the need for abortion and for supporting the proper facilities in which those abortions are performed.

A bigger problem than discovering new rights in the Constitution is the way that many rights were understood and stated in eighteenth-century language. The strangest debate in the country is over the Second Amendment on the "right to bear arms."[251] The authors of the amendment, based on what had been their recent experience, thought that a "well-regulated militia" (but not, of course, a standing army) was needed to defend the country. For many people in the country, it is close to religious belief that they need a gun for their security. For many other people, the belief borders on insanity.

In 2012, Rep. Martin Stutzman, Indiana Republican, said of the right to carry a concealed weapon, "Mr. Speaker, rights do not come from the government. We are, in the words of the Declaration of Independence, endowed by our creator with certain inalienable rights."[252] This view was carried further by Newt Gingrich in a speech before the National Rifle Association in April 2012. Gingrich said there was no doubt that the Second Amendment referred to an inalienable right. He criticized the NRA for being too timid! During a Gingrich presidency, he said, a human right to bear arms would be affirmed for every person on Earth. Sadly or not, the country does not seem destined to experience a Gingrich presidency.

It seems certain that the standoff over guns will not be resolved by the debate over exactly what the authors of the Second Amendment intended. Opponents of gun control laws have a case if the only question is the intention of the eighteenth-century writers. By "militia," the authors apparently meant every man who could carry a gun; that was the way to guarantee that the government would not become tyrannical. The Supreme Court in 2008 ruled that the individual does have the right

---

251 Only two other national constitutions include such a right: Guatemala and Mexico.
252 *New York Times*, November 17, 2011, A31.

to bear arms. It added that there can be regulations that apply to that ownership.[253]

The rest of the world looks on this debate with a mixture of amusement and horror. An outsider would think that some sensible steps might be taken to reduce the violence. But the underlying problem is the intense distrust of government and the strong regional and class differences in the country. The inability to reach any agreements on the control of firearms is symptomatic of the government's paralysis on numerous important issues. Other countries could make a very helpful contribution if the United States were open to learning from them. Canada, in particular, has many lessons to teach the United States, including the Canadian Charter of Rights and Freedoms.[254]

Also debated these days is the Fourth Amendment, which guarantees the right of citizens to be secure against unreasonable searches and seizures. The word "unreasonable" is up for debate, although one would think there could be consensus that some practices of the police are outrageously unreasonable. In this area there has been a startling change in the last two decades as to how much intrusion of the government is necessary for "security." Requiring "government papers" to travel across the country was unheard of until a short time ago; but soon body scans at airports were deemed necessary. Closed-circuit television cameras that can track an individual's movement within a city have quickly spread, and now one's movement can be tracked through GPS and one's thoughts and interests can be exposed through computers.

There is danger from government intrusions, and there is also a danger from a lack of government help where it is needed. In recent years, the relations between the police and inner-city communities has posed a new problem of Fourth Amendment rights. Or perhaps it is not a new problem but the cell phone has made it visible. A program called "stop-and-frisk" became a focus of the tension. No one would dispute the right of police

---

253 *District of Columbia v. Heller* 554 US 570 (2008). A 2010 decision in *McDonald v. Chicago* affirmed that the ruling applies to the states as well as to the District of Columbia.

254 For success in reducing violence, see Franklin Zimring, *The City that Became Safe: New York's Lessons for Urban Crime and its Control* (New York: Oxford University Press, 2012).

to stop and search someone when there is evidence of that person having committed a crime. But in New York City, the police in one year stopped seven hundred thousand people, 90 percent of whom were young black men. Not only was the policy ineffective in catching criminals, but it also soured relations between the police and the community. The Supreme Court condemned that version of stop-and-frisk as unconstitutional.

The Fifth to Eighth Amendments are concerned with crime and the protection of citizens who are accused of crimes. These amendments hold out beautiful ideals; but without the application of these provisions to every citizen, the rights exist only on paper. In a country that has a suspicion about any government actions and an opposition to almost all regulations, these amendments are treated dismissively. The most vulnerable populations are those that suffer the consequences. Black people in the United States have reason to be especially concerned with these protections.

The one provision of these amendments that does touch many people is in the Sixth Amendment: "The accused shall enjoy the right to a speedy and public trial, by an impartial jury." That ideal is carried out in numerous television programs but not in many courtrooms. The system has been overwhelmed for decades. A few celebrity cases are handled in public with care for every legal detail. Even here, whatever was meant by "speedy trial" surely was not a trial that would take many months or years. For the poor who are given the counsel of an overburdened public defender, the chances of the system giving them a fair deal are not good. In any large city, the great majority of cases are handled by plea bargaining—something not found in the Bill of Rights. But there is no way that everyone accused of a crime can have his or her speedy trial before an impartial jury.

The Bill of Rights is mainly about procedures, many of which are invaluable protections. But the Bill of Rights was not intended to deal substantively with the nature of justice and how to make sense of complicated cases—especially those of crimes that involve young people. There are many intelligent, dedicated, and honest judges who are prevented from making fair and sensible judgments because they are caught in an unworkable bureaucracy that no one intended.

The First Amendment, with five different provisions, is a hallmark of the United States; its rights are said to be at the heart of the sacred cause of liberty. The first provision is a clumsy formula for religious liberty. The

United States is one of the most religious countries in the world, but it has never worked out an adequate language of religion and government. Of course, it is not clear that any country has. The authors of the first amendment used a cryptic formula of sixteen words, simply prohibiting Congress from supporting "an establishment of religion" (a confusing phrase then; an unintelligible phrase now) or interfering with anyone's practice of a religion. It provided no guidance for how the government should act in its unavoidable dealings with the religions of the country and the members of those religions.

Thomas Jefferson later introduced the European language of "church and state," which had never made much sense in the American colonies and is patently inadequate for describing today's United States. Not even the Baptists, whom Jefferson was addressing when introducing the metaphor of "a wall of separation between church and state," ever used that language. In the 1880s the separation of church and state was discovered to be useful in resisting the rising power of the Roman Catholic Church.[255]

The Supreme Court's decisions, which in the 1940s introduced the language of "church and state," have mostly just confused things further. When, in the 1960s, the court outlawed state-mandated prayer in public schools, there were protests, and there is still resistance to the ruling. Many groups, such as the Moral Majority, rightly protested that they were not a church. The Supreme Court also made clumsy gestures toward the public schools having an obligation to deal academically with religion. Church-state language is simply an obstacle to thinking about that question.[256]

The First Amendment's other four provisions relate to the citizens' right to speak individually, in the press, in assemblies, and in petitions to the government. Each provision tries to assure the citizens that the government will not interfere if they wish to speak. One can imagine an eighteenth-century village in which the citizens came together and each

---

255 For Jefferson's intention, see Daniel Dreisbach, *Thomas Jefferson and the Wall of Separation between Church and State* (New York: New York University Press, 2003), 65; for the history of the metaphor of wall of separation between church and state, see: Philip Hamburger, *Separation of Church and State* (Cambridge, MA: Harvard University Press, 2004).

256 The Supreme Court did not help. Justice Arthur Goldberg introduced a distinction between "teach religion" and "teach about religion" that immediately became an unhelpful orthodoxy.

had a chance to speak his (and maybe even her) mind. No one would be arrested for having negative things to say about the government. The newspapers and journals of the late eighteenth century suggest that many citizens did engage in rollicking debates and were not hesitant to speak critically of the government.

The United States has been resistant to any attempt to rethink these provisions of the first amendment. The guarantee of freedom of speech is now usually referred to as "free speech," which is misleading. Whenever a few people wish to speak, there are decisions about who speaks, where they speak, for how long, on what topic, and in what manner. Right-wing political groups have recently discovered that the demand for "free speech" gives them a power to object to any regulation of their spreading hatred. Speech is regulated in one way or another; the removal of such regulations gives power to whoever shouts the loudest or has the most money.

A. J. Liebling famously commented that "freedom of the press is guaranteed only to those who own one." The meaning of "the press" has expanded in ways that the eighteenth century, or even the early twentieth century, could not have imagined. With the advent of the internet, Liebling's problem may seem to be solved; that is, everyone who has a computer owns a printing press.

Although the possibilities of communication have expanded in amazing ways, the avalanche of words has also highlighted the difference between the liberty to speak and a freedom of speech in which words have meaning and effect. Blogs and tweets can be entertaining and sometimes informative. There remains a difference between the clever remark of someone scoring a point and the researched and thoughtful writing of a person whose work is to search for (if not always to arrive at) the truth. An avalanche of words undermines the careful use of words to achieve intelligent and fair results.

A lack of standards and controls in public discourse in the United States leads to social controls that may or may not make sense. It has been a complaint of visitors to the United States since the country's beginning that everybody in "America" thinks alike. Alexis de Tocqueville is surprisingly harsh in his judgment that "freedom of opinion does not exist in America ... I know of no country in which there is so little independence of mind and real freedom of discussion as in America."[257] Liberty of speech does not of itself produce free-wheeling thought. There are areas—for example, in the sciences—where the United States has been highly creative. But that is the case where there are standards and a "community of discourse" for the exchange of ideas that are the products of careful experimentation and reflection.

The problem for most public discourse in the United States is that it is controlled by the ideology of America. Anyone who steps outside that ideology can be perceived as a threat to the existence of the country. The government has, on some occasions, come down hard on dissent (e.g., the alien and sedition laws in the late eighteenth and early twentieth centuries), but the pressures of social conformity are the regular way in which freedom of speech is severely curtailed. Herbert Croly, at the time of World War I, wrote that "the freedom of American speech and thought has not been essentially different from the freedom of speech a group of prisoners might enjoy during the term of their imprisonment."[258]

The Ninth and Tenth Amendments may appear to be throwaway lines; they do not specify any liberty that the individual has. Actually, both amendments are crucial to the Constitution. The Ninth Amendment was a simple admission by the authors that they had not covered everything. They were more open-minded than many people today who think that the Constitution and the Bill of Rights form a sacred scripture from which the country cannot stray. The ninth amendment said that "the people" had rights other than those enumerated in the Bill of Rights. That gave the country some room for acknowledging new situations.

The tenth amendment hardly belongs in a Bill of Rights, but it is probably the most important of the ten amendments. In the Articles of Confederation, the second article said, "Each state retains its sovereignty, freedom and independence, and every Power, Jurisdiction and right, which is not by this confederation expressly delegated to the United States in Congress assembled." The Tenth Amendment to the US Constitution started from that formula of the Articles of Confederation and made adaptations of it. The final form of the amendment was "The powers not

---

257 Alexis de Tocqueville, *Democracy in America*, I: 275.
258 Herbert Croly, *The Promise of American Life* (Cambridge, MA: Harvard University Press, 1965), 422.

delegated to the United States by the Constitution, nor prohibited by it to the states, are reserved to the states respectively, or to the people."

This amendment is often summarized as one that restricts the power of the federal government or that balances state and federal powers, but that is not its wording. The writers of the Tenth Amendment wisely left out "sovereign, free and independent" for describing the states. They also left out "expressly" which made later developments possible. But strangely, they also left out "in Congress assembled" which resulted in creating a contrast between "states" and "the United States" rather than between state and federal governments. One might dismiss the significance of this use of "United States" as legal shorthand, but it suggests a continuing confusion over whether what existed was a United States or an assemblage of united states. The Eleventh Amendment, penned in 1795, illogically refers to "one of the United States."

The United States of America and British North America

The secession of the thirteen colonies that produced a republic inevitably created a tension with British North America, which remained a part of the empire. The people who called themselves "the Americans" kept a close eye on their neighbor to the north. The geographical line dividing the two peoples was disputed at many places. And the values of the two peoples differed, although not radically. French Canada did have a different history and was especially suspicious of their fast-growing neighbor to the south. Upper Canada (Ontario) invited immigrants from the United States in the 1790s, who seem to have been more interested in cheap land than loyalty to the empire.

The colonies of British North America that remained part of the British Empire eventually became the Dominion of Canada in 1867. That move was spurred by the United States' purchase of Alaska from Russia in western Canada and the fear that the United States was a threat to invade eastern Canada. The formation of Canada, however, was not based on rebellion; England was willing to have this evolution and even gave a push to the Maritime Provinces to become part of the dominion. The federal union of the Canadian provinces was fragile, but it received stability from its continuing bond to the British Empire. And a motivator of national union was resistance to the United States, which from its birth had proclaimed that its destiny was continental. Before the Dominion of Canada could emerge in 1867, it had to fend off several incursions from the south, starting in 1775 and coming to its most dramatic point in 1812.

Both Canada and the United States have had a problem of national identity, although the problem has taken a different shape in the two countries. Canada began as an uneasy combination of French Canada and English Canada; English Canada was distinctly Protestant in religion; French Canada was overwhelmingly Roman Catholic. Ever since the Quebec treaty of 1775, in which Britain took control of French Canada but was tolerant of the French language and the Catholic religion, the relation has always been prickly.[259]

When the Dominion of Canada was formed from ten provinces, each with a sense of its own autonomy, a fragile unity of enormous size but small population began an endless search for a national identity. The thing that Canadians are sure of is that they are not Americans. A Canadian writer professes the belief that "without at least a touch of anti-Americanism, Canada would have no reason to exist."[260] A like sentiment is expressed over and over in Canadian literature. Canadians, it is said, are deeply un-American or anti-American.

This linguistic problem is a central example of the theme of this book. The United States, by equating itself with America, creates an untenable situation for Canada (and countries south of the United States). If Canadians wish to be in North America, they cannot cede the term "America" to their southern neighbor. Whoever owns "America" owns "North America." If one is going to fight the United States, the place to begin is with the United States' arrogant claim to be America. For Canadians to be "anti-American" is to reinforce what they are opposed to. Admittedly, there is no simple way to refer to US people, but that is not a reason for Canadians to interchange "United States" and "America."

I know of many books with "Canada and the United States" in the title. There are few Canadian books with "Canada and America" in the

---

259 Seymour Lipset, *Continental Divide: The Values and Institutions of the United States and Canada* (New York: Routledge, 1990), 179.

260 Blair Fraser, *The Search for Identity: Canada, 1945-1967* (Garden City, NY: Doubleday, 1967), 301.

title.[261] Yet inside the books on Canada and the United States, there is regular use of "America" when "United States" is meant. Michael Adams's *Fire and Ice: The United States, Canada, and the Myth of Converging Values* is packed with statistics to show that Canada and the United States have different values, but the book interchanges "America" and "United States" without noting any problem in that equivalence. The book contains some strange statements, such as "Canadian youth are more 'American' than their parents and grandparents, but they remain vastly less American than Americans."[262]

Perhaps Canadian authors consider it hopeless to resist a language spoken almost everywhere. But Canada is in the best position to teach the rest of the world, including the United States, how to speak about both the United States and America. The United States is never going to change its way of speaking without some prodding by friendly but insistent critics.

US people are usually shocked when they discover the so called "anti-Americanism" of Canadians. Of course, US Americans are surprised when they discover anything about Canada. Whereas Canadians are overwhelmed with news of the United States, people in the United States are blissfully ignorant of the history, politics, and culture of Canada.[263] Sports fans in the US know at least the names of a few Canadian cities; that awareness of Canada is more than can be found in national news broadcasts on almost any day of the year.

The best way for a nation to get a sense of its identity is by comparison to other nations. The United States is not inclined to do such comparative study, because in its language, "America" is outside the boundaries of a mere nation. From its beginning, the United States believed that it had left Europe in the dust as it lit the way to the future. Rather than European countries, the United States' more fertile soil for cross-national comparisons would be other American nations. Despite much that the US shares with

---

261 From the US side, the failure to see the problem is shown in a 2013 book titled *Merger of the Century*, which carries the subtitle *Why Canada and America Should Become One Country*. Surely every Canadian can recognize that this "merger" is actually a proposal that Canada be dissolved.

262 Michael Adams, *Fire and Ice: The United States, Canada and the Myth of Converging Values* (Toronto: Penguin Books, 2003), 92.

263 What hardly needed proving was documented in an opinion survey, "Portrait of Two Nations," in *Maclean's,* July 3, 1989, 23-56.

the "Latin" part of America, there are language and cultural barriers that are not easy to surmount. The obstacles are much less imposing for the possibility of comparing the US and Canada. Many Canadian scholars are interested in such study, but few US writers have pursued such an interest. The United States is the loser from that neglect. As Robin Wink writes: "The reason Americans should study Canadian history is to learn more about themselves, about how they differ from and how they are similar to others."[264]

The United States has seldom been aware that it might learn from Canada. In recent years, the United States has had to grudgingly acknowledge that in banking practices, health care, immigration policy, and foreign relations, Canada may have some things to teach the United States. US people might say that Canada tends to negotiate peacefully with other nations because it does not have a trillion-dollar military. Canadians might reverse the proposition. Because the United States does not often negotiate with other nations, it needs a trillion dollars of military "defense."

In an earlier discussion of "American exceptionalism," I pointed out that a nation or an individual can be exceptional but in opposite ways and to varying degrees. The United States is exceptional in both good and bad ways, depending on how it relates itself to the idea of America. The attempt to realize a dream of "liberty and justice for all" has at times created hope for the downtrodden of the world, especially when the United States opened its doors to tens of millions of immigrants. In contrast, the presumption that the United States is the sole bearer of emancipation in the world has made the United States an exceptionally violent nation that uses its military power for what it decides is good for everyone else.

An American exceptionalism can be seen to have slowly emerged in Canada. Canada's geography and history give the country distinctive qualities—some that are shared with the United States, and some in contrast to its southern neighbor. In the United States, the individual always has to be vigilant lest the state intervene; Canadians have generally seen the state as a positive force for the distribution of goods.[265] Canadians

---

264 Robert Wink, *Relevance of Canadian History* (Lanham, MD: Universities Press of America, 1988), xvii.

265 Elizabeth Mancke, *Fault Lines of Empire: Political Differentiation in Massachusetts and Nova Scotia, 1760-1830* (New York: Routledge, 2005), 163.

are widely known as the "nice North Americans." In the refugee crisis of recent years, Canada has put the United States to shame in its openness to receiving immigrants, while the United States has accepted few people (after years of "vetting" them) and seems obsessed with securing its borders. Canada has become an exceptional country in providing an example of order and openness in a chaotic world.

In the past, the question of Canada's relation to America might have seemed to be whether the United States would let Canada into the category of American with what would be second-class status. But at this juncture of history, the question can be seriously asked: Is Canada more American than the United States? Is Canada a more exceptional embodiment of the best qualities of America? If America is a realistic hope for liberty and wealth, then Canada does seem to be more American than the United States.

American Civil War: Part 1

The first American Civil War usually goes under the strange name of the War of 1812, as if the only thing certain about the war is the year in which it officially began. When it ended is not as clear. It was an American Civil War in the two senses of America: it was a war for the northern part of the continent of America, and it was and still is a war enveloped by the myth of America, such that any factual statements about the war are suspect. The version of the war found in most US textbooks is heavy on patriotism and short on facts.

My intent for my treatment of this war is not to give a more factual account of the battles but to examine the war so as to show the difficulty of getting at the history of the United States, which can never be entirely separated from the myth of America. There are few instances in US history that demonstrate this problem as well as does the War of 1812. Not surprisingly, Canada (or the Canadas) gets almost no attention in what became the standard account of the war, even though the US attempt to conquer British North America was central to the cause and the execution of the war. The US attempt to extend its continental ambitions northward was a failure. To that extent, Canada was the winner in the war insofar as the provinces of British North America were pushed toward the union that would later emerge as the Dominion of Canada.

The big loser in the war was the American native population in both the northern and southern regions of the United States. Forced to choose sides, most of the native tribes sided with the British, viewing them as more trustworthy than the United States. In the negotiations to end the war, the British made gestures toward securing recognition of Indian lands but eventually abandoned the natives to the aggressive frontiersmen of the United States. The westward thrust of the United States was therefore facilitated by the treaty that ended the war.

The account of the war was quickly fixed by what today is called political spin. President James Madison proclaimed a glorious victory that the country could be proud of. The history was given further spin toward the end of the nineteenth century by the push of US leaders to build a powerful navy. The exploits of the USS *Constitution* ("Old Ironsides") in the war of 1812 hold a cherished place in the story of how "America" took on the British navy. Given the lack of preparation and the small size of its fleet, the US Navy performed well against the part of its navy that the British chose to send to the coast of the United States.

In recent years, a few US historians have contributed fine studies of the war of 1812. The two-hundredth anniversary of the war sparked some interest in what Donald Hickey's subtitle calls "A Forgotten Conflict."[266] Alan Taylor chose to call his history "The Civil War of 1812." The subtitle of his book is comprehensive: "American Citizens, British Subjects, Irish Rebels, & Indian Allies."[267] For a detailed account of the war, it is difficult to imagine a more comprehensive study than Jon Latimer's book with the simple title *1812*.[268] The subtitle of Latimer's book is puzzling: "War with America."

What is obvious about the subtitle of Latimer's book is that it is announcing that the book is written from the perspective of Britain.

---

266 Donald Hickey, *The War of 1812: A Forgotten Conflict* (Urbana, IL: University of Illinois, 1990).

267 Alan Taylor, *The Civil War of 1812: American Citizens, British Subjects, Irish Rebels, & Indian Allies* (New York: Knopf, 2010).

268 Jon Latimer, *1812: War with America* (Cambridge, MA: Harvard University Press, 2007).

Beyond that, however, it is difficult to make sense of "War with America." It is true that the British then and now tend to say "America" when they are referring to the United States. In this case, however, the United States of America and British North America were involved in a struggle for America. The British were supporting one part of America and fighting against another part of America. Whether by "America" one means the continent or the myth, Britain was not at war with America. "The War *for* America" would make more sense.

Recent US histories of the war have made admirable attempts to provide an unbiased account of the war. But penetrating the myth of America surrounding the war is extremely difficult unless one is prepared to resist the patriotic language in which the facts are hidden. Jon Latimer, who relies on diaries and official British sources, is not hampered in that way.

Latimer presents the war as a "distraction" that the British had from the "Great War" being fought in Europe. He is meticulous in describing the details of the war, and he cannot hide his disdain for the way the war is remembered in the United States: "Defeat was practically guaranteed from the moment Madison and Congress stepped onto the warpath with risible preparations that undercooked the navy and put a half-baked army in the field."[269] Reacting to US complaints that the British were not civilized in their burning of the White House in 1814, Latimer writes, "The United States had started the war, and American forces had rained destruction on British communities; America could not reasonably complain if the fates of war brought its effects home."[270]

The war, although a long time coming, still caught much of the United States by surprise when President Madison declared war in June 1812. From the 1780s onward, there had been numerous clashes between the new republic and the British Empire; but each time, diplomacy was able to keep the peace. The Federalists, who dominated US politics in the 1790s, attended to preparedness for war but generally had a "pro-British" outlook. An important accomplishment of theirs was the Jay Treaty in 1794. The British had seized US ships that were trading with the French West Indies. The Jay Treaty worked out an agreement that regulated commerce and

---

269 Latimer, *1812*, 59.
270 Latimer, *1812*, 322.

defined neutral rights in war. The British also agreed to abandon forts on the Great Lakes. The Grenville Treaty in 1795 opened up US settlements in Ohio, Kentucky, Illinois, and Indiana.

The British were starting into what became twenty years of war with France. They were not looking to start a fight across the ocean. When the Jay Treaty expired in 1806, the Monroe-Pinkney Treaty, which was quite favorable to the United States, was negotiated. The Democratic Republicans were now in charge, and President Jefferson refused to submit the treaty for Senate approval. Shortly afterward came the British Orders in Council banning neutral powers from trading with France; that decision was a major irritant for the United States. In the years after 1807, foreign trade drastically fell because of British blockades.[271]

In this period, a number of incidents stirred up conflict between Britain and the United States. At the center of the conflict was the British claim that many British nationals were posing as US sailors. The pay was much better on US ships, and the British desperately needed twelve thousand new sailors each year. What seems to be true is that there were many British men—estimates run as high as ten thousand men or a quarter of the US merchant marine—who were mixed in with US personnel. The difficulty was in telling the difference between British deserters and US citizens. Even if men were carrying US papers, there was no guarantee that the papers were not a product of widespread forgery. Desperate to fill the ranks of their navy, the British resorted to impressment—that is, boarding US ships and seizing men who were thought to be British subjects.

This aggressive action on the part of the British was bound to result in mistakes and incidents of violence. The most serious occurred in 1807 when the HMS *Leonard* fired on the USS *Chesapeake* because there were supposedly four deserters on board. The attack killed three US personnel and wounded eighteen. From 1807 to 1812, the French and the British seized nine hundred US ships. Both imports and exports were interfered with as the United States tried to thread a neutral path that would be to its economic advantage.

The onset of war was therefore not without provocation. But as is usual in war, each side said that since it had exhausted all other remedies and

---

271 Walter Russell Meade and Richard Leone, *Special Providence: American Foreign Policy and How it Changed the World* (New York: Routledge, 2002), 17.

had no other choice, then this war was not being started by it. Still, it was a surprise when a nation with seven thousand regular troops and a navy of sixteen vessels took on the British Empire. As historian Gordon Wood writes, "Perhaps the strangest thing about the War of 1812 was that the Americans actually initiated it. They told the world in 1812 that they were declaring war against Great Britain solely because of British impressment of American sailors."[272]

Was the US government being truthful in saying that impressment was the sole cause? It is unlikely that any wars have a single cause. In this case, the complex motives were difficult to unravel then, and they still present a puzzle. The impressment of the sailors was the most proximate cause, but the struggle for control of northern America had been going on since the 1770s. The contrast in identifying the central piece of the conflict can be found in statements by John Randolph, a prominent opponent of the war, and Henry Clay, Speaker of the House of Representatives and leader of the war hawks. Randolph said on December 17, 1811, "Agrarian cupidity not maritime right urges the war … We have heard but one word: Canada, Canada, Canada." However, Henry Clay, in a letter of December 1812, wrote, "Canada was not the end but the means, the object of the war being the redress of injuries and Canada being the instrument by which that redress was to be obtained."[273]

There is probably truth in both of these statements. The desire for land and a push to expand were characteristic of the young republic. The purchase of Louisiana in 1803 had not satisfied that appetite. Randolph was surely exaggerating in saying that Canada was the only word being spoken, but Clay was also being disingenuous by reducing Canada to a mere means for striking at Great Britain. The conquest of Lower and Upper Canada had long been a background of US policy. The war brought that policy to the center of planning.

In 1774, the First Continental Congress had issued an invitation to its northern neighbor to join a rebellion against Britain, and the invitation was renewed by the Second Continental Congress in May 1775. John Hancock proposed that a march on Canada would "open a way for the

272 Gordon Wood, "The War We Lost and Won," *New York Review*, Oct. 28, 2010, 38.
273 Hickey, *War of 1812*, 72.

Blessing of Liberty, and the Happiness of well-ordered Government to visit that vast Dominion."[274] An ill-fated march on Quebec was actually attempted on December 31, 1775, but had to turn back.[275] In 1787, the United States prequalified Canadian provinces as future states on the mistaken assumption that these provinces were longing to join the rebels to the south.

The picture changed with the Canada Constitutional Act in 1791. A new colony of Upper Canada (Ontario) was founded, populated in large part by emigrants from the United States. The shaping of the two Canadas into a new nation was a response to the French Revolution's attack on the church and aristocracy. In Canada, one-seventh of the land was to be owned by the Church of England. In addition to elected assemblies, there was to be a "House of Lords" to preside over a nation that would be proud of its conservative emphasis on "peace, order and good government."[276] On the eve of the war, General William Hull addressed Canadians: "You will be emancipated from tyranny and oppression, and restored to the status of freemen."[277] The United States was oblivious of the fact that there were few Canadians who were clamoring for liberation.

While many people favored a "limited maritime war," similar to what had happened in 1798, the Democratic Republicans pushed ahead with an army-led war as well. From the beginning to the end, the war was resisted in the US, especially in New England. Every Federalist in Congress voted against going to war; the Republicans voted ninety-eight to twenty-three in favor of war. The war fever was led by Irish immigrants to the United States, who were the majority of immigrants that had entered the country since 1783. The New York Irish newspaper *Shamrock* proclaimed, "Ireland will be rescued from British bondage on the plains of Canada."[278]

The war itself can be described in three acts and an epilogue roughly corresponding to the calendar years of the war. The year 1812 was mostly

---

274 Lester Langley, *America in the Americas: The United States in the Western Hemisphere* (Athens, GA: University of Georgia, 1989), 7.

275 Nash, *Unknown American Revolution*, 177. Smallpox, winter weather and a reinforced British force caused terrible casualties to the invaders.

276 Maya Jasanoff, *Liberty's Exiles: American Loyalists in the Revolutionary World* (New York: Knopf, 2011), 201.

277 *Boston Columbian Centinel*, August 5, 1812.

278 Taylor, *The Civil War of 1812*, 81, 354.

a disaster for the US Army, while the US Navy surprisingly fared better against the powerful British navy. The year 1813 was much more successful for the improving US Army, and the US Navy achieved a victory on Lake Erie. In 1814, the British counterpunched, although they failed to land a knockout at the battles of Plattsburgh and Baltimore. The treaty to end the war was signed on December 25, 1814, but before it was ratified in March 1815, the United States scored big at the battle of New Orleans. At the end, very little land had changed hands; as is the case with most wars, it did not solve any problems.

In invading Canada at the beginning of the war, the United States had enormous superiority in numbers—a population of over seven million people compared to Canada's three hundred thousand. The US Army was supplemented by state militia, although those troops often balked at crossing the border.

Henry Clay believed that "the militia of Kentucky alone [were] competent to place Montreal and Upper Canada at [their] feet."[279] In the summer of 1812, the United States was quickly disabused of this illusion. Losses at Detroit, Dearborn, and the western outpost of Mackinac exposed the whole northwest to attack. Not until Zachary Harrison's defense of Fort Harrison in September did the United States achieve a land victory. The victory of Andrew Jackson over the Creek Indians provided some cover for the west.

The United States had some success on water. The heralded victory of the USS *Constitution* coupled with victory on Lake Erie in 1813 boosted spirits, but the United States was never able to get control of the St. Lawrence waterway. The British retained control of Lake Ontario and the Niagara River. By the end of 1813, the entire coast of the United States was blockaded (except for New England, which continued an unpatriotic flow of provisions to Canada and the British West Indies). US naval ships fought valiantly but unsuccessfully.

More important than any individual battle was the changing face of war in Europe. With Napoleon's defeat at Leipzig in October 1813 (he abdicated the following April) and British victories in Spain, the British in 1814 could take to the offensive in the United States. The burning of Washington was humiliating, and the British seized one hundred miles

---

279 Andrew Cockburn, "Washington is Burning," *Harper's,* September 2014, 44.

of Maine coastline without the United States offering any resistance.[280] The United States' successful defense of Baltimore and Plattsburgh in September of 1814 gave it a better bargaining position at peace talks.

Negotiations for peace took place at Ghent, Belgium, from August 8 to December 24 in 1814. By October the two sides were still far apart. The British demanded concession of much of Maine and Minnesota. In the end, both sides agreed to the possession of land as it was before the war. The British stopped impressing sailors, because the war in Europe had ended. Disputes about the Canadian-US border were referred to postwar commissions. "The Anglo-American War was over. After at least fifteen thousand combatants had been killed or wounded, on paper it had barely changed a thing."[281]

The Treaty of Ghent was signed on December 24, 1814. It took six weeks for it to reach Washington, where the Senate unanimously approved it on February 16, 1815, and the British countersigned. The war thus officially ended on February 17, 1815. During those six weeks, the battle of New Orleans occurred, in which the British suffered the loss of two thousand men. Andrew Jackson's defense of New Orleans began his political career. This victory at the end (or after the end) of the war led to an exalted cry: "We have triumphed – let snarling discontents say what they will – we have gloriously triumphed."[282]

With the generous terms of the peace treaty, the United States could be said to have lost the war but won the peace. That is not the way the emerging myth was forged. "The War of 1812 passed into history not as a futile and costly struggle in which the United States had barely escaped dismemberment and disunion, but as a glorious triumph in which the nation had singlehandedly defeated the conqueror of Napoleon and the Mistress of the Seas."[283]

US history books play up the bright spots while playing down the fact that the war accomplished little. It did stir up more patriotism, although it revealed a deep regional split. America may have been strengthened, but the United States was not. The East Coast carried most of the economic

---

280 Lattimer, *1812*, 347.
281 Jasanoff, *Liberty's*, 329.
282 *Worcester National Aegis*, February 22, 1815.
283 Latimer, *1812*, 400.

burden of the war, north and south forming a united opposition on this issue. Trade with the enemy continued throughout the war. The west was enthusiastic for war and profited the most from it. Custom duties were doubled, and internal taxes were postponed.

The most serious crack in national union was a meeting of New England leaders in Hartford in 1814 that proposed serious reform of the US Constitution. The Hartford Convention was actually the more moderate part of the rebellion in New England, where secession was seriously discussed. The Hartford Convention might have led to some drastic results, except that it did not actually convene until December 1, 1814, when the news from Europe was of an imminent peace treaty. Although the Hartford Convention was quickly dismissed as a joke and relegated to a footnote in history books, it was a prelude to later secession and the US Civil War.[284]

After the war, the United States dismantled its navy but spent millions of dollars on fortifying its coastline. An animosity toward the British continued throughout the nineteenth century. It is surprising, therefore, that before the end of the decade the British foreign minister, George Canning, proposed a joint agreement to keep other European nations from interfering in America. During the war, the British had opened new trade arrangements in the southern part of America. What they feared was a restoration of the Spanish Empire now led by the French. Canning warned the French that the British navy would intercept any French ships that were bringing Spanish arms to America.

Eventually, what won out in the United States was a unilateral announcement (much to the chagrin of George Canning) that the Western Hemisphere was now closed to the rest of the world. President Monroe incorporated this statement into his annual message to Congress in 1823.[285] Although it was never made into a Senate resolution, the Monroe Doctrine became famous as the United States' announcement that it was in charge

---

284 Hickey, *The War of 1812*, 274-80.
285 Edward Widmer, *Ark of the Liberties: America and the World* (New York: Hill and Wang, 2008), 91. Canning's response to Monroe's statement was "We cannot acknowledge the right of any country to proclaim such a principle, much less to bind other countries to the observance of it."

of all America. "The United States would tolerate in the Americas no imperialism but its own."[286]

The rest of the world paid little attention to the Monroe Doctrine. Predictably it was ridiculed by the French: "Who is this president to pose as a dictator armed with a right of suzerainty over the entire new world?" [287] For many decades, the only force that the Monroe Doctrine had was the British navy; the British, for their own purposes, wished to see southern America free of European intervention. If the United States had formed a joint alliance with Britain, it would have had a stronger hand, for example, when Napoleon III sent an army to invade Mexico in 1861. However, that would have been to admit that the United States was not America. Until the twentieth century, "the Monroe Doctrine was a tissue of highly exaggerated claims about what the United States would do, if it could, in response to a European invasion that was not going to happen, in places the United States had no jurisdiction over."[288]

The Losers in the War

There had been four major players in the first American Civil War: the United States of America, British North America, Great Britain, and coalitions of American natives. The one big loser of those four was the last—the native tribes in both the northern and southern regions of the United States. The Shawnees in the Great Lakes area had cast their lot with the British, who eventually abandoned them. The Creeks in the Mississippi Valley and across the south were losers in a struggle that would continue for decades. In the peace treaty, both Great Britain and the United States paid lip service to the rights of the Indians, pledging "to restore to such tribes … all the possessions, rights, and privileges which they may have enjoyed, or been entitled to, in 1811, previous to such hostilities."[289]

The real meaning of the treaty was that Britain relinquished all attempts to support an Indian buffer state, and the west became wide open

---

286 Felipe Fernandez-Armesto, *The Americans: A Hemispheric History* (New York: Modern Library, 2009), 165.
287 The Parisian journal *L'Etoile,* January 4, 1824.
288 Widmer, *Ark of the Liberties*, 93.
289 Hickey, *The War of 1812*, 296.

to the land-hungry settlers of the United States. The relation between the United States and the Indians was fixed in myth and imagery that would continue for the next century and a half. President Madison expressed the self-deluded vision of US Americans: "Whilst the benevolent policy of the United States invariably recommended peace and promoted civilization among that wretched portion of the human race ... the enemy has not scrupled to call to his aid their ruthless ferocity."[290] It is possible that Madison actually believed what he was saying. A benevolent United States could not understand why that wretched portion of the human race was not grateful.

"America" is always benevolent in its intention. The Indian was a centerpiece of the myth that the promised land had to be civilized and Christianized. The American hero was the lone cowboy protecting the vulnerable white settlers against the depredations of Indian warriors, who were barely human. The tide of battle was usually turned when the US calvary arrived with guns blazing. Hollywood movies fixed the scene indelibly and spread the image around the world.

The misunderstanding and conflict between the two worlds began at the first moment of the Europeans making landfall. Even before "America" was invented, the native people had been given the name "Indians." The strange name stuck, and it was not until the second half of the twentieth century that white people began to make a serious effort to change their way of speaking. Not all Indians were grateful for this new benevolence, but this time it was at least a clumsy beginning to rethink a shameful history. The name "Native American" has been a success, although it has not entirely replaced "Indian."

There is a case that can be made for the name "Native American" as a description of the people who were there when "America" was invented. The simpler name for Native Americans would simply be Americans. But people who call themselves "the Americans" can miss the irony of the name. In the US meaning of "America," the Indians from the beginning, far from being the original Americans, were cast as the ultimate opposite. The "American man" was defined as white in opposition to black and red men. Erik Erikson wrote that "if the Americans had not had the Indians

---

290 Hickey, *The War of 1812*, 107.

and the blacks ... the new Americans would have had to invent somebody else in their place."[291]

The Naturalization Act of 1790 limited citizenship to "free, white persons." This white population needed to have their lives and property protected from the Indians. "In return they pledged their loyalty to the state. In this fashion, then, Thomas Jefferson's 'empire of liberty' took root, a continental domain conceived in the ambitions of Washington and dominated by people who defined the fundamental ideals of the young republic in the rhetoric of liberty and color."[292]

The Indian population continued to decline until the middle of the twentieth century. The population then underwent a remarkable reversal, more than doubling between 1960 and 1980.[293] Aboriginal populations of Canada, Australia, and New Zealand had better chances of being heard because they constituted much larger percentages of their lands' total populations. For example, the natives in Canada made up about 3 percent of the population. In the United States, the census of 1980 showed that, even after explosive growth, Native Americans constituted 0.6 % of the population.[294]

The Treaty of 1783 between Britain and the United States was the first of several times that the Indians lost out in a treaty with the new republic. The Iroquois nations in the north were not even mentioned in the Quebec/US border agreement that ceded Indian lands to New York. During its first years, the United States suffered repeated defeats by the Indians, but that changed with Anthony Wayne's victory in 1794 at Fallen Timbers in Ohio. The following year, diplomats turned over most of Ohio to the United States, as well as lands beyond.[295] From that point on, the

291 Erik Erikson, *Dimensions of a New Identity* (New York: W. W. Norton, 1974), 78.
292 Langley, *America*, 11; Carroll Smith-Rosenberg, *This Violent Empire: The Birth of American National Identity* (Chapel Hill, NC: University of North Carolina Press, 2010), 205: "All who threatened the new American's delicate psychological and ideological balance—effeminate men, transgressive women, Native Americans—became objects of rage and violence."
293 Alvin Josephy, *Now that the Buffalo's Gone* (Norman, OK: University of Oklahoma Press, 1984), xiii. In 1960, the population was 552,000; in 1980, it was 1,418,000.
294 Lipset, *Continental Divide*, 176.
295 Holton, *Unruly Americans*, 269.

United States treated the Indians "as a 'subdued people' to whom the United States would dictate the terms of their retreat and the advance of white settlement."[296]

The Constitution allowed for territories to become states on equal terms with the original states. That provision seemed anti-imperialist, but it assumed that western lands were empty.[297] The land was seen as wilderness that needed conquering instead of territory that had been occupied for many centuries. In his autobiography, Chief Luther Standing Bear notes that only to the white man, nature was a wilderness infested with wild animals. "When the animals of the forest began fleeing from his approach, then it was that for us the 'Wild West' began."[298]

Leading into the American Civil War of 1812, the battle of Tippecanoe took on special symbolic importance. The United States lost far more men than did the Indians, but the battle was considered a US victory because it broke up an Indian confederacy that had been established by the Shawnee leaders Tecumseh and the Prophet. William Henry Harrison, governor of Indiana, was determined to crush the Indians. He burned the Prophet's town in 1811. The United States attributed to the British the instigation of Indian attacks—an accusation that was a proximate cause of the war that began shortly afterward.[299]

Indian wars in the southern United States also overlapped the 1812 war and lasted long afterward. A war with the Seminoles and Creeks in 1818 led to the US acquisition of Florida. Andrew Jackson's raids into east Florida practically dared Spain to do something. In the Adams-Onís treaty of 1819, the United States purchased Florida from Spain; the United States renounced a claim to Texas.

During the next decade, the United States removed a number of tribes to land west of the Mississippi. The Indian Removal Act of 1830 authorized the president to buy tribal lands in the east in exchange for territory in the west. When Georgia became involved in a dispute with the

---

296 Thomas Bender, *A Nation among Nations: America's Place in World History* (New York: Hill and Wang, 2006), 105.
297 Bender, *A Nation*, 183.
298 Chief Luther Standing Bear, *My Indian Boyhood* (Lincoln, NE: Bison Books, 2006)
299 Hickey, *War of 1812*, 25.

Cherokees in 1831, the Supreme Court sided with the Indians by declaring that they are "distinct, independent, political communities." As a result, said the court, they are "entitled to federal protection from states infringing on their sovereignty."[300] President Andrew Jackson disregarded the ruling, and after his reelection in 1832, he conciliated the South by moving more aggressively for withdrawal of the Indians.

At stake in this long effort to displace the Indians was their leaving their homes and traveling hundreds of miles to an inhospitable environment so that whites could seize the valuable real estate on the East Coast. It would be difficult to surpass the hypocrisy of US officials. Andrew Jackson's address to the Creeks epitomized this stance: "Beyond the great river Mississippi, where a part of your nation has gone, your father has provided a country large enough for all of you, and he advises you to remove to it. There your white brothers will not trouble you; they will have no claim on the land, and you can live on it, you and all your children, as long as the grass grows or the water runs, in peace and plenty. It will be yours forever."[301]

The Indians were still slow in moving, and in 1838 President Martin van Buren sent seven thousand troops to oversee the relocation. It has often been noted that the Cherokees, Chickasaws, Creeks, and Choctaws, who were the main tribes in the march westward, had done what the whites had asked of Indians; that is, they had been "civilized and Christianized."[302] They were still at fault because they were Indians. On October 1, 1838, there began the eight-hundred-mile journey known as the Trail of Tears. Of the fifteen thousand who began the journey, at least four thousand died along the way.

During the following decades of the nineteenth century, United States policy did not vary much from one of continuous efforts to displace the Indians from remaining strongholds. From 1865 to the mid-1890s, the US Army engaged in a thousand military battles with the Indians. During that

300 *Worcester v. Georgia* (1931).
301 William Goetzmann, *Beyond the Revolution: A History of American Thought from Paine to Pragmatism* (New York: Basic Books, 2009), 283-84.
302 Nicholas Guyatt, *Bind Us Apart: How Enlightened Americans Invented Racial Segregation* (New York: Basic Books, 2016).

time, the United States took in millions of immigrants, which entailed continuing pressure to open new lands for cultivation.

Legislation and court decisions produced a crossfire of Indian policies. In 1884, the US Supreme Court ruled that Indians were not citizens of the United States. John Elk, who had been born on a reservation but renounced allegiance to his tribe, claimed the right to vote under the terms of the Fourteenth Amendment's definition of a citizen as anyone born in the United States and not subject to any foreign power. The Supreme Court ruled that since Elk was born on a reservation, he did not qualify as a US citizen.[303]

Only three years later, the Dawes Act went in the opposite direction by trying to assimilate Indians into US society. The US government broke up Indian communities by allotting their land to individuals. The concept of individual ownership of land had always been foreign to Indian tribes. In 1908, the Curtis Act completed the Dawes Act by abolishing tribal jurisdiction of Indian lands. Health and education concerns of Indians were administered by the Bureau of Indian Affairs, which, since its founding within the US War Department in 1824, did not have a distinguished record for responding to Indian needs.

A change finally began under Commissioner John Collier, who was responsible for the Indian Reorganization Act of 1934. Signed into law by President Franklin Roosevelt, the new law reversed much of the Dawes Act and related legislation. Land that had not been allotted to individual ownership was preserved, and the act also allowed the US government to assign some non-Indian land to Indian control (casinos would later make this provision controversial).

What was still needed was a radical change in whites' attitudes to Indians and an understanding of the history of "America." Such a change might then eliminate the conflict between the two words in the name "American Indian" or else make sense of the term "Native American."[304]

---

303 *Elk v. Wilkins* 112 US 94 (1984). This ruling was reversed in the Indian Citizen Act of 1924.

304 In Canada, the term First Nation (or First Nations) began to be used in the 1980s for aboriginal groups. First Nation people have been able to influence Canadian culture and government far more than Native Americans in the United States

That revolution began in the 1970s when Indians became organized to protest for their rights. The radical group called the American Indian Movement posed the danger of stirring up stereotypes, myths, and fears of Indians on the rampage. However, other forces were at work that provided a context for Indian demands for justice. Historians were producing revised accounts of the nineteenth-century Indian wars. A 1970 movie, *Little Big Man*, with its reversal of stereotypes, signaled that even Hollywood was ready to change its standard story line. The professional sports world, with its resistance to relinquish offensive names, was slower to respond.

The 1970s in the United States saw the beginning of an environmental movement that continues to this day. The movement depends on scientific data that some people simply dismiss. At a deeper level, the environmental movement is philosophical and religious in nature; it is a call to change a deeply rooted attitude about "man's relation to nature." Indian attitudes to the earth may have something to teach the people who considered themselves to be nature's masters.

Young people in the United States, who were in search of a new spirituality based on respect for the natural world, discovered spirituality close to home. Sudden conversions can produce romanticized views rather than critical-minded histories. Time is still needed before it becomes clear how deep is the change in appreciating the history and culture of the people whose ancestors greeted Columbus. As environmental problems worsen, perhaps the claim of Indian activist Vine Deloria about the United States will no longer seem outlandish: "The only answer will be to adopt Indian ways to survive. For the white man even to exist, he must adopt a total way of life. That is really what he had to do when he came to this land. It is what he will have to do before he leaves it once again."[305]

The long, shameful history can therefore include an optimistic note that white people no longer think of Indians either as a people to be exterminated or as people to be cared for as dependent children. Respect for a people and its history needs to be reflected in any policies that affect people who are now called Native Americans. For that term to be meaningful, the United States would have to stop calling itself America. "American" can include the descendants of the white Europeans who

---

305 Vine Deloria, *We Talk, You Listen* (New York: Dell, 1974), 197.

came to the continent of America, and "American" also has to include descendants of the people who were here when America was invented. Thus, the Americans today are people descended from the mixture of Europeans, Africans, and Asians who joined the original Americans.

5

Conflicts over America

The conflict in the nineteenth century between the United States and the American natives was central to the continuous expansion of the United States under the rubric of America. There were also severe conflicts within the United States itself. The presence of slavery was a constant testimony to the failure by the United States to be the ark of liberty for the world. Negro slavery was the dystopian side of the dream of America.

The second part of the American Civil War broke out in 1846. The drive was for further expansion of US territory to the south, but the issue of slavery could no longer be hidden. A political realignment around that issue led to sectional conflict in the 1850s and finally to secession. When the United States descended into its civil war, each side was ideologically certain of its position, and the result was horrific violence.

Blacks: Waiting for America

The place of Negroes in the struggle for America paralleled the plight of the Indians but with significant differences. Both groups functioned as the "other" to the American identity of the Anglo-Saxon man as the light to all nations. Both groups had a long history in America; the Indians were there at the birth of America; the Africans arrived only shortly after, in 1619, in the English colonies of North America. The United States attempted to eliminate the Indians and so nearly succeeded that for much of the United States today, the Indian is but a haunting presence. Negroes, on the other hand, were an important cog in the United States economy.

The two themes that are emphasized in this section are, first, that the myth of America continues to obstruct a realistic perception of how

African Americans suffered in the United States because of their race; and second, that an extraordinary belief in America sustained Negro slaves and their descendants. The second theme might be construed as an illusion that was generated by the first theme. A religion of belief in another world could be a way of perpetuating obedience in this world. In this case, however, there have been numerous African Americans who clearly perceived the difference between an ideal America and an existing United States.

Poetry and music were central to the slave's culture in the nineteenth century, and African Americans have continued to inspire some of the best of the arts that the United States contributes to the world. Poetry can contain minority protests that are not heard in the main channels of politics. The poet can reshape the language that has been carelessly or callously used in the oppression of people. But the poet cannot entirely replace that language with a better one. He or she sets to the task with the language that is at hand. The word "America" presents a special problem. The person in the United States who suffers from religious or racial discrimination may appeal to the idea of America, but the oppressor is often the "America" of popular piety and political rhetoric. The task becomes one of reminding people in the United States that America as the freedom for all does not (yet) exist.

Slavery was not exclusively a problem of the southern colonies. Recent scholarship has brought out the part that New England and New York played in the slave trade.[306] For North and South, slavery was at first a difference in economic development, but that created a cultural abyss. The Southern states were eventually forced into defending a culture built on slavery as equal or superior to Northern industrial states, in which work was indeed dehumanizing.[307] When war came, both sides tried to avoid stating what was obviously the cause—namely, the United States' original sin of slavery. In the course of the war, that fact could no longer be kept

---

306 Wendy Warren, *New England Bound: Slavery and Colonization in Early America* (New York: Liveright, 2016).

307 George Fitzhugh, *Cannibals All!; or, Slaves without Masters* (Richmond, VA: A. Morris, 1857) argued that the northern laborer was more of slave than a negro because he works longer and harder for less allowance than the slave.

from center stage. But to this day, there are politicians who are affected by amnesia when they refer to the glorious traditions of the pre-Civil War era.

The pre-nineteenth-century sources for writing black history are limited by the fact that most slaves were illiterate. In the nineteenth century, it was illegal in the Southern states to teach a slave to read. To their credit, some children of the slaveholders did teach the slaves. The rate of literacy was only 10 percent at the beginning of the US Civil War, but there were writings by negroes, both slave and free. The Freedmen's Bureau, established in 1865, preserved diaries and other writings from slaves, but that source was neglected. Similarly, the twenty-three hundred interviews done by the Federal Writers Project in the 1930s were not much used by historians. There were a half dozen other collections of testimonies that were capable of correcting possible distortions in the historical record.[308] Not until the 1960s were all these slave testimonies finally given some of the appreciation that they deserve.

The colonial histories of the seventeenth and eighteenth centuries written by whites provide material that is only indirectly about the life of the slave. White people simply assumed that Africans were an inferior race of people who were content with their condition of permanent indenture. In the British American colonies, half of the slaveholding families had four or fewer slaves. In other parts of the new world, large groups of slaves lived on plantations. The good side of the arrangement in the Southern US colonies was that white families were often paternalistically kind to the slaves. The bad side was the limits that a small group of slaves would have in maintaining a cultural continuity of religion and a community that would be supportive of their lives.[309]

While there may have been some genuine concern for treating slaves well, there was little outcry for abolishing the system of slavery. Before 1750, there were about fifteen known condemnations of slavery in the

---

308 John Blassingame, *The Slave Community: Plantation Life in the Antebellum South* (New York: Oxford University Press, 1972), liv.

309 Philip Curtin, *The Rise and Fall of the Plantation Complex* (Cambridge, MA: Cambridge University Press, 1998). The survival of Africanism despite the obstacles was addressed in Melville Herskovits, *The Myth of the Negro Past* (Boston: Beacon Press, 1958).

colonies, all of them made by Quakers.[310] This small, peace-loving religious group, centered in Pennsylvania, was considered a threat to established order. Baptist and Methodist missionaries, unlike Anglican and Roman Catholic leaders, did extend a welcome hand to the African population, but they were careful to avoid inciting rebellion. People trying to convert the slaves "went out of their way to stress that Christianizing Negroes would make them much better slaves not worse."[311]

In the 1770s, the colonists portrayed their position in the empire with images of slavery. The use of such language was ironic. "The patriots knew what slavery was because they owned slaves."[312] When it came time to declare the independence of the colonies, Thomas Jefferson penned the famous lines "We hold these truths to be self-evident: that all men are created equal, that they are endowed by their Creator with certain unalienable rights, that among these are life, liberty and the pursuit of happiness."

How could Jefferson have reconciled his belief that all men have an inalienable right to liberty with the fact that he was a slaveholder? He was not alone among the nation's founders in accepting slavery, but the self-contradiction in Jefferson's case seems the most severe. There are several Jefferson quotations acknowledging that slavery is a terrible evil that must be ended. On the Jefferson Memorial are the words "Nothing is more certainly written in the book of fate than that these people are to be free." In 1820, after a shaky compromise to balance free and slave states, Jefferson wrote that the agreement "like a fire-bell in the night awakened and filled me with terror. I considered it at once as the knell of the nation." He thought there would be new and deeper irritations and doubted that the Union would be of long duration.[313]

The Declaration of Independence's grand rhetoric could be understood as philosophical speculation. No such explanation or excuse is available for

---

310 Winthrop Jordan, *White Man's Burden: Historical Origins of Racism in the United States* (New York: Oxford University Press, 1974), 92.

311 Jordan, *White Man's*, 91.

312 Catherine Albanese, *Sons of the Fathers: The Civil Religion of the American Revolution* (Philadelphia, PA: Temple University Press, 1977), 26.

313 Thomas Jefferson, *Notes on the State of Virginia* (New York: Forgotten Books, 2012), 272; Thomas Jefferson, "Letter to John Holmes," April 22, 1820, in *Portable Thomas Jefferson* (New York: Penguin, 1977), 568.

the US Constitution. Slavery is referred to three times in the document, but the word itself is avoided. Article I, section 2, on apportioning of representatives, refers to "three-fifths of all other persons." Article I, section 9, says that the importing of "such persons in any of the states now existing should think proper to admit" would not be prohibited prior to 1808. Article IV, section 2, states that no person "held to service or labor in one state, under the laws thereof, escaping into another" can be discharged from labor by the laws of the latter state.

The first of those references, which counts a slave as three-fifths of a person, seems especially demeaning. "The debate over the three-fifths rule took place with a near total absence of anything resembling a moral dimension."[314] It is a completely illogical provision despite James Madison's attempt at the convention to defend its necessity.[315] Clearly it is a compromise between something and nothing. Ironically, the power of the slave owners would have been strengthened if slaves had counted as persons. And "in this one instance, the slave's interest would have been better served if they had not been considered persons at all."[316]

Although Jefferson had changed John Locke's formula from "property" to "pursuit of happiness," the right to one's property became inviolable in nineteenth-century thinking. Slaves were owned as property, and any plan to liberate slaves was claimed to be a violation of the right to private property. The culmination of that principle was the Supreme Court's scandalous Dred Scott decision in 1857, which said that the United States government did not have the power to alter a white citizen's property.[317]

An 1831 revolt in Southampton County, Virginia, sent a shock wave throughout the South. The revolt was led by Nat Turner, who claimed to have visions and was called "the Prophet" by his followers. The revolt caused the deaths of sixty whites and more than a hundred Negroes. Turner was executed along with fifty-six others who had participated in

---

314 Richard Beeman, *Plain, Honest Men: The Making of the American Constitution* (New York: Random House, 2015).

315 Thelma Wills Foote, *Black and White Manhattan: The History of Racial Formation in Colonial New York* (New York: Oxford University Press, 2004), 228.

316 Woody Holton, *Unruly Americans and the Origin of the Constitution* (New York: Hill and Wang, 2007), 189.

317 Don Fehrenbacher, *The Dred Scott Case: Its Significance in American Law and Practice* (New York: Oxford University Press, 1978).

the bloody rampage. There was a swift reaction in many states, where laws were passed that restricted the movement of slaves. The *Richmond Enquirer* asserted, "The case of Nat Turner warns us. No black man ought to be permitted to turn a preacher through the country. The law must be enforced – or the tragedy of Southampton appeals to us in vain."[318] William Styron's *Confessions of Nat Turner* in 1967 introduced Turner to a generation of white students that was largely innocent of black history.

The whites were right to fear that education might result in blacks getting ideas about liberation. It was thought that Nat Turner got his radical ideas from reading the Bible. The slave owner could instruct the slaves using Paul's *Letter to Philomen* on the proper conduct of a slave. But if slaves could read for themselves, they might discover the book of Exodus and read it in a way that would inspire resistance to slavery. A second restriction on the slaves was a prohibition against the right of assembly; they could not gather in groups larger than five. A third requirement was that a white minister had to be present at all religious services.

There was a special fear of black preachers. Preaching the gospel was fine so long as it was done by white preachers. But there was no telling what could happen if black preachers awakened the emotions of a black congregation. Mississippi saw the need to pass a law that said "it is unlawful for any slave, free Negro, or mulatto to preach the gospel upon pain of receiving thirty-nine lashes upon the naked back of the preacher."[319]

Despite such prohibitions, the slaves often gathered for their own religious service after the standard indoctrination by white preachers. The slaves would "slip off into the woods" for "stealin the meetin," a religious service of their own. If these Sunday gatherings were found out by the master, the slave might be whipped on Monday but still return the next Sunday.[320] To this day, the art of preaching flourishes mainly among black ministers and politicians. Similarly, the religious music of the slaves still lives on in much of the music of the United States. Slave music was laced

318 Vincent Harding, *Is There a River? The Black Struggle for Freedom in America* (New York: Mariner, 1993), 102.
319 Harding, *Is There a River*, 102.
320 Thomas Webber, *Deep Like the River* (New York: W. W. Norton, 1980), 181-94. The slave Amanda McGray describes "A praying ground where the grass never had a chance ter grow fer the troubled knees that kept it crushed down."

with double meanings. "Every tone was a testimony against slavery, and a prayer to God for deliverance from chains."[321]

The stereotype of the slaves' religion was that it was "otherworldly" as opposed to "this-worldly." The religion preached to them by whites was undoubtedly that kind of religion; that is, obedience in this world would be rewarded by happiness in the next. And no doubt there were slaves who saw no other alternative except to hope for justice in the next world. But there was another strand of slave religion that differentiated between the Christianity they experienced in the churches and a true Christianity that existed somewhere else. They believed that there was a real Bible different from the Bible the master read from. When the slave said, "Thank God that where Christianity exists, slavery cannot exist," he was not ignorant or delusional. "To the black men and women of the quarter community, slavery and Christianity were so antithetical that they did not think of the slaveholding South as a Christian land."[322]

The slaves' religion was therefore a mixture of consolation for what they were experiencing together with the hope for a better future in this world as well as the next.[323] The slaves' ability to distinguish between the church they experienced and a true Christianity paralleled their distinction between the United States and America. While patriotic celebrations of liberty in America were everywhere around them, they knew very well that the equivalence of the United States of America and the land of liberty was a sham. Nonetheless, many of them were able to hold on to another idea of America that they were heirs to. Anna Cooper, an educator and activist, could later write, "America is the land of destiny for the descendants of the enslaved race, that here in the house of bondage are the seeds of the promise for their ultimate enfranchisement and development."[324] Schemes to return Negroes to Africa were rejected; the true America did not belong to the white man.

---

321 Frederick Douglass, *Narrative of the Life of Frederick Douglass* (Cambridge, MA: Harvard University Press, 1967, 24.

322 Webber, *Deep Like the River*, 85.

323 Albert Raboteau, *Slave Religion: The 'Invisible Institution' in the Antebellum South* (New York: Oxford University Press, 2004), 317.

324 Anna Cooper, "The Ethics of the Negro Question," in *Can I Get a Witness?* ed. Marcia Riggs (New York: Orbis Books, 1997), 143. It was originally published in 1902.

The distinctions between an oppressive church and a true Christianity as well as between the United States and America came together in David Walker's 1829 *Appeal to the Colored People of the World*—the first sustained attack on slavery and racism written by a US Negro. Walker referred in numerous passages to "christian Americans," in contrast to genuine followers of Jesus. His use of "America" and "United States" is generally consistent. He denounces "the Americans" more than a hundred times, drawing upon the racial meaning that was inherent to the concept. At the same time, Walker says, "I appeal and ask every citizen of these United States and of the world, both black and white" to reject the idea of recolonizing free blacks of the United States in Africa. He wished to be a citizen of the United States but not an "American."

Walker repeatedly refers to "the continent of America," but in one place he says, "America is more our country than it is the whites – we have enriched it with our blood and tears." He is not claiming political control of the country but a share in the meaning of America that blacks refused to cede to "the Americans." Sean Wilentz points out that "even in his bitterest passages Walker did not repudiate … republican principles or his native country."[325]

Like Martin Luther King Jr. in the twentieth century, Walker called on the principles stated in the Declaration of Independence. The appeal was for an America of justice by those who claimed the name America. "O Americans! Americans!! I call God – I call angels – I call men to witness that your Destruction is at hand, and will be speedily consummated unless you repent."[326] In the style of "American" jeremiads used by many black preachers, Walker's call for political justice was supported by a biblical cadence and biblical content.

The most famous Negro opponent of slavery was Frederick Douglass. His themes are similar to those in Walker's passionate attack on the United

---

325 Sean Wilentz, "Introduction," David Walker, *Appeal to the Colored People of the World* (New York: Hill and Wang, 1995), xvii.
326 David Walker in Herbert Aptheker, *One Continual Cry: David Walker's Appeal to the Colored People of the World: Its Setting and its Meaning* (New York: Humanities Press, 1965), 108.

States and the Christian church.[327] Like Walker, Douglass was a reformer from early in life; but unlike Walker, he was able to continue his efforts until the 1890s. He wrote three autobiographies, the first published in 1847.[328] Douglass wrote simply and brilliantly of his life in slavery and his escape from slavery.

Douglass seldom uses the term "America" in his writings. At all times, he is clear that he is talking about the United States and its laws. Early in his career, he agreed with the abolitionist William Lloyd Garrison's moral condemnation of slavery and Garrison's description of the US Constitution as "a covenant with death and an agreement with hell." That view led to Douglass's near despair over the possibility of any progress in getting rid of slavery. In an 1847 speech, on the occasion of his return from twenty months out of the country, Douglass voiced his most complete condemnation of the country: "I have not, I cannot have any love for this country, as such, or for its Constitution. I desire to see its overthrow as speedily as possible and its Constitution shivered in a thousand fragments rather than this foul course continue to remain as now."[329]

By 1851, however, he had come to a very different position. He had concluded that the Constitution was not "pro-slavery." He had arrived, he said, "at the firm conviction that the Constitution, construed in the light of well-established rules of legal interpretation, might be made consistent in its details with the noble purposes of its preamble."[330] William Lloyd Garrison was furious at Douglass's about-face. But as a result of his changed view, he set to work at changing the laws, politics, and economics of the United States—a task he pursued for forty years.

Although Douglass was steadfast and consistent in his convictions, he swung back and forth in his hope for "colored persons of the United States." In perhaps his most famous speech, "The Meaning of July Fourth for the Negro," he tore into the country's hypocritical celebration of liberty. But even in that speech, he concluded, "Notwithstanding the dark picture

---

327 Douglass in many places is critical of the churches' stand on slavery; "The Meaning of July Fourth for the Negro" in *Selected Speeches and Writings* (Chicago: Lawrence Hill Books, 1999), 200-203.

328 Douglass, *Narrative of the Life of Frederick Douglass.*

329 Douglass, *Selected Speeches,* 77.

330 Douglass, *Selected Speeches,* 173.

I have this day presented of the state of the nation, I do not despair of this country. There are forces in operation which must inevitably work the downfall of slavery."[331]

Douglass was very critical of Abraham Lincoln's policies in the first two years of Lincoln's presidency. Douglass was especially critical in the fall of 1862 of a plan to recolonize Negroes.[332] A few months later, however, he was overjoyed at the announcement of the Emancipation Proclamation: "The fourth of July was great but the first of January, when we consider it in all its relations and bearings, is incomparably greater."[333] In 1876, Douglass delivered an honest evaluation of Abraham Lincoln, who was "not either our man or our model" but who nonetheless brought about emancipation of the slaves. Is it a coincidence that in a speech that looks realistically at the country, the term "America" does not appear while "United States" is used ten times?[334] In 1888, however, he spoke under the title of "I Denounce the So-Called Emancipation as a Stupendous Fraud." Better than almost anyone else, he recognized that the reconstruction of the nation had failed to be realized and that a proclamation of liberty was not automatically followed by freedom.

Evangelical religion was so dominant in the first half of the eighteenth century that it affected both the defense and the condemnation of slavery. Religion did not replace economic considerations, but economic arguments were usually entangled with moral and religious themes. The white abolitionists in the North used fiery sermons of condemnation that sometimes drove away possible supporters. Defenders of slavery invoked the Bible, which does contain passages that could be used to support their

---

331 Douglass, *Selected Speeches*, 204.

332 Douglass had to fight against a succession of such preposterous plans to rid the country of Negroes. Lincoln never proposed colonization after he issued the Emancipation Proclamation. One reason was that Negro soldiers became indispensable to the Union war effort. During Reconstruction, other politicians picked up the colonization idea. Douglass, in his last speech in 1894, was still defending the right of Negroes to their homes in the United States, including the southern United States. Douglass, *Selected Speeches*, 750-76.

333 *Douglass' Monthly*, September 1862 and October 1862.

334 "Oration in Memory of Abraham Lincoln," April 14, 1876, at the dedication of the Freedmen's Monument, Washington, DC.

cause.[335] Several of the Christian denominations split in the 1850s over the question of slavery. However, for Negroes, both free and slave, the issue was simple. Frederick Douglass wrote, "I was just as well aware of the unjust, unnatural and murderous character of slavery, when nine years old, as I am now. Without appeals to books, to laws, or to authorities of any kind, I knew that to regard God as 'Our Father' condemned slavery as a crime."[336]

In addition to the assumption that slave religion was otherworldly, another stereotype imposed on the slaves was that family life was destroyed by slavery. It is undeniable that the southern system of slavery had devastating effects on Negro families. After the revolution, the breakup of big estates also meant the breakup of slave families at auctions that had no regard for ties of kinship.[337] The courts did not recognize marriage contracts between slaves.

What is surprising is that any semblance of family life could survive—a fact that was not evident when historians neglected the slaves' own testimonies. Since the 1960s, the testimonies of slaves together with other data (court files, newspapers, church records, and abolitionist publications) have produced a different picture of the family under slavery. "Scarcely a narrator speaks of his slave experience without dwelling upon the ways in which a specific family member or the family as a unit 'kept him up' during hard times."[338] By 1870, a majority of blacks lived in two-parent households.[339]

The belief that the family was destroyed under Southern slavery was the thesis of E. Franklin Frazier's *The Negro Family in the United States*. That view was adopted by some political leaders in a well-intentioned effort to provide help for blacks who were living in poverty.[340] The most

---

335 Robert Lewis Dabney, *A Defense of Virginia, and through Her, of the South* (Harrisburg, VA: Sprinkle, 1977), 103: "We assert that the Bible teaches that the relation of master and slave is perfectly lawful and right."

336 Webber, *Deep Like the River*, 80.

337 Alan Taylor, *The Internal Enemy: Slavery and War in Virginia, 1772-1832* (New York: W. W. Norton, 2014).

338 Webber, *Deep Like the River*, 111, 117, 162.

339 Eric Foner, *A Short History of Reconstruction, 1863-1877* (New York: Harper, 1988), 38.

340 E. Franklin Frazier, *The Negro Family in the United States* (Chicago: University of Chicago Press, 1939); also influential was Stanley Elkins, *Slavery: A Problem*

famous application of this position was Daniel Patrick Moynihan's *The Negro Family: The Case for National Action* as part of President Lyndon Johnson's war on poverty. At the end of the 1960s, there was a shift of emphasis from Negroes as past victims and present dependents to blacks as having assertive voices of their own. (The shift from "Negro" to "black" at that moment of history is not mere coincidence.)[341]

A forceful revision of the view that slavery had destroyed the Negro family was made by Herbert Gutman's *The Black Family in Slavery and Freedom 1750-1925*.[342] Gutman relied on a wide array of data that traced the effects of slavery beyond the Civil War and into the twentieth century. Other historians came to similar conclusions about the survival of the Negro family under the terrible conditions of slavery.[343] John Blassingame writes that "however frequently the family was broken it was primarily responsible for the slave's ability to survive on the plantation without becoming totally dependent on and submissive to his master."[344] Part of the misperception of black families comes from the fact that as the meaning of family among whites narrowed to two parents and children, black families continued to have an extended kinship system in which many adults might care for the children.[345]

The issues of religion, family, poverty, and discrimination continued long after the end of slavery. The United States has been scandalously slow in becoming a nation in which white and black have an equal chance in the pursuit of happiness. While white people have a responsibility to help their fellow black citizens, they also have to be willing to listen to and to

---

in American Institutional and Intellectual Life (New York: Universal Library, 1959).

341 Daniel Patrick Moynihan, *The Negro Family: The Case for National Action* (Cambridge, MA: MIT Press, 1970).

342 Herbert Gutman, *The Black Family in Slavery and Freedom, 1750-1925* (New York: Pantheon, 1976).

343 Eugene Genovese, *Roll, Jordan Roll: The World the Slaves Made* (New York: Vintage Books, 1976).

344 Blassingame, *The Slave Community*, 151.

345 George Rawick, *From Sundown to Sunup* (Westport, CT: Greenwood, 1972); the later effects upon the pattern of black child care was brilliantly captured in Carol Stack, *All Our Kin: Strategies for Survival in a Black Community* (New York: Harper, 1975).

learn from the black experience of the past and present. "America" remains a hope for many people who have suffered oppression. First among those groups are people whose ancestors have been in the English American colonies and United States of America for four centuries and who have made such great contributions to those things that are admirable in the American culture of the United States.

American Civil War: Part II

The story of slavery receded to the background but by no means disappeared in the continuing struggle for the land of America by the small republic that believed its destiny was "continental." One strange event in the march toward the United States' Civil War was a war with Mexico, a nation that was nearly dismembered by the war. In the end, the United States took almost half of Mexico's territory. The debate of whether to annex none, all, or part of Mexico was very much tied to the issue of slavery and how to keep a balance of free states and slave states.

Similar to the first American Civil War in 1812, this second war for America in America receives only brief mention in most US history books, despite its embodying a crucial turn in that history. This war is looked on more favorably than the earlier war because the United States clearly won by land and sea as well as by the terms of the peace treaty. When the war started, the United States had about the same size army as it had in 1812; but the seven thousand troops were now well trained, and they were fighting a Mexican army that, although large in size, proved to be incompetent. The US Navy had largely been dismantled, but now they were fighting a country that could not mount a naval force. US military leadership was fragmented, but it was still superior to Mexico's. Santa Anna was reputed to be a great general, but he did not achieve victory in any of the main battles. A young George Meade said at the time: "Well may we be grateful that we are at war with Mexico. Were it any other power, our gross follies would have been punished severely."[346]

Mexico had become a republic in 1824 with a liberal constitution that was influenced by the US Constitution. However, the country was not able

---

346 Otis Singletary, *The Mexican War* (Chicago: University of Chicago Press, 1960), 147.

to reach anything close to political stability. The trajectory of Mexico can be seen in the fact that in 1824 the country had 1.7 million square miles and 6 million people, compared to the United States' 1.8 million square miles and 9.6 million people. But by 1853, Mexico had 0.7 million square miles and 8 million people, while the United States now had 2.8 million square miles and 23 million people.

The northern part of Mexico was sparsely populated, and the United States was as concerned as ever about a European power getting a foothold in America. The area that became Texas was flooded with immigrants from the United States; by 1830 there were twenty thousand "Anglos" in Texas and only three thousand Mexicans. Mexico was too weak to control the northern part of its territory.[347] Despite smashing the Texans at the Alamo and at Goliad in 1836, Santa Anna eventually signed a treaty acknowledging the independence of Texas. From there it was a short step to the United States' annexation of Texas. When Mexico protested this annexation, the US response was that the arrangement was strictly the business of the United States and Texas. What remained in dispute was whether the boundary line between Texas and Mexico was the Rio Grande River or the Nueces River, the latter of which was 150 miles farther north.

The US Navy made a premature attack on California in 1842 on the mistaken assumption that war had been declared. In 1845, Polk sent his ambassador John Slidell to discuss a treaty with Mexico that would take up questions of California, the Texas boundary, and the $2 million in claims that US citizens had against Mexico. When Mexico refused to receive Slidell, Polk, in January of 1846, ordered General Zachary Taylor to move his troops south to the Rio Grande. The advance of the US Army into the land under dispute was enough to provoke hostile gunfire.

On April 25, 1846, President Polk announced that Mexico had exhausted the "cup of forbearance." Then he used the most famous phrase of the war: "Mexico has passed the boundary of the United States, has invaded our territory and *shed American blood on American soil.*"[348] It was the clever claim that US presidents ultimately employ, namely, *American*

---

347 Timothy Henderson, *A Glorious Defeat: Mexico and its War with the United States* (New York: Hill and Wang, 2008), 98, 188.

348 Joseph Wheelan, *Invading Mexico: America's Continental Dream and the Mexican War, 1846-1848* (New York: Public Affairs, 2007), 95.

blood and *American* soil. By crossing the disputed boundary of the United States, Mexico had violated the sacred land of America. Anyone could have pointed out that whether the soil belonged to the United States or to Mexico, it was certainly American. But to this day, in US history books there is regular reference to America fighting a war with Mexico and almost half of Mexico becoming part of America.

The president asked Congress for authority to bring a war that did not yet exist to a "speedy and successful conclusion." John Calhoun challenged Polk for saying that "a state of war exists"; Calhoun stated that war does not exist until Congress declares it. But as usually happens in such circumstances, the tide was unstoppable, and the Senate immediately voted 40-2 for war. (Calhoun abstained.) In a letter to Commodore David Conner, Calhoun presciently noted that "it sets the example which will enable all future Presidents to bring about a state of things in which Congress shall be forced, without deliberation or reflection, to declare war, however opposed to its convictions of justice or expediency."[349]

On the eve of the war, General William Hull addressed Mexicans: "You will be emancipated from tyranny and oppression, and restored to the status of freemen."[350] There was very little popular dissent either at the war's beginning or in the course of the war. What did exist in the country were several conflicts: between civil and military authority, between segments of both the Whig and Democratic Parties, and between northern and southern regions of the country. But so long as the issue was America and its mission, there was enthusiastic support for the war. Religious supporters spoke of "extending the area of freedom and realizing the destiny of the godly republic."[351] The war would "extend the Redeemer's Kingdom." Newspaper editorials pronounced, "To liberate and ennoble – not to enslave and debase – is our mission. Well may the Mexican nation, whose great masses have never yet tasted liberty, prattle over their lost phantom of nationality."[352]

---

349 John Schroeder, *Mr. Polk's War: American Opposition and Dissent, 1846-1848* (Madison, WI: University of Wisconsin Press, 1973); for the Congressional debate, *Congressional Globe* 29th Congress 1st Session, 795, 800-803.

350 *Boston Columbian Centinel*, August 5, 1812.

351 Schroeder, *Mr. Polk's War*, 109.

352 *New York Sun*, October 22, 1847.

In 1845, John L. O'Sullivan, in the *New York Morning News*, asserted that it is "the right of our manifest destiny to overspread and to possess the whole continent which Providence has given us for the development of the great experiment of liberty and federated self-government."[353] The phrase "manifest destiny" had staying power. It seemed to capture United States' belief in itself as America and as the bearer of liberty to the whole continent and even beyond the continent to the rest of the world. O'Sullivan had previously written, "The glittering diadem of England must fade, the colossus of Russia must crumble, but who can foresee the decline of American freedom?"[354]

The first theater of war was in northern Mexico, where the United States military quickly defeated a much larger Mexican force. As would be true in subsequent wars, the United States' superior artillery made the difference. By the end of 1846, almost all of northeastern Mexico had fallen. US troops under Taylor took Matamoros. In a second area, Mexico could offer little resistance to the US fleet, which deposited Winfield Scott and his troops at Veracruz. After a series of engagements, the United States reached Mexico City in September 1847. The United States had again faced an army superior in size, but at Contreras and Cherubusco, Santa Anna lost one-third of his effective troops to casualties and sickness.[355]

A third area of fighting was in northern California. The navy had been prepared to strike as early as 1845. As soon as war started, Commodore J. D. Sloat seized San Francisco and Monterey. After Commodore Robert Stockton replaced Sloat, US troops moved south toward Los Angeles and Santa Barbara—areas that the United States occupied by August 1847. Stockton later had to return to Los Angeles to quell a rebellion, but Mexican resistance had no chance of success.[356]

The fourth area of fighting that linked up with the California conquest was the US march across today's New Mexico with a destination of the Pacific coast. Colonel Stephen Kearny led the successful conquest of New Mexico and continued the march to California. A brief rebellion at Taos was put down by Colonel Stanley Price early in 1847.

---

353 *New York Morning News*, December 27, 1845.
354 *New York Morning News*, October 13, 1845.
355 Singletary, *The Mexican War*, 32, 53.
356 Singletary, *The Mexican War*, 56, 67.

The battlefield victories were a story of complete success, but by the end of 1847 the country was tired of the war.[357] One reason for the war having become unpopular was its cost. The land would come cheap: thirty-seven cents for each square mile of the 530,706 square miles acquired. The cost in human lives, however, was surprisingly high. Among US wars, this one had the highest per capita rate of death for the military who participated in the war: 125 out of 1,000. One-third of Massachusetts volunteers did not return, although they had seen no combat. The big killer in the war was disease. While 1,721 soldiers died in battle, 11,155 died of disease—that is, almost seven times as many.[358]

Protest against the war itself was very limited. The main dispute was whether to annex Mexican territory, and if so, how much of it. The Whig party settled on a "no territory" strategy. They feared that any addition of Mexican territory would endanger not only the unity of the Whig Party but the Union of the states.[359] The Whig press said that the party wanted neither Mexican soil nor the "wretched population" that went with it.[360] Henry Clay, in trying to bridge northern and southern Whigs, embraced the "no territory" position.

The "all Mexico" supporters, in contrast, said that Mexico was incapable of governing itself. The *New York Herald* announced that "like the Sabine virgins, [Mexico] will soon learn to love her ravisher."[361] Those who assumed that "America" was destined to spread across the world did not have any qualms about the United States using its might to remove a repressive government in the name of emancipation. An added irony in this situation was that people enthusiastic for taking over Mexico were motivated by a desire to spread slavery into territory where slavery did not exist. In the end, another bad compromise over slavery would not be enough to save the Whigs—and eventually the Union as well.

---

357 Schroeder, *Mr. Polk's War*, 51.

358 Wheelan, *Invading Mexico*, 414-16. Amy Greenberg, in *A Wicked War: Polk, Clay, Lincoln, and the Invasion of Mexico* (New York: Random House, 2012) makes this claim about the war with Mexico. Others claim that the US Civil War had a higher death ratio. See James McPherson, "America's 'Wicked War'" *New York Review*, February 7, 2013, 32-33.

359 Schroeder, *Mr. Polk's War*, 86.

360 *Richmond Whig*, May 19, 1847, in Schroeder, *Mr. Polk's War, 123.*

361 Wheelan, *Invading Mexico*, 395.

What became a centerpiece of discussion was an amendment attached to the first war appropriation bill in August 1846 by Representative David Wilmot. What was quickly named the Wilmot Proviso said, "As an express and fundamental condition of any territory from the Republic of Mexico ... neither slavery nor involuntary servitude shall ever exist in any part of said territory, except for crimes."[362] Since the Missouri Compromise of 1820, the country had managed to keep slavery out of the center of political debate. A precarious balance of free states and slave states had kept things quiet. The Wilmot Proviso forced a discussion of slavery that almost no one wanted.

The standard position in the North was that the federal government had neither the desire nor the power to eliminate slavery in states where it existed but that the government could outlaw it in the territories. The South was convinced, probably correctly, that if slavery was not allowed to spread, it would be ended by the shift of political power. An Augusta newspaper accurately perceived the implications of the debate: "Nothing appears plainer to us than the North is united on the Wilmot Proviso. The South is united against it. Hence rises a question of lurid and fearful portent."[363]

The slavery issue threatened to split the churches along regional lines. Not much protest against the war came from religious leaders. The main criticism came from three religious groups: Quakers, Unitarians, and Congregationalists. The first two of these groups had no difficulty in advocating equality. However, the Congregationalists in New England were united in opposition to the war but were affected by the almost universal racism of the time, which assumed the superiority of the white race. In this case, racism helped avoid an annexing of all Mexico because of the need to avoid "America mingling with an inferior people who embrace all shades of color."[364]

The great New England writers of the time were unanimous in their opposition to the war but did not engage in much public protest. Theodore

362 Chaplain Morrison, *Democratic Politics and Sectionalism: The Wilmot Proviso* (Chapel Hill, NC: University of North Carolina Press, 1967), 18.
363 *Augusta Chronicle and Sentinel*, June 17, 1847.
364 The words are those of Congressman Delano of Ohio; Howard Zinn, *A People's History*,157.

Parker, Margaret Fuller, Ralph Waldo Emerson, James Russell Lowell, and Herman Melville viewed the war as a symptom rather than a cause of what was wrong with the country. Emerson did write that "the United States will conquer Mexico, but it will be as the man who swallows the arsenic, which brings him down, in turn. Mexico will poison us."[365] The most famous protest was staged by Henry Thoreau, who said that paying taxes would "enable the Senate to commit violence and shed innocent blood."[366]

By the end of 1847, the United States was in financial trouble because the president had hidden the true cost of the war and refused to raise duties and taxes. Mexico had stubbornly refused to surrender despite its terrible losses on the battlefield. President Polk assigned Nicolas Trist to accompany the army under Winfield Scott and open negotiations with the Mexican government. His initial attempts were unsuccessful, and Polk recalled Trist on October 10, 1847. But before the message reached Trist, he had opened negotiations with a new interim president in Mexico who indicated a willingness to sign a peace treaty.

The treaty to end the war was thus written by an unemployed diplomat who had no authority. Although Polk denounced Trist as an "impudent and unqualified scoundrel," the terms of the treaty were accepted by Polk and subsequently ratified by the Senate in February 1848 as the Treaty of Guadalupe-Hidalgo. Mexico agreed to nearly all the demands that the United States had earlier made. The main provisions were as follows: the Rio Grande River was accepted as the boundary between Texas and Mexico, the United States assumed what had grown to $3.25 million in claims on the Mexican government by US citizens, and the United States would pay $15 million for five hundred twenty-five thousand square miles of Mexican land (which would become eight US states).[367]

The *National Intelligencer* spoke for many critics of the war: "A peace which everyone will be glad of, but no one will be proud of."[368] The payment of $15 million was mostly to avoid admitting the fact that the land was taken rather than purchased by a free exchange. The "all Mexico"

---

365 *Journal of Ralph Waldo Emerson* quoted in Schroeder, *Mr. Polk's War*, 116.
366 Henry Thoreau, "Resistance to Civil Government," in *Civil Disobedience* (New York: Empire Books, 2011).
367 Singletary, *Mexican War*, 161.
368 Schroeder, *Mr. Polk's War*, 158.

supporters lost out on their cause although they interpreted the fall of
monarchies in Europe (the French monarchy a few days after Senate
ratification of the treaty) as an extension of their fight to spread liberty
to the whole world.[369] Eight million Mexicans came with the annexed
territories—a problem for those who had feared the mingling of a colored
race with that of "America." John Calhoun said, "I protest against the
incorporation of such a people. Ours is the government of the white
people."[370]

One of the most admirable pieces of writing during the war was a
pamphlet entitled *Peace with Mexico*, written by eighty-six-year-old Albert
Gallatin, who had long served in the US government. A feature to be noted
in the long essay is that Gallatin uses "America" only half a dozen times
compared to the several hundred times he refers to "United States." He
was against the annexation of any territory. He thought that the "mission
of the United States [was] to be the model republic, to show that men are
capable of governing themselves."

In Mexico the war was a cause of continuing instability that would
lead to several European attempts to intervene. In the United States, the
war with Mexico was a prelude to war within the United States. There
was an immediate effect in the realignment of the political parties. A
group called the Conscience Whigs refused to support Zachary Taylor's
nomination for president. They joined the antislavery Democrats to form
the Free Soil Party in 1848. The Whigs would give way to a new party
called the Republicans.

A group known to history as the Know Nothings, whose actual name
was the American Party, was dangerously mixed with the new Republican
Party. The American Party embodied the worst of American traditions.
Abraham Lincoln wrote: "As a nation, we began by declaring that *all men
are created equal*. We now practically read it 'all men are created equal,
except negroes'. When the Know-Nothings get control, it will read 'all men

---

369 Frederick Merk, *Manifest Destiny and Mission in American History* (New York:
 Vintage Books, 1963), 195-201.
370 John Calhoun, *The Works of John C. Calhoun*, vol. 4, ed. Richard Cralle (New
 York: Appleton, 1874), 410.

are created equal, except negroes, *and foreigners and Catholics*."[371] The
American Party did not survive beyond the 1856 election; unfortunately
some of its sentiments did not die so readily.

The War within the United States

This section is centered on a horrifying set of battles between the years 1861
and 1865. It is estimated that there are fifty thousand books and articles on
what is usually called the Civil War, even though it was anything but civil.
In some parts of the southern United States, it is known by other names,
such as "the War between the States." The name "American Civil War"
is somewhat misleading. The *land* of America was not at stake; perhaps
one could argue that the *idea* of America was at issue in a war between
the United States of America and the Confederate States of America. But
to the extent that it is recognized as a civil war, it was a war between the
authority of the United States government and a section of the country
that was in rebellion.

Perhaps one thing that can be agreed upon is that the war is central
to United States history. Beyond that it is unclear how to describe the war
and the years that immediately followed. The war bears comparison to the
revolutionary war of 1775-1781, when the military battles were only part
of a revolution. The rebellion of 1861-65 had at least a decade of events
leading up to it and a decade or more afterward in which reconciliation
was attempted.[372] It is doubtful that a full reconciliation has ever occurred.

My interest is an issue that is both political and philosophical. What
did "United States" mean after the war in contrast to what it had meant
before the war? One clue is that before the war, "United States" usually
took a plural verb; after the war, "United States" has practically always
taken a singular verb. This fact has often been noted, and it is taken to
mean that the country became more unified after the war.[373] While that

---

371 *Abraham Lincoln: His Speeches and Writings*, vol. 1, ed. Roy Basler (Boston: Da
   Capo Press, 2001), 360.
372 James Oakes, *Freedom National: The Destruction of Slavery in the United States,
   1861-1865* (New York: W. W. Norton, 2012).
373 Samuel Huntington, *Who Are We? The Challenge to America's National Identity*
   (New York: Simon and Schuster, 2005), 119; James McPherson, *Battle Cry of*

implication may be true, a deeper and more complex truth gets hidden if one does not explore the relation between the usage of "United States" and "America."

A telling comparison of usage is found in the speeches of Abraham Lincoln, whose brooding presence hovers over the war and subsequent US history. In his first inaugural address, Lincoln used "union" twenty times and "nation" not at all. In the Gettysburg Address, three years later, he used "nation" five times (in the 270 words). In his second inaugural address, which proved to be his farewell address, Lincoln spoke of the South's effort to dissolve the union and the North fighting to preserve the nation. He did not use the word "America."

Until the US Civil War, the "United States were a federal republic." Loyalties were mainly to the states that made up the federation of the United States. Power was in the states, with a few powers stingily assigned to a federal government. Some creative reading of the US Constitution, especially by Supreme Court Justice John Marshall, allowed the US president and US Congress to exercise some needed authority. "Interstate commerce" was and is an elastic phrase for that purpose.

There is nothing like a war against an external enemy to unify a country; the United States engaged in several actual wars and a few other threatened wars. In those wars, the United States had an inadequate army; the federal government had to rely heavily on state militias. A turn toward the future was the founding of the United States Military Academy at West Point, New York, in 1802. Its great influence would be shown when the Civil War was led on both sides by the strategists who knew each other from their days at West Point.

Until 1860, ordinary citizens had their main contact with the federal government through their visits to the post office. There were more employees in the post office department than in any other department of government. Periodically there were elections, although the president was not (and still is not) elected by popular vote. Neither were US senators elected by the vote of the people. The people did elect a representative to the US House of Representatives, but the politicians in the town and the state governments were likely to be a bigger help to citizens in local matters.

Freedom: The Civil War Era (New York: Oxford University Press, 2003), 859.

During the second quarter of the nineteenth century, there were forces at work that would stretch the need to regulate "interstate commerce." Some smart politicians, preeminently Abraham Lincoln, sensed that a unification of the United States was taking place. The most powerful symbols were the steam engine, the railroad, and the telegraph. If it takes someone several days to travel to a neighboring state or even to know what is going on there, it is difficult for people to feel that they share a common life. Compared to today, the railroad and the telegraph represented a primitive stage of communication, but they were ushering in a new world of neighborliness. One of Lincoln's momentous decisions during the war was to order completion of a transcontinental railroad—the first solid link of a nationally unified country. The railroad was central to how the war was fought.

The forces at work to unify the United States of America were in tension with the drive to keep extending the landmass of the country. From the time of its infancy, the tiny republic on the Atlantic coast was convinced that its destiny was continental. By means of a few smart purchases, especially that of Louisiana, and by the use of firepower against the Native American nations, the United States of America became an overgrown adolescent, uncertain of its own strength. It constantly expanded westward by way of the Indian Wars, and it tested its control of America northward and southward in the American Civil Wars. But what took center stage immediately after the second of those wars was the issue of slavery, which threatened to tear apart the nation that was still in the making.

The question of slavery occasioned a public and passionate debate in 1850. The debate was carried out by three old-time political rivals who did not outlive the debate: Henry Clay, John C. Calhoun, and Daniel Webster. The main question was how to decide about slavery in the vast territory taken from Mexico. Clay and Webster tried to compromise, but Calhoun would not accept any compromise. Clay's position was that slavery was a terrible evil but trying to get rid of it in the Southern states would bring on worse evils. Webster spoke not for the abolition of slavery but for the preservation of the union. Within months, all three antagonists had passed from the scene; Stephen Douglas took up Clay's compromise proposals, which were eventually accepted; the compromise of 1850 averted, for a while, the showdown over union.[374]

The compromise let stand the old dividing line of slavery for former territories. But popular sovereignty would determine whether a territory from the Mexican annexation would be slave or free. The compromise included a fugitive slave law and promised noninterference by Congress in the interstate slave trade. The fugitive slave law was thought a minor provision that revised a 1793 law, but its effect was to make every Northerner an accomplice in protecting slavery. Northerners were forced to think about slavery in a way that they had previously avoided. In a series of famous debates, Abraham Lincoln opposed Stephen Douglas on the question of submitting slavery to popular vote in a territory.

The compromise of 1850 led to a series of events that produced what Daniel Webster had foreseen as a "yawning abyss." Three key events of the decade can be noted. The first was the publication of *Uncle Tom's Cabin* in 1852. The novel brought home the meaning of slavery in a way that politicians had not been able to duplicate.[375] Then, in 1856, the new territory of Kansas fulfilled Lincoln's fears of a bloody conflict over the status of slavery. At least two hundred people were killed in "bleeding Kansas" before federal troops intervened. John Brown was involved in a "retaliatory strike" against the proslavery forces in Kansas that led on to his more famous attack at Harpers Ferry, for which he was hanged.[376] In 1857, a decisive event for splitting the country was a Supreme Court opinion of Justice Roger Taney. According to Taney's ruling, a slave named Dred Scott could not appeal to the court because he was not a citizen of the United States. Scott belonged to a race that was "an inferior class of

---

374 Allen Guelzo, *Fateful Lightning: A New History of the Civil War and Reconstruction* (New York: Oxford University Press, 2012), 68-69.

375 Harriet Beecher Stowe, *The Annotated Uncle Tom's Cabin*, ed. Henry Louis Gates (New York: W. W. Norton, 2007).

376 John Stauffer and Zoe Trodd, *The Tribunal: Responses to John Brown and the Harpers Ferry Raid* (Cambridge, MA: Harvard University Press, 2012); Tony Horwitz, *Midnight Rising: John Brown and the Raid that Sparked the Civil War* (New York: Picador, 2012). For a careful reading of John Brown's writings, see Louis DeCaro, *The Last Days of John Brown in Virginia* (Lanham, MD: Rowman and Littlefield, 2015).

beings" and "had no rights which the white man was bound to respect ...
the Negro might justly and lawfully be reduced to slavery for his benefit."

Taney went on to offer a further opinion—namely, that Scott's claim
that residence in a free territory freed him from slavery did not legally
stand up. In effect, Taney did away with all the previous compromises and
denied that the federal government had the power to restrict slavery in any
way. Until 1864 Lincoln would exercise his presidency with awareness that
Justice Taney was always looking over his shoulder.

When secession was already in the air in 1860, a final attempt at
compromise was put forward by Senator John Crittenden. President
James Buchanan, while still in office after Lincoln's election, encouraged
this compromise that would revive the line of the Missouri Compromise
of 1820. Congress would not interfere with the slave trade and would
compensate slave owners whose runaways were sheltered by Northern
courts and legislation. The Crittenden Compromise was killed in the
Senate. Lincoln would have nothing to do with the *extension* of slavery
into any of the territories.

Abraham Lincoln's position on slavery until 1860 did not differ
essentially from that of many other politicians, including Thomas Jefferson
and Henry Clay.[377] These men held two beliefs which went in opposition
directions: slavery is evil; and slavery cannot be eradicated where it already
exists. The way to reconcile these two beliefs was by the hope that slavery
would die out from its own inner dynamic. That seemed realistic in the
early days of the Republic; the importing of new slaves was to end in 1808.
Until 1830 slavery in Virginia (the home of four of the first five presidents)
was just an embarrassing fact of life. No rationales were put forward to
defend a "peculiar institution."

After 1830, Virginia, with its tobacco crop, was no longer the clear
leader of a Southern way of life. The explosive growth of cotton as the basis
of the southern economy brought with it what seemed to Southern people
a necessary and positive role for slavery. By 1850, the South had 68 percent
of a rapidly expanding world market for cotton. A more brutal form of
slavery that had its origin in the West Indies via South Carolina came to

---

377 Nicholas Guyatt, *Bind Us Apart: How Enlightened Americans Invented Racial
   Segregation* (New York: Basic Books, 2016).

represent the "deep South."[378] South Carolina had flexed its muscle in 1832 with a claim to have the power to nullify federal laws and to secede from the Union. Although President Andrew Jackson gave no support to these claims, they never died out. When the question of slavery came to the front in the 1850s, it was clear to Lincoln that "a house divided against itself cannot stand. I believe this government cannot endure permanently half slave and half free."[379]

Although Lincoln was no doubt firm in this conviction, he did not go further in his debates with Stephen Douglas than to say that the federal government should prohibit slavery in the territories. In the election of 1860, the Southern states suspected that Lincoln's convictions would carry him further if he were elected; they were right. He received no electoral help from the South and was elected with 40 percent of the popular vote. He tried to calm Southern fears by insisting in his first inaugural address, "I have no purpose, directly or indirectly, to interfere with the institution of slavery in the States where it exists. I believe I have no lawful right to do so, and I have no inclination to do so."[380] A subsequent letter to Horace Greeley at the *New York Tribune* on April, 20, 1862, continued Lincoln's insistence that "my paramount object in this struggle is to save the Union, and is not either to save or destroy slavery. If I could save the union without freeing any slave, I would do it; and if I could save it by freeing all the slaves I would do it."[381] Lincoln seems here to be motivated by crassly political calculations. But in his attitude to slavery, Lincoln showed in the few remaining years of his life what Eric Foner refers to as an "extraordinary capacity for growth."[382]

When South Carolina in 1861 declared that it was resuming its status as an independent nation, Lincoln treated the act as a rebellion against the Union. He never recognized the Confederate States of America as

378 Colin Woodard, *American Nations: A History of the Eleven Regional Cultures of North America* (New York: Viking Press, 2011), 200.

379 Abraham Lincoln, "'A House Divided Speech' at Springfield, Illinois, in *Collected Works of Abraham Lincoln*, vol. 2: 461-66.

380 Abraham Lincoln, "First Inaugural Address," *Abraham Lincoln: His Speeches and Writings*, 579.

381 Lincoln, *Abraham Lincoln: His Speeches and Writings*, 652.

382 Eric Foner, *The Fiery Trial: Abraham Lincoln and American Slavery* (New York: W. W. Norton, 2011).

a nation. To him they were rebels who had to be brought back to their proper place in the United States of America. Lincoln came increasingly to use the term "nation" in reference to what must be preserved. But in a way, he was not trying to preserve the nation so much as trying to bring it to birth. His task was to make the United States become a single nation with a national government.

"Nation" is a word that did not seem appropriate to what the United States of America had been trying to do. The root meaning of "nation" is that a group of people share common ancestors. The language, religion, and social practices have been handed down from the distant past that make "my people" different from those others who might not even merit the term "a people." Nationhood gives people identity, support, and a place of their own. The drawback in the claim to nationhood is that it sets up conflict with anyone who threatens the life, liberty, and happiness of "my people." As a cynical European saying puts it, "A nation is a group of people united by a common error concerning their ancestry and by shared hostility to their neighbor."

A nation's claim to unity involves a feeling of solidarity. Modern technology can be at the service of that feeling. The railroad and the telegraph in the nineteenth century made possible shared experiences across a great stretch of territory. In the twenty-first century, the effect of television, email, Facebook, Twitter, and not-yet imagined technology is unpredictable for creating either separate technological islands or national unities.

The assumed ideal was that the nation has a state and the state contains only one nation—for example, the French people have a French government that serves France and its people. The presence of a common language was the chief sign that a state was a nation-state. In addition to having one language, the long and destructive religious wars in Europe made it seem desirable that each nation-state have a single religion or else one dominant religion that might tolerate the existence of other religions.

In the first half of the nineteenth century, the United States had acquired some of the characteristics of a nation. It had a common language, even if English had been borrowed from the mother country. It had no "established church" but it had a dominant religion—the Protestant

Christian religion. It became a leader in the practical arts ("technology")—inventions with the potential of unifying a huge territory and a diverse immigrant population.

Nations require rituals, which are often adapted from traditional religions; the holy day becomes a holiday. In colonial America, there were religious days of thanksgiving; the practice continued in many of the states, most prominently in New England. During the Civil War, each side regularly called for days of fasting, and less often for a day of thanksgiving. Lincoln made an enduring contribution when he established a national holiday of Thanksgiving on the fourth Thursday in November. The Thanksgiving on November 25, 1864, was in gratitude for the devastating destruction by General Sherman in Georgia and by General Sheridan in the Shenandoah Valley.[383] Thanksgiving Day joined the Fourth of July in a celebration of the mythical beginning of a nation called America. Even after the Civil War, Thanksgiving was most closely identified with New England, but today it is a national celebration of family gatherings, with turkey dinners and football games—but no mention of Sherman and Sheridan.[384]

What the United States of 1860 lacked as a nation-state was a government that could command obedience from the people of the emerging "nation." The term "individualism" was coined to describe the attitude of people in the United States, but that term does not capture the fragmented nature of the rebellious groups that made up the country. Alexis de Tocqueville, a French visitor in the 1830s, had given a face to "the Americans." It was a mostly positive portrait, but Tocqueville worried that the democratic dynamic of the country would demolish the safeguards that the authors of the US Constitution thought were indispensable for a republican form of government.[385]

---

383 Harry Stout, *Upon the Altar of the Nation: A Moral History of the Civil War* (New York: Penguin Books), 390-91.

384 In the New England town where I grew up, Thanksgiving was still mainly the Yankee holiday; Christmas was for Irish Catholics; New Year's Day was for French Catholics. My mother, who worked in the textile mill, said the Yankee owners took particular delight in making the Irish Catholic girls work on Christmas.

385 Alexis de Tocqueville, *Democracy in America*, ed. Henry Reeve (New York: Bantam Press, 2000).

Lincoln made his case for a nation and a national government in a speech whose most obvious inaccuracy was the line "The world will little note nor long remember what we say here." This funeral oration at the battlefield of Gettysburg, where fifty thousand young men had been "sacrificed," had a more lasting effect than anything else Lincoln said.[386] The Gettysburg Address on December 8, 1863, made the case that a nation existed whose basis was the equality and liberty of all men.

The Gettysburg Address was a beautiful oration, although one might take issue with its opening pronouncement: "Four score and seven years ago our fathers brought forth on this continent a new nation conceived in liberty and dedicated to the proposition that all men are created equal." No nation was brought forth in 1776; instead, a tenuous collection of "free and independent states" agreed upon fighting a common enemy. As Joseph Ellis points out, Lincoln was off by eleven years in referring to when the nation came into existence.[387]

Would Lincoln reconsider his apotheosis of the Declaration of Independence if he could see today's Tea Party, Freedom Caucus, and other right-wing groups? His favorite metaphor of the US Constitution as a mere picture frame for the truths of the Declaration of Independence does not seem helpful for dealing with the fractured country of today.[388] For Lincoln, the Declaration of Independence has the effect of a chord binding the nation together; today for both the far right and far left, the declaration affirms a right to dismiss the authority of a national government.[389]

The Declaration of Independence was mainly concerned with achieving liberty from Great Britain. That specific liberty was included in an assertion of self-evident truths, starting with "all men are created equal."

---

386 Garry Wills, *Lincoln at Gettysburg* (New York: Simon and Schuster, 1992), 37: "The Civil War is to most Americans what Lincoln wanted it to mean. Words had to complete the works of the guns."

387 Joseph Ellis, *The Quartet: Orchestrating the Second American Revolution, 1783-1789* (New York: Alfred A. Knopf, 2015.

388 Abraham Lincoln, *Abraham Lincoln: His Speeches and Writings*, 531,536.

389 *Collected Works of Abraham Lincoln*, vol. 2: 484-500; Pauline Maier in *American Scripture: Making the Declaration of Independence* (New York: Knopf, 1997), 202, writes that Lincoln "never had a feeling politically that did not spring from the sentiments embodied in the Declaration of Independence." Perhaps that is admirable, but it could also be too much of a good thing.

In Lincoln's Address, that was the "proposition" the nation was dedicated to. But there is no way that a nation could come into existence on the basis of a proposition, and the United States of America clearly did not. It needed to establish a working unity with agreed-upon centers of authority. That was an especially daunting challenge for the United States and a task that had not been completed when Lincoln spoke.

The positive effect of the Gettysburg Address is more in its conclusion than in its beginning; Lincoln resolves that "government of the people, by the people, for the people shall not perish from the earth." Thomas Bender notes Lincoln's difference from the Declaration of Independence in 1776: "He transformed Jefferson's proposition into a challenge that 'this nation under God shall have a new birth of freedom'. Liberal nationalism for Lincoln was thus 'aspirational', demanding resolute and continuous pursuit."[390]

The challenge at the end of 1863, unfortunately, was to continue the massacre, which still had no end in sight. It was clear by then that what began as a rebellion against the Union was now what had been feared by writers on the nature of warfare: "total war," which did not exclude women, children, the elderly, the homes, and the productive capacity of the enemy's land. In wars between "civilized nations," it had seemed wise not to completely destroy the enemy's homeland. Plato had warned that in a war between Greeks, it would be unwise to destroy the productive capacities of the foe, as eventually both sides would have to live together. In his view, war should be conducted as army against army according to agreed-upon rules. For as long as there were wars, however stupid and immoral war may be, the need for some restraints was recognized.[391]

The war had begun by being imagined as a sporting match. The two teams were variously named North and South, Yankees and Rebels, Blue and Gray. The opening kickoff was at Bull Run, which brought out rich people in carriages to watch the scrimmage. The spectators were stunned

---

390 Thomas Bender, *A Nation among Nations: America's Place in World History* (New York: Hill and Wang, 2006), 176.

391 The idea of total war is found in Carl von Clausewitz, *On War*, vol. 3 (London: Wordsworth, 1997) 3, 49; Plato, *The Republic* 471b; the Christian theology laid down principles for justice in going to war and fighting a war; the Geneva accords are a modern adaptation.

to see their boys taking a beating; five hundred Union soldiers were killed, and twenty-six hundred were wounded. The crowd quickly scurried back to town.[392]

The US Civil War was a prelude to the world wars of the next century that eventually engulfed the whole population. General William Tecumseh Sherman's "march to the sea" is the most infamous example of the devastation of the land and people.[393] Grant had persuaded Lincoln to let Sherman cut a fifty-mile swath through Georgia in which the army could "forage liberally." That was the culmination of the constantly increasing slaughter of the war.

A string of place names for the key battles is known to every US schoolchild: Antietam, Shiloh, Fredericksburg, Chancellorsville, Gettysburg, Vicksburg, Atlanta, and the rest. Students usually have little understanding of how these battles are related to any larger purpose. And no textbook conveys the astounding butchery of the war. The Currier and Ives lithographs of the war emphasize heroic battle scenes. In the actual war, the generals threw tens of thousands of young bodies against well-defended positions until corpses filled up the farmland. The wounded soldiers who were not immediately killed were likely to die of infection after hours or days of agonizing suffering.[394] As usual, the generals were fighting the last war instead of recognizing that the technology of war had changed. A line of men in close-order formation rushing across an open field into the guns of an entrenched army was insane.

The presidents, Abraham Lincoln and Jefferson Davis, urged their generals to attack. Lincoln ran through a series of generals before finally finding his man in 1864: Ulysses S. Grant. General Grant had been successful in the western theater of the war—especially the victory at Vicksburg, from which the South never recovered. The grinding battle at Vicksburg had cut the Confederacy in half.

By this point, the South's hope for help from the British had disappeared. Britain had had a large stake in the South's cotton. The naval blockade of

---

392 Guelzo, *Fateful Lightning*, 154-55.
393 On the same day in 1862 that Lincoln issued the preliminary Emancipation Proclamation, he also issued an executive order permitting commanders to seize or destroy civilian property—so long as it was not done wantonly or maliciously.
394 Guelzo, *Fateful Lightning*, 265.

the South by the North had angered Britain. But Britain found other outlets for its cotton goods. Grant's mission was "get Lee"—that is, crush Robert E. Lee's army in Virginia.[395] Grant, with the help of Sherman coming up from the South, did just that. The two gentleman warriors, Lee and Grant, shook hands at Appomattox. Lee, in a letter dated April 20, 1865, wisely advised President Davis against continuing a guerrilla war. Grant was lenient in his terms of surrender and, surprisingly, so was Sherman.[396] Lincoln was not consulted beforehand, but the generals were acting in the spirit of Lincoln's Proclamation of Amnesty and Reconstruction, which had been issued in December 1863.

Despite the fury of the war, the soldiers were ready for peace. There is a form of pity that develops among men in battle. They have been conscripted or have volunteered to fight for their country, but after a while it is simply a matter of survival. They fight to get the war over. Many of the people who had celebrated the war were, of course, disappointed at the terms of surrender; they wanted "unconditional surrender" and revenge. The military battles were concluded, but the fight for the meaning of the war and the spoils of war was just beginning.

In 1864, Lincoln had come from behind to win a second term on the newly named National Union Party. As the war was about to conclude, Lincoln gave the last great speech of his life, his second inaugural address, which consists of 701 words. The last paragraph of the speech is well known: "With malice toward none; with charity for all; with firmness in the right as God gives us to see the right, let us strive on to finish the work we are in; to bind up the nation's wounds; to care for him who shall have borne the battle, and for his widow, and his orphan – to do all which may achieve and cherish a just and lasting peace, among ourselves, and all nations." It would be difficult to find anyone who would disagree with its sentiments.

It needs to be noticed, however, what preceded this conclusion. Many books, especially by people who praise America, are not so comfortable

---

395 Stout, *Upon the Altar of the Nation*, 322.
396 Ulysses S. Grant, *Memoirs and Selected Letters* (New York: Library of America), 736-41.

with the harsh words that lead up to Lincoln's irenic conclusion.[397] As in his first inaugural address, Lincoln did not use the term "America" in the speech. In his second inaugural address, he used the word "American" only once—to describe slavery. He expressed no joy that our boys would win the war and that our side would have been proved right. Instead Lincoln displays an evenhanded skepticism about both sides. "Both parties deprecated war; but one of them would *make* war rather than let the nation survive; and the other would *accept* war rather than let it perish. And the war came." In this passage, he places the greater burden on the South, but the final sentence is frighteningly fatalistic: "And the war came."

Christian language played a major part on both sides. Ministers regularly and scandalously presumed that God was on their side of the massacre. Lincoln had been formed from the cradle in a stern Calvinistic Christianity. Although the image of the Calvinist God had been softened during the first half of the nineteenth century, Lincoln's God was still the harsh but fair judge. The man who was saved should be grateful for God's mercy; the man who was damned had no basis for complaint about God's justice.

In his search for some meaning to the massacre, Lincoln suggested that the war as "a woe due to both sides" might be God's punishment for the "bondsman's two hundred and fifty years of unrequited toil." And there is no guarantee that the punishment is now concluding. Lincoln eerily foresaw that "every drop of blood drawn by the lash [would] be paid for by one drawn with the sword." At the founding of the country, there were approximately six hundred thousand slaves, which is a close match for the number of soldiers killed in the war.[398] And even if the shedding of blood continued, Lincoln said, "still it must be said that the judgments of the Lord are true and righteous altogether."

The last five words of the speech should be noted: "among ourselves, and all nations." Lincoln was aware of the need for the United States to

---

397 For example, Larry Shweikart and Michael Allen, *A Patriot's History of the United States: From Columbus's Great Discovery to the War on Terror* (New York: Penguin Books, 2004), 347.

398 Recent estimates of the number that were killed place it as high as seven hundred fifty thousand. See J. David Hacker, "A Census-Based Count of the Civil War Dead," *Civil War History* 57, no.4 (December 2011).

concentrate on self-healing so that it would be able to take its place among the nations of the world. But what emerged after Lincoln was a nation that claimed to be America with the mission and power to lead all mankind.

After the War

The period immediately following the war is usually called Reconstruction. One thing that is largely agreed upon is that Reconstruction failed, but the reason for the failure is not agreed upon. For more than half a century, a dominant view was that at war's end, Northern "carpetbaggers" went south to supposedly help the ex-slaves but in fact went there to exploit the situation for their own benefit. The freedmen, it was claimed, were not capable of directing their own lives and became part of the corruption that attended Northern attempts to punish southern whites. A different view was signaled by the publication of W. E. B. DuBois's *Black Reconstruction in America*, which began unearthing the racist assumptions in the white view of Reconstruction. The Federal Writers' Project in the 1930s gathered up memoirs of what had happened.[399] But a large-scale scholarly revision of history did not begin until the 1960s.

A first question that can be raised is whether the connotations of "reconstruction" are helpful to understanding the period. At the least, "reconstruction" should be supplemented by other metaphors, such as rebirth, repair, or development. What was needed was not simply a rebuilding of damaged sites and a fixing of the economy but rather a transformation of fundamental attitudes about race, class, and culture. Such a "reconstruction" of attitudes was needed in the North as well as the South. Southerners had a legitimate complaint that they were not the only ones who needed some reworking if a unified nation was to emerge.

The period in question began in 1865, at the end of—or shortly before the end of—the war.[400] Lincoln had begun planning what would be needed "to bind up the nation's wounds." Black people were saying to Union officials, "Do not abolish slavery and leave us landless ... They

---

399 Eric Foner, *A Short History of Reconstruction, 1863-1877* (New York: Harper, 1988), 259.

400 Richard White, *The Republic for which It Stands: The United States during Reconstruction and the Gilded Age* (New York: Oxford University Press, 2017).

distinguished between *abolishing slavery* and *freeing people*."[401] Some admirable experiments were tried but did not have the time to develop fully. The war to liberate the Negro population was followed by an inadequate political and economic revolution to realize black freedom. The former class of white plantation owners reemerged; they were bizarrely named "redeemers." An end to the period of Reconstruction is apparent by the 1876 election

Lincoln's successor, Andrew Johnson, was not up to the task. Congress took the initiative away from Johnson and passed a series of radical Reconstruction Acts. The South was divided into five military districts with fairly lenient rules for the readmission of states to the union. By 1870, all the states had new constitutions and had been readmitted. The Freedmen's Bureau was established in March 1865, initially for one year to provide food, clothing, and fuel, but it was renewed as a permanent agency. Its mandate was "the supervision and management of all abandoned lands, and the control of all subjects relating to refugees and freedmen … in areas declared to be in insurrection." The agency was given power to divide up plantation lands that had been seized for nonpayment of taxes or confiscated for retribution.[402]

The Freedmen's Bureau led the way in a series of laws and investments that signaled new authority for a national government. The government was deeply involved in the development of the railroad, in a national bank and national currency, in a national system of higher education, and in a homestead policy by which any immigrant could purchase federal lands for $1.25 per acre. The government also used the tariff to protect domestic industry and to provide an economic base for its ambitious programs. The aim was not to create a dependency of the blacks on government. In fact, "black participation in southern public life after 1867 was the most radical development of the Reconstruction years."[403]

---

401 Ibram Kendi, *Stamped from the Beginning: The Definitive History of Racist Ideas in America* (New York: Perseus, 2016), 230.

402 Guelzo, *Fateful Lightning*, 486. Many proposals for national reform died in Congress: a bureau of health, a federal railroad commission, a federal role in public education, and a nationalizing of the telegraph.

403 Foner, *A Short History of Reconstruction*, xv.

The intention to create a new nation was embodied in the passing of three amendments to the US Constitution. The Thirteenth Amendment in 1865 outlawed slavery in the whole country. It solidified the legality of Lincoln's Emancipation Proclamation. The Fourteenth Amendment in 1868 provided a definition of citizenship and in effect reversed the Dred Scott decision. By this amendment, the ten amendments of the US Constitution applied in the states; it overturned "black codes" that restrained blacks from moving and made it possible for them to sue and to testify in court. The Fifteenth Amendment in 1870 was intended to protect the voting rights of blacks against new restrictions in southern states.

The ratification of these three amendments was a significant achievement. Still, there was timidity in much of the wording. The Thirteenth Amendment did not entirely exclude slavery. It reads, "Neither slavery nor involuntary servitude, *except as a punishment for crime*, whereof the party shall have been duly convicted, shall exist within the United States or any place subject to their jurisdiction." The parenthetical phrase "except as a punishment for crime" is not just a historical curiosity. It is the basis of the slave-like treatment of the two million prisoners in the United States. Not surprisingly, most of the prisoners are black.

The Fourteenth Amendment was cramped in its view of sexual or gender equality when it could have included women in the protection of rights.[404] It adopted representation according to the number of eligible male voters; for the first time, the term "male" appeared in the Constitution. An early version of the Thirteenth Amendment that referred to "all persons" was rejected because it could mean "a wife would be equal to her husband and as free as her husband before the law."[405] The right of women to vote was postponed until 1920. The Freedmen's Bureau, which was concerned with the promotion of families headed by males, was wary of the "woman's movement." Leaders of the woman's movement, such as Susan B. Anthony and Elizabeth Cady Stanton, complained of the recognition of black men as "political superiors of all the noble women."[406] The tragic opposition

---

404 Kendi, *Stamped from the Beginning*, 245-47.

405 Bender, *A Nation among Nations: America's Place in World History* (New York: Hill and Wang, 2006), 165.

406 Ibram Kendi, *Stamped from the Beginning*, 245. The words are those of Anthony.

between freedom movements for (white) women and blacks was not helpful to either cause.

The Fifteenth Amendment was weak in the application of a nice-sounding principle of equality. The defenders of the voting rights of Negroes were in for a long fight against obstructions by way of rules on literacy, property, and education. The amendment said nothing about the right of blacks to hold office. The failure to bar discrimination reflected in part the fact that the North did not wish to change its own suffrage qualifications. And the failure to achieve "social rights," starting with integrated schools, perpetuated scandalous discriminatory practices for another century.

Just as blacks were gaining significant political power and making strides educationally, the country was hit by an economic depression in 1870. The problem was greatest in the South, where the value of cotton fell by 50 percent; tobacco, rice, and sugar were also hard hit.[407] Proposals to help blacks economically had trailed the concern with voting rights. Civil equality lacking economic power eventually fell apart. Black workers were forced into labor contracts and plantation discipline that resembled slavery. The police and judiciary remained firmly under white control. A weak civil rights bill of 1875 left blacks still unprotected in practice. For example, a clause on integrated schools was dropped to make the bill more palatable.[408]

The end of Reconstruction is signaled by a Supreme Court decision in 1875: *United States v. Cruikshank*.[409] The case concerned the conviction of several men for violating the rights of black citizens. The Supreme Court decided that the federal government did not have jurisdiction over local practices, except for states acting as states. Violations of rights by individuals were not covered in the application of federal laws. The decision ended the country's push for the full emancipation of the black race. Tied to that reversal was a failure of the United States to emerge as a fully functioning nation-state.

---

407 Foner, *A Short History of Reconstruction*, 227.
408 Foner, *A Short History of Reconstruction*, 235.
409 *United States v. Cruikshank* 92 US 542 (1875).

The premise of the Court's decision is found in its seemingly logical statement that "the people of the United States resident within any State are subject to two governments: one State and the other National; but there need be no conflict between the two. The powers which one possesses the other does not." Ideally there would be no conflicts between state and "national" governments, but in fact there were severe conflicts. Which one would then take precedence? If the answer is the state, then there is no national government; there is a confederacy of states.

This interpretation was made explicit in the court's conclusion: "The Constitution of the United States has not conferred the right of suffrage upon anyone and ... the United States have no voters of their own creation in the States." The plural verb after "United States" is not a grammatical slip. The court was saying that the Civil War had come and gone, and the attempt to create a unified nation was at an end. The South might seem to have lost the war, but confederacy had triumphed.

The amendments and laws were to establish a framework for a nation, but the political movement was not accompanied by a moral reconstruction. "Redeemer governments" in the South would disenfranchise black citizens by means of a poll tax or a literacy test. Jim Crow laws segregated blacks into the poorest housing, and public education was especially hard hit.[410] The United States lacked a national government that would effectively enforce national laws.

What would emerge or reemerge by the end of the century for joining the states was belief in America. The United States of America and the Confederate States of America had fought each other in a horrifying set of battles; in the end, what could be agreed to was that the participants were all Americans. "America" now came forward as a name for the nation. The "United States" had moved linguistically from plural to singular, but "United States" then began a slow decline in usage relative to "America" as the name of the nation that sought to lead the world.

The nation that Lincoln hoped for did not come into existence. Some of the reasons are obvious: the deeply held prejudice that blacks are an inferior race affected the North as well as the South, the death and destruction of the war were on a scale that had effects no one could calculate, and men were deeply prejudiced against the obvious conclusion that a nation of

---

410 Guelzo, *Fateful Lightning*, 510.

equality meant that women and men had to be recognized as having equal rights. The new nation was struggling to emerge as a world power while it was still trying to create a workable structure to heal the wounds of war and assimilate millions of immigrants.

The United States' American Empire

This chapter documents one of the most crucial turns in the history of "America" since its invention in 1507. At its origin, America was an idea of liberation imposed on a landmass that had been "discovered" by European adventurers. This invention of America involved a rethinking of the whole earth and its place in the world. In the sixteenth century, the idea of America was fused with the newly discovered land; America as liberty was thought to consist of a place of escape from the geography of Europe and the burden of history. America, the continent, was the place for trying to realize the idea or dream of America. For more than two centuries, this America was a place of experiments in novel approaches to human history. Then a more radical experiment began when a small group of British American colonists declared themselves to be "the Americans" in a place named the United States of America.

Although the land of America and the idea of America arose together, it was possible to distinguish between them. A group who believed themselves to be "the Americans" might try to spread the idea of America beyond the continent called America. There was a movement toward universality implicit in America as a new world. But what is universal is always embodied in a particular reality. People who try to free other people have to be aware that professed liberators have their own particular limitations. If someone resists the gift of liberty, it might be that the gift wrappings represent some unacknowledged limitations on the gift.

Between friends, gift-giving is a natural, almost continuous, process. But human gift-giving is liberating only when it is part of a mutual process; otherwise, the supposed gift becomes coercive. The recipient of the gift is placed into a role of dependence. "America's liberty" as a gift of emancipation might succeed within a mutual exchange of many aspects of human life. But the attempt to spread American liberation by means of military conquest is the place where a self-contradiction emerges.

The United States throughout its history has thought of itself as a beacon of freedom in an unfree world. Based on that assumption, conflict with the forces of darkness were and are inevitable. According to most US textbooks, the country reluctantly took up arms in each of its wars for the defense of freedom after being attacked by enemies of freedom. And in nearly every war, the United States supposedly won a glorious victory. The sociologist Robert Nisbet voices a distinctly un-American opinion in stating, "The stark, agonizing truth is we Americans have not been good at war, and particularly conventional war fought on land."[411]

Human power functions by nonviolent exchanges that are mutually liberating. Military power arises when there is an absence of human power. The impatient use of firepower to spread an idea of freedom is not a failure that is exclusive to the United States. For example, Spain sent both soldiers and Christian missionaries to the land of America. It was believed that the gospel by itself would take too long to succeed; guns gave the illusion of quick success. But a government that supports human freedom cannot be built on oppression.

In many ways, the United States has had success in spreading America *despite* its wars in the name of liberation. The country was receptive to people who were imaginative and had ideas for invention. The United States was a leader in developing the technology of communication and travel. "In the decade 1940-50 the United States was behind 82 percent of major inventions, discoveries and innovations."[412] Its culture (a word whose modern meaning it helped to invent) has been a wildly eclectic mixture that has spread around the earth. This "popular culture" is a mixture that can include the best and the worst of humanity when it is let loose from most historical constraints. People who try to preserve the best of what

411 Robert Nisbet, *The Present Age: Progress and Anarchy in Modern America* (New York: Harper Collins, 1988), 16.

412 Geir Lundestad, *The Rise and Decline of the American "Empire"* (New York: Oxford University Press, 2012), 12.

"culture" meant before the twentieth century ("the best of humanity") are horrified by "American culture."[413] They often have good cause for this reaction, but they also have to wonder about the attractiveness of the food, clothes, movies, music, sports, and all other things that now jump across continents with ease.

Here is where the term "empire" fits. From the beginning of the twentieth century, the United States developed what some people call an empire. Other people dispute this claim or at least maintain that whatever empire the United States had was a passing phenomenon.[414] A debate over whether the United States has an empire does not get far, especially when authors use "United States" and "America" interchangeably.

A question here is whether "empire" is being used equivocally or analogously. Until fairly recently, "empire" described imperial control by the Chinese, Babylonians, Romans, British, or other people. Military conquest was the usual means to empire. After the conquest, the mother country was in administrative control of a subject people. Empires were the common way by which the world was organized before the advent of the nation-state, and empires continued right into the twentieth century.[415]

The United States, almost by accident, changed the meaning of empire. It tried to dominate the world by spreading an idea (backed by military might) instead of by acquiring colonies. Like Rome, the United States claimed only to be interested in peace.[416] Despite that claim, the United States has mainly relied on awesome stockpiles of missiles and planes instead of the spread of hope for a better life. Millions of people who do not trust the military arrogance of America might be receptive to a United States example of a peaceful and just order.

---

413 The phrase "the best of humanity" as the meaning of culture is from Matthew Arnold's *Culture and Anarchy*.

414 Elizabeth Cobbs Hoffman, *American Umpire* (Cambridge, MA: Harvard University Press, 2013) dismisses the idea of an American empire, except for 1898-1946. Her counterclaim is that the United States has been an "umpire." At the very end of the book, she admits that "umpire" often does not fit US history and suggests "player-umpire," a phrase that is close to a self-contradiction.

415 Jane Burbank and Frederick Cooper, *Empires in World History: Power and Politics of Difference* (Princeton, NJ: Princeton University Press, 2010).

416 Thomas Madden, *Empires of Trust: How Rome Built—and America is Building—a New World Order* (New York: Dutton, 2008).

In the description of empires, the most common way to describe their movement is "rise and fall." It is fairly easy to trace the rise of the United States' American empire. An "empire of liberty" was claimed from the beginning of the country, although the story of a worldwide empire is mostly a story of the twentieth century. In the first decade of that century, "the borders of American nationhood were well secured while the borders of American power remained limitless."[417]

The other half of the metaphor—the fall of America—is of doubtful applicability. The more appropriate image would be a "decline" of its empire—one that seems likely to be occurring.[418] Anyone expecting an implosion similar to that of the Soviet Union will probably be disappointed. The relation between Russia and the Soviet Empire was very different from the relation between the United States and the American empire. The Soviet Empire was a tightly bound collection of ethnic and religious groups. The attempt to loosen some of those bonds led to a crash. The last chapter will raise a different kind of question about the American empire—a question not about whether America is collapsing but about whether the United States is being swallowed by America.

In the 1890s, a conflict arose in the United States between groups called imperialist and anti-imperialist. That conflict was a distraction from understanding the era in which "America" was being spread worldwide. Neither side of the argument was against the establishing of empire.

The imperialists argued that the United States had a responsibility to help spread liberty around the world. If war was necessary for that mission, that was just part of the responsibility. The anti-imperialists did not differ about the mission of spreading liberty, but they wanted the United States to have control of other nations without the burden of governing territories, and especially without incorporating people of "mixed race" in any new state of the United States. They favored a society in which "some nations were more equal than others, in which American commercial agents were

---

417 Steven Hahn, *A Nation without Borders: The United States and its World in an Age of Civil Wars, 1830-1910* (New York: Viking Books, 2016).

418 Lundestad, *The Rise and Decline of the American "Empire"*, is a balanced examination of a contemporary decline—not a fall. It is unclear why the word "empire" is put in quotation marks in the title. Throughout the book, the author accepts the term "empire" as an appropriate description.

granted special privileges, American government officials were treated with special deference, and the American navy was allowed special access to harbors and coaling stations."[419] Imperialists and anti-imperialists might have spent their energies better by examining the arrogance and racism on both sides of US policies.

The United States is not unusual in seeing itself as legitimately dominating others; the British had no qualms in doing so. But the United States is unusual in the degree to which it can obscure the fact that its intention is to dominate. Its success in inventing a new kind of empire depended on the ability of its political, economic, and cultural leaders to convince the people of the United States that their nation always uses its power benevolently. The claim that American activity is always benevolent is sometimes made with transparent cynicism, but more often it is a claim that is made with a simple and fervent belief in America.

"America" has always been a good land, and "Americans" are a good and innocent people. It follows that American blood and American soil are sacred; any violations call for retribution, if necessary by war. It should be noted that "American blood" might be shed anywhere in the world that "the American" chooses to travel, including the oceans. "American soil," when circumstances warrant the claim, can be any place on the American continent, extending to the Caribbean Islands.

Mark Twain wrote a famous essay in 1901 that severely criticized US activity in the Philippines. One statement in the essay has often been quoted: "There must be two Americas, one that sets the captive free, and one that takes a once-captive's new freedom from him, and picks a quarrel with him, with nothing to found it on, then kills him to get his land." What is seldom quoted is the immediately preceding sentence: "[We] lost the chance to add another Cuba and another honorable deed to our record." How could Twain not see by 1901 that what the United States had already done in Cuba was almost as dishonorable as the US actions in the Philippines that he was condemning?[420]

---

419 Robert Beisner, *Twelve Against Empire: The Anti-Imperialists* (New York: McGraw Hill, 1968), 105.

420 Mark Twain, "To the Person Sitting in Darkness," *North American Review* 172 (February 1901), 109-117b. In most respects, the United States war against the Philippines was more shameful than its quick suppression of an independent

The answer to that puzzle is that Twain was not comparing United States policies in the two countries. His contrast was in the form of "two Americas," in mythical language that obscures obvious facts. In the essay, Twain refers to the "European game," which is "un-American"—not the way Americans act. What was happening in the Philippines, he said, was "uncharacteristic, foreign to our established traditions." The real America would not destroy a newly formed government. But Twain's language hid the fact that the "established traditions" of the United States did include the suppression of freedom; the war against the Philippines was not uncharacteristic of US tradition.

The Fateful 1890s

The last decade of the nineteenth century opened the United States to the exercise of its power in world affairs. Since then, the country has never been the same. The fundamental change can be pinpointed as happening between 1893 and the end of the decade. There were years of buildup before those decisive years, and the United States had been involved with other nations from the time of its founding, but it had played down any entanglements beyond the American continent.

Since the 1890s, the record of the United States in using its power has been mixed. It has not been a monster out to destroy all opposing powers, but it has also not measured up to the usual claims of its leaders that it is just trying to help others. All nations pursue their own interests; they usually incorporate a generous amount of self-deception into their practices. What makes the United States different and dangerous is the level of self-deception engendered by speaking of the country as America.

In the background to the 1890s is the story of the United States emerging as a powerhouse of agricultural and industrial production. After the US Civil War, millions of immigrants arrived at its shores. The large and increasing population had the benefit of open land at cheap prices. If someone did not like the looks of the neighborhood, the impulse was to

---

Cuba. However, the United States finally came to grips with Philippine independence; the United States is still coming to terms with an independent Cuba.

move west. For white people, the frontier meant openness, liberty, and the growth of the republic.

This freedom of the US republic and its people was achieved at the expense of the native population. The long trail was coming to an end in 1890 with the massacre of the Lakota nation at Wounded Knee.[421] The violence was supposedly justified by the need to pacify an inferior race. Buffalo Bill Cody proclaimed at the 1893 World's Fair, "The bullet is the pioneer of civilization, for it has gone hand in hand with the axe that cleared the forest, and with the family Bible and school book."[422]

The movie industry that was born at the end of the nineteenth century had a big part in forming the image of "America." In his book *America in the Movies*, Michael Wood writes, "The movies did not describe or explore America, they invented it, dreamed up an America all their own, and persuaded us to share the dream."[423] Many people in the United States are unaware that "America" around the world is mainly what the movies and television show it to be.

It can seem ridiculous when looking back to the 1890s that there was a sense that expansion was coming to an end. By any measure, the United States was still very sparsely populated. In the cities, however, where rapid industrialization was occurring, there was the pressure not only of population but also of a growing underclass. Education could not keep pace with the number of new immigrants and the rapid growth of industry. As still happens in a capitalist system, the rewards were distributed very unevenly. In addition, the system was prone to cycles and, until some lessons were learned in the Depression of the 1930s, governments did little to soften the blows on vulnerable groups during economic downturns. The Democratic Party of the early 1890s, when faced with a collapsing economy, had a policy of letting the economic system correct itself.

As the split between rich and poor became pronounced, the members of the laboring class formed organizations to agitate for better working

---

421 Black Elk, *Black Elk Speaks* (Lincoln, NE: University of Nebraska Press, 1988), 276.

422 Lester Langley, *America in the Americas: The United States in the Western Hemisphere* (Athens, GA: University of Georgia Press, 1989), 78.

423 Michael Wood, *America in the Movies* (New York: Delta, 1976), 23; Russell Banks, *Dreaming Up America* (New York: Seven Stories Press, 2008).

conditions. Before some rules for bargaining had been established, the wealthy owners protected their investments by using coercive and sometimes violent means. The workers also felt the need for confrontations, which often turned violent. The strike was the labor union's only sure weapon, and when strikers prevented other workers from taking their jobs, violent conflict was likely to occur.

The unions were fighting against heavy odds, and they lost most of the early battles.[424] The Homestead strike against Carnegie Steel began in 1889 but became a full-fledged battle in 1892; the union suffered a crushing defeat. A strike with even larger implications began in the town of Pullman in 1894 and affected most rail travel west of Detroit. Pullman was one of the first company towns in which workers were provided with services in their private lives as part of their working for the company. On paper it may have looked good, but as the economy turned bad in 1893, the people rebelled against the stifling paternalism of the town. The overlord of the town, George Pullman, was shocked at the ingratitude of the workers. "'I was like a father to them', Pullman lamented, puzzled and hurt that they could go on strike."[425] A commission that investigated the strike interestingly called the town "un-American."

The severe economic depression of 1893 coincided with one of the most famous lectures in US history. Frederick Jackson Turner delivered a paper at a meeting of the American Historical Association entitled "The Significance of the Frontier in American History." In 1890, the Census Bureau had issued a report that was mainly a celebration of the United States' great progress. The report included a sentence stating that until 1880 the country had had a frontier line but that the line was now so broken by various bodies of settlement that a frontier line no longer existed. Turner seized on that one sentence to argue that the egalitarian and innovative character of the United States was produced by the frontier. "The most significant thing about the American frontier is that it lies at the hither

---

424 H. W. Brands, *American Colossus: The Triumph of Capitalism, 1865-1900* (New York: Doubleday, 2010).
425 Richard Sennett, *Authority* (New York: Vintage Books, 1980), 68.

edge of free land."[426] It is significant that Turner's speech was in belated celebration of the four-hundredth anniversary of Columbus's voyage.

The idea of the frontier has come in for constant criticism from historians of the "American West," but as Patricia Limerick, one of the prominent critics, writes, "Scholars who are holding on to the use of the word 'frontier' and scholars who have rejected it hold one thing in common: the public is paying no attention to either of us."[427] One reason that the public has not changed its view is that the story of "America" is a myth not subject to historical correction, especially when the historians themselves use a language in which the United States and America are not clearly distinguished.

A striking thing about Turner's essay is that it is about "America." The United States gets scant mention. That fact is crucial in understanding what the United States was soon to do in the name of America. Turner wrote that "up to our own day American history has been in a large degree the history of the colonization of the Great West." That premise could support the argument that "American" history no longer should be bound by the Great West of the states and territories of the United States.

Over the next few decades, Turner himself pointed out the implication that the United States had to find a "new frontier." In an *Atlantic Monthly* article in 1896, Turner suggested the need for (US) American influence in "outlying islands and adjoining countries." Turner thus contributed to the thinking that took hold among politicians between 1893 and 1898. As Theodore Roosevelt wrote, "[The war of 1898] finished the work begun a century before by the backwoodsman … The question of expansion in 1898 was but a variant … of the great western movement."[428] It was time for the United States to expand beyond the continent not as the nation of the United States but as America, the empire of liberty.

---

426 Turner's original speech and subsequent essays are collected in Frederick Jackson Turner, *The Frontier in American History* (New York: Holt, Rinehart and Winston, 1962).

427 Patricia Limerick, "The Adventures of the Frontier in the Twentieth Century," *The Frontier in American Culture* (Berkeley, CA: University of California Press, 1994), 79.

428 Theodore Roosevelt, *Winning the West* (New York: Current Literature Publishing Company, 1906), preface.

The purchase of Alaska in 1867 had been a first step beyond the contiguous states of the nation; it was the acquisition of a territory for the building of an empire. Alaska was still on the continent of America. Other ventures to the south were explored as contributions to an American empire. As early as 1856, a wild warrior named William Walker seized hold of Nicaragua and proclaimed himself president. Although Walker received no official endorsement by the US government, he had some enthusiastic support in the southern United States, especially for his reintroduction of slavery into the country. Slaveholders in the southern United States envisioned an expansion of America southward.[429]

In the latter part of the nineteenth century, there were many soundings of the possibility of a canal across the isthmus at Panama. The United States was fearful of a European attempt to build such a canal. President Hayes, in 1880, said it had to be an "American" canal or no canal. A canal, Hayes said to Congress, would be "virtually a part of the coastline of the United States." There was also a serious move by the US government in 1870 to buy the Dominican Republic. The issue was intensely debated, and it divided liberal political leaders. President Grant was unable to convince the Senate to ratify the treaty.[430]

The first US venture into empire beyond the American continent—by two thousand miles—was the annexation of Hawaii. The United States became involved in Hawaiian affairs in 1874 when businessmen secured a reciprocity treaty in which the United States received exclusive rights to commerce and to military bases in Hawaii. President Grant readily agreed to the favorable conditions of the treaty; a renewal of the treaty in 1884 provided further concessions. Trouble arose for Hawaii in 1890 when, under pressure from the sugar industry in the US, a tariff was imposed on sugar that reduced the value of Hawaiian exports in two years from $13 million to $8 million.

---

429 Walter Johnson, *River of Dark Dreams: Slavery and Empire in the Cotton Kingdom* (Cambridge, MA: Harvard University Press, 2013).

430 Joseph Smith, *The United States and Latin America* (New York: Routledge, 2005), 39, 43. As usual, the question of race was a complicating factor in imperialism versus anti-imperialism.

Queen Liliuokalani, who came into power in 1891, was not as compliant to US wishes as her brother had been.[431] There ensued a series of conflicts in Hawaii sparked by the economic problems and the fear of the upper class at a possible loss of power. A "Committee of Safety" was formed that cited "general alarm and terror." The US cruiser *Boston* moved in to protect Americans. After intrigues by US ambassador John Stevens, and with some local help and 162 marines from the *Boston*, the government of Hawaii was overthrown in January 1893. Just weeks before leaving office, President Harrison signed a treaty with leaders of the coup. President Cleveland was less enthusiastic about acquiring Hawaii. Eventually Hawaii was annexed by a joint resolution on May 4, 1898.[432]

The United States intervened in a dispute between Great Britain and Venezuela over the boundary with British Guyana. The dispute had simmered since the 1840s, but a serious conflict arose in the 1880s with reports of the discovery of gold in the disputed region. Venezuela had previously looked in vain for help from the United States. In 1895, President Cleveland, seeing Britain as a good target for resentment by US farmers, took the side of Venezuela. In May 1895, Cleveland appointed the aggressive Richard Olney as secretary of state, who promptly informed the British that "today the United States is practically sovereign on the continent, and its fiat is law upon the subjects to which it confines its interposition."[433]

The British were shocked at this arrogant assertion of US "sovereignty" over the entire continent and considered it a threat of war. Many politicians in the United States thought the country was in need of a war to toughen its youth.[434] Fortunately, in January 1896, Britain became preoccupied with problems in South Africa stirred up by Kaiser Wilhelm; the dispute

431 Stephen Kinzer, *Overthrow: America's Century of Regime Change from Hawaii to Iraq* (New York: Henry Holt, 2006), 16.

432 William Russ, *The Hawaiian Republic (1894-1898) and its Struggle for Annexation* (Selinsgrove, PA: Susquehanna University Press, 1961).

433 Walter Karp, *Politics of War: The Story of Two Wars Which Altered Forever the Political Life of the American Republic* (New York: Harper Collins, 1980), 43.

434 Kristin Hoganson, *Fighting for American Manhood: How Gender Politics Provoked the Spanish-American and Philippine-American Wars* (New Haven, CT: Yale University Press, 1998), 144.

with Venezuela was dropped. The United States moved on to a much weaker nation to have its war.[435]

The economic crisis of the United States in 1893 impelled the nation outward toward the establishment of world markets. By late 1893, five hundred banks had failed, along with sixteen thousand businesses. The secretary of the treasury, John Carlisle, said in 1894 that "the prosperity of our people depends largely on their ability to sell their surplus products in foreign markets at remunerative prices."

This realization coincided with one of the most important books in US history, *The Influence of Sea Power upon History*.[436] The author, Alfred Thayer Mahan, saw the ocean as a domain of power, and he argued persuasively that the United States had to develop a powerful navy to rule the seas. Thayer also urged the building of a canal to connect Atlantic and Pacific Oceans, as well as the establishing of naval bases in the Caribbean, the Pacific, and wherever else the United States wished to trade. Mahan was the toast of Washington and was praised by Theodore Roosevelt and Henry Cabot Lodge, chief advocates of expansionism.

In 1888, the US Congress authorized the president to hold "an international American Conference" (which did not include Canada and the British West Indies). The purpose on the US side was to form a customs union and to set up machinery for arbitration of any disputes with European countries. The United States' slogan was "America for the Americans," which did not fool any delegates from the South. In the US understanding of that slogan, "America" meant the continent; "Americans" meant the people of the United States. At the conference, the Argentine leader Sáenz Peña offered an alternative saying: "Let America be for Humanity." That was a saying that was difficult for the US government to oppose, but its implication was unacceptable because it would take control of "America" from the people who called themselves "the Americans."[437]

435 Karp, *Politics of War*, 47.
436 Alfred Thayer Mahan, *The Influence of Sea Power upon History* (Boston: Little, Brown and Company, 1890).
437 Arthur Whitaker, *The Western Hemisphere Idea: Its Rise and Decline* (Ithaca, NY: Cornell University Press, 1954), 84.

Cuba

Cuba, which was heavily dependent on the US market, suffered from a tariff change in 1894 that removed Cuban sugar from its duty-free status.[438] Cuba had experienced an economic depression since the early 1880s; the new US tariff added to Cuba's political unrest. Cubans had been struggling for independence from Spain since the unsuccessful Ten Years' War of 1868-1878. President Ulysses Grant, in 1875, said that the unsettlement in Cuba meant that "under these circumstances, the agency of others, either by mediation or intervention [seemed] to be the only alternative which must sooner or later be invoked for the termination of the strife."[439] The United States did not intervene then, but a new Cuban war of independence began in 1895.

Cubans were inspired by the writing of José Martí who organized a multiracial army to overthrow Cuba's creole elite.[440] Martí had lived in New York and had a good understanding of the United States. He was killed in the first battle of the revolution in 1895, but he had had the time to rejoice that "the Cuban war [had] broken out in America in time to prevent ... the annexation of Cuba to the United States."[441] Martí urged his compatriots "to prevent, by the independence of Cuba, the United States from spreading over the West Indies and falling, with that added weight, upon other lands of our America."[442]

The United States always feared an independent Cuba, supposedly on the basis that Cubans would not know how to rule themselves. The United States was therefore in agreement with Cuba's elites that Spanish rule was the best available arrangement. At the beginning of the Cuban rebellion in 1895 the official position of the United States was neutrality. However, there was considerable sympathy among US people for the

438 Louis Pérez Jr., *Cuba and the United States* (Athens, GA: University of Georgia Press, 1997), 13-23, 60-62.
439 Ulysses A. Grant, Annual Message to Congress, December 7, 1875.
440 José Martí, *Our America: Writings on Latin America and the Struggle for Cuban Independence*, Philip Sheldon Foner, ed. (New York: Monthly Review Press, 1977).
441 Philip Sheldon Foner, *The Spanish-Cuban-American War and the Birth of American Imperialism 1895-1902* (New York: Monthly Review, 1972), xxxiv.
442 Kinzer, *Overthrow*, 35.

revolutionaries. The support was heightened by the cruelties of Spanish commander General Valeriano Weyler, who was appointed in 1896 to crack down on the revolutionaries.

Weyler was removed in 1897, in part because of US pressure but mainly because his cruel and destructive methods were not working.[443] Sympathy for the Cubans in the United States was surprising given the country's tendency to consider a nonwhite population to be inferior. The Spanish, however, had a bad reputation in the United States, and the Cuban revolutionaries were somewhat romanticized in their struggle for liberty. When the United States actually encountered the Cubans in their drive for independence, there was a reversion to the stereotype of a nonwhite population as an inferior and belligerent race.

In 1896, both political parties in the United States stated support for *Cuba libre*. The Republican platform supported what was known as a "large policy," which meant taking military steps toward an American empire. The policy included annexation of Hawaii, enlargement of the navy, application of the Monroe Doctrine "in its fullest extent," and "the ultimate union of all English-speaking parts of the continent by the free consent of its inhabitants." Finally, the platform also declared that "American citizens and American property must be absolutely protected at all hazards and any price."[444]

William McKinley, the Democratic nominee that year, reassured Republicans that he would continue President Cleveland's policy of neutrality toward Cuba. In his inaugural address, McKinley reaffirmed a "policy of non-interference with the affairs of foreign governments." That meant "we want no wars of conquest" and "we must avoid the temptation of territorial aggression."[445] McKinley, like his predecessor, was not truly neutral. The United States supported Spanish sovereignty, and the US denial of "belligerent status" to the revolutionaries made it difficult for them to obtain supplies.

In 1897, McKinley endorsed an offer that the Spanish leader, Praxedes Mateo Sagasta, made to Cuba (and Puerto Rico) for home rule. Spain, however, would still be the ruler. The revolutionaries, sensing victory after

---

443 Foner, *The Spanish-Cuban-American War*, 76-97, 1272-78.
444 Karp, *Politics of War*, 66.
445 Karp, *Politics of War*, 68.

their decades of struggle, rejected the offer. The revolutionaries struck fear in US businesses that had invested fifty million dollars in Cuba. McKinley made a remarkable statement about Cuba in his annual address to Congress on December 2, 1897: "If it shall hereafter appear to be a duty imposed by our obligations to ourselves, it shall be without fault on our part and because the necessity for such action will be so clear as to command the support and approval of the civilized world."[446]

In Cuba, riots broke out in January 1898 between loyalists and revolutionaries. In response to the disorder, McKinley sent the battleship *Maine* to Havana. The arrival of the *Maine* was said to be for a "friendly visit," but a battleship in a country's harbor was sure to send mixed signals. On February 15, 1898, the *Maine* exploded in Havana harbor and 250 US sailors were killed. Conspiracy theories circulated, but while the cause was never entirely determined, it seems certain that Spain was not responsible.[447] Nonetheless, this incident ignited what was already a hankering in the United States for war against Spain. Newspapers played a major role in stirring up the popular clamor to "remember the Maine."

War for the American Empire

There was added pressure on McKinley to defend the honor of the country after an indiscreet letter from the Spanish Minister in Washington was revealed. The letter said that McKinley was "a would-be politician … who tries to leave open a door behind himself while keeping on good terms with the jingoes of his party."[448] The United States refused Spain's offer to arbitrate the *Maine* affair. Senator George Perkins said, "There are questions that do not admit of arbitration. Men do not arbitrate questions of honor. Neither do nations."[449] An editorial in the *Atlanta Constitution* on April 1 was headed "Wanted – A Man, an American." The nation's honor was at issue, and manly strength was needed, the editorial said. "At

446 *A Compilation of the Messages and Papers of the Presidents of the United States*, ed. James Richardson (New York: BiblioBazaar, 2008), XIV: 654-83.
447 Foner, *Spanish-Cuban-American War*, 245.
448 Charles Olcott, *William McKinley*, vol. 2 (Boston: Little, Brown and Company, 1914), 9.
449 Hoganson, *Fighting for American Manhood*, 72.

this moment there is great need of a man in the White House. The people need a man – an American – at the helm."[450]

This identification of manliness and "American" was not entirely new in the 1890s, but a younger generation of political leaders made it the centerpiece of US policies. The commonly used analogy was that the United States was like a young man who is ready to enter adulthood. He has to find good outlets for his newly found physical strength; he cannot back down from exercising this power. His only choice is to act like a man or become soft and effeminate.

Some of the causes of this dominant imagery that affected the direction of US policy are evident, although none of them completely explains the urge to go to war. Three overlapping reasons can be cited for the war fever. First, there was the simple fact that the United States had indeed become an industrial powerhouse with the need for overseas markets. In 1852, William Seward had proclaimed that "commerce is the empire of the world." and urged the United States to confront the rising powers in Asia.[451] By 1898, the United States for the first time exported more than it imported. With 5 percent of world population, it was supplying 32 percent of the world's food supply. To Senator Albert Beveridge, the implication was clear: "American factories are making more than the American people can use; American soil is producing more than they can consume. Fate has written our policy for us. The trade of the world must and shall be ours."[452]

Second, the late 1890s were just enough distant from the United States Civil War to create a fantasy of heroism and adventure among young men. In the debate between the imperialists and the anti-imperialists of the 1890s, there was a pronounced division by age. The men who opposed military conquests, including McKinley, were old enough to remember the real horrors of the Civil War. The men who were eager for war in 1898 were in their forties; of course, they were not likely to be the foot soldiers in a new war, but they eagerly sought to have a war that would prove their manly valor. Senator Beveridge, for example, had wanted to be a drummer

---

450 Hoganson, *Fighting for American Manhood*, 90.

451 William Henry Seward, *The Works of William H. Seward* (New York: Forgotten Books, 2012), 618.

452 Claude Bowers, *Beveridge and the Progressive Era* (Boston: Houghton Mifflin, 1932), 67.

boy during the Civil War but was too young. Theodore Roosevelt was the most outspoken and influential advocate of war as a necessary test of manhood. After the war, he wrote to a friend that "in the biggest thing since the civil war we did actually do our part, and had the luck to get into the fighting."[453]

A third reason for an obsession with manly strength was that social Darwinism was reaching a peak at that time. Darwin had resisted applying his biological theory to the history of society, but some of his disciples were not averse to doing so.[454] In this scheme of evolution, the white man was at the top, or the forward point, of history's movement. It was the "burden" of the white man to take care of the inferior races. The United States had still not come to grips with its "Negro problem," and as a result, racist attitudes influenced the images US representatives carried around the world. Another part of this evolutionary story was a condescending attitude toward women, who were considered inferior to men. But by the 1890s, women were pushing back. The reaffirmation of manhood was set in opposition to the growing strength of a movement for women's equality.

These three reasons could be gathered into the single term "America." An implied claim that America could be fully realized only when embodied in a middle-aged, white, Anglo-Saxon male now became orthodoxy. Any other example of the human species was not fully American. This ideology not only allowed but demanded that the blessings of American liberty, both religious and secular, should be spread worldwide. No one better articulated what the country was doing at the end of the nineteenth century than Josiah Strong. Raising money that was needed for foreign missionaries, Strong wrote in *Our Country*, "Our plea is not America for America's sake, but America for the world's sake. For if this generation is faithful to its trust, America is to become God's right arm in his battle with the world's ignorance, oppression and sin."[455] European countries looked

---

453 Letter to Winthrop Chanler, March 23, 1999, in *Letters of Theodore Roosevelt*, vol. 2, Elting Morison, ed. (Cambridge, MA: Harvard University Press, 1951), 969.

454 Influential proponents of social Darwinism were Thomas Huxley, *Man's Place in Nature* (New York: Dover Books, 2003) (published five years after Darwin's book); and Herbert Spencer, *The Principles of Ethics* (New York: Ulan Press, 2011).

455 Josiah Strong, *Our Country: Its Possible Future and its Present Crisis* (New York: American Home Mission Society, 1885), 253.

on with mixed feelings about the rise of the United States to world power, but no country was willing to come to Spain's defense.[456]

By the early months of 1898, it seemed inevitable that the United States would intervene in Cuba. Cuban planters and Spanish property owners were ready to welcome US intervention. The revolutionaries were less enthusiastic. A leader of the rebels, Gonzalo de Quesada, said on April 7, "We will oppose any armistice or intervention which does not have for its expressed and declared object the independence of Cuba."[457]

On April 18, President McKinley delivered a war message to Congress in which there was no mention of Cuban independence. He said that intervention might be needed "in behalf of endangered American interests which give us the right ... to act." When Congress submitted a resolution authorizing the president to intervene in the war, Spain immediately severed relations with the United States. On April 22, the United States imposed a naval blockade on Cuba, and on April 24, Spain declared war. On April 25, President McKinley asked Congress for a war resolution because "a state of war already exists." Congress readily agreed and predated its declaration of war to April 21.

The revolutionary leaders still hoped for independence because of an attachment to the war resolution called the Teller Amendment. It began with the statement that "the people of the island of Cuba are, and of right ought to be, free and independent." The amendment concluded that "the United States hereby disclaims any disposition or intention to exercise sovereignty, jurisdiction or control over said island except for pacification thereof, and asserts its determination, when that is accomplished, to leave the government and control of the island to its people."[458] McKinley accepted the amendment, but its provision that the United States would be the sole judge of when the island was pacified opened the door to decades of US mischief in the name of peace and order.

456 Ernest May, *Imperialist Democracy* (New York: Harper Torch, 1973), 181-95.
457 Pérez, *Cuba and the United States*, 95.
458 The Senate version of the bill was stronger than the House's in referring specifically to the Cuban government; the compromise bill was finally accepted in the Senate on April 20, 1898; for an extensive discussion, see Foner, *The Spanish-Cuban-American War*, 270-75.

The United States thus had what Secretary of State John Hay famously called a "splendid little war."[459] How any war can be called splendid is puzzling. As for "little," it was indeed little according to the standard account in US history books. If one refers only to what happened during a few weeks of 1898 in Santiago de Cuba and Manila Bay, the War of 1898 was a minor skirmish with so few US casualties that it hardly deserves to be called a war. If, however, one considers the war as what happened between 1898 and 1902 in Cuba and the Philippines, the war was not little and was anything but splendid. In Cuba, the United States struggled for almost four years to suppress the independence movement and keep Cuba under US control. In the Philippines, the United States sent one hundred twenty-six thousand military to fight against local resistance that, even after the declaration of victory in 1902, continued sporadically for years afterward.

On June 14, 1898, the United States landed seventeen thousand troops near Santiago de Cuba. The war lasted long enough for Theodore Roosevelt to have his "luck" in getting into battle. On July 1, he made a charge up San Juan Hill on the outskirts of Santiago—a feat for which he became famous. On July 3, the United States destroyed the decrepit ships of the Spanish navy near Santiago. As a result, the Spanish military were not able to bring in supplies, and the war was effectively over. While his men were dying of disease, General William Shafter waited for Santiago to surrender, which happened on July 16. The Spanish surrendered to the United States, not to the Cuban revolutionaries. Battlefield losses of life for the United States military were minimal. However, more soldiers died from sickness than from wounds. And civilians died in much greater number than soldiers.

Within days of the surrender, the Teller Amendment was disregarded. Attorney General John Griggs told the vice president of the Cuban provisional government that the United States was "an invading army that would carry with it American sovereignty wherever it went." The compromise version of the Teller Amendment had removed any reference to the Cuban government. When Spain surrendered, the United States became the ruler of a "conquered territory." On July 29, the *New York Times* declared, "If we are to save Cuba, we must hold on to it. If we leave

---

459 John Hay in a letter to Theodore Roosevelt; see Franklin Freidel, *The Splendid Little War* (Boston: Little Brown, 1958), 3.

it to the Cubans, we give it over to a reign of terror – to the machete and the torch, to insurrection and assassination."[460]

US Marines took the island of Puerto Rico without suffering any casualties. Puerto Rico was still in the process of organizing its cabinet for the home rule that had been granted by Spain. The US general Nelson Miles assured the population that "we have not come to make war upon the people of a country that for centuries has been oppressed ... This is not a war of devastation, but one to give to all within the control of its military and naval forces the advantages and blessings of enlightened civilization."[461]

While these blessings of civilization were being brought to Cuba and Puerto Rico, a similar process was occurring in the Philippine Islands. As in Cuba, Spain confronted in the Philippines a nationalist uprising that had begun in 1896. The US Commodore, George Dewey, met with the rebel leader Emilio Aguinaldo, who thought he had the support of the United States for a Philippine Republic. The Philippine Islands were attractive to the United States as a location for a naval station to serve a growing trade with China.

On February 25, 1898, Dewey was told to be ready to move US warships to the Philippines from Hong Kong. The assistant secretary of the navy, Theodore Roosevelt, told Dewey: "In the event of a declaration of war it will be your duty to see that the Spanish squadron does not leave the Asiatic coast and thus begin defensive operations in the Philippine Islands."[462] Dewey was ready when war was declared by Congress on April 25. Even before US troops landed in Cuba, the US fleet reached Manila. On April 30, Dewey moved into Manila Bay with four cruisers and two gunboats. In one day, they destroyed all ten ships of Spain's squadron, as well as most shore batteries. Dewey was hailed as a conquering hero of biblical proportions. "The Spanish fleet went down as miraculously as Jericho's walls."[463]

---

460 Perez, *Cuba and the United States*, 99.
461 Kinzer, *Overthrow*, 44.
462 Foner, *Spanish-Cuban-American War*.
463 Stuart Miller, *Benevolent Assimilation: The American Conquest of the Philippines, 1899-1903* (New Haven, CT: Yale University Press, 1984), 17.

The fall of the city of Manila took a little longer. Dewey waited for the arrival of US soldiers. Then, with the help of Aguinaldo's rebels on three sides of the city, the United States military occupied Manila on August 14. The United States suffered one military death—from heat exhaustion. Senator Henry Cabot Lodge immediately declared, "We must on no account let the islands go … The American flag is up and it must stay." The battle of Manila was hailed in some quarters as a great victory, although as Finley Dunne said, "Most Americans didn't know whether Philippines were islands or canned goods." It was even said that President McKinley "could not have told where those darned islands were within two thousand miles." It seems certain that most US leaders were hardly aware of the Philippines' long struggle for independence.

Although the nationalist rebels had helped in the US taking of Manila, signs of future problems quickly surfaced. On May 24, the provisional revolutionary government was established. On June 12, it published a declaration of independence, and on June 23 the Philippine Republic was declared. At the ceremonies initiating the new government, neither Dewey nor any US representative chose to attend. The United States went on to disregard the revolutionaries in the negotiations between the United States and Spain.

While there had been justifications offered for annexing Hawaii and the Caribbean Islands as forming a natural perimeter to the United States, those arguments did not apply to the Philippines. Annexing those islands could be understood only as a move into empire status. Such a move had immediate and long-range consequences. "As Japanese and Chinese observers clearly saw, the United States had become an imperial presence in eastern Asia."[464]

The clash between anti-imperialists and imperialists became intensified on the question of the Philippines. As with Cuba, the imperialists claimed that they had to take care of people who could not take care of themselves. The anti-imperialists were often opposed to letting in a nonwhite population mix with a superior race of people. The intensity of feeling at the time can be seen in a Thanksgiving sermon in 1898 entitled

---

464 Michael Hunt and Steven Levine, *Arc of Empire: America's Wars in Asia from the Philippines to Vietnam* (Charlotte, NC: University of North Carolina Press, 2012).

"The American Birthright and the Philippine Potage." Henry Van Dyke asked, "Are the United States to continue as a peaceful republic or are they to become a conquering island? God save the birthright of the one country on earth whose ideal is not to subjugate the world but to enlighten it."[465]

Peace Treaty and Continuing War

The peace treaty signed in Paris in December 1898 was the official end of the war in the Caribbean and in Asia. Spain relinquished sovereignty over Cuba and ceded Puerto Rico, Guam, and the Philippines to the United States. The treaty included a clause upholding the right of the United States to acquire new territories without a commitment to future admission as states. The US treatment of the Indians within the United States was the model for this arrangement. The US Supreme Court in 1901 referred to people "subject to the jurisdiction of the United States" but "not of the United States"; they would be "foreign to the United States in a domestic sense."[466] The term "colony" was avoided, but the language of American empire came into existence.

In the case of Cuba, the United States maintained a military government until May 20, 1902. There were more US soldiers on the island after the signing of the peace treaty than during the war.[467] The delay in removing the military was based on the claim that Cuba was not ready to rule itself. In 1899, President McKinley said that "the new Cuba yet to arise from the ashes of the past must needs be bound to us by ties of singular intimacy and strength if its enduring welfare is to be assured."[468] One of the parties in this relation was not seeking "singular intimacy." Cuba wanted independence, but that is not what was offered.

In the fall of 1900, Secretary of War Elihu Root and Senator Orville Platt wrote an amendment that generated intense opposition in Cuba and

---

465 Winthrop Hudson, *Nationalism and Religion in America* (New York: Harper and Row, 1970), 121.

466 The court decision, one of the "Insular" cases that referred to Puerto Rico, was Downes v. Bidwell (1901). Justice John Marshall Haran dissented.

467 Perez, *Cuba and the United States*, 108.

468 William McKinley, State of the Union address, December 5, 1999: http://stateoftheunion.onetwothree.net/texts/18991205.html.

was to shape Cuba's subsequent history. The Platt Amendment contained the following provisions: The United States would end its occupation as soon as the Cuban constitution gave the United States the right to military bases (including the now famous Guantánamo Bay); the United States could veto any treaty of Cuba's; the United States had the right to intervene for the maintenance of a government adequate for protection of life, property, and individual liberty.[469] General Leonard Wood, the US military governor in Cuba, candidly admitted in a private letter, "There is, of course, little or no independence left Cuba under the Platt Amendment."[470]

The Platt Amendment was passed in the Senate on February 27, 1901. Any resistance by Cubans to accepting the amendment was futile. They incorporated the Platt Amendment into their own constitution in 1901. In May 1902, the occupation was formally ended. Power was transferred to an elected president, Thomas Estrada Palma, a representative of the "better class" favored by the US military. Cuba was now unofficially a US protectorate.[471] The United States would see fit to intervene on several occasions, starting in 1906.[472]

After 1902, Cuba was flooded with US business interests. There were few alternatives to working for the *yanqui*. Economic success depended on accepting and mastering the methods of US business and being influenced by some of the cultural assumptions accompanying those methods, that is, to become *americanizado*. One of the few things that united all Cubans was opposition to *plattismo*—that is, a desire to get rid of the Platt Amendment. Unfortunately, Cubans, instead of adopting José Martí's language of "*nuestra América*," accepted the language of their oppressor and spoke a contorted language of "anti-Americanism." A traveler to Cuba in 1910 described what he found: "It is America who is the enemy; in the mind of the average Cuban – between American and Cuban no love exists."[473]

---

469 Louis Perez, Jr., *Cuba under the Platt Amendment* (Pittsburgh, PA: University of Pittsburgh Press, 1986).

470 Kinzer, *Overthrow*, 43.

471 Perez, *Cuba under the Platt Amendment*, 39.

472 Perez; *Cuba and the United States*, 187.

473 Herbert de Lisser, quoted in Perez, *Cuba and the United States*, 146.

The empire begun in Cuba and Puerto Rico was spread to other parts of the Caribbean, to the central part of America, and to the south of America. The opening of the Panama Canal in 1904 was a chief symbol of the dominance of the United States in that region. The political hegemony was signaled by the Drago Doctrine in 1902, which started as a proposal by Argentine Foreign Minister Luis Maria Drago to expand the Monroe Doctrine for protecting the finances of American nations against European intrusions. But a multilateral Monroe Doctrine was not acceptable to the United States, and the Drago Doctrine was transformed in 1904 into the Roosevelt Corollary. The United States appointed itself protector of the Western Hemisphere.[474] Roosevelt acknowledged that this role might "force the United States, however reluctantly, in flagrant cases of wrongdoing or impotence, to the exercise of an international police power."[475] In the following two decades, the United States found it necessary, "however reluctantly," to intervene twenty-one times in American nations.

The results of the Paris Peace Treaty were even worse for the Philippines than for Cuba. After the taking of Manila in May 1898, the United States seemed interested only in securing a naval base, similar to its taking possession of Guantánamo Bay in Cuba. But shortly before the peace treaty was signed, President McKinley decided that the United States should take all the Philippine archipelago. The United States offered Spain $20 million, which Spain accepted as part of the treaty.

On December 21, 1898, McKinley issued an executive order declaring US sovereignty over all the Philippines, despite the fact that most of the territory was under the control of the revolutionaries. Emilio Aguinaldo, who had cooperated with Dewey in the taking of Manila, had initially welcomed an alliance with "the great North American nation, the cradle of liberty, and therefore the friend to our people."[476] Aguinaldo was willing to turn over a naval base to the United States. When he saw that he had been deceived by his ally, he denounced the United States "in order that

---

474 For the full story of the Drago Doctrine and Roosevelt Corollary, see Whitaker, *Western Hemisphere*, 86-107.
475 Congressional Record 58th Congress, 3rd session, 19.
476 Miller, *Benevolent Assimilation*, 37.

the conscience of mankind may pronounce its infallible verdict as to who are the true oppressors of nations and the tormentors of mankind."[477]

Why did McKinley pursue this policy? There is a famous statement that McKinley himself made to explain his course of action. It is found in an interview of November 21, 1899. After examining what choices he had, McKinley said of his decision, "There was nothing left for us to do but to take them all, and to educate the Filipinos, and uplift and civilize and Christianize them, and by God's grace do the very best we could by them as our fellowmen for whom Christ also died."[478] McKinley said that he then slept soundly and the next morning told the chief engineer of the War Department to put the Philippines on the map of US possessions. McKinley's explanation makes painfully apparent his ignorance of and intolerance toward the Philippine people. The language of Christianizing the Filipinos is ironic, considering the fact that the great majority of them were Roman Catholic.

The Philippine rebels elected an assembly that wrote a constitution, and the Republic of the Philippines was proclaimed on January 23, 1899. Twelve days later, they declared war on the United States. As is the case in most US wars, it is disputed who fired first. The United States immediately claimed that they had been fired upon; later there was admission that the United States had at least provoked the attack.[479] The beginning of the war coincided with the Senate ratification of the peace treaty on February 6, 1899.

From the start of the war, it was obvious that the rebels could not defeat the United States' military force. But in a form of warfare eerily foreshadowing some future US wars, the local rebels could harass the superior army until a truce was acceptable to the invaders. Despite having more than one hundred thousand soldiers in the war, the United States had nowhere near enough resources to gain control of the seven thousand islands. The United States had to resort to torture, including a form of

---

477 Miller, *Benevolent Assimilation*, 54.
478 Charles Olcott, *The Life of William McKinley* (Boston: Houghton Mifflin Co., 1916).
479 Miller, *Benevolent Assimilation*, 61, 64.

waterboarding (the "water cure"), and to the killing of civilians along with soldiers when the US could not distinguish one from the other.[480]

While the United States claimed to be civilizing and Christianizing the Filipinos, many Asians looked on the proceedings with skepticism or revulsion. The leading Chinese nationalist, Jujia Ou, praised President Aguinaldo and his outmanned army for the "wind of freedom and independence blowing across Asia."[481] On March 31, 1901, the rebels suffered a grievous loss with the capture of Aguinaldo. He urged his followers to surrender, but the battles continued for another year.

The other face of the United States was shown with the arrival of five hundred schoolteachers in Manila in August 1901. This gesture has recently been described as "an endearing introduction to America – a precursor of the Peace Corps." The same author says that "we established something new in the Philippines – the global projection not just of American power but of American ideals."[482] In most US accounts, there was no war in the Philippines, only an insurrection that was quickly overcome together with the introduction of "American ideals."

Both the politicians at home and the generals in the field repeatedly proclaimed victory. General Elwell Otis, commander of the troops in the Philippines, wrote an article in June 1900 insisting that "the insurrection ended some months ago, and all we have to do now is protect the Filipinos against themselves and to give protection to those natives who are begging for it ... against the wild and savage bands who are too lazy to work." Theodore Roosevelt, speaking at the Republican National Convention the same month, declared that "the American people have conducted and in victory concluded a war for liberty and human rights."[483]

What finally brought an end to the fighting was a revelation of the savagery of the war. A Senate hearing in the first half of 1902 about a particular massacre led the *New York Times* to declare that "all Americans

---

480 Gregg Jones, *Honor in the Dust: Theodore Roosevelt, War in the Philippines and the Rise and Fall of America's Imperial Dream* (New York: New American Library, 2012). Jones begins his history with a description of the "water cure" of a Filipino mayor.

481 Karp, *Politics of War*, 93.

482 James Traub, *The Freedom Agenda: Why America Must Spread Democracy (Just Not the Way George Bush Did)* (New York: Picador, 2009), 26, 36.

483 Miller, *Benevolent Assimilation*, 101, 102.

have been shocked." On the other hand, the *Times* continued, "a choice of cruelties is the best that has been offered in the Philippines … The army has obeyed orders. It was sent to subdue the Filipinos. Having the devil to fight, it has sometimes used fire."[484] The reference of fighting the devil with fire referred to a massacre in the village of Balangiga on the island of Samar. The US assault on the village was revenge for the surprise attack of September 28, 1901, which had killed fifty-four marines. General Jacob Smith ordered Major Littleton Waller and his three hundred marines to Samar with these instructions: "I want no prisoners. I wish you to kill and burn; the more you kill and burn the better it will please me. I want all persons killed who are capable of bearing arms in actual hostilities against the United States."[485]

When Waller was tried for murder, he revealed Smith's orders. The responsibility went up the chain of command to the military commander General Adna Chaffee. When there was public demand for a thorough investigation, Theodore Roosevelt enlisted his friend Senator Henry Cabot Lodge to hold hearings and keep the lid on how the war was conducted. When Smith retired with no additional punishment, Roosevelt said that Smith's sin was "loose and violent talk" that got into the press.

On July 4, 1902, Roosevelt declared that the Philippines were pacified. That date is sometimes given as the official end of the war, although sporadic fighting continued. In three and a half years, the United States losses were 4,374 soldiers—ten times the loss in Cuba. The estimates of Philippine losses were 16,000 to 20,000 soldiers and 200,000 civilians.[486] Speaking in 1902, F. F. Elinwood, director of the Presbyterian Missions, said that the US conquest was "a Providential event of the widest reach and of the most momentous consequences and on whole a great step toward the civilization and evangelization of the world."[487] The war did have momentous consequences but not in any discernible way that added to the civilization of the world.[488]

---

484 *New York Times*, May 2, 1902.
485 Miller, *Benevolent Assimilation*, 219.
486 Hoganson, *Fighting for American Manhood*, 7.
487 Miller, *Benevolent Assimilation*, 248.
488 Gregg Jones, *Honor in the Dust*.

Critics of the war saw the reason for the war as economic, but it is important to identify not just a general economic interest but the issue of wealth entwined with a quasireligious ideology. In the United States of the 1890s, the American empire was born, with a promise of both secular and religious liberty for all who were brought under the umbrella of America's benevolent policies. The paradox of this stance was that reformers, who were noted for advocating legislation to protect the poor and the vulnerable at home, were prominent among the "imperialists," who resisted independence and freedom for people abroad. An understanding of that paradox requires an examination of an international movement called progressivism and its relation to the idea of America.

The Progressive Movement

The progressive movement has a prominent place in most US history books, but the treatment usually presumes that the movement was born in the United States and flourished between 1900 and 1917. A wider lens on the movement shows it to have roots in the mid-nineteenth century, with the United States lagging behind Germany, Great Britain, France, and other countries. In the 1890s, New Zealand was considered the showcase of progressive politics. The United States is not inclined to think of itself as ever having been behind European countries—or New Zealand. The United States did join the movement at the beginning of the twentieth century, but after some steps at reform, the progressive movement lost its credibility, especially because of its support of US entry into the Great War.[489] There was no longer a discernible movement after 1918, but the idea of progressive actions in politics, education, religion, and elsewhere continued to attract passionate adherents.

Calling something "progressive" was a clever move, because not many people—certainly not many people in the United States—would be against progress. But that did not guarantee support of *progressivism*. A progressive movement had a difficult time getting a foothold in the United States. For example, programs of social insurance for the sick, the elderly, or the unemployed met with strong opposition.

489 An excellent history of the movement is Daniel Rodgers, *Atlantic Crossing: Social Politics in a Progressive Age* (Cambridge, MA: Harvard University Press, 1998).

My main interest is how the United States' relation to America played a crucial part in the late arrival of the United States to the progressive movement and the limited success of progressivism in the United States. The identification of the existing United States with America, the land of liberty and justice for all, had a major role in the nation's reaction to proposed "social" reforms. The rise and fall of the progressive movement is worth investigating to understand how "America" can be an obstacle to such programs as immigration reform, urban renewal, support of labor unions, or government aid to children and the elderly. Roger Daniels suggests that for Indians, blacks, and immigrants, the 1890s to the 1920s could be called the "regressive era."[490]

At the turn of the twentieth century, progressive reforms were mainly the work of Republicans. "The conservative leaders of the [Republican] party, after 1908, began dropping the word conservative from their lexicon … and began calling themselves 'progressives.'"[491] It was a surprise when the Democratic nominee in 1912, Woodrow Wilson, proclaimed himself a progressive; he had opposed most progressive legislation.

Democrats were finding it difficult to describe what they stood for. Eventually the terms "liberal" and "progressive" were embraced by Democrats, but that was not an outcome that had been obvious. "Progressive" became a cover for the great turnaround by Democrats to become the party of government programs. The main enemy of freedom was now seen to be the enormous concentration of capital in business corporations. The individual was overmatched in dealing with corporations. Private associations, such as labor unions, needed help to make negotiations with corporations realistic and effective.

The eighteenth-century political revolution had not got rid of rich people; nor could the revolutionaries foresee the Industrial Revolution, which was to create a much wider gap between the rich and the poor. Liberals in the nineteenth century were in favor of individual freedom, by which they meant that the government should not interfere with a man's liberty. Their conservative adversaries highlighted reverence for the past, when society was regulated by tradition, as embodied in church and

490 Roger Daniels, *Not Like Us: Immigrants and Minorities in America, 1890-1924* (Chicago: Ivan Dee, 1997), 48.
491 Karp, *Politics of War*, 153.

monarchy. Neither liberals nor conservatives knew what to do about the plight of an increasing number of people left behind in the nineteenth century's economic revolution.

Starting in Germany, ideas arose that were a challenge to the widely accepted theory that dominated economic thinking—what the Germans called "the English school." In that way of thinking, the laws of economics are "natural" and therefore unchangeable. Thus, when a famine in 1816 threatened a third of the population with starvation, David Ricardo wrote that he was "sorry to see a disposition to inflame the minds of the lower orders by persuading them that legislation can afford them any relief."[492]

The new reformers refused to accept this fatalism. They speculated that if society is threatened by destruction of needed resources and by a growing number of people who are becoming disconnected to society, government has to play a positive role. The French Revolution's political revolution needed to be completed by "a social revolution that would bring about full human emancipation."[493] The most famous and influential document of the time was *The Communist Manifesto* in 1848, which led in the twentieth century to a state takeover of individual and society.

Less ostentatious was the movement to initiate reforms that might improve the lot of the individual vis-à-vis concentrations of wealth and power. The progressive movement was a way of dealing with the "social question." The social emphasis was a reaction against individualism—that is, the ideology that only individuals exist and that each human individual acts independently of other human beings. The progressive movement was an affirmation of one form of socialism against other forms of socialism. The people who argued for progressive reform offered it as a defense of capitalism against *state* socialism.

One of the first moves of the nascent progressive movement in England might seem minor, but it had profound effects: the control of the water supply. In those parts of the world where water is abundant and safe

---

492 Quoted in Amartya Sen, *Idea of Justice* (Cambridge, MA: Harvard University Press, 2009), 388. Ricardo is responding to a letter from his friend James Mill, in which Mill had suggested "it would be a blessing to take them [the starving poor] into the streets and highways and cut their throats as we do the pigs."

493 Costas Douzinas, *The End of Human Rights: Critical Legal Thought at the Turn of the Century* (Oxford: Hart Publishing, 2000), 159.

to drink, it is easy to forget how indispensable clean water is and the effort that is needed to guarantee its safety. In the nineteenth century, the main reason for improvement of health in "advanced" nations was the improvement in water. Until the middle of the century, water was under the control of private suppliers. What was obvious to reformers is that water for drinking, like air for breathing, is a public not a private good. It should not be subject to the profit motive by people lucky enough or assertive enough to control the availability of potable water. Municipal water supplies became a model for how other public goods might be regulated by government.[494]

From its beginning, the progressive movement was centered in the cities, where there were huge increases in the number of people. The factories required great numbers of workers; millions of immigrants crowded into the cities to run the machines. Manhattan Island became one of the most crowded places on earth. Marx and Engels saw the city as a cesspool of human suffering and poverty. They were right, but they neglected another aspect of urban life—namely, its communal possibilities as an alternative to both individualism and the isolated family. While the populist movement in the United States was distrustful of cities and their corrupt politics, the progressives in the United States were sympathetic to the urban masses, even though the outlook of the reformers was often tainted by condescension toward blacks and immigrants.[495]

The US attitude to cities was central to the limited success that the progressive movement had in the United States. From its beginning in the sixteenth century, "America" was not a place of cities. America was where you went to escape the crowded city. The British American colonies, more than other American colonies, emphasized America as abundant land that guaranteed liberty. The United States, from the time of its founding, continued this tradition. Each man was to have his own tract of land, and Americans would not live in crowded and corrupt cities. States were the focus of the US Constitution; cities were not part of the plan.

The abundance of land in the United States, combined with a particular form of Protestant Christianity, fed this antiurban bias. The

494 Rodgers, *Atlantic Crossing*, 119.
495 Michael McGerr, *A Fierce Discontent: Rise and Fall of the Progressive Movement in America, 1890-1920* (New York: Free Press, 2003), 216.

nineteenth-century mantra was that "God made the country; man made the city." And it was not the man who is made in the image of God who populated cities, but man the sinner, who is constantly tempted by Satan. The influential writer Josiah Strong wrote in 1898, "The first city was built by the first murderer, and crime and vice and wretchedness have festered in it ever since."[496]

There was, in fact, plenty of corruption that was evident in cities, but much of it was a self-fulfilling prophecy. Both the advocates of reform and the critics of urban living could accept Andrew White's assessment in 1890 that "with very few exceptions, the city governments of the United States are the worst in Christendom – the most expensive, the most inefficient, and the most corrupt."[497] The country had not yet adjusted to the earlier immigration of German Jews and Irish Catholics when it had to confront an even bigger wave of immigration. In 1890, four-fifths of the people in New York City were immigrants or children of immigrants. In every large city, one could meet languages and ritual practices that had not been eliminated by Americanization. Religious and racial biases were mixed together in antiurban sentiments.

Although religion played a central role in an antiurban bias, resulting in a neglect of the poor, there were also countermovements that were religiously motivated. The progressive movement was inspired by evangelical Protestantism.[498] That fact was played down by some prominent reformers, such as John Dewey, who did not wish to emphasize their evangelical upbringings. The progressives who stayed within the church gave a new twist to their Christian beliefs, which they called the "Social Gospel." The Christian movement, they pointed out, first spread in cities among the poor and other social outcasts (a *pagan* in Roman times was a country dweller). Jesus did not spend his time with the rich and powerful. The

496 Josiah Strong, *The Twentieth-Century City* (New York: Forgotten Books, 2012[1898]), 181. See also the author's *Our Country: Its Possible Future and its Present Crisis* (New York: American Home Mission Society, 1885).
497 Richard Hofstadter, *The Age of Reform* (New York: Vintage Books, 1960), 175.
498 McGerr, *A Fierce Discontent*.

social gospel movement rejected the late nineteenth century equivalence of wealth and virtue—a view scandalously held by some church officials.[499]

The Protestant reformers found allies among both Roman Catholics and Jews, the great majority of whom lived in cities. Catholics were supported by a papal encyclical in the 1890s, in which the Roman Catholic Church began to back away from opposition to the modern world. Pope Leo XIII affirmed labor unions and government support for vulnerable people.[500] The universal principles that the pope articulated had immediate effects upon those Catholics in the United States who were working for "social justice." John A. Ryan, an activist monsignor, could cite papal support for "all reasonable measures of protective legislation," including laws protecting child and female labor; a minimum wage; and insurance for the sick, elderly, and unemployed.[501]

Jewish thinkers were central to social and progressive reforms. Starting with the first large wave of Jewish immigrants in the mid-nineteenth century and continuing throughout the twentieth century, Jews were prominent in progressive causes in numbers far beyond their proportion of the national population.[502] Jews were subjected to widespread discrimination by people who identified "America" as a Christian nation. Despite all obstacles, Jewish success in a great many areas of US life was remarkable. And even with the economic success that moved Jews out of urban ghettoes, Jews continued to be strong supporters of progressive policies.

The attempt to reform the cities was not generally successful. Cities remained places of activities suspected of being un-American. In the 1630s William Bradford had wondered why Plymouth lost much of its population to its "suburbs."[503] The process has continued throughout the

---

499 Bishop William Lawrence, "The Relation of Wealth to Morals," in *God's New Israel*, ed. Conrad Cherry (Englewood Cliffs, NJ: Prentice Hall, 1971), 246: "In the long run, it is only to the man of morality that wealth comes. We believe in the harmony of God's Universe."

500 The Encyclical is known by its first words in Latin, "*Rerum Novarum.*" Unhelpfully, the same pope shortly afterward published *Testem Benevolentiae*, an encyclical condemning "Americanism."

501 John A. Ryan, *Distributive Justice: The Right and Wrong of Our Present Distribution of Wealth* (New York: Macmillan, 1942 [1916]).

502 Nathan Glazer, *American Judaism* (Chicago: University of Chicago, 1957), 179.

503 William Bradford, *Of Plymouth Plantation* (New York: Dover Books, 2006), 334.

history of the United States. The railroad made it possible for people to live in suburbs, which were a few miles from the center of the city; the automobile multiplied those distances. But everyone cannot move out of town; there could not be suburbs if there were no "urbs" in the middle. The alternative to the urban center was simply a sprawl of highways.

The "American" solution for an economic underclass was for each man to work his way up the social ladder to success. The "American" ethos of the nineteenth century was taught to almost every schoolchild in the textbook series the McGuffey Readers. The books hammered home slogans that are still common in the US today: "If at first you don't succeed, try, try again." "Where there's a will there's a way." The preacher in the late nineteenth century thundered, "It is all in the will. For every man in the house tonight, it's I will or I will not."[504]

The United States has never been quite the land of social mobility that is imagined to exist in America. One of the few literary allusions that most people in the country are familiar with is the "Horatio Alger" story, referring to a character in popular novels at the end of the nineteenth century. What is meant by the Horatio Alger story today is that a poor boy with a will to succeed can work hard and achieve success. The actual novels told a different story. The books arrived at that moment when it was becoming evident that working a seventy-hour week and saving one's pennies was not the way that most people became rich. One of the novels admitted that "worldly prosperity doesn't always go by merit; plenty of mean men prosper." The boy in the novels actually succeeds by attracting the attention of a rich man who gives him the needed boost to get out of poverty.[505]

A central problem of most cities was and is the absence of adequate transportation. Early in the twentieth century, the United States fell in love with the automobile, a driving machine for the open road but a machine that is worse than useless in the city. At the beginning of the twentieth century, it had seemed that the United States would be a leader in urban transportation; by the middle of the twentieth century, public transport

---

504 William Holmes McGuffey, *McGuffey's Eclectic Readers* (New York: John Wiley and Sons, 1989).

505 Bernard Wishy, *The Child and the Republic* (Philadelphia, PA: University of Pennsylvania Press, 1968), 83.

was bad and getting worse. While water was publicly controlled in the 1920s by sixty of the sixty-nine main cities of the United States, only four of those cities controlled the means of transportation.[506] Instead of urban transit being seen as a necessity of life, similar to clean air and drinkable water, transportation was in the hands of private companies who tried to make it a profitable business. The result was easily predictable. Fares rose as the service steadily declined. The technological marvels of "America" are not apparent in the urban transportation systems of the United States.

One of the areas in which "progressive" and "progressivism" have been most prominent is the discussion of education. The connection is hardly surprising. Effective reforms would have to include an educational system to sustain progress. The peculiar thing is that "progressive education" made its big entrance just when the progressive movement is said to have ended.

In the 1890s, the adjective "progressive" was attached to education, especially through the influence of John Dewey. Dewey had begun advocating a reform of school curricula emphasizing the sciences. He was particularly enthralled by the new psychology that would make it possible to match the student's development with the mastery of science, art, and mathematics. Until World War I, progressive education was a central element within the progressive movement's attempt at political and economic reform. The progressive movement suffered a fatal blow by supporting US entrance into the war.

The Progressive Education Association was founded in 1919 and continued until 1955. The president of the association, Burton Fowler, stated its basic principle as "we do endorse by common consent the obvious hypothesis that the child rather than what he studies should be the center of educational effort."[507] The idea of a "child-centered school" was attributed to Dewey, but Dewey's opinion of that idea was, "Such a method is really stupid. For it attempts the impossible, which is always stupid, and it misconceives the conditions of independent thinking." Dewey was still complaining in 1950: "Why do writers and teachers insist on saddling me with the 'child-centered' school?"[508]

506 Rodgers, *Atlantic Crossing*, 152.
507 Lawrence Cremin, *Transformation of the School* (New York: Knopf, 1961), 258.
508 Cremin, *Transformation of the School*, 234; a letter to Bob Rothman, cited in Jay Martin, *The Education of John Dewey* (New York: Columbia University Press,

Dewey had not foreseen that his celebration of psychology would lead to psychological language swallowing educational discussions.[509] The result was that "progressive" came to refer to attention to the psychology of children in rich suburban schools rather than an intellectually challenging curriculum for students in all schools. Dewey was appalled at schools that dismissed curriculum questions and undermined the authority of classroom teachers. He was most chagrined by the fact that people quoted him in support of schools whose curriculum consisted of letting students have "experiences." Dewey's, *Experience and Education*, published in 1938, is a protest against "progressive schools," but Dewey never admits in the book that he was part of the problem. At the beginning and end of the book, Dewey proposes eliminating the word "progressive," but throughout the book he continues to oppose "progressive" to "traditional," just as he had fifty years earlier.[510]

My main interest in the history of progressive education is the use of "American." In both scholarly and popular discussions of education in the United States, the adjective "American" is omnipresent. Nearly all discussion of "American education" is actually concerned with US public elementary and secondary schools. Obviously those schools are a major part of US education. But everything left out is also important. In a world where education, both good and bad, goes from birth to death and involves innumerable settings, the obsessive attention with the five-to-sixteen age group and with buildings called schools is patently inadequate. In the 1930s, Dewey was still stuck in the educational language of the 1890s. Shockingly, the country has still made little progress in reformulating the questions of education. American education is assumed by most people in the United States to lead the world, but United States elementary and secondary schools are in the rear internationally.

The United States' entrance into the Great War was not the work of progressivism, but progressives thought that war might serve their cause. In the long lead up to the war, progressives rejoiced in a decline

---

2003), 498.

509 Richard Hofstadter, *Anti-Intellectualism in American Life* (New York: Knopf, 1963), 369.

510 John Dewey, *Experience and Education* (New York: Collier Books, 1963), 6, 90.

of individualism and the rise of collectivism, or a social outlook.[511] They naively believed that after the war, the newly expanded government would be put at the service of progressive reforms. Although by 1916 the Progressive Party had already made its last stand and returned to the Republican Party, its rhetoric lived on. Richard Hofstadter said that "the war was justified before the American public – perhaps had to be justified – in the Progressive rhetoric and in Progressive terms."[512] Reforms to aid the vulnerable populations of the United States had given way to remaking the world "in the image of America."

The progressive movement may have been near its conclusion even without the war. Wilson had declared in 1914 that the "high enterprise of reform" had come to an end; the legislation of the previous year and a half had remedied the "dangerous ill-humors" of the previous dozen years.[513] Wilson was blind to the continuing plight of the Negro, who was still being denied the basic rights of an American. There was still an abundance of poverty in the cities. There was also a rise of anti-immigrant feelings in many parts of the country, and the charge of disloyalty was aimed at people called "hyphenated Americans." A particularly vicious example was an influential book in 1916 entitled *The Passing of the Great Race*. The author, Madison Grant, worried that if the melting pot is allowed to boil without control then "the native American of Colonial descent will become extinct."[514]

---

511 McGeer, *A Fierce Discontent*, 299; Rodgers, *Atlantic Crossing*, 279.
512 Hofstadter, *Age of Reform*, 273.
513 *New York Times*, November 18, 1914.
514 Madison Grant, *The Passing of the Great Race; or, The Racial Basis of European History* (New York: C. Scribner's Sons, 1916).

7

America and the United States in a World at War

It is sometimes said that the twentieth century lasted from 1914 to 1989. Marking off history with periods of a hundred years is obviously arbitrary. If history can be said to have periods, each period begins and ends with events that cause, or at least symbolize, a new direction. In the case of the twentieth century, the First World War, which began in 1914, marked an abrupt end to the optimism of the nineteenth century in which intellectual leaders had celebrated the triumph of reason.[515] The years that followed 1914 were sobering evidence that the human race was still afflicted by violent infighting that was made much worse by the advances of technology. At the other end of the century, the balance of terror that followed the Second World War came to an abrupt end with the collapse of the Soviet Empire in 1989. The world seemed ready for something different.

"America's" twentieth century began in 1898 and ended in 2001. This chapter examines "America" in the first half of the century; the next chapter continues the story after midcentury. The previous chapter laid out evidence that the "American century" began with the US wars in Cuba

---

515 A striking example is the statement of the great historian James Bury on the eve of the Great War: "The struggle of reason against authority has ended in what appears to be a decisive and permanent victory for liberty. In the most civilized and progressive countries, freedom of discussion is recognized as a fundamental principle" (James Bury, *A History of the Freedom of Thought* [New York: Henry Holt and Co., 1913], 247).

and the Philippines.[516] As for the end of the American century, the current perspective is that the United States abruptly changed on September 11, 2001, and can never return to what it had been. The contention that "America" is in decline may or may not be accurate. But clearly what has been shaken up is the United States in its relation to America. The idea and the term "America" (unlike "Soviet Union") has existed for five centuries and is not likely to disappear any time soon. The future of the United States, on the other hand, is anyone's guess.

It may seem ridiculous to try to cover twentieth-century history in this chapter and the next. Hundreds of books have been written about each decade and every major event of the century. My focus is the twentieth-century history of "America." That history can be described with a number of broad strokes. "America" was, and still is, the quasireligious idea that was a driving force of the United States in its mission to spread liberty around the world. In the twentieth century, there were two crises of faith for US belief in America. The first was the severe depression of the 1930s; the second was the hangover in the 1970s that followed upon war and chaos in the 1960s. Whether the United States is suffering another crisis of faith in the present era will be discussed in the last chapter.

This chapter examines what Winston Churchill once described as the second Thirty Years' War.[517] The Great War of 1914-18 was a warm-up for the much greater war in the years 1939-45. The years in between were an interlude that began with an armistice for the battlefield, but the era was hardly one of peace. The outbreak of military conflict in 1939 was

---

516 A strange fact about the phrase "American century" was that it did not get coined until 1941. Henry Luce, in *Life* magazine, February 17, 1941, is the author of the idea, which proved to have great staying power. Luce was supremely confident of where "America" stood in history: "Unlike the prestige of Rome or Genghis Khan or 19th century England, American prestige throughout the world is faith in the good intentions as well as the ultimate intelligence and ultimate strength of the American people." However, the essay was not entirely celebratory. Luce sought to evoke a "new vision of America as a world power which is authentically American," because at present "we Americans are unhappy about America. We are not happy about ourselves in relation to America." For recent reflections on Luce's idea, see Andrew Bacevich, ed., *The Short American Century: A Postmortem* (Cambridge, MA: Harvard University Press, 2012).

517 Winston Churchill, *The Gathering Storm* (Boston: Houghton Mifflin, 1948), iii.

an almost inevitable result of policies put in place after 1918. The United States came late to both wars, but it was able to mobilize its resources quickly. "America" was exalted in both instances so that by the end of World War II, the United States seemed to rule the world.

World War: Part 1

In 1915, the *New York World* ran a five-part series on Germany's "elaborate scheme to control and influence the press of the United States."[518] Like most conspiracy theories, it completely missed the mark in that the press was almost entirely oriented to the Allies' side; any criticism of Britain risked being called un-American. Even today the political right wing in the United States remains suspicious of the big ideas that came out of nineteenth-century Germany and led to progressive or "socialistic" causes. A contemporary author warns that "before the left's avant-garde became captivated by the Soviet Union, it fell in love with Germany."[519]

It took three years after the war's beginning in 1914 to generate the anti-German sentiment that eventually led to US entrance into the war. Germany violated international law by its submarine attacks on US ships—a tactic that Wilson denounced as opposed to "the rights of humanity." It should be noted that the allies also acted illegally in their blockades. As part of a big push called preparedness, the United States armed its ships and provided instruction on how to destroy submarines. Any profession of neutrality was undermined. The most famous incident in the submarine warfare was the 1915 sinking of the *Lusitania*, which raised a cry for retaliation against Germany. After a few months, the anger subsided. Later, when the Germans reinstituted their policy, they knew the consequences of the move but saw no other way to survive.

Paul Fussell, in his classic study of the Great War, notes that "every war is ironic because every war is worse than expected. Every war constitutes an irony because its means are melodramatically disproportionate to its presumed ends. In the Great War eight million were destroyed because

---

518 Walter Karp, *The Politics of War: The Story of Two Wars Which Altered Forever the Political Life of the American Republic* (New York: Franklin Square, 1979), 231.
519 Charles Kesler, *I am the Change: Barack Obama and the Crisis of Liberalism* (New York: Harper Collins, 2012).

two persons, the Archduke Francis Ferdinand and his consort had been shot."[520] It was assumed on both sides that the war would last only a few months; but Europe settled into a war of attrition in which each side waited for the other side to eventually exhaust its resources.

Fussell points out that the war cannot be narrated as a series of battles because it was unlike earlier wars, in which an army would win a victory and take control of enemy territory. Instead, tens of thousands of bodies were thrown against the new machinery of war, and when no advance was made, the commanders simply did the same thing again. Two of the most striking examples of this insane strategy were the struggle for Gallipoli in the Dardanelles and the senseless assault of the British and French at the Somme. In both cases, the initial move was a disastrous loss of life, but leaders refused to face the fact that continuing this course of action simply added to the casualty lists.

The struggle for Gallipoli at least made some strategic sense. The British and French forces were aiming at Istanbul to open the trade route to Russia. The great British navy could not accomplish the mission, and soldiers were brought in to make a landing under what were impossible conditions. The main body of soldiers was from a newly formed army of Australian and New Zealand troops (ANZAC). The date of the 1915 attack, April 25, is still memorialized in Australia as establishing the very identity of Australia. In John Keegan's description, the soldiers marched into Gallipoli as colonials, those who survived marched home as Australians.[521]

The fighting at Gallipoli within a two-square-mile area went on until the following January. The forces of the Ottoman Empire were the winners insofar as the allied attack was a failure. The loss of life on both sides was staggering. One statistic is emblematic of the whole war: The New Zealanders had 8,566 men in the fight, and they suffered 14,720 casualties. That is, getting wounded was the first step to a return to get wounded again—or, this time, to get killed.[522]

---

520 Paul Fussell, *The Great War: War and Modern Memory* (New York: Oxford University Press, 1975), 7.

521 John Keegan, *The First World War* (New York: Vintage Books, 2000), 249.

522 Keegan, *The First World War*, 248; Rachel Billington, *Glory: A Story of Gallipoli* (London: Orion Press, 2015).

On the Western Front in France, the struggle at the Somme was, according to Fussell, "the largest engagement fought since the beginning of civilization."[523] It was also one of the stupidest. After a stalemate of the opposing armies in their trenches for almost two years, the British decided to launch one great assault that would break through the German lines. The British bombarded the German trenches for a week with one and a half million shells that were supposed to "soften up" the defenses. In reality, the Germans were dug in so deeply that the bombardment had little effect. On July 1, 1916, at 7:30 a.m., the whistle blew and the British troops came up out of their trenches, having as their destination the German line a few hundred yards away. Unfortunately, at 7:31 a.m. the Germans, having foreseen what was about to happen and having gotten their machine guns in place, opened fire. The troops who were not cut down by bullets landed on the barbed wire. By the afternoon, sixty thousand men lay dead or wounded in the short space between the trenches.[524]

In 1916, Woodrow Wilson's campaign slogan was "He kept us out of war." That was obviously true, but it avoided the question of what was soon going to happen. War was everywhere in the air, and Wilson would not have dared to run as a pacifist. Two months after the election, the United States and Germany began the slide into war. Germany announced that it was reinstituting its submarine attacks against any vessels in the zones around Great Britain, France, Italy, and the eastern Mediterranean. On January 22, 1917, Wilson gave his "peace without victory" speech, in which he set out conditions for a viable peace. But the United States had by then lost its claim to be a neutral intermediary. Germany tipped the balance toward war with a cable to Mexico on January 16 that was intercepted by the British. In it, Foreign Minister Arthur Zimmerman proposed to the

---

523 Fussell, *The Great War*, 12.

524 There are many accounts of the Somme Offensive. Martin Middlebrook, *The First Day on the Somme* (Baltimore, MD: Penguin Books, 1971); William Philipott, *Bloody Victory: The Sacrifice on the Somme and the Making of the Twentieth Century* (Boston: Little Brown and Co., 2000). For grasping a sense of the event, the novel by Sebastian Faulks, *Birdsong: A Novel of Love and War* (New York: Vintage Books, 1997), may be more helpful than a straightforward report of the facts.

Mexicans an alliance "as soon as the war breaks out" in which Mexico might reacquire Texas, New Mexico, and Arizona.[525]

When President Wilson spoke before Congress on February 3, he was still talking peace, but he warned that any attack on US ships would lead to war. On the same date, the United States broke off diplomatic relations with Germany, and the stage was set for Wilson's speech of April 2 in which he proposed that "the world must be made safe for democracy." He concluded, "The day has come when America is privileged to spend her blood ... for the principles that gave her birth and happiness and the peace which she has treasured. God helping her she can do no other." One might argue that "she" could surely have done other. More importantly, she—"America"—was not "privileged to shed her blood." The blood was about to be shed by several hundred thousand young men from the United States.

As usual in such situations, the president did not ask Congress to declare war. He asked that "it formally accept the status of belligerent which has been thrust upon us."[526] A majority of Congress was supportive of war, the Senate voting 82-6 for war. Only one senator had the fortitude or folly to provide a point-by-point rebuttal to the president's speech. Robert LaFollette, a Republican progressive who had labored for reform of taxes and the regulation of corporations, took on his biggest fight as opponent of the war. A significant fact about LaFollette's lengthy speech is that it has almost nothing to say about "America"; it is about the actions of the United States and its government that had led to the brink of war.[527]

After a House of Representatives debate, which lasted until 3:00 a.m. on April 6, the vote was 373-50 for war. LaFollette and others who were opposed to the war were denounced in the press as near traitors. The day after the vote, the *New York Tribune* had a striking three-word headline: "America in Armageddon." Interestingly, the editors assumed that most people were familiar with the meaning of "Armageddon." Theodore Roosevelt's speech at the National Progressive Party Convention in 1912

---

525 Karp, *Politics of War*, 309.

526 Woodrow Wilson, "War Message," 65th Congress, 1st Session, Senate Document No. 5, Serial 7264, Washington, 1917.

527 For LaFollette's speech, see Walter Mills, *Road to War: America, 1914-1917* (New York: Houghton Mifflin, 1935), 451.

("We stand at Armageddon and we battle for the Lord") had helped to make the term widely known.[528] The word is biblical in origin, referring to the final conflict between good and evil. One meaning of "America" has always been "the end of history." Thus, instead of America *in* Armageddon, "America" *is* Armageddon.

The rhetoric of "America" in Woodrow Wilson's description of the war and its expected outcome gave support to belief in a world beyond the conflicts of history. That rhetoric has been a dangerous way of hiding political and economic problems in a religious language. It was hardly an encouraging sign of a fight for freedom and democracy that the United States passed an espionage act in June 1917, followed by a sedition act in 1918. It became a felony, punishable by twenty years in prison, to say anything that might postpone an "American" victory. In June 1917, the president of Columbia University said to the faculty, "This is the university's last and only warning to any among us, if such there be, who are not with whole heart and mind and strength committed to fight with us to make the world safe for democracy." Not surprisingly, such people did exist. Professor James McKeen Cattell was fired for sending a petition to three congressmen about excluding draftees from battle.[529]

After the war, the xenophobia only worsened. The hopes of progressives for reform continued for about six months after the war and then were thoroughly dashed. The US attorney general shipped several hundred people to the Soviet Union and scooped up four thousand supposed radicals. During the "Red Scare," the American Protective League generated a suspicion of disloyalty by three million US citizens. A revived Ku Klux Klan reached a membership of five million.[530] The year after the war produced the most labor strikes in history.

The socialist leader Eugene Debs, who had been sentenced in 1918 to ten years in prison for questioning the war effort, was freed by President

---

528 Theodore Roosevelt, "Case against Reactionaries," Chicago, June 17, 1912.

529 Louis Menand, *The Metaphysical Club: A Story of Ideas in America* (New York: Farrar, Straus and Giroux, 2002), 418; Morton White, *Social Thought in America: The Revolt against Formalism* (New York: Galaxy, 1976), 179.

530 Michael McGerr, *A Fierce Discontent: the Rise and Fall of the Progressive Movement in America, 1890-1920* (New York: Free Press, 2003), 306. Adam Hochschild, "When Dissent Became Treason," the *New York Review of Books*, September 28, 2017, 82-85.

Harding in 1921.[531] The Supreme Court eventually gave some protection for "free trade in ideas." It rather tardily endorsed freedom of speech while upholding the Espionage Act. The court warned that "the most stringent protection of free speech would not protect a man in falsely shouting fire in a theater and causing a panic."[532] The metaphor is clear enough and is regularly invoked, but it is unclear how it applies to protesters against war who are not trying to start a stampede of killing but to stop one.

The Great War caused an estimated sixteen million deaths and left another thirty-seven million people wounded. The only "good news" was that death by disease radically declined from its rate in nineteenth-century wars. However, a worldwide flu epidemic, which killed 5 percent of young people in the world, was spread through war camps.[533] In the war itself, United States deaths were a tiny fraction of the war's total casualties: one hundred seventeen thousand dead and two hundred five thousand wounded. The Second World War would dwarf all of those numbers, but the war that began in 1914 devastated any optimistic hope that the human race was making progress. In a sense, the world has never recovered from the war; world conflicts without end seem to have become inevitable.

The seeds of the future disaster were already present in the way that the war had been fought and especially in the way that it concluded. George Kennan, writing in 1951, could bring a perspective on the war that the victors had not had in 1918: "The progress of World War I did not bring reasonableness or humility or the spirit of compromise to the warring peoples ... The Allies came to be interested only in a total victory of national humiliation, of crushing reparations."[534]

Before the war, Wilson had said, "My dream is that ... America will come into the full light of day when all shall know that she puts human rights above all other rights, and that her flag is the flag not only of

531 White, *Social Thought in America*, 177. The court decision, the last of three espionage cases, is *Abrams v. United States* 250 US 616 (1919).
532 *Schenck v. United States* 249 US 47 (1919).
533 John Barry, *The Great Influenza: The Story of the Greatest Pandemic in History* (New York: Penguin Books, 2005), 398.
534 George Kennan, *American Diplomacy, 1900-1950* (Chicago: University of Chicago Press, 1951), 62.

America but of humanity."[535] In Wilson's vocabulary, the nation called "America" was "a determining factor in the history of mankind ... the light of the world." The war gave Wilson the world stage that he had hoped for. He encouraged his compatriots to think of themselves as "citizens of the world." The case was difficult to make to a citizenry whose wish was simply to get "back to normalcy."

In a speech in January 1918, Wilson laid out a peace plan of fourteen points, the last of which was the creation of "a general association of nations ... for the purpose of affording mutual guarantees of political independence and territorial integrity to great and small states alike." This general association came into existence as the League of Nations. Many of Wilson's fourteen points were reasonable, but either they could not have been achieved immediately or the problems could not be solved within his rhetorical framework. His first point began with the well-known phrase "open covenants of peace, openly arrived at" which sounds desirable, but he ends the sentence with "no private international understandings of any kind but diplomacy shall proceed always frankly and in the public view." That stipulation goes too far; it is inherent to the nature of diplomacy that it cannot proceed if every step in the process is exposed to public view.[536]

Some form of international association was an idea whose time had come, but Wilson and others at that time did not grasp the complexity of such an association and how many steps would be needed for such an organization to gain any credibility. For example, Wilson made a shocking confession before the Senate Foreign Relations Committee. He said, concerning a statement he had made at the peace conference, that all nations have a right to self-determination: "When I gave utterance to those words I said them without the knowledge that nationalities existed, which are coming to us day after day ... You do not know and cannot appreciate the anxieties I have experienced as the result of many millions

---

535 A speech at Independence Hall, July 4, 1914: www.presidency.uscb.edu/ws/?pid=65381.

536 John Milton Cooper, *Breaking the Heart of the World: Woodrow Wilson and the Fight for the League of Nations* (Cambridge, MA: Cambridge University Press, 2001).

of people having their hopes raised by what I have said."[537] At least Wilson was honest enough to admit his mistake, but presidential rhetoric can have effects much more traumatic than causing anxiety for a president. Wilson was not able to convince his own people of the wisdom of an international organization to prevent wars.

It is interesting that while the United States never joined the League of Nations, twenty other American nations became members. Yankee imperialism was one reason for the league's popularity in the rest of America. The League of Nations seemed to "provide more guarantee of territorial integrity of Latin America than a unilaterally interpreted Monroe Doctrine."[538]

Senator Henry Cabot Lodge, in his criticism of Woodrow Wilson's rhetoric, used a helpful distinction between a man having ideals and a man being an idealist.[539] Wise leaders offer ideals that lead to action for bettering a human situation. Idealism is a philosophical system that places ideas above existing realities. Wilson said, "Sometimes people call me an idealist. Well, that is the way I know I am an American. America, my fellow citizen … is the only idealistic nation in the world."[540] Wilson's idealism led

537 Kalevi Holsti, *The State, War, and the State of War* (Cambridge, MA: Cambridge University Press, 1996), 53; Geir Lundestad, *The Rise and Fall of the American "Empire"* (New York: Oxford University Press, 2012), 153: "Nobody knows how many 'nations' there are in the world since it is up to the various inhabitants to decide how they want to define themselves, but it has been estimated that there are at least 3,500. In only half of the world's states are there a single ethnic group that comprises at least 75 percent of the populations."

538 Arthur Whitaker, *The Western Hemisphere Idea: Its Rise and Decline* (New York: Cornell University Press, 1954), 74.

539 William Widenor, *Henry Cabot Lodge and the Search for an American Foreign Policy* (Berkeley, CA: University of California Press, 1980), 352.

540 Woodrow Wilson, *Public Papers* (New York: Harper and Brothers, 1925), VI: 52. Much of Wilson's rhetoric echoes sentiments that John Stuart Mill expressed about England (e.g., "acts only in service to others," "no benefit to itself," "a novelty in the world," and "policies that are blameless and laudable"). Mill's claims were more exposed to criticism because he was describing the real nation of England. Wilson was describing America, which is an idea about the nation of the United States. John Stuart Mill, "A Few Words on Non-Intervention," *Foreign Policy Perspectives* 8. London: Libertarian Alliance, 1859.

him to confuse an ideal America with a nation-state that acts according to its interests—something that is intrinsic to being a nation-state.

Upbeat 1920s, Pessimistic 1930s

The United States does not deserve all the blame for the international failures that led to the second part of the world war in 1939. Nevertheless, the US was now a major player in world affairs and had to take a share of the blame. The two-decade interlude between wars or within the war was a peculiar time of radically shifting moods. While the shift does not exactly correspond to a change between the decades of the 1920s and the 1930s, the enthusiasm of the early '20s was clearly gone toward the end of the '30s.

In the 1920s, the United States turned away from ambitious progressive programs and returned to its deeper belief in America. Calvin Coolidge, in his inaugural address, followed the same path as Wilson had in claiming that America was something the world had never seen before—namely, an altruistic nation concerned only with peace and moral order. Coolidge made no reference to the United States in his speech. He finished with a declaration that "America seeks no earthly empire ... The higher state to which she seeks the allegiance of all mankind is not of human, but of divine origin. She cherishes no purpose save to merit the favor of Almighty God."[541]

Even allowing for the exalted rhetoric that is typical of inaugural addresses, the delusion manifest in this claim is striking. America is beyond national selfishness; it is concerned with a new world order in which peace will reign. Belief that America could lead the world was not well reflected in the United States' refusal to engage in international politics. Perhaps the weaknesses of the League of Nation's charter would have doomed the organization anyway, but if the United States had been involved, a reform might have happened.

The United States did sponsor the first of several conferences on naval disarmament. A limit on naval forces was perceived to be the key to peace. Several treaties were signed at the Washington Conference in 1923; the most important was a treaty joining Japan, Great Britain, and the United

---

541 Calvin Coolidge, Inaugural Address: www.bartleby.com/124/pres47.html. Accessed 12 Dec, 2017.

States in limiting tonnage of battleships and the guns on cruisers. A second meeting in Geneva in 1927 was somewhat frustrating but led to increased efforts at the London conference in 1930.[542] It also led to a treaty that outlawed war.[543] At the beginning of the 1930s, there seemed to be evidence for progress toward permanent peace.

Two factors intervened. The technology of war drastically changed in the 1930s. During the 1920s, there had been no discussion of aircraft carriers—a development that along with newer submarines changed the face of war. The second factor was the Great Depression of the 1930s. One might think that economic collapse would cool the appetite for war. However, there was a cruel irony in the effect of economic bad times: "Disarmament fell from favor in Britain because the public and politicians beheld shipyards as important for employment."[544]

Until the bubble burst in 1929, the United States concentrated on its own cultural upheaval and economic prosperity. One of the changes at the beginning of the decade seemed to herald a new burst of progressivism. The Nineteenth Amendment, which was ratified by the states in 1920, finally enfranchised women. By the time the United States followed many other countries, such as Great Britain, Sweden, and New Zealand, there was little resistance left. Some groups had argued that the women's vote was needed to correct the problems of society. Other groups had argued that the women's vote would not upset anything because women would not vote as a bloc. The two contrasting arguments together carried the day.

The women who had adopted the recently coined term "feminist" looked forward to a transformation of women's lives and of society as a whole. Progress did come about, but it proved to be a long journey to equality of opportunity, equal pay, and entrance into the most prestigious

---

542 Richard Fanning, *Peace and Disarmament: Naval Rivalry and Arms Control 1922–1933* (Lexington, KY: University of Kentucky Press, 1995), 160. Fanning notes that even the setback at the 1927 conference led to a French–British naval pact. That agreement angered the United States.

543 An agreement between French prime minister Aristide Briand and US secretary of state Frank Kellogg led to this treaty to outlaw war. The treaty has usually been dismissed as hopelessly idealistic, although it was given a serious hearing in Oona Hathaway and Scott Shapiro, *The Internationalists: How a Radical Plan to Outlaw War Remade the World* (New York: Simon and Schuster, 2017).

544 Fanning, *Peace and Disarmament*, 162.

professions and national political offices. What was striking in the 1920s was the freeing up of sexual mores.[545] Many women made use of the new sexual freedom, although a larger social revolution would not be completed until the 1960s and beyond. Other cultural changes were brought on by the automobile and the movies—innovations that carried the stamp of America.

Some key events in the United States showed that the country was something less than America. Immigration policy was one indication of the limits of the great "melting pot." The simplistic evolutionary theories associated with social Darwinism were still very much alive in the assumption of who could be a true American in contrast to those who were "hyphenated Americans." The IQ test, which was developed during the Great War, was put to use in the 1920s to show that immigrants from Southern and Eastern Europe were mentally, physically, and morally inferior. Lewis Terman, a founder of the IQ test, warned that "all the feeble-minded are at least potential criminals ... Moral judgments, like business judgments, social judgments or any other kind of higher thought process, is a function of intelligence."[546]

The immigration act of 1924 set quotas for the immigration of each ethnic group. A series of bills had become increasingly restrictive until the final version in 1924 set a limit of 2 percent of each group that was resident in the United States before 1890.[547] The effect of basing the quota on that date was to drastically reduce immigration from the countries of Eastern and Southern Europe. A massive report by the US Immigration Commission warned about the difference between the "old immigration" and these new immigrants whose "only purpose in coming to America [was] to temporarily take advantage of the greater wages." The whole discussion of immigration was clouded in nativism and racism. Edward Ross, a leading social scientist, wrote "that the Mediterranean peoples

---

545 Nancy Cott, *The Grounding of Modern Feminism* (New Haven, CT: Yale University Press, 1989), 149.

546 Clarence Karier and Joel Spring, *Roots of Crisis* (Chicago: Rand McNally, 1973), 115.

547 Roger Daniels, *Not Like Us: Immigrants and Minorities in America 1890–1924* (Chicago: Ivan Dee, 1997).

are morally below the races of northern Europe is as certain as any social fact."[548]

Chinese immigrants had been largely excluded starting in 1875; the 1924 act made this exclusion complete. Only after 1965 did immigration from Asian countries recommence. An Indian Citizenship Act was passed in 1924, but it was not put into practice by the states until 1948. As for Negroes, they were contributing much of the best in American culture, but they were not getting a fair share of the country's wealth. The large cities in the northern United States, where millions of Negroes went in search of work, were badly neglected. The United States had reverted to a more individualistic kind of country.

Two significant events of the 1920s are linked in relation to evolutionary theory, which pitted "progressives" against the poor and uneducated. In 1925, a trial in Dayton, Tennessee, was one of the most important religious events of the twentieth century. John Scopes, a secondary-level schoolteacher of biology, was tried on the charge of violating the law in Tennessee by teaching evolution. The trial became a circus for journalists and social commentators. People today who know anything about the trial are likely to have their knowledge of it from the 1960 movie *Inherit the Wind*. The movie was based on a 1955 play that made the Scopes trial an analogy of McCarthyism. The movie was brilliantly done but somewhat biased in its portrayal of people who defended the law, especially William Jennings Bryan.

As "social Darwinists" drew out the application of evolution to human society, the fight against evolution had become a centerpiece of resistance for conservative Protestant Christians. No ground could be given in defending every word of the Bible. The term "fundamentalist" was coined in 1920 and proved to have staying power. "Fundamentalism" was a term that summed up the steadily increasing movement of the previous fifty years, which was helped by anti-German sentiment during and after the war. German philosophy and theology were seen to embody the modernist attack on Christianity. The fundamentalists were confident that they could control school curricula, and they moved to outlaw the teaching of evolution in schools.

---

548 Edward Ross, *The Old World in the New* (New York: The Century Co., 1914), 293.

The Scopes trial was a calculated move by the newly founded American Civil Liberties Union to test the law prohibiting the teaching of evolution. The forces opposed to evolution did not have much chance against the superior brain power of their opponents. Clarence Darrow, a powerful courtroom orator, led the attack. The spokesperson for the defense of the law was William Jennings Bryan, who was neither a historian nor a biblical scholar.

Commentators like H. L. Mencken zeroed in on Bryan. Richard Hofstadter described him as "a man who at sixty-five had long outlived his time."[549] The ridicule of Bryan is not entirely fair. Bryan's concern had long been that Darwinism was being used to justify laissez-faire economics, imperialism, and militarism. In 1904, he had described Darwinism as "the merciless law by which the strong crowd and kill off the weak."[550] He resigned from the office of secretary of state in Woodrow Wilson's cabinet rather than give his consent for entrance into the war. From the perspective of the northern press, the Scopes trial was a definitive defeat of fundamentalism. But as became evident a half century later, the religious and cultural division in the country had only been driven underground.[551]

The significance of Bryan's resistance to the applications of evolutionary theory is demonstrated in a 1927 Supreme Court decision, *Buck v. Bell.* The case concerned a Virginia law that authorized the involuntary sterilization of the "feebleminded." A young black woman, Carrie Buck, who had been raped, became pregnant at age seventeen and was sterilized. She was judged to be one of those feebleminded people, but her subsequent normal life demonstrated otherwise.[552] The court ruled 8 to 1 in favor of the law. The one dissenting vote was cast by Justice Pierce Butler who was the Catholic on the Supreme Court. The fact that a conservative Catholic was the one dissenting vote confirmed for many liberals that the

549 Richard Hofstadter, *American Political Tradition and the Men Who Made It* (New York: Vintage Books, 1989).

550 Edward Larson, *Summer for the Gods: The Scopes Trial and America's Continuing Debate over Science and Religion* (New York: Basic Books, 2006), 27.

551 Larson, *Summer*, 230.

552 Adam Cohen, *Imbeciles: The Supreme Court, American Eugenics, and the Sterilization of Carrie Buck* (New York: Penguin Books, 2016).

decision was truly progressive.[553] The background to this decision was the eugenics movement, which had originated in the United States in the late nineteenth century. There were many public campaigns in the 1920s to impose eugenic restrictions on reproduction. In the 1930s, Adolf Hitler gave eugenics a bad name.[554]

The most shocking part of *Buck v. Bell* was the majority opinion written by Oliver Wendell Holmes Jr. Holmes said that the state had every right to call upon those who would sap its strength to sacrifice for the common good. He stated that "it is better for all the world if instead of waiting to execute degenerate offspring for crime, or let them starve for their imbecility, society can prevent those who are manifestly unfit from continuing their kind. The principle that sustains compulsory vaccination is broad enough to cover cutting the Fallopian tubes. Three generations of imbeciles are enough." Far from regretting such harsh words, Holmes later wrote that "[he] was getting near to the first principle of real reform" and that the decision "gave [him] pleasure."[555]

The domestic events of the United States might seem to be irrelevant to what was happening in international affairs. But one of the most important writers on the 1920s, Edward Carr, charged that "nearly all popular theories of international politics between the two world wars were reflexions, seen in an American mirror, of nineteenth-century liberal thought."[556] What he is referring to is Woodrow Wilson's setting the context of the 1920s, in which it was believed that an abstract system of collective security devised by the Allies could keep the peace.[557]

The 1920s approach to peace is often dismissed with the single word "pacifism." Walter Lippmann would later write that "the preachment and the practice of pacifists in Britain and America were a cause of the

553 Carl Degler, *In Search of Human Nature: The Decline and Revival of Darwinism in American Social Thought* (New York: Oxford University Press, 1992), 47.

554 On the intimate relation of Hitler's laws and US eugenics theory, see James Whitman, *Hitler's American Model: The United States and the Making of Nazi Race Law* (Princeton, NJ: Princeton University Press, 2017).

555 Degler, *In Search*, 47.

556 Edward H. Carr, *The Twenty Years Crisis1919–1939*, 2nd ed. (London: Macmillan, 1945), 27.

557 Carr, *The Twenty Years' Crisis*, 74.

[Second] World War."[558] At least he limited pacifism to being only one cause of the war. That still grants a lot of power to the "preachment and practice of pacifists." William James pointed out in his famous essay on the moral equivalent of war that "pacifism makes no converts from the military party."[559]

The weakness of pacifism starts with its name. "Pacifism" was coined in 1901 at the Tenth Universal Peace Conference in Glasgow. Since then, "pacifism" has called up the idea of simply negating the military power that leads to war.[560] Groups that withdraw as far as they can from political life and try to give an example of peaceful existence can be admirable, and their lives may have political reverberations. But that way of life does not directly supply an ethical basis for international exchanges.

Force

The single most important term for discussing international morality is "force," a term that is constantly used but without much reflection on its meaning. If in a contest between the military party and the peace party the term "force" is ceded to the military side, there is no possibility of peace having an effective voice in public affairs. Force is always present in human life. In most contexts, the term "force" does not connote violence. Unfortunately, in international discussions, the term "force" almost always is associated with violence and is even regularly used as a synonym or euphemism for "war." If "force" means "war," the game is over; the military party wins.[561]

Carr attacked Lord Cecil's speech to the Imperial Conference in 1923, in which he said that the method of the League of Nations "is a method of consent and its executive instrument is not force, but public opinion."[562] In

---

558 Walter Lippmann, *U.S. Foreign Policy: Shield of the Republic* (Boston: Little, Brown, and Co.,1953), 53.

559 William James, *Pragmatism* (New York: Dover Publications, 1995), 295.

560 David Cortright, *Peace: A History of Movements and Ideas* (Cambridge, MA: Cambridge University Press, 2008), 8.

561 John Dewey, "Force and Coercion," in *Middle Works*, vol. 10 (Carbondale, IL: Southern Illinois University, 1980), 246. John Dewey had tried to distinguish force and violence, but he did not pursue that distinction after the World War.

562 Carr, *Twenty Years' Crisis*, 35.

reality, public opinion is itself a force, but it is one that needs the support of other forces. An extraordinary misuse of "force" is in the Atlantic Charter, where Winston Churchill and Franklin Roosevelt pronounced that "all the nations of the world ... must come to the abandonment of force."[563] Such rhetoric might be amusing if it were not so deadly. These men were not pacifists holding up signs of protest but leaders of nations who used a range of force in daily governance but seemed unwilling to investigate and admit their own practice.

One of the most influential essays of the twentieth century that still shapes today's language of ethics arose from a lecture by Max Weber to German students in 1919. Weber's intention was to warn students that simply being against war does not stop wars. He invited to return in ten years "those ... who [felt] that they [were] genuine followers of the 'politics of intention' and share in the frenzy which this revolution amounts to."[564] Ten years later, in 1929, Weber was dead and Germany was on its way to war.

Weber created a radical dichotomy—namely, that all morality "can be subsumed under one of two maxims, which are fundamentally different from and irreconcilably opposed to each other. Ethics may be based on intentions or responsibility."[565] The morality of intention, he said, is exemplified by the Sermon on the Mount, which excludes force of any kind. In contrast, "politics has quite different goals which can only be achieved by force." Weber never distinguishes between force and violence. Ever since Weber's essay, the Sermon on the Mount has been routinely referred to as "otherworldly," and while it might be admirable in the lives of otherworldly individuals, politicians have to be "responsible."[566]

---

563 Atlantic Charter, eighth paragraph.

564 Max Weber, "Politics as a Vocation," in *Max Weber: Selections in Translation*, ed. W. G. Runcinan (Cambridge, MA: Cambridge University Press, 1978), 224.

565 Weber, "Politics as a Vocation," 222. There is no logical opposition between intention and responsibility. And Weber ends the essay (224) by saying that in the vocation of the politician, the two come together.

566 For a more accurate commentary on the Sermon on the Mount, see Walter Wink, *Jesus and Nonviolence: A Third War* (Minneapolis, MN: Fortress Press, 2003), 10–11. It is ironic that Weber excludes a *true* Christian from being responsible. Jewish and Christian religions were central to the development of

Weber's essay found an echo in the United States in Reinhold Niebuhr's *Moral Man and Immoral Society*, which has reverberated throughout the decades since it appeared in 1932.[567] It is astounding that a Christian minister and theologian had such an influence on the foreign policy of the United States. The self-proclaimed "realism" of US policymakers has been influenced by Niebuhr's dichotomy of the moral individual and the immoral society.

Niebuhr had some doubts later in life, especially during the Vietnam War, about his dichotomy; he admitted that he should have read more Jewish and Catholic literature. He said jokingly that perhaps the title of his book should have been "The Not so Moral Man in His Less than Moral Communities."[568] But he was unable to offer a new framework, and he left a lasting imprint on US policy since World War II. In Niebuhr's theology, individuals are not moral on their own; only God's grace of redemption can lead to a life of unselfishness, but "the unselfishness of individuals makes for the selfishness of nations." The Christian can live a life according to the Sermon on the Mount, but there is no carryover to society; in fact, the contrary is true. "As individuals, men believe that they ought to love and serve each other and establish justice between each other. As racial, economic and national groups, they take for themselves whatever their power can command."[569]

Secular political leaders skipped over the part of Niebuhr's contention that the individual needs to be redeemed from original sin. What they loved was the idea that as individuals they could be moral even while they were unleashing large-scale violence. War is terrible—as they always say—but sometimes it is a tragic necessity in a world that is governed not by morality but only by "power." The belief is that the only security in

---

the idea of responsibility. See Gabriel Moran, *A Grammar of Responsibility* (New York: Crossroad, 1996).

567 Reinhold Niebuhr, *Moral Man and Immoral Society: A Study in Ethics and Politics* (New York: Charles Scribner's Sons, 1960 (1932).

568 Reinhold Niebuhr, *Man's Nature and His Communities* (New York: Charles Scribner's Sons, 1965), 22. In several other places, Niebuhr tried to soften the contrast into one of degree, not kind: *Interpretation of Christian Ethics* (New York: Seabury Press, 1979), 76.

569 Niebuhr, *Moral Man*, 91, 9.

such a world is for one's own nation to have more guns, ships, and planes than any other nation.

Moral Man and Immoral Society arrived just as Hitler was skillfully taking control of Germany. In an amazingly short period between 1933 and 1936, German prosperity was re-established, the army was reconstituted, opposition to the Nazi movement was destroyed, and the unfair treaties that had been forced upon Germany by the Allies were abrogated. Hitler was simply being "realistic," and some intellectual leaders (most famously Martin Heidegger) and church leaders welcomed Hitler's plan to reverse the humiliating position that Germany had been placed in.[570] An impressive body of reporters from the United States saw what was happening after Hitler came to power, but their reporting did not capture the attention of the United States until 1941. William Shirer made daily reports from Berlin on what was happening as early as September 1934: "He [Hitler] is restoring pageantry and colour and mysticism to the drab lives of twentieth-century Germans."[571]

The moment for the Allies to offer resistance was early in the 1930s. George Kennan, who was a young diplomat on the scene, later wrote: "Firmness at the time of the re-occupation of the Rhineland would probably have yielded even better results than firmness at the time of Munich."[572] However, there was little energy for Allied resistance. The German movements into the Rhineland, Austria, Czechoslovakia, and eventually Poland were justified by Germany as simply restoring what was rightfully Germany's. The Molotov-Ribbentrop nonaggression pact of

---

570 Exactly how close Heidegger was to the Nazis has been debated. He certainly welcomed Hitler's advent in 1933, when Heidegger was installed as rector of the University of Freiburg. More pertinent to my interest is Heidegger's equivalence of "America" and Russia in the 1930s and even after the war. He introduced this idea in *Introduction to Metaphysics* in 1935: "From a metaphysical vantage, Russia and America are the same dreary technological frenzy, the same organization of the average man." He suggested in his 1948 "Letter on Humanism" that "America" is worse than Marxism because it does not engage history.

571 William Shirer, *Berlin Diary: The Journal of a Foreign Correspondent 1934– 1941* (New York: Knopf, 1941), 18; Andrew Nagorski, *Hitlerland: American Eyewitnesses to the Nazi Rise to Power.* (New York: Simon and Schuster, 2012).

572 George Kennan, *American Diplomacy 1900–1950* (Chicago: University of Chicago Press, 1951), 79.

August 1939 was an ominous sign that worse was coming. France, Great Britain, and other European countries had no strategy except to try to "appease" Germany with new agreements.[573]

In 1932, Albert Einstein wrote a letter to Sigmund Freud asking Freud to join with a group of intellectuals in a peace forum. Freud politely but cavalierly dismissed the idea: "Any effort to replace brute force by the might of an ideal is, under present conditions, doomed to fail. Our logic is at fault if we ignore the fact that right is founded on brute force and even needs today violence to maintain it."[574] Freud's claim that right is based on "brute force" that is maintained by violence is shockingly cynical and pessimistic. Humans resort to "brute" force when other human sources of force have been neglected. And, unfortunately, when humans make use of "brute force," they do so without the restrictions built into brutes so that the effect of human violence far outstrips the destruction that a brute's force can cause. Humans have to use physical, political, economic, and diplomatic forces in international relations.

The United States, where the Great Depression began in 1929, was too distracted by domestic problems to pay much attention to European problems or to Japanese attacks on Manchuria and China. After 1932, the United States did have the benefit of an extraordinary president who was able to initiate some badly needed programs, such as Social Security, that had been stoutly resisted during the Progressive era. A striking feature of Roosevelt's rhetoric was his constant reference to "the nation" and "the United States." In his key speeches, there is almost no use of the term "America."[575] Roosevelt was interested in solving real problems in the nation of the United States. There was serious doubt about the survival of the "American dream" in a country that Roosevelt described as "one-third of a nation ill-housed, ill-clad, ill-nourished."

---

573 John Keegan, *The Second World War* (New York: Penguin Books, 1989), 43.

574 Sigmund Freud, "Why War?" *Standard Edition of the Works of Sigmund Freud*, vol. 22: 199–215.

575 In Franklin Roosevelt's first inaugural address on March 4, 1933, the word "America" does not appear. In his famous "four freedoms" address on January 6, 1941, he uses "America" once. In his message to Congress the day after Pearl Harbor, the word "America" appears only in the phrase "United States of America."

The United States had no appetite for war, but it had not lost its fascination with violence at home. The twentieth-century inventions of radio, movies, and television sometimes made it difficult to sort out the difference between real and fictional violence. Some criminals in the 1920s and 1930s became popular heroes. Bank robbers, bootleggers, and other criminals with a romantic flair held the country's attention. Against the spread of crime, one-man armies fit in with an American belief in the incorruptible individual. A lone hero is needed to clean up the mess, whether it is in the metropolis or on the frontier. The imaginations of US Americans in the 1930s were filled with American heroes in novels and movies.

Probably no fictional character ever fit the American myth better than Superman, introduced in June 1938 to fight for "truth, justice and the American way." The meek Clark Kent, at a moment's notice and with a phone booth, was revealed as a man of steel. However, this incomparable force for good restricted his fight against evil to petty urban crimes, not international uprisings or organized crime at home. Similarly, the Lone Ranger, with silver bullets and a fast horse, was unstoppable in wiping out criminals simply because it was the right thing to do. Almost every boy in the country was familiar with the William Tell Overture, which introduced the Lone Ranger on Monday, Wednesday, and Friday evenings. Between 1933 and 1954, 2,956 episodes of the masked man's lonely battle against injustice were broadcast.[576]

It can easily be forgotten in today's media world that radio was such a great influence on the popular mind during the 1930s and 1940s. (Right-wing talk radio continues to play a more important role today than is usually recognized.) Hitler, Churchill, and Roosevelt were radio preachers; they would have had a difficult time succeeding in a television and internet world. During the Depression years, Roosevelt made good use of the radio. He was able to command the attention of a big part of the country with his "fireside chats." But radio was (and still is) a medium that can serve the rants of extremist politicians. One preacher who achieved a following of tens of millions was Father Charles Coughlin, whose original support of Roosevelt was reversed in the mid-1930s. With the slogan "America First,"

---

576 John Lawrence and Robert Jewett, *The Myth of the American Superhero* (Grand Rapids, MI: Eerdmans Press, 2002), 188.

Coughlin began as a critic of both capitalism and Communism. His turn against Roosevelt was accompanied by anti-Semitism and an approval of fascist developments in the world.[577]

World War, Part II: The Greater Insanity

By 1939, the stage had been set for the unrolling of a conflict the enormity of which no one could have imagined. It was not Wilson's war that ended all war, but it may have been the next-to-last war. Albert Einstein said that he did not know what weapons would be used in World War III but he did know that World War IV would be fought with sticks and stones. Steven Toulmin points out that "thirty years of slaughter in the name of religion preceded the setting up of the modern system of nation-states; thirty years of slaughter in the name of nationhood were needed before Europeans and Americans were ready to acknowledge its shortcomings."[578] Toulmin's comparison of the periods 1618–1648 and 1914–1945 is appropriate, although one might suggest two qualifications. Nationalism is itself a form of religion; in addition, nationhood survived the war and continues to be central to today's conflicts.

As in the First World War, the United States played a secondary role, as reflected in the casualties of the war; the fact that the United States sent sixteen million men into the war and suffered 300,000 dead and 1.2 million wounded is indicative of the enormity of the war and how bad was the destruction in the countries with the primary losses. On the allied side, the Soviet Union bore the heaviest burden with at least 14 million military and civilian casualties. France, from being invaded, and Great Britain, from air strikes, suffered terrible losses of people and property. Countries in Eastern Europe were savaged by Germany from the west and the Soviet army from the east. Poland lost about five and a half million people—20 percent of its population.

Where the United States played the major role was in the production of arms, including tanks, ships, and aircraft. The United States was

---

577 Donald Warren, *Radio Priest: Charles Coughlin, the Father of Hate Radio* (New York: Free Press, 1996).

578 Steven Toulmin, *Cosmopolis: The Hidden Agenda of Modernity* (Chicago: University of Chicago Press, 1990), 160.

already supplying material to Great Britain and the Soviet Union before it entered the war in 1941. The United States sent one hundred eighty-three thousand modern trucks to the Soviet Union; even more important were thirteen million felt boots made in the United States according to Soviet specifications. The battles at Moscow and Leningrad in the harsh winter were won in part by the Soviet army having superior protection against frostbite.

At the end of the 1930s, the United States economy had still not recovered from the Depression. Suddenly the military market was open, and the United States was astoundingly productive of armaments. During the war, the man-hour productivity of the United States was twice that of Germany and five times that of Japan. In 1940, the US share of the production of war material was negligible; by 1945 its share of the world's arms productions was 40 percent. It has never looked back when the production of armaments is on the table.

By the end of the war, other nations were exhausted and in ruins. The United States had not been invaded or bombed. Its economy was in great shape. It was easy to believe that "America" reigned over the whole world. It has been common to refer to the war as "the good war," which seems a grotesque way to refer to an event that killed fifty million people.[579] In recent years, the phrase "greatest generation" was coined as a tribute to the men who fought in the war and the women who kept the machines going in the factories. The phrase is either mawkish or meaningless. What can be rightly asserted is that the country pulled itself together and helped its allies to stop the rampage of Hitler and the escapades of the Japanese leaders.

The Second World War is dated from September 1, 1939, when Germany invaded Poland even after Britain and France had warned that the step would mean war. Germany had assurance from the Soviet Union that it would not oppose a German move on Poland; in fact, the Soviet

---

579 One source for the phrase "good war" was Studs Terkel, *"The Good War": An Oral History of WWII* (New York: New Press, 1997). Many times the book is cited without the crucial quotation marks around the title. Terkel may have been too optimistic in thinking people would understand the title as ironic; he said in a note at the beginning of the book that he used quotation marks because "the adjective 'good' mated to the noun 'war' is so incongruous."

Union would annex a large part of eastern Poland for itself. When Germany faced west, it moved with lightning speed (*blitzkrieg*) against Belgium, the Netherlands, and France, and all three countries quickly capitulated. The British army was nearly overcome, but it managed to escape from the port at Dunkirk and live to fight another day. The British were heavily bombed in 1940 before what was planned to be a German invasion of England.

During the period of 1939–1941, the United States proclaimed that it was a neutral nation, although Roosevelt said in 1939, "I cannot ask that every American remain neutral in thought as well … Even a neutral cannot be asked to close his mind or his conscience." Hitler had his backers in the United States during the 1930s. Henry Ford, William Hearst, and Joseph Kennedy expressed admiration if not complete approval of the rising power of Germany. Most famous was Charles Lindbergh, who had become a quintessential American hero with his solo flight over the Atlantic in 1927. Lindbergh, who had soured on the US after the hoopla surrounding the kidnapping and death of his infant son, was susceptible to German propaganda and the exploitation of his name.

The people of the United States were not interested in getting involved in another European war. However, there was little resistance to a buildup of arms in 1940. The size of the US fleet was doubled, the army was increased from two hundred thousand to one million men, and money was appropriated for seventy-eight hundred aircraft. Some people have speculated that President Roosevelt was looking for a way for the United States to enter the war. That does not seem to have been Roosevelt's character; unlike his European counterparts, Roosevelt was never an enthusiast of the war. He told Churchill that he would wage war but not declare it. If the Germans did not like US actions, they could attack US forces. To his secretary of the treasury, Henry Morgenthau, Roosevelt had said, "I am waiting to be pushed into the situation." The Germans seemed to do that in August of 1941 when they sank the USS *Reuben James*, killing 115 sailors. That could have been an immediate cause for war, but Roosevelt still held back.

In August 1941, Franklin Roosevelt and Winston Churchill met on a ship at Placentia Bay, near Newfoundland. The meeting produced a document—actually a telegram—called the Atlantic Charter. Although it was only eight short paragraphs, the document had powerful effects both immediately and in the long run. Churchill had wanted the meeting to get the United States support of the Allied cause. He was also trying to shore up sagging morale back home. What Churchill was not enthusiastic about was Roosevelt's use of the occasion to put forward a statement of global principles in the form of "four freedoms:" Freedom of speech and of belief, as well as freedom from fear and from want.

Roosevelt resisted inclusion of a declaration to set up an "effective international organization." He finally did agree to a call for the disarmament of aggressors, "pending the establishment of a wider and permanent system of general security."[580] The seed for the founding of the United Nations was contained in that promise, and in January of 1942, twenty-six nations at a meeting in Washington issued a United Nations declaration to conquer the Axis powers. By February 1942, Roosevelt had the name for the new international organization: the United Nations.[581]

The part of the Atlantic Charter that caused unease, if not embarrassment, for Churchill was the promise of a "peace which will afford assurance that all men in all lands may live out their lives in freedom from fear and want." In 1941, the English had no plans to relinquish their empire. However, in subsequent struggles against colonialism, prominent leaders, such as Nelson Mandela, took notice of the charter's promise of freedom for all men in all lands. Churchill would subsequently say that the Atlantic Charter "is not a law – it is a star" to provide guidance.[582] The fact that Churchill left the meeting before Roosevelt, who put both of their names on the document, suggests that Churchill was playing down the document's proclamation of universal principles. Churchill did get his immediate aim—the increase of US material for the war, including extension of lend lease to the Soviet Union, which was in desperate need of help.

---

580 Townsend Hoopes and Douglas Brinkley, *FDR and the Creation of the U.N.* (New Haven, CT: Yale University Press, 1987), 36–40.
581 Stephen Schlesinger, *Act of Creation: The Founding of the United Nations* (New York: Basic Books, 2003), 38.
582 Elizabeth Borgwardt, *A New Deal for the World: America's Vision for Human Rights* (Cambridge, MA: Harvard University Press, 2007), 45.

The Battles on Land and Sea

Throughout 1941, the Soviet Union was fighting for its life against the assault of the German army. The nonaggression pact of 1939 was quickly forgotten as Germany, having formed a new pact with Japan and Italy, moved against its former ally. The Germans found that blitzkrieg by itself does not conquer another country. The lightning strike works only if it is followed by surrounding the enemy. In the Russian winter, the Germans became stymied at Moscow and Leningrad. They reached the very outskirts of Moscow but could not finish the job. An important factor was that the Soviet Union was aware that Japan planned to strike the United States rather than enter the Soviet–German standoff at Moscow. That information allowed Stalin to bring in reinforcements that would otherwise have been concerned with Japan.

From the perspective of the United States, the big event was the Japanese attack on Pearl Harbor. It is difficult to imagine today how the Japanese could have pulled off their devastating attack in secret. "There had never been anything remotely like it in the history of naval warfare."[583] The Japanese launched 353 planes from aircraft carriers. In the space of a few hours, twenty-four hundred lives were lost and much of the US Navy was destroyed; however, the destruction of ships was not as complete as it had first seemed. Significantly, no airplane carriers were destroyed—the kind of ship that would prove most important in the war. The United States was able to repair all but a few of the ships. One of the battleships, the *Arizona*, was sunk with a heavy loss of life; it remains today as a tourist attraction where it sank.

President Roosevelt did not have to do much to generate anger in the country and a determination to retaliate in kind. From the US side, the attack had been a vicious unprovoked action. George Kennan notes that "the emotional fervor which we Americans are able to put into a war … goes far in explaining the difficulty we have in employing force for rational and restricted purposes."[584]

---

583 Steve Twomey, *Countdown to Pearl Harbor* (New York: Simon and Schuster, 2016).
584 Kennan, *American Diplomacy*, 84.

Japan, from its side, saw no alternative to its attack because the United States was strangling the Japanese economy. The United States had joined with the British and the Dutch in July 1941 to tighten an embargo on Japan. Japanese foreign trade was cut by three-quarters; oil imports were cut by 90 percent.[585]

In an amazingly short time, US factories were refitted to produce the weapons of war, and young men volunteered to join the army, navy, and marines (the air force was not yet a separate branch). The speed of the transformation is shown by the fact that a crucial naval battle was fought at Midway Island in June 1942, just seven months after Pearl Harbor. After seemingly going down to defeat, the United States was able to free up a group of dive bombers that destroyed the Japanese fleet of planes on the aircraft carriers. Here was a new kind of war: an enormous naval battle in which the fleets could not see each other. It was the first of many times that the tide of battle depended on the superiority of US air power.

Four days after the bombing of Pearl Harbor, Germany declared war on the United States. The US was faced with a herculean task of fighting two wars simultaneously. Not surprisingly, there were disagreements among the generals and admirals about the allocation of resources. Roosevelt had agreed with the other Allied leaders on a "Germany first" strategy. Most of the naval actions would happen in the Pacific, although there was still a need in Europe for ships, especially landing carriers.

In the island-hopping war in the Pacific, the US Marines were the mainstay, suffering terrible losses in places that hardly anyone in the United States had previously heard of. A United States possession, the Philippine Islands, was quickly overwhelmed and became the scene of the horrifying Bataan death march.[586] General Douglas McArthur, leaving the Philippines for Australia, pronounced in his usual flair for the dramatic, "I shall return." He did keep the promise, but it was a long journey and, especially for the marines, a terrible journey.

One of the major issues in the European theater of war was the argument over a "second front"—that is, a landing of allied troops to

---

585 Keegan, *Second World War*, 248.
586 Michael Norman and Elizabeth Norman, *Tears in the Darkness: The Story of the Bataan Death March and its Aftermath* (New York: Farrar, Straus and Giroux, 2009).

engage the German army from the west while the Soviet army fought from the east. George Marshall, who was in charge of the US forces, advocated an invasion of France in 1943. Fortunately, the British were persuasive in delaying that move until June 1944. If the attempt had been made a year earlier, it would almost certainly have been a disaster. The Allied forces took measured steps with an invasion of northern Africa, followed by Sicily and Italy. The Italian campaign was long and arduous.

After a massive buildup in England, the Allied forces were ready for an invasion. The Germans thought it would occur at Calais, the place in France closest to England. The US and British command fed that belief with false information while they prepared to land at Normandy. On June 6, 1944, they struck at five beaches; the United States had developed superior landing craft that gave much better protection than former landings, in which many of the troops drowned or were cut down by enemy fire before they could leave the ship. Only at Omaha beach were US losses severe. Given how complex the whole operation was, it was considered a great success.

For six months after the invasion, allied forces moved steadily through France and appeared to have the war going their way. Then Hitler threw his remaining forces into a desperate counterattack. The Battle of the Bulge showed that the war was not going to be over quickly; however, Allied forces were able to stabilize their position. The western front had the intended effect of strengthening the Soviet push from the east.

By early 1945, it was becoming evident that however long it might take to finish the war, Hitler's domination of Europe was over. Lives and property could have been saved if Hitler had accepted that fact instead of perpetuating the punishment that was leveled in the last months of the war against the whole German nation. On the ground, the culmination of that destruction was the Soviet siege of Berlin. The Soviet army suffered its worst losses since the desperate defense of its homeland in 1941. In the siege of April 16 through May 8, three hundred thousand men were killed or wounded.[587]

The punishment from the air was unrelenting because the Germans had very little air defense and the United States, along with Great Britain, could launch massive air strikes. Until 1940, there had been an agreement

---

587 Keegan, *Second World War*, 533.

that cities were not to be the targets of air attacks. The bombing of England in 1940 changed that; of course, the Germans claimed that they were retaliating for an earlier British attack on Freiburg. The German decision proved to be strategically unwise; in the course of the war, German cities took a horrible beating. The Germans, on September 8, 1944, launched the first of nine thousand "guided missiles," which returned some of the punishment on England, but it was too late to shift the tide of war.

Hamburg was subjected to four nights of bombing in July 1943. The bombs, together with the right weather conditions, caused firestorms of fifteen hundred degrees and destroyed 80 percent of the city. The death toll was about forty thousand. The morality of this policy was debated in Washington, but "reasons of war" won out. Lewis Mumford wrote that "more than any other event that has taken place in modern times this sudden radical change-over from war to collective extermination reversed the whole course of human history."[588] Once the concern for civilian populations was discarded, the death and destruction in German and Japanese cities was destined to keep getting worse up to the atomic bombings.

The culmination in German cities was the destruction of Dresden, a city that did not have any strategic military value—just people. On the night of February 13, 1945, three waves of Allied bombers destroyed the city from the middle outward. As women and children fled out of the city, the fires caught up with them. The estimated number of dead varied wildly. Perhaps one hundred thousand people died. Afterward, the US communiqué noted that "the Dresden raid was designed to cripple communications. The fact that the city was crowded with refugees at the time of the attack was coincidental and took the form of a bonus."[589] Hundreds of thousands of people were fleeing from the Soviet army in its movement across Eastern Europe. They were the "bonus" for the Allied bombs.

Dresden was one of the inspirations for the policy initiated in March 1945 by General Curtis Lemay, who was in charge of bombing strategy in the Pacific theater. Between May and August, the United States dropped

588 Lewis Mumford, *Breakthrough*, 18.
589 Paul Addison and Jeremy Craig, *Firestorm: The Bombing of Dresden, 1945* (New York: Ivan R. Dee, 2006).

one hundred fifty-eight thousand tons of explosives, two-thirds of which were incendiary bombs. Fifty-eight Japanese cities were firebombed in night attacks; 60 percent of the area was destroyed. All claims to be fighting a "just war" were jettisoned with the policy of burning to death as many people as possible. The hope was that such a brutal treatment of people would break their will to resist, although that had not happened in previous bombing onslaughts.

The bombing of Tokyo was particularly horrific, even though it is not as well-known as Dresden or Hiroshima. On the night of March 9, 1945, 325 US bombers filled with incendiary bombs came in low over Tokyo and burned down sixteen square miles of the city. The death toll was eighty-nine thousand people. The US suffered only a 2 percent loss of planes. In the following month, five of Japan's largest cities were also firebombed, bringing death to two hundred sixty thousand people and leaving many millions homeless.

In the ground battles of the Pacific, the United States had been making its way up from the south, starting from its first victory at Guadalcanal in 1943. The objective was to invade the Japanese homeland and end the war. The combination of naval and air power in support of US troops was a winning strategy even though the fighting conditions were extremely difficult. Japanese losses were far greater than those of the US. The Japanese had communication and logistical problems across the vast territory that they were trying to defend.

The retaking of the Philippine Islands was a big step for US morale as well as US strategy. On October 23, 1944, the US invasion began in the Leyte Gulf. The Japanese were expecting an attack on the island of Mindanao, where they had concentrated their defenses. At Leyte, the United States met only sixteen thousand Japanese troops. The Japanese navy did not go so quietly. The battle in the gulf of Leyte was the largest naval battle in history. After a long struggle, the United States emerged as the winner.

Two of the islands closest to Japan were Iwo Jima and Okinawa, both of which the United States invaded and subsequently controlled, although the US suffered some of its worst losses. The decision was made in October 1944 to take the two islands as staging points for bombers. In February 1945, a landing was made at Iwo Jima. Over a third of the US force that landed on the island were killed or wounded. Nearly all of the twenty-one thousand Japanese soldiers died in a struggle to the end. Their thoughts as they faced certain death were captured in letters they wrote to loved ones. In 2005, Hollywood made an extraordinary movie based on those letters.[590]

In April 1945, Okinawa was an even deadlier battle than Iwo Jima. About the same number of men from the US Army and US Marines were killed; the Japanese losses were horrific, with as many as one hundred thousand killed. Besides the gruesome battle to take each bit of the ground on the island, Okinawa was a grim naval battle in which the US Navy suffered greater losses than ever before in its history. A huge concentration of US ships was offshore when the Japanese unleashed seventy-eight hundred aircraft, including one thousand kamikazes. There was nowhere for the ships to go, and they simply took direct hits from the planes crashing into the ship decks. Okinawa did prove to be a valuable air base, although its continued use by the United States has been a point of considerable friction in US–Japanese relations.

One of the bad results of Iwo Jima and Okinawa was an Allied conclusion about the intended invasion of Japan. If the Japanese had fought to the last man in defending those islands, they would do the same in their country. It was thought that a million men would be needed for invading Japan and that the casualties would run into the hundreds of thousands. Thus, when the possibility of a quick end to the war by using the new "weapon of mass destruction" arose, there was little opposition. Churchill said of the use of the atomic bomb that "to avert a vast, indefinite butchery … at the cost of a few explosions seemed, after all our toils and perils, a miracle of deliverance."[591] One of the US generals involved in

---

590 The movie is *Letters from Iwo Jima*, directed by Clint Eastwood; it complemented his movie *Sons of Our Fathers*, which showed the war from the side of the US soldiers. Iwo Jima became known to much of the US public because of a (staged) photo showing a group of marines raising the flag. Later the country tried to make heroes of the men in that group, who mostly wished to be left in peace.

591 Mark Kurlansky, *Nonviolence: The History of a Dangerous Idea* (New York: Modern Library, 2008), 142.

choosing the site for these "few explosions" described President Harry Truman as a "boy on a toboggan."[592]

In the context of the time, amid the butchery of the war, one more bomb on one more city did not seem to be a big leap in kind. From a later perspective, the United States is seen to have perpetrated a terrible act that is difficult to justify. On August 6, 1945, the B29 bomber *Enola Gay* dropped the atomic bomb on Hiroshima, killing an estimated seventy-eight thousand people and scarring untold numbers. The whole world could see that a jump in magnitude had occurred and that humanity had entered uncharted territory.

What is more difficult to understand is the use of the bomb on a second city, Nagasaki, a mere three days later. The deaths there were fewer in number, but the psychic and physical destruction was as great. The United States' explanation was that Japan had made no response after the first bombing. US officials therefore continued to believe that the Japanese would resist to the end and that an invasion of Japan would therefore be needed. It is possible, however, that Japanese officials were stunned and had not been able to consider fully their predicament. Also of crucial importance was that in between the two bombings the Soviet Union had declared war on Japan, as it had previously promised. The Japanese feared that their country would be split in a way similar to Korea. The Japanese quickly surrendered.

President Truman said that the development of the atomic bomb "probably represents the greatest achievement of the combined efforts of science, industry, labor, and the military in history." In a perverted sort of way, he was right. If one puts aside all questions of morality and humanity, the bomb was a stupendous achievement of "American" know-how and organization. The US public certainly agreed. The Gallup and Roper Polls at the time showed 75 percent of the population approving the bombings, and less than 2 percent in outright opposition.[593] One of the few strong voices in condemnation was that of literary and political commentator Dwight MacDonald. In August of 1945, he wrote, "This atrocious action

---

592 Frances Harbour, *Thinking about International Ethics* (Boulder, CO: Westview Press, 1998), 135.

593 Mark Silk, *Spiritual Politics: Religion and America since World War II* (New York: Touchstone, 1989).

places 'us', the defenders of civilization, on a moral level with 'them', the beasts of Maidenek." [594]

For an anniversary of Pearl Harbor, Japanese officials proposed that their prime minister lay a wreath at the battleship Arizona and that President Bush do the same at Hiroshima. The US officials "gagged at the stab at moral equivalence."[595]To most of the world, however, the United States could hardly claim to occupy the moral high ground in the comparison of horrors. Some mutual acknowledgment of the horrors was finally reached by President Barack Obama's visit to Hiroshima in 2015 and Japanese prime minister Abe Shinzo's visit to Pearl Harbor in 2016.

For the fiftieth anniversary of the bombing of Hiroshima, the Smithsonian National Air and Space Museum prepared an exhibit around the *Enola Gay* in an attempt to get US citizens to reflect on the horrifying destruction and the moral ambiguity of the war. There was an uproar of protest led by the *Wall Street Journal* and Republican politicians against this effort "to inculcate in American youth a revulsion toward America's past." One Republican senator was not joking when he complained that this is what happens "to America's view of its history when you start mixing in other countries' perspectives." Nothing was said about the history of the United States, which, unlike America's history, can indeed be seen from the perspectives of other countries.[596]

The Aftermath of the War

As of August 1945, the world was no longer at war, although to say it was at peace would not be quite accurate.[597] In China, where the war had brought a temporary truce between nationalists and Communists, the civil war recommenced in 1946. Fighting was focused in Manchuria as Japan withdrew from the region. Chiang Kai-shek's army had superior

594 Dwight MacDonald, *The Responsibility of Peoples and Other Essays in Political Criticism* (London: Gollancz, 1957), 102.
595 *Newsweek*, July 1, 2001.
596 Steve Levine and Michael Hunt, *Arc of Empire: America's Wars in Asia from the Philippines to Vietnam* (Chapel Hill, NC: University of North Carolina Press, 2012), 114. The first comment is by Patrick Buchanan, the second by Senator Wendell Ford of Kentucky.
597 Ian Buruma, *Year Zero: A History of 1945* (New York: Penguin Books, 2013).

numbers and US support, but Mao's followers were the better fighters, and they prevailed in China while Chiang withdrew to Formosa (Taiwan). In Indochina, Ho Chi Minh begged for US intervention, appealing to the Atlantic Charter's promise of self-determination rather than having the French return. The United States was not inclined to help him.

The Soviet Union's crushing of Eastern Europe involved continued violence and repression. Stalin set out to build a new social and political order.[598] The meeting of the big three at Yalta was criticized for giving away too much to the Soviets, but the Soviet army was already in control of the territory. Roosevelt accepted the Soviet occupation of Poland in exchange for a Soviet promise to enter the war against Japan. As of 1945, all of Europe east of the Elbe River was Soviet territory. The Soviet Union did not extend its territory farther, thanks in part to the North Atlantic Treaty Organization, which became a formidable military force.[599]

Despite its power and influence, the United States could do little to change events in Eastern Europe and China. That did not stop some Republican politicians from asking, "How could America so strong and so pure be defeated?" Their answer was treason; the big question became, Who lost China? Many reputations would be soiled in the decade after the end of the war. The "Red Scare" that existed after the First World War returned with more clout. The accusation of "Communist sympathizer" was made by Senator Joseph McCarthy and other politicians concerned with "un-American activities."

On the whole, however, the United States could bask in the light at the top of the world. Theodore White, describing China in 1945, wrote, "All was free: rooms, food, liquor, girls – because we were Americans. The whole world belonged to America."[600] That exaggerates the situation, but the United States had succeeded in fending off the challenges of Japan, Germany, and the Soviet Union. In addition, the United States was in a position to build a new economic order and take the place that Great

---

598 Anne Applebaum, *Iron Curtain: The Crushing of Eastern Europe 1944–1956* (New York: Doubleday, 2012).

599 Lundestad, *The Rise and Decline*, 115.

600 Quoted in Geoffrey Hodgson, *America in Our Time* (Garden City, NY: Doubleday, 1976), 463.

Britain had occupied for more than a century.[601] Even Pope Pius XII added to the United States' inflated view of its self-importance: "The American people have a genius for great and unselfish deeds. Into the hands of America, God has placed the destiny of an afflicted mankind."[602]

One of the last pieces of the war was the trial of war criminals in Japan and Germany. The trial in Nuremberg, Germany, began in November of 1945 and continued for 133 days of testimony. The signing of the Nuremberg Charter occurred on the same day as the bombing of Nagasaki. The two images of "America" were on display: the use of horrifying destruction and the genuine search for justice. At the Nuremberg trials, Robert Jackson of the US Supreme Court presided and spoke eloquently of the task that the judges faced. The legal basis for judgment was unclear, but the trial inspired important developments in international law and gave support to the beginning of the United Nations. In August 1945, the Allies had issued a charter called the Nuremberg Principles, which stated that a war of aggression that persecuted individuals or minorities on political, racial, or religious grounds was a crime against humanity.[603]

Of the twenty-one defendants, two were acquitted, eight were given prison sentences, and eleven were sentenced to death. At the conclusion of any war, "victors' justice" is always suspect. There were and still are critics of Nuremberg, but the judges themselves tried to be fair. Although many years passed before the Nuremberg Code was understood as applicable to subjects for medical experimentation, a leading medical journal said, "The Nuremberg Code is the most important document in the history of the ethics of medical research."[604]

---

601 Robert Skidelsky, in the third volume of his biography of John Maynard Keynes, *Battling for Britain* (New York: Penguin, 2002), goes so far as to say that the United States' three war aims were the defeats of Germany, Japan, and Great Britain.

602 Pope Pius XII, "Destinies of Humanity in U.S. Hands," *Collier's Magazine*, December 29, 1945.

603 For a summary of the Nuremberg trials, see Martha Minow, *Between Vengeance and Forgiveness: Facing History after Genocide and Mass Murder* (Boston: Beacon Press, 1999), 29–51.

604 Robert Burt, *Death is that Man Taking Names: Intersections of American Medicine, Law and Culture* (Berkeley, CA: University of California Press, 2002), 81.

The trials in Japan were inspired by Nuremberg but were not as meticulous in practice. As many as five thousand people were tried for crimes, and nine hundred of them were executed. The Tokyo trial of major government officials involved twenty-five people. Seven were condemned to death. In the brutality of the war, violations of law and basic morality were not all on one side. Robert McNamara had been an assistant to General Curtis Lemay while Lemay carried out the firebombing of Japanese cities. McNamara recounts a conversation in which Lemay said to him, "You know if we lose the war, we will be convicted as war criminals." McNamara wondered, "What makes it immoral if you lose and not immoral if you win?"[605]

United Nations

During the war, the founding of the United Nations had already begun. President Roosevelt had the name and an outline of the organization as early as 1942. A brilliant and dedicated man in the State Department, Leo Pasvolsky, began working on plans for a new international organization in 1939. Pasvolsky does not get much attention in history books, but the charter of the UN is largely what he conceived. Pasvolsky convinced Roosevelt that authority should be vested in a security council of eleven members rather than the four "policemen" that Roosevelt wanted. Security issues would be decided in the security council rather than in both council and assembly, as was the case with the League of Nations.

The United Nations was disappointing to some people—and still is—because the sovereign state is the rights-bearing subject that is prior to expressions of law. A system of sovereign states since the seventeenth century has repeatedly led to war; the twentieth-century wars between nations were unimaginably destructive. For at least two centuries, there have been voices calling for a supranational authority, but there has been a lack of knowledge for designing such an authority and a lack of wills for creating such a new world order. The United Nations left each member state inviolate on domestic issues. Not until 2005, when the UN General Assembly adopted a principle of the need to intervene, did the United

---

605 Interview of Robert McNamara in the 2003 film, *Fog of War*, directed by Errol Morris.

Nations assert the right of the international community to step in when there are atrocities that a particular state fails to stop.

A meeting to draw up a charter for the United Nations was scheduled for June 1945 in San Francisco as the war was nearing its end. Sadly, President Roosevelt died in April 1945. His successor, an inexperienced Harry Truman, made it his first order of business to go ahead with the meeting. In his first major speech at the signing of the UN Charter, Truman said he looked forward to the framing of an "International Bill of Rights."

A draft of the charter had been produced at a preliminary meeting at Dumbarton Oaks in Washington, DC. The document was subjected to severe criticism. A Pan American Union meeting of twenty-one nations met at Chapultepec in Mexico City during February and March of 1945; it offered a helpful critique concerning a broadening of the charter's vision to include human rights.[606] Although the draft at Dumbarton Oaks had restricted the extent of veto power by the UN Security Council and strengthened the ability of the United Nations to respond militarily, it still had little to say about the rights of persons. At San Francisco, a human rights commission was established with the mission of preparing an international bill of rights. In the final version of the charter, the terms "human rights," "justice," "full employment," and "education" were inserted.

Whatever the limitations of the UN Charter, the fact that it came into existence when it did was nearly miraculous. Much of the credit has to be given to the United States, which provided the organization as well as the intellectual drive. The secretary of the conference, Edward Stettinius, managed the meetings with efficiency and fairness. At one point, the Soviet delegate, Vyacheslav Molotov, threatened to abort the meeting with an intransigent position on veto power. Truman sent his chief negotiator, Harry Hopkins, to talk to Stalin, who overrode Molotov. Stettinius later said that "if Stalin had adamantly supported Molotov, there would have been no United Nations formed at San Francisco."[607]

---

606 Hooper and Brinkley, *FDR and the Creation,* 192–93.The meeting was also concerned about regional security; Stettinius negotiated an "Act of Chapultepec" that dealt with Latin American fears. One of the most notable critics of the Dumbarton Oaks draft was W. E. B. Dubois, the distinguished black leader in the United States; see Borgwardt, *New Deal,* 192–93.
607 Schlesinger, *Act of Creation,* 217.

The United Nations did come into existence and survived the Cold War standoff between the United States and the Soviet Union. Some people criticize it as merely a discussion club, but that is mainly what it is designed to be. The hope is that while people are talking with each other, they are not killing each other. When the United Nations has tried to intervene in international conflicts, it has not had much success. Regional associations, which were frowned on at the time of the founding of the United Nations, quickly emerged. These groups included the North Atlantic Treaty Organization (NATO), the Organization of American States (OAS), the European Council, and the African Union. They are a substitute for a worldwide supranational authority; their power can be a danger, but they can also be supportive of the United Nations' effort to maintain a balance of power.

The international bill of rights that was promised when the charter was approved has never appeared. Despite developments in international law and an international court, there is no power to enforce a world bill of rights. When the commission on human rights met, Eleanor Roosevelt was elected chairperson. She was advised by her consultants in the US State Department that the Senate would never pass a treaty on human rights. She was told to use as a model the Declaration of Independence rather than the Bill of Rights. An agreement was reached that the commission would divide its work into a declaration, a covenant, and measures of implementation. The covenant became two covenants that took eighteen years; the measures of implementation never appeared. The Universal Declaration of Human Rights appeared in 1948.

Eleanor Roosevelt was a surprise; she had not been looked upon as a political leader (even by herself), but she managed to get a declaration written and then approved by the UN General Assembly during 1948, when there were eruptions all over the world. Roosevelt constantly clashed with Soviet delegate Victor Koretsky, but she did not alienate him. A Mexican diplomat said of her: "Never before have I seen naiveté and cunning so graciously blended."[608] The final vote in the UN General Assembly was forty-eight in favor and eight abstaining (the latter being the

---

608 William Schulz, *In Our Own Best Interests: How Defending Human Rights Benefits the United States of America* (Boston: Beacon Press, 2002), 4.

Soviet bloc, Saudi Arabia, and South Africa). The fact that no one voted against the declaration was a victory of sorts.

In the committee charged with writing the declaration, the United States and Soviet Union had disagreed on what should be the contents of the document. The disagreement produced a bad compromise that led to the split of the covenant into two covenants: one concerned with political and civil rights, and a second with economic, social, and cultural rights. This dichotomy continues to haunt any discussion of human rights long after the dissolution of the Soviet empire. Rights that belong to every person by the fact of their being human should not be divided into so-called liberty rights and welfare rights.

Despite the fact that the authorship of the declaration included writers from east and west, north and south, the document was often seen as "western" in its conception.[609] Roosevelt assumed that liberty rights were well established in the United States and in Western European nations. She wished to add economic rights, as her husband had advocated.[610] The declaration, in fact, does add economic rights to political rights, but an approach of addition rather than integration undercuts the meaning of human rights.

Starting with the Eisenhower administration in 1953, the political right wing in the United States has actively opposed the United Nations. Eisenhower's secretary of state, John Foster Dulles, announced that the executive branch did not intend to submit to the Senate any human rights treaties with their "socialistic conceptions."[611] Even US Ambassadors to the United Nations have sometimes been dismissive of the organization. Jeanne Kirkpatrick was quoted as describing a UN Human Rights Commission report as "a letter to Santa Claus." John Bolton, a known opponent of the United Nations, was appointed by George W. Bush as UN ambassador. Bolton's view was that "the U.N. is valuable only when it directly serves

---

609 Authors included P. C. Chang, from China; John Humphrey, from Canada; Charles Malik, from Lebanon; and René Cassin, from France. Important contributions were also made by Hernán Santa Cruz, from Chile; and Carolos Romulo, from the Philippines.

610 Mary Ann Glendon, *A World Made New: Eleanor Roosevelt and the Universal Declaration of Human Rights* (New York: Random House, 2001), 42–43.

611 Borgwardt, *New Deal*, 268.

the United States." As for negotiations to resolve international disputes, Bolton said "I don't do carrots."[612]

Michael Ignatieff writes, "Of all the ironies in the history of human rights since the Declaration, the one that would most astonish Eleanor Roosevelt is the degree to which her own country is now the odd man out."[613] The United States too quickly assumed that America would forever be supreme. The idea of America as a place of freedom and riches for all people has been enticing for many people. But the United States has still not become that place of liberty and justice where everyone enjoys the right to pursue his or her happiness.

---

612 David Boucher, *The Limits of Ethics in International Relations: Natural Law, Natural Rights and Human Rights in Transition* (New York: Oxford University Press, 2009), 367; Jimmy Carter, *Our Endangered Values: America's Moral Crisis* (New York: Simon and Schuster 2005), 98.
613 Michael Ignatieff, *Human Rights as Politics and Idolatry* (Princeton, NJ: Princeton University Press, 2001), 93.

8

Powerful America, Insecure United States

The second half of the twentieth century was a time of strange contrasts for the United States. For almost four decades, the United States was locked in a struggle for world supremacy. When its competitor rather suddenly dissolved, the United States was in new territory during the last decade of the century. There had been talk of a "peace dividend" when the Soviet Union was no longer a threat—that is, the United States could become demilitarized. No such revolution occurred. At the end of the century, a new threat was perceived and the vision of a peaceful America retreated far to the background.

Even between 1945 and 1950, the paradox of power and insecurity was set in place. The war had just ended when, in Winston Churchill's metaphor, an iron curtain came down to divide the world.[614] The "free world" was confronted with an implacable enemy. Once the enemy had "the bomb," each side sought to build a bigger arsenal of bombs, although each had enough nuclear power to destroy the world several times over.

Archibald MacLeish, writing in 1949, described what happened at the end of the war: "Never in the history of the world was one people as completely dominated, intellectually and morally by another as the people

---

614 The "iron curtain" is usually said to have originated in a speech in Fulton, Missouri, in March 1946; actually Churchill had used the image in a letter to Harry Truman nine months earlier. The image is somewhat misleading because there was much that was known about what was happening behind the curtain. See Anne Applebaum, *Iron Curtain: The Crushing of Eastern Europe 1944–1956* (New York: Doubleday, 2012).

of the United States by the people of Russia in the four years from 1946 to 1949. American foreign policy was a mirror image of Russian policy. Whatever the Russians did we did in reverse. All ... this took place not in a time of national weakness and decay but precisely at the moment when the United States, having engineered a tremendous triumph and fought its way to a brilliant victory in the greatest of all wars, had reached the highest point of world power ever achieved by a single state."[615]

At the end of the war in 1945, the dichotomy which had been used in the 1930s resurfaced in a choice between "realism" and "idealism." People who saw the choice in those terms believed that the right choice was obvious. "Idealism" had proved to be a disastrous policy that had led to the horrors of Hitler and World War II. The country should never again be lulled into dreams of a world in which everyone gets along with everyone else.

It was said that anyone who is "realistic" knows that the relations between states are governed only by "power," which necessarily includes violence and at least a credible threat of war. The opposite of "realistic," of course, is "unrealistic." Any criticism of "realism" could be dismissed as stating an ideal that is possible, perhaps even admirable, for individuals but one that is simply irrelevant in international affairs.

A crucial phrase in all these discussions is "national interest." It is usually the first and undeniable principle stated about international dealings: "No state has ever entered a treaty for any other reason than self-interest. A statesman who has any other motive would deserve to be hung."[616] There are, however, some questions about this apotheosis of "national interest," starting with the assumption that nations have only one instead of multiple interests. In the ordinary flow of politics around taxes, tariffs, or investments, the interests of one or several groups are served and other groups lose out. Wars fought for "the national interest" are actually fought for the interests of some people as opposed to the interests of other people.

---

615 Archibald MacLeish's essay "Conquest of America" was reprinted in *The Atlantic Monthly*, February 1980.

616 Johannes Haller, as quoted approvingly in Reinhold Niebuhr, *Moral Man and Immoral Society: A Study in Ethics and Politics* (New York: Charles Scribner's Sons, 1932), 84.

The idea of "self-interest" was invented by early social scientists in imitation of Newton's laws of motion. Helvétius, in the eighteenth century, proclaimed that "as the physical universe is ruled by the laws of motion so is the moral universe ruled by laws of interest."[617] Human actions were as predictable as natural things. All you had to do was consider the individual's self-interest—something that was assumed to be obvious. The murky idea of self-interest was bad enough when applied to individuals. When applied to nation-states, it was much worse. The "realist" talk about national interest was unrealistic.

Persons and nations act from their many interests. If two nations discuss their interests (the root meaning of "interest" refers to what is between us), they are likely to find some interests that are common to the two nations or even common to humanity, such as having food to eat. An individual finds it difficult to determine what his or her many interests are. At the level of a nation-state, interests are extremely complex, and no nation has worked out a perfect system for determining its interests and balancing competing interests within the country.

In today's world, with the "realistic" possibility of destroying life on earth, searching for common human interests, even when nations are in conflict, cannot be dismissed as unrealistic. Nations preparing for war have never been very successful at finding an alternative to the slaughter of war. The world has not learned a lesson here since Thucydides' account that "what made war inevitable was the growth of Athenian power and the fear which this caused in Sparta."[618] A mantra of the people called realists is that, of course, they are against war—except as a "last resort."

America vs Communism

The short period between the end of World War II and the war on the Korean peninsula set the direction for US foreign policy for at least the forty years that followed. Intense debate occurred in Washington concerning what to do about the Soviet Union, which at the end of the war was a

617 Helvetius, *L'espirit*, quoted in Albert Hirschman, *The Rhetoric of Reaction: Perversity, Futility, Jeopardy* (Cambridge, MA: Harvard University Press, 1991), 55. Hirschman has an illuminating history of "self-interest."
618 Thucydides, *Peloponnesian Wars*, vol. 1 (New York: Cassell, 1962), 24.

battered country but which nevertheless occupied all of Eastern Europe. Was there a plan for Communism to take over the world, and if any such expansionist policy was at play, what was the best way to oppose it? Europe was in bad shape physically and economically. The United States could not avoid decisions about a big plan for the world. There was no new world war; there was what was named a "cold war."

An important disagreement was whether the United States should confront Soviet outreach primarily in military terms. The United States was the only nuclear power, although such was the horror of the actual use of an atomic bomb that its place in military strategy was questionable. The United States had a powerful air force and navy, but the country had little enthusiasm for maintaining a large army or getting itself involved in any new land engagement.

The question for government planners as to whether military force should be primary or secondary is illustrated by two events in 1947. On March 12, President Harry Truman requested from Congress $300 million for Turkey and $100 million for Greece. Both countries were seen to be threatened by a Communist takeover. The metaphor in the speech was a spoiled apple in a barrel that would soon infect all the other apples.[619]

The speech crystallized what became known as the Truman Doctrine. Wherever there was a danger of Communist triumph—whether in Iran, the Turkish straits, northern Greece, Egypt, Africa, Italy, or France—the United States must intervene with economic and military aid. Truman said, "I believe that it must be the policy of the United States to support free peoples who are resisting attempted subjugation by armed minorities and by outside pressures."[620] Truman, like many presidents before and after him, presumed that a fight for freedom anywhere was "America's" fight.

The alternate approach was signaled by a speech that George Marshall gave at Harvard University on June 5, 1947. Marshall, who was then undersecretary of state and soon to replace Dean Acheson as the secretary, outlined a plan to provide help to Europe. Marshall had just returned from

---

619 Another of Acheson's influential metaphors was a tide of water sweeping through Turkey and Greece; see James Chace, *Acheson: The Secretary of State Who Created the American World* (Cambridge, MA: Harvard University Press, 1999).

620 Neil Sheehan, *A Fiery Peace in a Cold War* (New York: Random House, 2009), 89.

meeting with Stalin, who was insisting on German reparations. Marshall gave a graphic description of conditions in Europe. What he proposed in his speech became a policy known as the Marshall Plan.

William Boden describes the paradoxical position in which the United States found itself: "The sheer economic supremacy of the United States … caused a tremendous imbalance in the world economy that threatened both the prosperity of the United States and its foreign policy objectives."[621] The economic task was not to dominate others but to help European countries to gain in power relative to the United States. The United States had one-half of the world's monetary reserves and one-half of the world's manufactured goods. Other nations needed trade surpluses to get the dollars for food and reconstruction.

There was a question whether the Marshall Plan would even get started, because Truman was not expected to be re-elected in 1948. Once that happened, the money began to be appropriated, and it eventually amounted to $13 billion. The help was offered to every European nation, though it was presumed that Russia would not accept any help. Two of the countries under Soviet control, Poland and Czechoslovakia, indicated a willingness to work with the United States and Western Europe. They were quickly corrected of their wayward tendencies. Stalin perceived the Marshall Plan to be a kind of economic war, which it was. A major problem was to work out a system of payments to extend trade possibilities beyond pacts between two countries. The United States, without much consultation, devised a workable plan.

At the center of Europe was the great unresolved problem of Germany. When the war ended, the country was split between the Soviets in the east and the British and United States in the west. What was stranger still was that 110 miles into Soviet-controlled East Germany was the great city of Berlin, which was also split. Economic reform in West Germany included introduction of the deutsche mark, which the Soviet Union perceived as a direct threat. In response, the Soviets cut the land route for supplies into West Berlin. If the United States had used armed force to open the roads, there is no telling where the shooting might have led. Instead the United

---

621 William Boden, *The Pacific Alliance: United States Foreign Economic Policy and Japanese Trade Recovery, 1947-1955* (Madison, WI: University of Wisconsin Press, 1984), 5.

States used its ingenuity and its extraordinary air force to bring in supplies to Berlin by air. The Soviets did not think the airlift could be sustained, but it was. The Soviets finally gave up and lifted the blockade the following May. The world could breathe a sigh of relief.

How successful was the Marshall Plan? There is no debate about Western Europe's economic recovery in the 1950s. However, the part that the Marshall Plan had in the recovery has been a source of debate from the beginning. One can say that spokespersons in the United States went too far in claiming to be the saviors of the world. People who think that the country is America almost inevitably exaggerate the goodness, unselfishness, and success of US policies. In this case, the United States did engage in activities that were good and that contributed in part to a great success. The Europeans who have spoken on the matter will grant that the Marshall Plan was well-intentioned and did contribute to the recovery. They tend to play down the actual results. They also have varying degrees of resentment at the United States claiming to have singlehandedly saved Europe. A generally positive assessment of the Marshall Plan by a European commentator states, "The psychological success at the outset was so amazing that we felt that the psychological effect was four-fifths accomplished before the first supplies arrived."[622] The role of the Marshall Plan from 1948 to 1951 amounted to 2 percent of GDP of the recipient countries.[623] That does not sound like much, but at the very beginning of the recovery, it was an important help.

The United States was acting for its own interests, but it had some enlightened men in power, starting with George C. Marshall, the secretary of state. The politicians were assisted by knowledgeable people in several fields who contributed expert advice. "The narrow financial effects of American aid were strengthened by the effort to export to Europe the American model of cooperative labor relations and scientific management."[624]

---

622 Charles Mee Jr., *The Marshall Plan: The Launching of the Pax Americana* (New York: Simon and Schuster, 1984), 246.

623 Lucrezia Reichlin, "The Marshall Plan Reconsidered," in *Europe's Post-War Recovery*, ed. Barry Eichengreen (Cambridge, MA: Cambridge University Press, 1995), 42.

624 Reichlin, "The Marshall Plan Reconsidered," 64.

Whatever were the benefits of the Marshall Plan for Europe, its effect in the United States was to steer the country in a less belligerent direction. There were people who did not want war but wanted to "roll back" Communism in unspecified ways that could have led to war. In the second half of the 1940s, the United States began to demilitarize the country—a process that abruptly ended in 1950. Despite the numerous crises in the world during 1948, the United States was mainly engaged in peaceful efforts to restore international stability. The rhetoric of the Truman Doctrine to help freedom everywhere did not lead to military interventions.

A central character in the debates of that time was the diplomat George Kennan, who composed an eight thousand word telegram in 1946 that was pivotal in the US response to the Soviet Union from the 1940s until the end of the 1980s. The story begins on February 22, 1946, when Kennan, who was an analyst in the US embassy in Moscow, sent the "long telegram" to Washington. Stalin had recently given a bellicose speech, and the State Department in Washington asked for an assessment of the Soviet Union. Kennan, having extensive experience in diplomacy with Stalin's government and being a student of Russia and Russian history, was probably the best qualified person in the US government to provide guidelines for US policy. Most of the telegram is a description of the present situation of the Soviet Empire and what most likely were the intentions of the Soviet government. A last brief section proposed what should be the US response to an expansionist Soviet policy. Kennan followed up the telegram with a 1947 essay in *Foreign Affairs*, signed by Mr. X.[625]

The debate that followed was less about whether someone agreed with Kennan than over what Kennan meant. His views were claimed by both sides of the debate about how to deal with the Soviet Union. In the essay, Kennan used the term "containment" to describe what should be done. Containment would become official policy, but the debate continued over what containment meant.

There are two keys to understanding Kennan's proposal that commentators missed, leading to misinterpretations: (1) Kennan always

---

625 George Kennan, "The Sources of Soviet Conduct," *Foreign Affairs* 25 (July 1947), 566–82.

refers to the United States; the word "America" does not appear in the telegram, and (2) Kennan never equates "force" with military force.

The first point is important because anyone writing about US government policies who uses "United States" is at least referring to actual data and not religious myth. In "America" there is always a solution to any problem. Whatever America wants, America gets. But for United States actions in other countries, the will of America does not always prevail. George Marshall said that sometimes there is no solution to a problem and we have to learn to live with the imperfect conditions of the actual world. Patience is not a virtue that gets top billing in "America."

The second point is the heart of what Kennan was proposing—that is, the use of every kind of force except military force. The point is not obscure, but people in international relations are so accustomed to using "force" as equivalent to "violence" and "war" that they assume this meaning even when the person expressly denies that meaning. In all ordinary uses of "force," outside the arena of international dealings, there is recognized a distinction between force and violence. The statement that was most often quoted from the Long Telegram was "Soviet pressure against the free institutions of the Western world can be contained by the adroit and vigorous application of counterforce." Kennan repeatedly says that this counterforce should *not* be military action.

Looking back in 1996, Kennan said, "My thoughts about containment were of course distorted by the people who understood it exclusively as a military concept, and I think that, as much as any other cause, led to the forty years of unnecessary, fearfully expensive and disoriented process of the cold war."[626] In 1986, he said he had accomplished two of his three aims: (1) "Curing Washington of a naïve optimism," and (2) "Helping General Marshall design the program of European reconstruction." With those two successes, he had hoped to get to (3) negotiation.[627]

Kennan protested the inclusion of the atomic bomb in US military planning, and he opposed the founding of NATO. Disagreement with other officials led to his resigning from the Policy Planner Office in the State Department. His replacement, Paul Nitze, represented the other

626 Interview with George Kennan, CNN, May 1996.
627 George Kennan, *Nuclear Delusion: Soviet-American Relations in the Atomic Age* (New York: Pantheon, 1982), xii.

side of the policy debate, the trust in a buildup of military force.[628] In the Long Telegram, Kennan warned that "the greatest danger that can befall us in coping with this problem of Soviet communism is that we shall allow ourselves to become like those with whom we are coping." Kennan would later denounce the US venture into North Korea and our involvement in Vietnam. As he was approaching his one hundredth birthday, he opposed US war-making in Iraq.

One of the most pointed attacks on Kennan's position in 1947 was written by Walter Lippmann. As one reads their words many decades later, it seems that they were not as far apart as Lippmann thought. Both men wanted the United States to rely on diplomacy rather than military confrontation with the Soviet Union. Both men were seeking a kind of "containment." Lippmann, like so many other people, made one big mistake in reading Kennan: Lippmann assumed that by "force" Kennan meant military force—even though Kennan clearly said he did not.

That mistake led Lippmann to place Kennan on the side of the Truman Doctrine. He repeatedly uses Kennan's containment and Truman's military rhetoric as equivalent policies.[629] Kennan's essay in *Foreign Affairs* appeared four months after the Truman speech, so Lippmann thought it was an application of the Truman Doctrine. Lippmann published his book before he could have witnessed Kennan's strong support of the Marshall Plan, which Lippmann correctly saw as opposed to Truman's military approach. Kennan was stung by Lippmann's criticism and wrote him a letter that was never sent in which he insisted that "we need no aggressive strategic plans, no provocation of military hostilities, no showdowns."[630]

Neither man, of course, had a clear solution for what the United States should do about the Soviet Union. Kennan was vulnerable to Lippmann's criticism that he was very sketchy about how to use diplomatic and economic "counter-force" while avoiding military confrontations. Lippmann, for his part, thought that the most important thing was to get the Red Army to withdraw from Eastern Europe. But on how to get

---

628 Nicholas Thompson, *The Hawk and the Dove: Paul Nitze, George Kennan and the History of the Cold War* (New York: Picador, 2010).

629 Walter Lippmann, *The Cold War* (New York: Harper and Brothers, 1947), 29.

630 Nicholas Thompson, "A War Best Served Cold," *New York Times*, July 31, 2007. The letter and its context are described by Thompson in *The Hawk and the Dove*.

that to happen he was not clear, other than to say it should be done by diplomacy.[631] Lippmann thought it was unimaginable that we should have to wait for "ten or fifteen years" for the Soviet empire to fail. Kennan was ultimately right that the seeds of self-destruction were present in the Soviet system, but neither man could have envisioned a forty-year wait.

Kennan is regularly classified as a "realist." Walter Russell Meade made a helpful distinction in a discussion of realists. He used "continental realists" (referring back to Metternich and Bismarck as models) for people who dismissed moral questions by maintaining that the clash of national powers is all that counts. "The Nixon and Ford administrations represented the zenith of Continental Realism's influence in U.S. foreign policy. International life was seen as a morals-free zone."[632] Henry Kissinger was the embodiment of this realism.

Among writers of this 1950s version of realism, Hans Morgenthau stands out as a consistent and prolific advocate. His view of human nature and international politics was clear: "An essential and universal lust for power as an end in itself knows no limits; one's lust for power would be satisfied only if the last man became the object of his domination."[633] Morgenthau elsewhere says that in the "power politics" of national interest, "one of the great tragic antinomies of human existence" is "the contradiction between power politics and ethics."[634] However, Morgenthau admitted that "we cannot act but morally because we are men" and "all human actions in some way are subject to moral judgment." He was critical of human rights as an abstract principle that "America" should not be trying to apply to other nations. "One need only look at the unique characteristics of the American polity and at these very special, nowhere-else-to-be-found characteristics of our protection of human rights within

---

631 Lippmann, *Cold War*, 41.

632 Walter Russell Mead, *Special Providence: American Foreign Policy and How It Changed the World* (New York: Routledge, 2002), 72.

633 Hans Morgenthau, *Politics among Nations* (New York: McGraw-Hill, 2005).

634 Morgenthau, *Politics among Nations*, 201. Morgenthau was an early critic of the Vietnam War and outlined a path for the United States to extricate itself; *Newsweek*, January 18, 1965.

the confines of America. You have only to look at the complete lack of respect for human rights in many nations, or in most nations."[635]

Morgenthau even claimed that "a foreign policy derived from the national interest is in fact morally superior to a foreign policy inspired by universal moral principles."[636] He was fond of quoting Edmund Burke on the side of "realism": "Nothing universal can be rationally affirmed on any moral or any political subject."[637] If that were the only choice, he might be right. Deducing politics from supposedly universal principles is likely to be disastrous. But "national interest" might also be a concept too abstract and shortsighted to provide a way to relate people of many races, religions, ages, and sexual groups within today's nation-states as well as between them.

Mead contrasts his "continental realism" to an "American realism" that does acknowledge morality. His examples are George Kennan, Dean Acheson, Walter Lippmann, and Averill Harriman. But as Morgenthau's claim of moral superiority for national interest shows, something called morality can mean many things. Kennan is the most interesting of the people named by Mead as allowing morality into realism. Actually, Kennan insisted that morality should not come into play. He often sounds like Morgenthau (they did work together at one period) in his distrust of people who wish to "moralize" or anyone's claim to have "universal principles of morality."

Kennan was opposed to talk about morality, but like many other writers of the 1950s, the morality he opposed was a substitute for the hard work of politics. Morality was thought to be a personal code of conduct that someone tries to impose on international dealings. The assumption is that there is a separate realm called morality next to politics. But the human race has always had questions about whether an action, including a political action, is right or wrong based on some implied or explicit standard of moral judgment. For some people, such as Morgenthau,

---

635 Hans Morgenthau, "Human Rights and Foreign Policy," in *Moral Dimensions of American Foreign Policy*, ed. K. W. Thompson (New Brunswick, NJ: Transaction Publishers, 1994), 341, 344–45.

636 Hans Morgenthau, *Scientific Man vs. Power Politics* (Chicago: University of Chicago Press, 1974), 39.

637 Michael Joseph Smith, *Realist Thought from Weber to Kissinger* (Baton Rouge, LA: Louisiana State University Press, 1990), 164.

"national interest" is a *moral* standard—the answer to questions of morality. However, other people may be acting quite reasonably when searching for a more comprehensive standard than national interest without ceasing to be practical and realistic.

George Kennan was not impressed by the Universal Declaration of Human Rights. Simply declaring what is right does not accomplish much; it can even be a distraction from human efforts to improve the world. Human rights language is not a substitute for politics. But the issue, for example, of whether a government is torturing prisoners raises a question that resonates with millions of people who have a deep conviction that torture is not the way human beings should be treated.

Kennan's opposition to the Nuremberg trials is more difficult to understand. The Nuremberg judges refrained from universal declarations. They focused on particular actions during a particular war. It is true that their standard of judgment was not entirely clear. The Nazi wrongs were not just political miscalculations (though they were that); they were moral wrongs that most human beings can judge were wrong even if they know nothing about theories of morality and politics.

Kennan's objection to US wars in Vietnam and Iraq seemed to be based not only on their being political folly but also on their having been immoral. As Vietnam was on the horizon, he called for a foreign policy "unsullied by arrogance or hostility to other people or delusions of superiority."[638] In a later essay entitled "Morality and Foreign Policy," he described US policy in Vietnam as "unbridled cynicism, and brutality." Policymakers, he said, showed a "total lack of scruple on their own part but also a boundless contempt for the countries against which their efforts were directed."[639] Kennan begins that essay by complaining that his book of thirty years previous had been misinterpreted as advocating "an amoral or even immoral foreign policy."[640] But he refrained from drawing the only conclusion that logically follows—namely, a claim that the policy he advocated was moral or morally good. The "continental realists" would be comfortable calling their policies "amoral"; Kennan was not.

---

638 George Kennan, *American Diplomacy* (Chicago: University of Chicago Press, 1951), 54.
639 George Kennan, "Morality and Foreign Policy," *Foreign Affairs* 64(1985/86), 213.
640 Kennan, "Morality and Foreign Policy," 205.

Kennan's conflicted ideas of whether his policies were "moral" is captured in his question of "whether there is any such thing as morality that does not rest, consciously or otherwise, on some foundation of religious faith, for the renunciation of self-interest, which is what morality implies, can never be realized by purely secular and materialistic considerations."[641] There is a tragic misunderstanding here of both religion and the moral life, neither of which is renunciation of self-interest. People act from their interests and for their interests. But many religious people are convinced that humans ultimately have some interests in common and interests that transcend their narrowest individual interests.

When the United States identifies itself as America, and its interests as American, it can imply a universal standard for its moral judgments. When "realists" talk about national interest, they seldom refer to the United States' national interest; almost always the discussion has been about America's national interest. America's interests are religiously transnational; America's interest is the world's interest. But the United States' interests are its own, which at their best lead to US cooperation with other nations.

America's Asian Wars: Korea

By the end of the 1940s, the stage was set for worldwide struggles of liberty against oppression, "America" being another name for liberty. The first application of the fight for liberty happened on the Korean peninsula, where the United States had overseen the southern part of the country after the war's end. When the "forces of Communism" overran the south in June 1950, the United States resisted the invasion and then decided to "roll back" Communism. The result was a disastrous war that has never ended. US losses were 33,629 killed and 103,284 wounded. The United States, having intervened in a country that planners did not understand, tried to forget the war rather than learn a lesson from it. When a second civil war in Asia presented a similar problem, the United States repeated the disaster in Vietnam, only on a grander scale.

June 25, 1950, is the moment that the United States dates a beginning to the Korean War. The war actually started at the beginning of the 1930s and has roots that go back to the beginning of the twentieth century. To

---

641 Kennan, "Morality and Foreign Policy," 217.

this day, there is little understanding within the United States of the origin, the nature, or the effects of that war. The only thing that is obvious to the United States today is that North Korea is in the hands of a madman who for no good reason hates the United States.

In 1950, the United States was dealing at home with the phenomenon of McCarthyism. Senator Joseph McCarthy's book *McCarthyism: The Fight for America* has an accurate title insofar as "America" was at the center of debate about the international policies of the United States government. In a country nervous about all kinds of confusing things happening in countries with unfamiliar names, the charges of conspiracy and treason had their appeal.[642] The United States was not threatened, but America was being disrespected.

Ironically, McCarthy provided support to the US officials whom he was attacking. Truman, Acheson, and their colleagues at the State and Defense Departments were entangling the country in a war that did not have popular support. But getting attacked by McCarthy turned Truman and Acheson into heroes who stood up against McCarthy's bullying. Far from being dupes of communism, they were building a military state to defend America against Communism. "The Korean War was the crisis that, in Acheson's words, "came along and saved us." By that he meant that it "enabled ... passage through Congress of a quadrupling of American defense spending."[643]

During the late 1940s, the United States had begun a radical demilitarization from eleven million men in uniform at war's end to 554,000 in 1948. Aircraft sales dropped from $16 billion in 1944 to $1.2 billion in 1947. The navy budget went from $50 billion to $6 billion.[644] The United States wisely refrained from interfering in European and Middle Eastern conflicts. It supplied money to resist Communism, but it had no appetite to send its young men to die in defense of British or French possessions that were slipping away from them. In Europe, the confrontation of freedom and despotism was clearly framed. The Soviet

---

642 Landon Storrs, *The Second Red Scare and the Unmaking of the New Deal Left* (Princeton, NJ: Princeton University Press, 2012).

643 Bruce Cumings, *The Korean War: A History* (New York: Modern Library, 2010), 210.

644 Cumings, *Korean War*, 212.

army was kept in place east of the Elbe. But what was happening in Asia was not at all clear.

When World War II officially ended, older conflicts in Asia recommenced. The people of Korea, heirs to a long and impressive civilization, had been struggling for control of their country since at least 1905. Theodore Roosevelt had presided over the signing of a peace treaty between Russia and Japan in which Korea was part of the spoils of war for Japan. There began a period of repression by the Japanese that is deeply stamped in the minds and hearts of Koreans. China was a natural ally for Korea in its resistance to Japanese attempts to smother the language and culture of Korea. In 1931, a war flared up when the Japanese invaded Manchuria. Koreans sided with the Chinese and filled the ranks of the Chinese army. It was in Manchuria that Kim Il Sung began his long struggle to lead the Korean people to a determination of their own future.

In the last days of World War II, the Soviets had moved down the Korean peninsula. The United States established a provisional government in the south. One day after the bombing of Nagasaki, the United States simply drew a line across the thirty-eighth parallel as part of the Japanese surrender. The United States wished to keep Seoul, which is just south of the thirty-eighth parallel, and the Soviets were willing to accept that line of partition. The Korean people had no voice in what was done to their country. Korea was not actually a central concern of the United States.

The United States wished to get Japan on its feet after the devastation of the war. Korea was to be part of the plan to make Japan the industrial workshop of East and Southeast Asia. Korea became a pawn in the fight against Soviet and Chinese Communism. Some of the postwar leaders in the south had previously collaborated with the Japanese. Kim Il Sung's movement for Korean independence feared a growing industrial strength in the south shaped by United States and Japanese power. As many as ninety thousand soldiers who had fought with the Chinese Communists against the Japanese became available when the war drew to a close in 1950. A series of statements by top US officials early in 1950 indicated that the United States did not consider Korea to be part of its defense strategy.

On June 25, 1950, the North Koreans swept across the thirty-eighth parallel and within a few days were able to take Seoul. A decision to intervene in this civil war (the thirty-eighth parallel was not a recognized international boundary) was made by Dean Acheson. He was supported by the president, and the action was taken before any consultation with the Pentagon, the United Nations, or Congress.[645] President Truman ordered US air and sea forces to support the South Koreans before the UN Security Council was asked to ratify a fait accompli on June 27. Douglas MacArthur, on June 29, decided that US ground troops would be needed. He also gave an order on that same day to the US air command: "Take out North Korean airfields immediately. No Publicity."[646] But it was North Korean tanks, not airplanes, that were devastating South Korea.

In the United Nations, the Soviet Union was boycotting the UN Security Council, so the United States was able to get a 9–0 vote for UN support of the war. The possibility of mediation was immediately lost, and by June 30 Truman had authorized the bombing of military targets in North Korea, a naval blockade, and the use of US ground troops. MacArthur became the top authority, but he did not report directly to the United Nations. As has several times happened, the United States wished to have military support from other nations in the United Nations, but it wished to remain in command of the whole military effort.

Dean Acheson's response to congressional critics was to say, "We are in a position in the world today where the argument as to who has the power to do this, that or the other is not exactly what is called for from America in this very critical hour."[647] When "America" is at risk; the niceties of the US Constitution can be put aside. At a meeting of top US officials in Washington, it was concluded that "South Korea would be defended, not because its conquest would directly threaten America's vital interests but because a failure to meet Stalin's challenge there would be so morally derelict it might fatally damage America's prestige and lead to a collapse of the free world's will to resist Communist aggression in places that really counted."[648]

---

645 Cumings, *Korean War*, 12.
646 Clay Blair, *The Forgotten War* (New York: Times Books, 1987), 76.
647 Emmet John Hughes, *The Living Presidency: The Resources and Dilemmas of the American Presidential Office* (New York: Penguin Books, 1974), 243.
648 Blair, *Forgotten War*, 72; James Thomson and others, *Sentimental Imperialists: The American Experience in East Asia* (New York: Harper and Row, 1981), 239.

A policy paper in 1948 had said that Korea was not part of the United States' strategic defense; however, an attack by North Korea could be countered by a "police action" carried out by an "international force" to which the United States might contribute units. President Truman adopted this language of "police action," which was afterward ridiculed because the phrase seemed to be a clumsy attempt to cover up a terrible war. But the idea of "police action" by the United Nations was not a bad idea.

In police work, violence or the threat of violence is restricted to the offending party; wholesale violence against innocent people is excluded. The police are limited by legislation and review boards. Korea could have been an instance of international police work. If the United Nations coalition had restored the boundary at or near the thirty-eighth parallel and tried to determine who was responsible for the violent conflict, the restoration might have provided a good example for similar conflicts that would inevitably follow elsewhere in the world.

The first year of the war had swift movements first to the south, then to the north, and then back south; after that, there was a stalemate. In the first weeks of the war, the South Korean army, along with some US forces, were driven all the way down to a pocket around the port of Pusan. If the Soviets or Chinese had wished to do so, they could have driven US forces into the sea. Instead, the US and South Korean troops had time to build up their strength. On September 15, 1950, US Marines made a landing at Inchon, the port near Seoul. Despite the doubters, MacArthur's plan was a spectacular success. Two weeks later, US and South Korean forces recaptured the capital city, Seoul.

Peace was possible then and at several other points in the year that followed. Instead, on the very day of the Inchon landing, Truman told MacArthur that he should prepare to invade North Korea. The United States got United Nations approval for crossing the thirty-eighth parallel, and MacArthur swept up to Pyongyang by October 20. D. Clayton James wrote that the decision to invade North Korea "must rank in quixotism with the Bay of Pigs invasion in 1961."[649] Communism was to be rolled back to the border of China. But while MacArthur and Truman were meeting at Wake Island on Oct.16, Chinese troops in large number were

---

649 D. Clayton James, *Refighting the Last War: Command and Crisis in Korea 1950–1953* (New York: Free Press, 1992), xi.

moving into North Korea. China was not going to allow a powerful army on its doorstep. The Chinese troops pushed the US and South Korean forces back to the thirty-eighth parallel and once again down to the "Pusan Perimeter."

At Wake Island, MacArthur told Truman that if the Chinese intervened in the war, US air power would inflict "the greatest slaughter."[650] When the Chinese troops did enter the battle, MacArthur ordered air strikes between the Yalu River and the war front. His order was "to destroy every means of communication and every installation and factories and cities and villages." A policy of firebombing cities that had been used against Japan was introduced in Korea, although there were not many cities in North Korea to bomb. The United States, however, eventually lost its supremacy in the air. To the shock of US officials, the Soviet MIG proved to be a better fighter plane than anything the United States had.

The Chinese were concerned with attacks on the Manchurian border, where they had important power plants. MacArthur was miffed when he was told on November 6 not to attack targets within five miles of the border. He managed to get Truman to back down on that order. When things were going badly for UN forces in November, Truman was asked during a press conference whether the use of the atomic bomb was a possibility. He replied that "there [had] always been active consideration of its use."[651] His answer shocked his allies at the United Nations.

In a letter to the Joint Chiefs of Staff on December 30, MacArthur objected to the constraints that he was under in conducting the war. He advocated a war with Communist China that would include a blockade of China, a destruction of Chinese industry, and a use of Chiang Kai Shek's army for "diversionary action." After the Chinese crossed the thirty-eighth parallel on January 1, 1951, it became questionable whether US forces could maintain their position. On January 9, the Joint Chiefs responded to MacArthur's letter by saying that the US Eighth Army should try to stabilize the situation without the US attacking China. They also told MacArthur to consider a plan for evacuating the army if that became necessary. Truman wrote a personal letter to MacArthur assuring him that if an evacuation of the troops did occur, that would not be the end;

---

650 Blair, *Forgotten War*, 375.
651 Blair, *Forgotten War*, 522.

Chinese aggression would still be "rectified." Whatever Truman meant by that word, it was probably not wise to give MacArthur any illusion of support in his wish to attack the Chinese homeland.

The US position became stable after Matthew Ridgway was put in charge of the troops in the field. A counterattack was launched and by March 15 a largely abandoned Seoul passed back into South Korea's possession. On March 20, MacArthur was told not to cross the thirty-eighth parallel. MacArthur decided to engage in a public dispute with the Truman administration, and on March 23 Truman decided that MacArthur had to go. Truman had taken his time to be sure that he had the support of his whole government. After more provocative statements by MacArthur, Truman delivered the news to MacArthur through Ridgway on April 12. MacArthur's own explanation for why he was fired was that Truman was mentally unbalanced.

MacArthur came home to a hero's welcome, complete with a ticker-tape parade in New York on April 20 that drew seven million people. MacArthur gave a speech before Congress; the concluding line of that speech is what most people remember: "Old soldiers never die they just fade away." What that was supposed to mean is anyone's guess. McArthur's speech was a bombastic defense of himself as standing up to the worldwide Communist conspiracy. On March 20, MacArthur wrote to Representative Joseph Martin, "If we lose the war to Communism in Asia the fall of Europe is inevitable, win it and Europe most probably would avoid war and yet preserve freedom. As you pointed out we must win. There is no substitute for victory."[652] A movement to nominate MacArthur for president quickly died down as the country regained its senses.

On July 4, President Truman gave a speech in which he warned that even if the Korean War were to end, humanity would "face a long period of world tension and great international danger."[653] General James Van Fleet, who was Ridgway's successor, spoke for many US officials: "Korea has been a blessing. There had to be a Korea either here or some place in the world."[654] "America" was in a worldwide battle for freedom; a few little

---

652 Blair, *Forgotten War*, 760.
653 I. F. Stone, *The Hidden History of the Korean War* (New York: Monthly Review, 1952), 281.
654 *New York Journal American*, January 19, 1952.

countries might have to bear the scars of the battle. But as for widening the war in Korea by attacking China, General Omar Bradley spoke sanely to a Congressional hearing: "Frankly, in the opinion of the Joint Chiefs of Staff, this strategy would involve us in the wrong war, at the wrong place, at the wrong time, and with the wrong enemy."[655]

Peace talks began on July 10, 1951, but they were caught up in the politics of the great powers. The Korean peace talks began just before the conference on the Japanese peace treaty took place on September 4, 1951. The United Nations was also set to meet in October when the question of Communist China's membership in the body was to be discussed. US officials expressed suspicion that Korean peace talks were a Russian or Chinese ploy to improve their position with the United Nations.

While the United States continued to be suspicious of Chinese motives for wishing to reach an agreement, the talks dragged on. Ridgway kept up pressure on North Korea, including an attack on Pyongyang with 450 aircraft. The approximate truce line was agreed upon by November 27, 1951. During the five months of talks, UN forces had suffered sixty thousand more casualties.[656] And yet the wrangling continued for more than a year and a half before an armistice was signed by North Korea, China, and the United States on July 27, 1953. The Republic of Korea refused to sign the armistice; technically the South is still at war with the North. The armistice provided for a buffer zone of two to five miles, creating a demilitarized zone (DMZ). The United States, which has never left the area, maintains an uneasy relation with the heavily militarized North.

The Korean War was a particularly brutal affair. As many as three million Koreans died, half of them civilians. Lurid stories of North Korean atrocities circulated in the United States. The war produced a new word in the English language: "brainwashing." While the North Koreans were in fact guilty of brainwashing prisoners (quite effectively in getting the majority of captured soldiers to make false confessions and accusations) and committing other war atrocities, the South engaged in more of the same. A Korean truth commission a half century later unearthed some of the horrors committed on both sides. The present situation remains volatile

---

655 Omar Bradley, *A General's Life* (New York: Touchstone, 1984), 640.
656 Blair, *Forgotten War*, 960.

and unresolved. "A new Korean War could break out tomorrow morning, and Americans would still be in their original state of overwhelming might and unfathomable cluelessness; armies ignorant of each other would clash again, and the outcome would again yield its central truth: there is no military solution in Korea (and there never was)."[657]

The cluelessness of the United States was unfortunately not restricted to the Korean peninsula. I. F. Stone wrote in 1952 that "if peace came in Korea, there might be new Koreas in the making in Indochina and Burma."[658] And indeed, before the Korean War was over, the United States was already beginning to get itself entangled in the area known as French Indochina. Documents released in 1971 show that the United States began shipping military aid to the French in Indochina in 1950.[659]

From Eisenhower to Kennedy

When commentators today bewail the decline of standards in the country, they frequently invoke the 1950s for its idyllic family life and civic order. Dwight Eisenhower is portrayed as presiding over a pacified country in which women returned to their rightful place in the home, Negroes were not complaining about the violations of their civil rights, and young people obeyed their parents and schoolteachers.

The 1950s, however, were hardly the model for a normal world. The decade was an interlude between the horrors of world war and the social eruptions of the 1960s. The attempt to cover over the changes brought on by the war, especially for women and Negroes, was only briefly successful. Underneath the placid surface of the time, there was a simmering of major social change that would become visible at the end of the decade. Protests in the name of a more inclusive society, with less discrimination against minorities and poor people, might have progressed with a minimum of chaos except that over the calls for change there hovered one enormous change that was the contribution of the 1950s: the militarization of the country.

---

657 Cumings, *Korean War*, 241.
658 Stone, *Hidden History*, 348.
659 Cumings, *Korean War*, 215.

President Eisenhower, on leaving office, coined a phrase for which he is famous: "the military-industrial complex." Unfortunately he does not seem to have had much success in counteracting the growth of that complex during his eight years in office. Truman and Acheson had become imprisoned in an economy that was linked to war-making. Eisenhower oversaw the end of the war but not a radical shift in the economy. The principle had been established that every young man in the country had to be ready to fight for freedom in the next international conflict. Education and industry were to be shaped along the lines of military discipline.[660]

John Kennedy's inaugural address in 1961 is remembered as beautiful rhetoric, but it is a speech that contributed to the unrealism of what "America" can do in the world. In his famous promise, Kennedy said "we shall pay any price, bear any burden, meet any hardship, support any friend, oppose any foe, in order to assure the survival and the success of liberty." Who is the "we" in that sentence? There is not a single reference in the speech to the United States and its government. The last paragraph begins, "Whether you are citizens of America or citizens of the world ..." It has sometimes been noted that no one is a "citizen of the world." But the stranger category is "citizens of America"; one can be a citizen only of the United States. Presidents have a license for hyperbole in inaugural addresses. Still, in Kennedy's speech the United States was almost swallowed in the mythical language of America.

Cuba Again

Two of the major events of Kennedy's short presidency are related to this inflated language of America and its support of the cause of liberty: the Cuban missile crisis and the beginning of US military involvement in Vietnam. Both events were tied to the great battle of the superpowers: the United States of America versus the Union of Soviet Socialist Republics. The choice for the world, according to the United States, was America or Communism. America meant liberty; Communism meant enslavement. Although Kennedy proclaimed the arrival of a new generation, his rhetoric was that of the late 1940s.

---

660 David Noble, *America by Design: Science, Technology, and the Rise of Corporate Capitalism* (New York: Galaxy Books, 1979), 225.

Early in Kennedy's presidency, he was embarrassed by a botched invasion of Cuba at the Bay of Pigs. The whole venture was so inept it could have been dismissed as comedy, except it highlighted the inexperience of the new president and the United States' inability to come to terms with Cuba. As recounted earlier, the United States has had a Cuba problem since the nineteenth century. In 1898, the United States squelched the movement for the independence of the Cuban people. Instead of helping Cuba to become a well-functioning state after breaking from Spain, the United States exercised political and economic control of the island. An independent state in the Caribbean was not something the United States would allow.

In 1933, Cuba's government of Gerardo Machado was in crisis, and President Roosevelt sent a special envoy, Sumner Welles, to mediate the conflict. Welles's efforts tended to undermine Machado; several opposition figures arose. One of those, Fulgencio Batista, was said by Welles to be "the only individual in Cuba today who represented authority."[661] And indeed Batista as chief of the armed forces controlled the Cuban presidency until he took over that office in 1940. After serving one term and living in the United States for a time, he led a military coup in 1952. He presided over an increasingly corrupt government that worsened the split between rich and poor. The US tried to ease out Batista and set up a caretaker government to prevent Fidel Castro from taking over. But Castro's July 26 Movement succeeded with its revolution on January 1, 1959.[662]

Once again there was a chance for a reorientation of Cuba-US relations, but things quickly went bad. The fiasco at the Bay of Pigs convinced Castro that the United States would not stop until the Cuban government was overthrown. Castro aligned himself with the Soviet Union, which found Cuba to be a convenient ally where missiles could be located ninety miles from the US mainland.

What followed was "the most dangerous moment in human history" (Arthur Schlesinger Jr.). The full story did not emerge until the release of

---

661 Louis Pérez, *Cuba and the United States: Ties of Singular Intimacy* (Athens, GA: University of Georgia Press, 1997), 200.
662 Pérez, *Cuba and the United States*, 235.

classified material in 1991.[663] The crisis was brought on by the Soviet response to the United States encircling the Soviet Union with intercontinental ballistic missiles. In the American myth created immediately after the event, Kennedy was the brilliant statesman who saved the world instead of a politician who feared for America's credibility. On October 15, 1962, US spy planes discovered long-range missiles in Cuba, courtesy of the Soviet Union. While efforts were made for a week to resolve the issue, the press kept quiet—something unimaginable today. Kennedy finally went on television to warn the nation and to demand that the missiles be removed. The missiles were easily capable of hitting the US mainland. (They were primarily aimed at New York City.) The scary conflict was between the Cold War adversaries: America and Communism. Cuba was in the middle, a small country that might act unpredictably.

The United States instituted an illegal blockade challenging Soviet ships on the way to Cuba. On Saturday, October 26, the crisis became most intense. Dean Rusk told Richard Holbrooke that he went to bed that night not knowing whether he (and the rest of us) would be alive in the morning.[664] Castro wrote to Khrushchev in the middle of that night: "If they attack Cuba, we should wipe them off the face of the earth."[665] In his memoirs, Khrushchev says he asked his generals if they could assure him that holding fast would not result in the death of five hundred million people. "They looked at me as if I were out of my mind or worse a traitor ... the biggest tragedy would be that the Chinese or Albanians would accuse us of weakness or appeasement."[666]

Khrushchev took the initiative in avoiding the ultimate showdown. "Let us display statesmanlike wisdom," he wrote to Kennedy in proposing a diplomatic solution. Kennedy agreed, resisting the belligerent advice of some of his advisers. The two leaders would agree to one thing in private

---

663 James Blight and Janet Lang, *The Armageddon Letters: Kennedy, Khrushchev, Castro in the Cuban Missile Crisis* (Lanham, MD: Rowman and Littlefield, 2012); Sheldon Stern, *The Cuban Missile Crisis in American Memory* (Stanford, CT: Stanford University Press, 2012).

664 Richard Holbrooke, "Superpower Nuclear Confrontation but Real," *New York Times*, October 15, 2004.

665 Blight and Lang, *The Armageddon Letters*.

666 Quoted in Jonathan Schell, *The Unconquerable World* (New York: Holt, 2004), 56.

and allow the other to make a different and face-saving statement in public. The United States said to the Soviets that removing the Jupiter missiles from Turkey was not "an insurmountable obstacle." Their removal a few months later would not to be tied in public to a trade. In private, the United States agreed not to invade Cuba. The Soviets would make a public statement that would indicate the USSR was not backing down, but in private they agreed to defuse the situation. The Soviet ships stopped short of the blockade. The public reaction in the United States was that the Soviets had "blinked first." Khrushchev later said to his son: "The one who blinks first is not always the weaker one. Sometimes he is the wiser one."[667]

One might have hoped that this incident would open a new era of communication between the United States and Cuba, as well as between the United States and Central American nations where struggles for a better life were caught up in the geopolitical game of America versus Communism. Twenty years after the Cuban crisis, Ronald Reagan would make some of his worst moves in the Caribbean and in Central America, and the United States' Cuban problem seemed destined to never end.

At home, the United States was undergoing a massive change. Just as fifty years later the Cuban missile crisis does appear to be as frightening as it then seemed, so the cultural upheaval of the 1960s, which seemed like radical change then, has indeed proved to be a radical shift in US history. There were so many interrelated changes that no one can say with certainty which one led and which one followed. According to the dates assigned to various movements, one can say that the struggle for African American rights was followed by the women's movement, followed by the gay rights movement, followed by the environmental movement. There were many other movements (focused on children, Native Americans, old people, and so on), but the date for when each movement began is mostly symbolic. The black civil rights movement had been stirring for years, if not decades, before Rosa Parks refused on December 1, 1955, to move to the back of a Montgomery bus. Gay men had been asserting their rights before June 28, 1969, when they resisted what was then the customary police harassment in Greenwich Village. Still, it helps to have markers for when much of the country took notice of these protests.

---

667 Sergei Khrushchev, "The Thwarted Promise of the 13 Days," *New York Times*, February 4, 2001, op-ed page.

Most, if not all, of these movements were interconnected simply by a desire of protesters to be accepted as full citizens. But why did all these things suddenly happen in the 1960s? The precondition of this upheaval was a transformation of the media of communication—a revolution that has continued since the 1960s. The match that lit the fire of widespread protest was the increasing involvement of the country in the Vietnam War and the government's need to find hundreds of thousands of young men to fight the war. Much had happened since the early 1950s, when young men dutifully went off to fight a war in Korea. A larger population of young people—and, especially, their presence in universities—was a catalyst for organized protest against what was seen to be a discredited adult authority. The government eventually sent five hundred thousand young men into the battle between North and South Vietnam. But hundreds of thousands of young men and women sustained public protest against the policies of their country.

The Rights of Black Americans

The movement for black civil rights got a head start on the war. It is significant that the black struggle is usually just called the civil rights movement. Among all the struggles in America and for American rights, black people hold a preeminent place. At the beginning of the United States, "the American" was defined as a free white person. Leaders of the women's movement in the nineteenth century were upset that the Negro received the right to vote by the passing of the fifteenth amendment in 1869, while women had to wait until 1920.[668] The unfortunate tension between white women and black people that was unhelpful to both groups remained in the emerging movements of the 1960s.

The denial of rights to black people was a question of not only civil rights but also of human rights. Although the term "human rights" was uncommon until the 1970s, the black person's exclusion from "America" was a complete denial of his or her humanity. The confusing choice for the descendant of the slave was to be assimilated into white culture or to try to establish a new category of "black American." Negroes who advanced in

---

668 Louise Michelle Newman, *White Women's Rights: The Racial Origins of Feminism in the United States* (New York: Oxford University Press, 1999).

a world of white people were forced to have a double consciousness: their own identity and their awareness of how they were perceived by whites. Perhaps no one embodied this acute problem better than the brilliant W. E. B. Du Bois. His task expressed in the book *The Souls of Black Folk* may sound simple to a white reader: "He simply wishes to make it possible for a man to be both a Negro and an American."[669]

The movement found a leader in a talented young preacher—Martin Luther King Jr. After protests against discrimination in the southern United States, starting with the Montgomery bus boycott in 1955–56, King was able to galvanize a national movement. He wrote to President Kennedy in May 1962 that "the struggle for freedom … of which the Civil War was but a bloody chapter, continues throughout our land today." King wanted not mere integration but a reimagination of American citizenship as a citizenship of racial equals.[670]

Like black leaders before and after him, King was immersed in the language of "America" while fighting against the "America" of his experience. King often used as a theme: "In a real sense America is essentially a dream – a dream yet unfulfilled." His most famous speech, which was delivered at the Capitol on August 28, 1963, filled out what this dream included, starting with the sons of slaves and the sons of former slave owners sitting together at the table of brotherhood. It is often forgotten that, while King harshly criticized "America" at the beginning of the speech, he ended with the first lines of the song "America."

Martin Luther King Jr. was unavoidably a polarizing figure. He cautioned his followers that "we must rise to the majestic heights of meeting physical force with soul force"—a formula that showed his indebtedness to Gandhi's strategy of nonviolent protest. King was keenly aware that nonviolent protest can lead to violent reactions, frequently directed at the person who refuses to engage in violence. Toward the end of his life, which was cut short by violence, King expanded his message to include the war in Vietnam. Many of his associates warned him that he would lose if he took a stand that would be seen as unpatriotic (un-American). King

---

669 W. E. B. Du Bois, *The Souls of Black Folk* (New York: Dover Publications, 2012), 2.

670 Kwame Anthony Appiah, "Battling with DuBois," *New York Review of Books*, December 22, 2011, 84.

correctly saw that the war and the treatment of black people at home were inextricably linked.[671]

The protest against the war, passionately led by young people ("don't trust anyone over 30"), was even more polarizing than the civil rights movement. The saying of opponents was "America: love it or leave it." Some of the young did leave for Canada or Europe, but most of them stayed and fought a contorted battle over "America." The generation born after World War II had been immersed in a patriotism that proclaimed America to be the greatest place in the world. Suddenly the young people became aware that this great power could do terrible things. For the young, as typically happens with sudden conversions, "America" became the name for everything that was wrong.

The young protesters thought that "America" was fighting a senseless and immoral war. Their cause was admirable, but their language unnecessarily isolated them from many of their elders, who also sensed that the war was wrong but who, despite that, still loved their country. No one gets very far in the United States by attacking America. The young had more potential supporters than the surface indicated. "America" was undergoing a crisis that would continue for at least a decade.

America's Asian Wars: Vietnam

At a Geneva conference in 1954, a peace treaty was signed between the French and the Vietminh. Vietnam was divided at the seventeenth parallel with a Communist government in the North. In February 1950, the United States had recognized the government of a French puppet, Bao Dai; that action made the United States an opponent of Ho Chi Minh's government in the North. In April 1950, a prescient article by Harold Isaacs, "A New Disaster in Asia," described what would happen in the following twenty years, as the "ill-conceived adventure" of fighting Communism in Vietnam was doomed to failure.[672] The situation was eerily similar to

---

671 King was confronted by Whitney Young of the Urban League at a 1967 meeting. Young feared that King's antagonizing the president would harm the civil rights movement; see David Halberstam, *The Best and the Brightest* (New York: Ballantine Books, 1993), 640.
672 Harold Isaacs, "A New Disaster in Asia," the *Reporter*, April 11, 1950, 25-27.

Korea, but few people saw looming the repetition of a failed policy to stop the advance of Communism. A striking feature of Isaacs's essay is that he refers to the "United States" several dozen times while the word "America" appears once. He was talking about an actual country instead of a mythical America.

There were efforts at a diplomatic solution to Vietnamese unrest during 1961-1963. France's Charles de Gaulle issued numerous warnings to the United States about the danger of its becoming involved in a Vietnamese war. United States officials consistently disregarded and even resented de Gaulle's advocacy of a "neutral" Vietnam. By the beginning of 1963, the United States had sixteen thousand military advisors in South Vietnam and was spending a million dollars a day in aid. In May 1963, a crisis occurred when the corrupt government of Ngo Dinh Diem opened fire on a Buddhist assembly. Later that year, the United States participated in a coup to replace Diem, but his successor was no better. In 1964, the US finally got a general to their liking—Nguyen Khanh.

The most crucial factor in 1963 was the assassination of John Kennedy. There has been debate in recent decades whether or not Kennedy would have kept the country from launching an all-out war in Vietnam.[673] Despite Kennedy's hawkish rhetoric in his inaugural address, he was a practical politician who had experienced war at close range. He learned from his experience with Cuba that an escapade such as the Bay of Pigs invasion could be disastrous and that negotiation with Khrushchev was the right way to go. Kennedy's successor, Lyndon Johnson, proclaimed on his first day in office, "I will not lose in Vietnam." Johnson's trusted advisor, Robert McNamara, said thirty years later, "We were wrong, terribly wrong."[674]

Lyndon Johnson was a clever and effective politician, but his view of world history was clouded by the mythical meaning of "America." He repeatedly asserted that "we learned from Hitler at Munich that success only feeds the appetite of aggression."[675] He was very aware of the attacks on Truman and Acheson for "losing China." During the 1950s, Johnson

---

673 James Blight and Janet Lang, *Virtual JFK: Vietnam if Kennedy Had Lived* (Lanham, MD: Rowman and Littlefield, 2010).

674 Robert McNamara, *In Retrospect: The Tragedy and Lessons of Vietnam* (New York: Times Books, 1995), xiii.

675 Halberstam, *The Best and the Brightest*, 600.

had criticized Eisenhower for not being aggressive enough. When a counter revolt was engineered in Guatemala by the United States, Johnson's response was "We've got to be for America first."[676]

With his insecurity on foreign affairs, Johnson trusted only a few people. In addition to McNamara, there were Dean Rusk and McGeorge Bundy, who urged Johnson to deepen the involvement of the United States in the war. Only a few people spoke out publicly against war; foremost among political leaders was Senator Mike Mansfield, who drew a comparison to Korea and urged a negotiated settlement. At the beginning of 1964, David Nes, deputy chief in Saigon, warned that the South Korean government had very little will to fight a war. McNamara was sent to Vietnam in March 1964 to evaluate the situation. His report was pessimistic, but he kept his doubts in check out of loyalty to the president.[677]

The key moment in the march to war was August 2, 1964. The US destroyer *Maddox* was fired upon in the Gulf of Tonkin. After the United States issued a warning to North Vietnam, a second attack supposedly occurred on August 4. The president, mindful of the Democratic National Convention in mid-August, received nearly unanimous backing in the Senate to take all steps necessary in retaliation. Many years later, General Alexander Haig said, "If he [Johnson] had not found the Gulf of Tonkin there would have been another excuse. This was tailor-made. It gave him an excuse and it gave him a massive level of support from the legislature."[678]

A sustained effort by U Thant, the secretary general of the United Nations, to bring North Vietnam to peace talks went nowhere on the part of the United States. Johnson kept secret during the presidential campaign that he was in fact moving in the direction that candidate Barry Goldwater was urging. Johnson won the election by one of the biggest margins in any presidential election. "If any American president had ever promised anything to the American people, then Lyndon Johnson had promised

---

676 Frederick Logevall, *Choosing War: The Lost Chance for Peace and the Escalation of War in Vietnam* (Berkeley, CA: University of California Press, 1999), 76.

677 Logevall, *Choosing War*, 125–28.

678 CNN, *Vietnam Twenty Years Later*, May 1995. The only senator who opposed Johnson was Wayne Morse of Oregon.

to keep the United States out of the war in Vietnam."[679] Immediately after the election, Hanoi sent a message that it was willing to talk; in addition, the government in Saigon was a mess. The respected journalist James Reston wrote on December 24, 1964, that Johnson had often said "intervention was needed to help a government defend its freedom; in view of the infighting in Saigon and a rising anti-Americanism in the South, US defense was now neither necessary nor warranted."[680]

The first stepping up of the war was by air—a regularly repeated illusion by the United States. Ambassador Maxwell Taylor, appearing before the US Senate Committee on Foreign Relations on December 3, said that the United States could attack by air and "let it go at that." Senator William Fulbright, one of the strongest opponents of the war, replied, "America never fails – once it engages in [bombing] they will just go all out."[681] Fulbright precisely stated what was happening and what would be the tragic story of the years to come: America never fails. To the extent that the United States government thinks that it is defending America, the only direction is to plow straight ahead. On January 27, 1965, while reinstating destroyer patrols in the Gulf of Tonkin, Johnson said, "We will move strongly, stable government or no stable government." All that he needed was an incident to spark an attack on the North, which he got on February 7. The Vietcong attack on a US helicopter near Pleiku killed 8 and wounded 126 US soldiers. Within hours, four preselected sites in North Vietnam were bombed.

What is still a puzzle is how the United States could get itself involved in an Asian land war only a dozen years after getting out of its disastrous war in Korea. The argument that the United States was defending a freedom-loving government against Communist aggression was preposterous. Dwight Eisenhower, describing Vietnam in the 1950s, wrote, "I have never talked or corresponded with a person knowledgeable in Indochina affairs who did not agree that had elections been held at the

---

679 Thomas Powers, *The War at Home: Vietnam and the American People, 1964-1968* (New York: Grossman, 1973), 17.

680 *New York Times*, December 24, 1964.

681 William Gibbons, *The U.S. Government and the Vietnam War: Executive and Legislative Roles and Relationships*, vol. 2 (Princeton, NJ: Princeton University Press, 1986-1995), 377.

time of the fighting, possibly 80 percent of the population would have voted for the communist Ho Chi Minh as their leader rather than Chief of State, Bao Dai."[682] The United States was on the wrong side of a civil war that it should not have been in at all.[683]

Foreign policies cannot be reduced to psychological profiles, but the character of political leaders is an undeniable part of the mix. Eisenhower acquired his fame from directing a world war. He was not inclined to exaggerate the gravity of a situation, for example, when the Chinese bombed the islands of Quemoy and Matsu. Lyndon Johnson, in contrast, was a bundle of insecurity, from which the people of the United States and millions of people in Southeast Asia would suffer the consequences. "Johnson's profound insecurity led him not only to personalize all the goals he aspired to but also to personalize all forms of dissent."[684] The small circle of people whom he trusted reinforced his isolation from thoughtful critics, both in the United States and around the world. Johnson was defending his manhood (as numerous vulgar statements he made in private show) and unfortunately did not separate that from "America's manhood."[685]

The war continued to escalate throughout 1965. After meeting with General Westmoreland in Saigon, McNamara recommended having four hundred thousand troops deployed by the end of 1965 and six hundred thousand by the end of 1967. Westmoreland was a conventional general whose policy was to win the war by attrition; his strategy was "search and destroy," which never had a chance of ending the war. By 1966, there was increasing protest in the country against the steady escalation of the war. Johnson seemed untouched.

The situation in Vietnam did get to McNamara. When increased bombing of North Vietnam by June 1966 was a failure, McNamara began

682 Dwight Eisenhower, *Mandate for Change, 1953-1956* (New York: Signet Books, 1965), 449.

683 Evan Thomas, *Ike's Bluff: President Eisenhower's Secret Battle to Save the World* (Boston: Little, Brown and Company, 2012).

684 Logevall, *Choosing War*, 298. Logevall relies in large part on the portrait of Johnson by Johnson's press secretary, George Reedy, *Lyndon B. Johnson: A Memoir* (New York: Andrews and McMeel, 1982). Reedy's book *Twilight of the Presidency* (New York: Dutton, 1987) argues that the White House isolates all presidents and has the effect of making worse any bad qualities they already had.

685 Logevall, *Choosing War*, 393.

trying to cap the war. On returning from a trip to Vietnam in October, McNamara told Johnson: "I see no reasonable way to bring the war to an end soon."[686] He resisted Westmoreland's call for more troops (the limit became five hundred twenty-five thousand), but McNamara had to cope with another true believer in Walter Rostow, who replaced Dean Rusk at the State Department. The double role that McNamara was forced to play led him to resign. He was replaced by Clark Clifford, who was first welcomed by Johnson, but Clifford offered stiffer criticism than Johnson had previously received. In January 1968, the Tet Offensive showed that even Saigon and other cities were not safe. Westmoreland's promises of victory were discredited. And within weeks, Johnson withdrew from the presidential primaries. Johnson's war became Nixon's war.

During the 1968 campaign, Richard Nixon repeatedly said he had a plan to end the war. No such plan appeared after Nixon won a close election against Hubert Humphrey. Henry Kissinger became the great mastermind of the war. "Vietnamization" was the grand new strategy, but it involved an "incursion" into Cambodia and the bombing of Laos. It is astounding that a war that obviously could not be won would drag on for another five years. There had been thirty-one thousand US deaths when Nixon took office, which means that almost half of US deaths came while the wrangling continued over how to get out of Vietnam.

Nixon laid out the picture as he saw it in an address to the nation on November 3, 1969. "The great question," Nixon said, "is how can we win America's peace." After pinning responsibility for the war on his three predecessors, Nixon put the blame for stalled peace talks on the North Vietnamese. Nixon appealed over the heads of protesters to "Middle America." These were the good Americans who loved their country and their flag and who wanted "peace with honor." In his inaugural address of January 20, 1973, Nixon said, "Our children have been taught to be ashamed of their country … we have been beset by those who find everything wrong with America and little that is right." Nixon asked his audience to pledge "to make these next four years the best four years in America's history, so that on its two hundredth birthday America will be as young and vital as when it began." Indeed, four years later "America" was as young as ever, but Nixon had long since departed in disgrace.

---

686 Halberstam, *Best and the Brightest*, 631.

Nixon and Kissinger did not get their peace with honor. The United States was rudely pushed out of Vietnam. The human cost of the war had been horrific. No one has a sure number for Vietnamese deaths, but it was at least two million. The precious credibility of "America" that both Johnson and Nixon were so anxious to preserve was badly tarnished. The war's economic cost, which had never been made clear during the war, was enormous. The political split in the United States between antipatriotism and "middle America" has never been healed.

William Manchester, in *The Glory and the Dream*, wrote that "the American Dream – that American democracy and prosperity were exportable – died in the jungles of Southeast Asia."[687] That requiem was premature. As soon as memory of the war became clouded, there would be new leaders who were sure that they knew how to export the American dream.

The New Morning in America

Nixon's pledge about the next four years pointed to the "two hundredth birthday of America" in 1976, which was actually the two hundredth anniversary of the Declaration of Independence. In 1976, there was a lot of flag-waving, and there were bigger fireworks than usual on July 4. There was no noticeable study of how the Declaration of Independence is related to the Constitution or the history of the United States.[688] The Vietnam War and the Watergate scandal had soured much of the country. After an interim administration of Gerald Ford, the country went with Jimmy Carter, a southerner with a sense of sin. Carter introduced most of the country to the issue of "human rights," especially in Latin America.[689] Very quickly, however, the United States decided that it did not want a president who had suggested that the country was in a "malaise" and that the United States might be on the wrong side in many freedom struggles.

---

687 William Manchester, *The Glory and the Dream* (Boston: Little, Brown and Company, 1974).

688 Thurgood Marshall, *Thurgood Marshall: His Speeches, Writings, Opinions and Reminiscences*, ed. Mark Tushnet (Chicago: Lawrence Hill Books, 2001), 281-85.

689 Samuel Moyn, *The Last Utopia* (Cambridge, MA: Harvard University Press, 2010).

Commentators from abroad expressed concern about the United States' wallowing in its own anxieties. Henry Fairlie wrote that "the future of the world lies with America … it would be a tragedy if, in the rage that must be endured, America wearied of its own idea."[690] Gunnar Myrdal, a sympathetic critic, wrote in 1977 that "Americans have, to an unprecedented extent, lost confidence in their national institutions." The fact that US citizens were in rebellion against their own institutions was not a new phenomenon. But Myrdal sensed a different kind of crisis that would arise if Americans ceased to believe in America. "What is at stake in the present many-faceted crisis in America is nothing less than the nation's soul."[691]

In 1979, an Islamic republic suddenly emerged in Iran, replacing the US-backed government of Shah Mohammad Reza Pahlavi. Iran boldly defied the United States and took hostages at the US embassy in Tehran. A new era was signaled with signs reading, "Death to America." ABC television began a nightly program that eventually was called *Nightline*. For its first 444 episodes, it was called *America Held Hostage*. Some people protested against that title; they said that it was embassy personnel that were being held hostage, not America. But ABC had it right; it was precisely "America" that Iran was defying and controlling. President Carter certainly learned that lesson when inept handling of the situation was the final factor in his being turned out of the presidency.

A symbolic but crucial event occurred at the Winter Olympics in 1980. The United States hockey team pulled off an unlikely victory over the Soviet Union. At the end of that game, the United States flag was draped over the team's goalie. At that moment, the gloom of Vietnam seemed to lift and "America" was back. Working from that change of mood, and feeding it with his own patriotic rhetoric, was an improbable politician named Ronald Reagan.

---

690 Henry Fairlie, *The Spoiled Child of the Western World* (Garden City, NY: Doubleday, 1975).

691 Gunnar Myrdal, "A Worried America," *Christian Century*, December 14, 1977, 1161-66; Rick Perlstein, *The Invisible Bridge: The Fall of Nixon and the Rise of Reagan* (New York: Simon and Schuster, 2014), documents the political and cultural shifts of the 1970s in exhaustive detail.

Reagan's background as a movie actor and a host of a television program fit quite well with the return of a sunny America. The movies did not invent America, but they were a chief contributor to America's meaning. The great film critic Pauline Kael reported in 1973, "The Vietnamization of American movies is nearly complete. Today, movies say that the system is corrupt, that the whole thing stinks."[692] Who better to restore America than a movie actor? Reagan's career in films was untouched by what Kael described as "a flipover from their prolonged age of innocence to this age of corruption." The oldest president in US history announced in his soaring rhetoric that it was "morning again in America." His favorite quotation was Thomas Paine's "We have it within our power to begin the world over again."

Reagan was paired with two other national leaders: Margaret Thatcher and Mikhail Gorbachev. The US president and British prime minister made an odd pair, but they each led a conservative reaction against the "welfare state," which had previously triumphed in Britain and had also, to a lesser extent, triumphed in the United States. They generated loathing among their respective opponents, but they had enough popular support to make dramatic changes in the economic structure of their countries. Reagan had the easier time in selling a program that was skewed to the rich because the rhetoric of America's greatness could cover over what was happening to workers in the United States.

Part of the economic package that Reagan sold was a big increase in defense—that is, military spending. Conservatives in the United States profess belief in reducing the federal budget to its bare bones—except for military spending. Reagan was a master of portraying a great race between America and Communism for superiority in bombs and missiles. It can be argued that he was successful in his strategy of challenging the Soviets to keep up with his pouring money into armaments. The Soviet Union, which was slowly unraveling, could not keep up the pace. Gorbachev either had to make a deal or else come down hard, as some of his predecessors had.

The world can be thankful that Gorbachev accepted the dissolution of the empire without making a last desperate crackdown. Once Gorbachev opened the door to change, the process overwhelmed him and any hopes and plans he had to reform the Soviet system. The beginning of the end of

---

692 Pauline Kael, *Reeling* (New York: Marion Boyars Publisher, 1977), 225.

the Cold War occurred at the Twenty-Seventh Congress of the Communist Party of the Soviet Union in 1986.[693] And Gorbachev's speech at the United Nations in 1988 revealed that the Soviet Union could no longer participate in an arms race.[694] Reagan was lucky to have had Gorbachev to deal with rather than an earlier Soviet leader who might have reacted very differently to Reagan's bellicose rhetoric. It is clear that the Soviets lost the Cold War; it is not so clear that the United States won, even if America did.

In Reagan's mission to triumph over Communism, several Central American and Caribbean nations became pawns in the battle between the superpowers. Any movement for social change was classified as either pro-American or pro-Communist (anti-American). The least infiltration of Communist influence was taken to be a threat to America.

Reagan had an obsession with Nicaragua and El Salvador, two Central American countries that were trying to get some distance from the United States and improve the lot of their people. Nicaragua had struggled since the mid-nineteenth century to get out from under US control. In 1927, Nicaraguans led by Augusto Sandino had unsuccessfully rebelled against the United States. In 1980, a group called the "Sandinistas" took up the fight.[695] From the US side, no one else around the "American lake" would be allowed to follow Cuba.

Some reporters in the 1980s became aware of how language worked against "Central American" nations in their conflict with "America." On the front page of the *New York Times*, the reporters in Nicaragua and El Salvador struggled to distinguish "America/American" from the US government's policies and the US military. The editorial writers at the *Times* seemed not to be reading the front page of their newspaper, as they continued to expound on what America should do and what American policy should be.

---

693 Robert Gates, *From the Shadows: The Ultimate Insider's Story of Five Presidents and How They Won the Cold War* (New York: Simon and Schuster, 2007), 380.

694 Geir Lundestad, *The Rise and Decline of the American "Empire"* (New York: Oxford University Press, 2012), 143.

695 Peter Smith, *Talons of the Eagle: Dynamics of U.S.-Latin American Relations* (New York: Oxford University Press, 1996), 109-10.

At a 1983 press conference, Ronald Reagan said of Nicaragua, "This is the first real Communist aggression on the American mainland."[696] Later in the same press conference, he said, "There is no thought of sending American combat troops." No one at the press conference and no one in later reports on the press conference asked the obvious question: If there is Communist aggression on the American mainland, why would American troops not be sent? The answer, of course, is that there was an equivocation in Reagan's use of "American." A US president can refer to the American mainland as including Central America when that suits US policy, and he can refer to troops as American when it is the US military that is meant.

How conscious Reagan was of his equivocal use of "American" is not the main point. He knew how to use America/American to suit his purposes, and no one in the press or the opposition party challenged him. The equivocation was an intrinsic part of the United States deciding what kind of government was acceptable in nations throughout America. After the fall of the Soviet empire, the United States returned to its general indifference about life in Central America.[697]

The presidency of George H. W. Bush was highlighted by the first war in Iraq. Saddam Hussein made a move into Kuwait, perhaps because he thought he had a green light from the United States. For most war activity in the twentieth and twenty-first centuries, presidents have easily manipulated public support. The Gulf War of 1991 did involve Senate debate. The Senate passed a war resolution by a four-vote majority. The vote was affected by what proved to be a calculated lie. On October 10, 1990, a fifteen-year-old girl named Nayirah testified before the Congressional Human Rights Caucus. She described how, as a volunteer in a Kuwaiti maternity ward, she had seen Iraqi troops storm the hospital, steal the incubators, and "leave 312 babies on the cold floor to die." Seven senators referred to this story as supporting evidence for going to war.

In January 1991, just before the US bombing began, press reports questioned the truth of the story. It was learned that Nayirah was the daughter of the Kuwaiti ambassador to Washington and had no connection to the Kuwaiti hospital. She had been coached by senior executives of Hill

---

696 *New York Times*, July 16, 1983.

697 Albert Fishlow and James Jones, eds., *The United States and the Americas: A Twenty-First Century View* (New York: W. W. Norton, 1999).

and Knowlton, a public relations firm that had a contract with Kuwait, to make the case for war. Brent Scowcroft, the national security advisor, said in a 1995 interview, "We didn't know it wasn't true at the time." He acknowledged that "it was useful in mobilizing public opinion."

If one believes Scowcroft that the government was not lying, one can only conclude that their willingness to be taken in by a shaggy-dog story is breathtaking. Why would they not check out who this fifteen-year-old girl was and whether there was any basis for her story? The story itself stands in a long line of tall tales that have been told about an enemy's inhumanity. What would be the point of killing 312 babies (by her count?) except to prove that you are evil incarnate? The US government in this case may not have been lying; it outsourced the job to a public relations firm.

Bush impressively organized an overwhelming military force to push Hussein back into Iraq. Hussein never had a chance in a landscape where US tanks and bombers had unrestricted power to aid a ground force that had time to prepare for an invasion. The hundred-day war ended in humiliation and the slaughter of Iraq's army. Bush wisely decided not to have the United States take Baghdad, because that would mean acquiring a problem that the United States did not need. The United States did institute a "no fly zone" that remained in place for ten years and was the cause of terrible suffering for innocent people in Iraq.

During the 1990s, after the fall of the Soviet empire, the United States seemed to be riding high. President Bill Clinton presided over good economic times; some people predicted that new technology and more flexible banking rules meant the good times were now here to stay. Clinton actually managed to balance the budget, and some people began worrying about the government running too big a surplus.

Clinton had to struggle against an opposition determined to bring him down. He was not very vulnerable on economic policy or on a cautious foreign policy, but his lack of personal discipline, especially in the Lewinsky scandal, gave his enemies the arrow they needed. The final part of Clinton's time in office was a wasted opportunity. Clinton would make an amazing comeback years later as he devoted himself with great energy to good causes. Unfortunately his impeachment proceedings put his vice president in a bind when he ran for president in 2000. The decade of high hopes ended with the election of George W. Bush.

9

Is the "United States" Disappearing?

The practice of calling the country "America" goes back to the beginning of US history. The shorthand at first seemed harmless, although many people in other nations of America did not think such usage was a trivial matter. Throughout the nineteenth century, the significance of the US claim to be America became more evident. At the conclusion of the US Civil War, there was one thing that joined the Confederate States of America and the United States of America: the idea of America. After the war, "America" increasingly became the way to refer to the reunited country.

Despite this increased dependence on "America" as the name of the country, it would not have seemed necessary in the first half of the twentieth century to ask whether "United States" was in danger of being replaced by "America." Franklin Roosevelt's first inaugural address in 1933 does not contain the word "America." His whole attention was on fixing the problems of "the nation." In his message to Congress on December 8, 1941, carrying the country into war, Roosevelt referred repeatedly to the United States and not at all to "America."

The seeds of a new way of speaking emerged immediately after World War II as an "iron curtain" divided the world into America and Communism—two ideologies backed by military power. Anyone in the United States who seemed not sufficiently anti-Communist was said to be un-American.

The ideological wars of the 1960s, including attempts to justify what the United States was doing in a small Asian country, hardened the binary view of the world. The disastrous war could be explained only as a necessary part of the world conflict between "America" as leader of the free world and Soviet Communism, which was intent on enslaving people everywhere. Unfortunately, opponents of the war absorbed the same language of America. Instead of criticizing the policies of the United States, they attacked America and ridiculed patriotic symbols. It was a hopeless strategy. Then and now, no one gets anywhere in the United States by attacking America.

Although Barry Goldwater's extremism in defense of liberty was too extreme for the country in 1968, his presidential campaign prepared the way for Richard Nixon and Ronald Reagan. As the black civil rights movement and the women's movement gained steam, the American way seemed to be under threat from within and without. The sour conclusion to Nixon's presidency left the country mired in self-doubt. Jimmy Carter's promise that he would never lie and that he would guarantee a government as good as the people provided a respite. But when Carter asked the country to examine its own moral malaise and to stand for a new idea called human rights, the president found himself increasingly isolated.

Ronald Reagan had not the slightest doubt that the question was, Whose side are you on—that of America or that of the evil empire? Reagan brilliantly manipulated the positive feeling for "America" that had been obscured during the Vietnam fiasco. The country enthusiastically followed Reagan's positive message of morning again in America.

Although Ronald Reagan had seemed to go as far as anyone could go in conflating the United States and America, George W. Bush outdid him. US presidents regularly manipulate feelings for America, but other presidents did not sever almost all linguistic ties to the "United States." In his inaugural address of January 20, 2001, Bush referred nineteen times to "America"/"American" but not once to the nation whose presidency he was assuming.[698] It might have been predicted then that the country was destined for some bad times with a man who thought he was becoming the president of America.

---

698 George W. Bush, inaugural address: www. pbs.org/newshour/inauguration/ speech.html.

A Shock to America

George W. Bush's linguistically living in America became even more pronounced in 2001 with the bombing of the Pentagon and the World Trade Center. Bush led the way for the country in the increasing use of "America." Immediately after September 11, it was widely said, "Everything has changed." Of course, *everything* did not change, but much did, including the defense of America. What had happened to America's security, and what should America do now?

The bombers in 2001 aimed at humiliating America, and they chose suitable symbols of military and economic power. If they had meant to attack New York, which is an actual part of the United States, they would have bombed buildings dear to New Yorkers rather than the World Trade Center, which had been widely ridiculed by locals. Bombing the Empire State Building or the Chrysler Building would have caused far more death and destruction. Instead the bombers went at what they imagined was a symbol of America and a center of American financial dominance.

Most people who watched the collapse of the towers felt sympathy for the thousands of people who were incinerated. It was difficult not to feel bad for the victims of the attack. But for many people around the world, it was also difficult not to feel a thrill that America the bully had suffered a bloody nose. The twofold reaction was exemplified in the pages of *Le Monde* in Paris. An editorial on September 12, 2001, proclaimed, *"Nous Sommes Tous Américains."* That rather extravagant claim was more modestly stated in the editorial: "How can we not feel profound solidarity with those people, that country, the United States ..."[699] A few months later, the writer of the editorial, Jean-Marie Colombiani, had second thoughts, asking, *"Tous Américains?"* and giving a decidedly negative answer: There is no solidarity, he wrote, with a place that violates all the world's laws, glories in the death penalty, treats its minorities in a racist fashion, and is a fundamentalist Christian state.[700]

The French may have led the way in this dichotomous reaction, but the split was common both within the United States and in numerous other

---

699 *Le Monde*, September 12, 2001.
700 Jean-Marie Colombiani, *Tous Américains? Le monde après le 11 Septembre 2001* (Paris, 2002).

countries.[701] If America is a place of innocence that tries only to do good in the world, the bombing was a dastardly and unprovoked attack. If America is a technological horror that is corrupting the world, then the bombing was a long overdue retaliation against the world's biggest bully.[702] Both reactions suffered from an inability to distinguish between a mythical America and the policies and people of the United States.

Osama bin Laden released a statement on October 7, 2001, expressing satisfaction at what had happened on September 11: "America, hit by God in one of its softest spots ... There is America, full of fear from its north to its south, from its west to its east. Thank God for that. What America is tasting now is something insignificant compared to what we have tasted for scores of years." Bin Laden gave no indication of a knowledge of the United States, but he was confident that he knew America, and he was certain that God was going to destroy America, with a little help from suicide bombers.[703]

Within the United States, not surprisingly, the dominant feeling was that America was the innocent victim of an unprovoked attack. Not many people dared to suggest that actions by the United States had been a contributing factor to the context of the attack. Instead there were endless renditions of "God Bless America." When critics both within and outside the United States reacted against the mawkish sentiments, they tended

---

701 In England, the Classics scholar Mary Beard drew a strong reaction with her comment that "however tactfully you dress it up, the United States had it coming." (See *Question Time,* September 13, 2001.) Interestingly, Beard referred to the United States, not America. She later complained that people neglected the fact that the statement simply referred to what "many people openly or privately think." Six years later, she was still trying to defend her original comments while apologizing for the way they came across. (See *London Review of Books,* November 22, 2007.)

702 Charlotte Raven wrote in *The Guardian,* September 18, 2001, "America is the same country it was before September 11. If you didn't like it then, there's no reason to pretend to now....A bully with a bloody nose is still a bully."

703 Amy Chua, *World on Fire: How Exporting Free Market Democracy Breeds Ethnic Hatreds and Global Instability* (New York: Doubleday, 2003), 257.

to go to the opposite extreme in attacking America: "America is evil." "America brought this attack upon itself." "America deserved it."[704]

If, instead of talking about a mythical America, US citizens had taken the opportunity to reassess their place in the world and the policies of their government, some helpful changes might have happened. Instead of their political leaders declaring that the bombing was a "declaration of war on America" and that some country or countries would have to pay, the leaders might have concluded that if the schoolyard bully could be sucker-punched, then a new cooperation might be needed for order in the yard. The United States, chastened with a little humility, might have found a wide receptiveness to proposals for better international cooperation.[705] For a while, other nations did seem to leave the door open to a new order, but the metaphor and then the reality of war quickly took over the thinking of US officials.

A revealing contrast is found in two letters of 2002, each signed by a long list of academics. The first letter is entitled "What We're Fighting for: A Letter from America"; the second letter is called "A Critical Response: A Letter from United States' Citizens to Friends in Europe."[706] From merely looking at those two titles, it is easy to guess the contents of each letter.

The "Letter from America" is a shrill defense of "America" and "American values." Much of the letter is about "just war theory" which is invoked to justify the course that the US government had set out on. After acknowledging that "some values sometimes seen in America

---

704 Jean Baudrillard in *Le Monde*, November 3, 2001, declared that the perpetrators had acted out what was the dream of "all the world without exception....It is they who acted but we who wanted the deed."

705 A PEW research poll two months after the attack found that more than one-half of the world's "opinion makers" agreed with the statement that American policies were a major cause of the attacks; two-thirds agreed that Americans now knew what it was like to be vulnerable. After six years, the favorability rating of the United States fell in almost every country; from 61 to 29 percent in Indonesia, from 30 to 9 percent in Turkey, and from 60 to 30 percent in Germany. (See James Traub, *The Freedom Agenda: Why America Must Spread Democracy (Just not the Way George Bush Did)* [New York: Picador, 2009], 146.)

706 "What We're Fighting For: A Letter from America," *The Responsive Community*, Fall 2002, 30-41; "A Critical Response: A Letter from United States' Citizens to Friends in Europe," *The Responsive Community*, Fall, 2002, 43-48.

are unattractive and harmful," the letter says, "At the same time, other American values – what we view as our founding ideals and those that most define our way of life – are quite different from these, and they are much more attractive, not only to Americans but to people everywhere in the world." These American values are said to be human dignity, freedom of conscience and religion, openness to other views, and universal moral truths. "The best of what we too casually call 'American values' do not belong only to America, but are in fact the shared inheritance of humankind, and therefore a possible basis of hope for a world community based on peace and justice."[707]

The second document, "A Letter from United States' Citizens to Friends in Europe," attempts a sober assessment of US policies and why so many people hate the country. This letter is especially critical of the claim that equates American values and universal values. People who wish to spread American values may think they are being generous. Indeed, some of the values that the United States imperfectly embodies can be usefully shared with other nations. But if the United States and US Americans casually call their nation America, then "American values" cannot be shared with other nations.

The United States tends to cover its failings and defects under a rhetoric that exalts America. Objective observers speak a different language. A 1998 Amnesty International study of human rights in the United States has almost nothing to say about America. The horrific statistics about prisons, health care, and child poverty are not an attack on America, as critics charged, but facts about the United States.[708] A 2005 Amnesty International report on US torture was dismissed by George W. Bush as having been written by "people who hate America."

Similarly, the International Red Cross report on abuses of prisoners during the Bush administration has almost nothing to say about America but reveals much about US policies. The report cited practices at Guantanamo prison that amounted to "cruel, inhuman or degrading

---

707 "What We're Fighting For," 33.
708 Amnesty International, *United States of America: Human Rights for All* (London: Amnesty International UK, 1998).

treatment."[709] Although some US officials tried to play down the findings as based merely on the testimony of prisoners, the accounts by the fourteen interviewees were remarkably uniform in describing practices that the Red Cross Committee, famous for its neutrality, called "torture."

Barack Obama, immediately after his election in November 2008, was interviewed on *60 Minutes*. Obama's response to the question of torture was "I have said repeatedly that America doesn't torture. And I'm going to make sure that we don't torture. Those are part and parcel of an effort to regain America's moral stature in the world."[710] Those three sentences do not go together. The first sentence, "America doesn't torture," is not a factual statement; it refers to an ideal called America. The second sentence is what the president of the United States intends to do. The third sentence acknowledges that the United States has indeed engaged in torture, has lost moral stature, and needs to regain a standard that is suggested by the term "America."

In August 2014, President Obama somewhat casually admitted, "We tortured some folks."[711] The ambiguous meaning of "We" in that statement was worsened by his saying that he understood the context in which "We" used torture. The torture was used and approved by individuals who blatantly violated the law and have never been held accountable. It is difficult to understand why particular officials in the US government should not have been treated as war criminals.

It is frightening to listen to presidents and other powerful men who seem to be oblivious of the fact that they are talking about a mythical land where there is equality, liberty, and justice for all. In 2012, presidential candidate Mitt Romney in his acceptance speech at the Republican National Convention used "America" fifty-three times while saying little about what he would do as president of the United States.[712] Donald

---

709 International Committee of the Red Cross, *Report on the Treatment of Fourteen "High Value Detainees"* (Washington: ICRC, 2007); Mark Danner, "U.S. Torture: Voices from the Black Sites," *New York Review of Books*, April 9, 2009, 69-77.

710 *60 Minutes*, November 16, 2008.

711 A press briefing on August 1, 2014.

712 *New York Times*, August 30, 2012.

Trump in his 2018 State of the Union address used "America" eighty-two times while not confronting any of the problems that the United States has.

Hillary Clinton's campaign book, *Hard Choices*, contained some hard facts framed within the mythical language of America. The book's beginning is disconcerting. In the "Author's Note" before page 1, there is a collection of standard clichés about the greatness of America. The rhetoric improves when Clinton recounts in detail the diplomatic negotiations between the United States and other nations. But at the end of the book, she says that "the most important questions anyone considering running for president must answer are: 'What is your vision for America' and 'Can you lead us there'?"[713] A clearer and more relevant question to ask would have been, How can the US government move from its present gridlock toward fulfilling the well-known ideals of America?

Donald Trump talked about a vision for America during the campaign and did some new and ominous manipulation of "America." Because he described the country in such a bleakly negative way, he occasionally slipped in references to the United States.[714] America, he argued, could easily be as great as ever, but it was being held hostage by a vast conspiracy. What was needed to reveal the conspiracy was someone who would not be restrained by the usual rules of political discourse and who would speak simple truths. Trump's speeches contained innumerable lies and factual errors, but his language fit the narrative of letting America be as great as it once was. In mythical America, statements are not to be judged as true or false but according to whether they advance the cause of the greatest nation in the history of the world.

Wars and More Wars

There is a direct line from the bombings on September 11, 2001, to two wars that the United States got itself involved in. Practically no one denied that the bombings were the work of international criminals. The response of the United States understandably involved a hunt for those criminals so that justice could be served. As I have noted above, the United States could

---

713 Hillary Clinton, *Hard Choices* (New York: Simon and Schuster, 2014), 602.
714 Ddonald Trump, in his acceptance speech, used "United States" four times and "America" twenty-five times.

have also engaged in some self-examination and a review of its foreign policies. To start a war was hardly the answer, but using its military might was not a surprising move by the United States.

Immediately after the attack of September 11, 2001, George W. Bush addressed Congress and used apocalyptic rhetoric: "On September 11, enemies of freedom committed an act of war against our country." Bush's response was to declare war on terror, which he warned would be a long war: "Our war on terror begins with al Qaeda, but it does not end there. Every enemy of terror must be overcome. This is not, however, just America's fight. And what is at stake is not just America's freedom. This is the world's fight. This is civilization's fight … Either you are with us or you are with the terrorists."[715]

Bush announced, in his Thanksgiving address of 2001, "America has a message for the nations of the world. If you harbor terrorists you are terrorists … We will not be secure as a nation until all of these threats are defeated. Across the world and across the years, we will fight these evil doers."[716] Any country that "harbored" terrorists could be declared an enemy. By that standard, almost every country in the world (including perhaps the United States) might find itself an enemy of America. Bush was committing the United States to an endless attempt to drive out evil; the nation will be insecure so long as the job is not finished.

First up for punishment was the broken country of Afghanistan, where a band of international terrorists were thought to be hiding. Numerous observers warned the United States that starting a war in Afghanistan was unwise and unjustified. The Russians, most recently, had had a disastrous experience in Afghanistan to offer as a warning. If the United States had reliable information regarding where the terrorists were, it might have made sense to use its ability to make a quick strike against them. As soon as it was apparent that no quick "police action" would succeed, the United States should have taken itself out of the country.

A few billion dollars in aid would have been appropriate for whatever havoc the United States had caused in Afghanistan. Instead the United States decided to fix a place that it did not understand and that no one

---

715 *New York Times*, September 21, 2001.
716 Charles Townshend, *Terrorism: A Very Short Introduction* (New York: Oxford University Press, 2011), 118.

else knows how to fix. For a short while, there did seem to be progress, especially for women who were freed from an oppressive dictatorship. Perhaps some gains might have been secured, but instead the United States decided to start another war. Afghanistan was left to a hopeless and seemingly endless fight in which US troops were never certain who the enemy was. The United States poured in billions of dollars, which did not seem to do much good.

Next up was Iraq. It seems that many of George W. Bush's advisers were waiting for a casus belli to finish off the Iraqi dictator Saddam Hussein. He had once been a favorite of the United States, but now he was someone who dared to tweak the whiskers of Uncle Sam.[717] Hussein was an aging dictator presiding over an impoverished country that was still suffering from the beating that the United States had given it in the previous decade. However, the United States claimed that Hussein was building "weapons of mass destruction."

Bush's inner circle were intent on taking the war to Iraq, even though there was no evidence that Iraq was connected to the September 11 attack. The Senate voted seventy-seven to twenty-three "that the president is authorized to use all necessary force against those nations and organizations or persons he determines planned, authorized, committed or aided the terrorist attacks that occurred on Sept.11, 2001 or harbored such organizations." Twenty-one Democrats voted against the resolution, along with one brave Republican, Lincoln Chaffee. Many of the Democrats who gave Bush the green light for war soon regretted their vote and tried to get a reversal of the act in 2003, but it was too late. Some of them claimed that they were against the war and had not authorized Bush to go to war. They had failed to distinguish between "force" and "war," which allowed Bush to interpret the vote as an authorization of war.

Bush, in an address to the nation on October 16, 2002, used "force" as an equivalent of "war." He cited Senate support for his policy: "Though Congress has now authorized the use of force, I have not authorized the use of force. I hope the use of force will not be necessary ... Our goal is

---

717 Testimony of Richard Clarke before the 9/11 Commission, March 24, 2004; also Richard Clarke, *Against All Enemies: Inside America's War on Terror* (New York: Free Press, 2004).

to fully and finally remove a real threat to world peace and to America. Hopefully that can be done peacefully."[718]

In his State of the Union address in January 2003, Bush said "that the British Government [had] learned that Saddam Hussein recently sought significant quantities of uranium from Africa." As everyone later learned, Bush was either lying or misinformed. George Tenet, the CIA director, more or less took the fall for the misstatement. He sort of apologized, but his main point seemed to be that the dangerous offense against truth consisted of only sixteen words. But when peace or war is at stake, a few words in a presidential speech can be a powerful deed.[719]

The Bush Administration seemed keen on going to war despite the protests of most of the nations of the world. Secretary of State Colin Powell insisted on getting international support if the United States was to start a war. Powell was the most internationally respected of the Bush team. He opposed the Cheney-Rumsfeld-Wolfowitz lust for war; he actually knew what war is like. Nonetheless, Powell eventually agreed to make the case for war to the UN Security Council. Dick Cheney said to him, "You've got high poll ratings; you can afford to lose a few points."[720]

On February 5, 2003, Powell argued before the UN Security Council (while waving a vial) that "there [could] be no doubt that Saddam Hussein [had] biological weapons and the capability to produce more, many more." Powell also claimed that Hussein was undoubtedly trying to obtain components for a nuclear bomb. Powell would later regret this performance that smoothed the path to war. In a 2005 interview, Powell said, "It will always be a part of my record. It was painful. It's painful now."[721]

On February 17, 2003, the European Union directly addressed the US president in a badly flawed statement: "War is not inevitable. Force should only be used as a last resort."[722] Similar to the Senate and the president, the European Union played with the ambiguity of "force." What the European Union could truthfully have said to Bush was "Force is inevitable. Iraq is

718 Mark Danner, "Secret Way to War," *New York Review of Books,* June 9, 2005, 70.
719 Peter Eisner, "How a Bogus Letter Became a Cause for War," *Washington Post,* April 3, 2007.
720 Karen De Young, "Falling on his Sword," *Washington Post,* February 3, 2007.
721 Interview on ABC television with Barbara Walters, September 8, 2005.
722 *New York Times,* February 18, 2003, 1.

already being subjected to several kinds of force. Iraq is not an imminent threat to the world. War, if it is ever justified, should only be used as a last resort and the world is nowhere near that point."

A Pew Research Center poll at the time showed that 54 percent of Germans and 75 percent of the French thought that "the United States [wanted] to control Iraqi oil." A US military historian reacted: "They just can't seem to accept that we might be acting for, say, the general safety and security of the world. After more than two hundred years, Europe still hasn't figured out what makes America tick."[723] Only if one sorts out the difference between the United States and America can one make sense of this disagreement. America always acts only for the safety and security of the world, but the United States did have an interest in oil. Europe fails to understand America, but the United States also misunderstands its own relation to America.

As has happened repeatedly in US wars, leaders insisted that the enemy would melt away in the face of America's superior military power. And the further delusion was that the local population would greet the invading force with gratitude for the liberation of their country. It was famously said by advisor Kenneth Adelman that "liberating Iraq would be a cakewalk."[724] The initial show of US firepower was indeed awesome; the Iraqis had no air force and not much air defense. The US troops on the ground had their way. Resistance was light as the US military drove straight toward Baghdad.

Someone might have wondered at that moment whether Iraq was using the age-old tactic of allowing an enemy force to break through the line of defense and then surrounding them. That ancient tactic may have seemed outdated because of air power, but a variation on the tactic did occur. The US soldiers were not surrounded by a superior army; they were surrounded by a country and a population that they did not understand. When the US took Baghdad, they were not greeted as liberators who could solve the country's problems. Instead chaos and destruction followed the defeat of Hussein—a situation for which the United States was totally unprepared.

---

723 Max Boot, "A War for Oil? Not this Time," *New York Times*, February 13, 2003.
724 Kenneth Adelman, "Cakewalk in Iraq," *Washington Post*, February 13, 2002; "Cakewalk Revisited," *Washington Post*, April 10, 2003.

Without the dictator, Iraq was torn by competing factions. Instead of oil production paying for the war, as US officials had promised, the country's economy ground to a halt and billions of US dollars were needed to sustain the country. The elusive weapons of mass destruction were never recovered, so the purpose of the war became "nation building," which Bush had ridiculed before his election.[725]

The war was not the quick victory that "shock and awe" was supposed to bring about. On May 1, 2003, Bush made himself look ridiculous by landing in a jet plane on the aircraft carrier USS *Abraham*. Speaking in front of a huge banner that said "Mission Accomplished," Bush declared that "major combat operations" in Iraq were concluded. But in fact, the guerrilla war had just begun and would drag on for a decade. In later years, Bush and his supporters tried to explain what he really meant on that occasion—for example, that the "Mission Accomplished" banner referred to the carrier's completion of ten months' deployment in the Persian Gulf, and also that he did not say the war was finished. The twists and turns of explanations only added to the embarrassment.[726]

In a war in which the enemy was not clear and attacks could come from any quarter, the use of brutal tactics of suppression was not surprising. The US soldiers in these bewildering surroundings often lashed out at suspected terrorists. The US engaged in torturing prisoners, which is not so unusual in wars, but with the existence of the internet, the shocking pictures of torture quickly spread around the world.[727] The prison at Abu Ghraib had thousands of prisoners who, according to the army's own report in February 2004, were subjected to "sadistic, blatant and wanton criminal abuses."[728] Some of the reaction around the world was hypocritical, a posturing by nations that readily employ torture. But "America," according to US claims, is supposed to be better than that.

---

725 Fred Kaplan, *The Insurgents: David Petraeus and the Plot to Change the American Way of War* (New York: Simon and Schuster, 2013).

726 "Mission Accomplished Whodunit," *CBS News*, October 29, 2003.

727 Jane Mayer, *The Dark Side: The Inside Story of How the War on Terror Turned into a War on American Ideals* (New York: Doubleday, 2008).

728 This report prepared by Major General Antonio Taguba was leaked to the press: Seymour Hersh, "Torture at Abu Ghraib," *New Yorker*, May 10, 2004.

What led up to revelations of prisoner mistreatment at several sites was the supposed need to rethink international rules for the treatment of prisoners. The attack on September 11, 2001, it was claimed, had changed the rules. Bush's motto was "No freedom for the enemies of freedom."[729] In 2004, there came to light an infamous memo of 2002 written by White House Counsel Alberto Gonzalez. The part of the memo that attracted the most attention and condemnation was as follows: "In my judgment, the new paradigm [in the post 9/11 era] renders obsolete Geneva's strict limitations on questioning of enemy prisoners and renders quaint some of its provisions."[730] Gonzalez later complained that news reports did not include his examples of the Geneva provisions that he was referring to as "quaint," such as "commissary privileges" or "athletic uniforms." What could not be denied, however, was that the United States was using what it called "enhanced interrogation techniques," which most of the world calls torture.

The younger Bush was out to better his father's one-term presidency and complete the job that, in his view, his father had failed to do.[731] Concerning his father's decision not to march troops into Baghdad, the younger Bush told his biographer, "My father had all this political capital built up when he drove the Iraqis out of Kuwait and he wasted it ... If I have a chance to invade ... if I had that much capital, I'm not going to waste it." He did, in fact, have the opportunity, and he did what he said he would do. The result showed that the older Bush had been wiser than the younger.

When George W. Bush was getting ready for war, he was asked whether he consulted with his father; his answer was that he consulted a greater father in heaven. Actually, in his memoir, *Decision Points*, he does recount a conversation with his father about going to war. The father says, "You know how tough war is, son, and you've got to try everything

729 Ian Buruma, *Taming the Gods: Religion and Democracy on Three Continents* (Princeton, NJ: Princeton University Press, 2010), 110, points out that although Bush was not an enthusiast of the French Revolution, the motto comes from the Terror of 1793.

730 The memo was written on January 18, 2002; the *Newsweek* publication of its contents was on May 24, 2004.

731 George Bush and Mickey Herskowitz, *A Charge to Keep: My Journey to the White House* (New York: William Morrow, 2001).

you can to avoid war … But if the man won't comply, you don't have any other choice."[732] It is difficult to imagine worse advice from father to son. Everyone else in the world knew that there were other choices. If only it had been true that the son knew "how tough war is," he might not have recklessly started a war. Infrequent participation in the Texas Air National Guard had not conveyed the horrors of war.

America: Conqueror of Evil

The United States, when it is conflated with "America," has a strong tendency to turn its wars into crusades against evil. During World War II, Franklin Roosevelt said to Congress, "No compromise can end that conflict. There never has been – there never can be – successful compromise between good and evil. Only total victory can reward the champions of tolerance, and decency, and freedom, and faith." [733] Dwight Eisenhower wrote of his participation in the war: "Daily as it progressed there grew within me the conviction that as never before in a war between many nations the forces that stood for human good and men's rights were this time confronted by a completely evil conspiracy with which no compromise could be tolerated. Because only by the utter destruction of the Axis was a decent world possible, the war became for me a crusade in the traditional sense of that often misused word."[734]

One of George W. Bush's most fateful lines was spoken at Washington's National Cathedral on September 18, 2001: "Our responsibility to history is already clear: to answer these attacks and rid the world of evil."[735] The last phrase, "rid the world of evil," is breathtaking in its naïveté and arrogance. If history is clear about anything, it is that attempts to rid the world of evil unleash death and destruction. Getting rid of evil is not a political

---

732 George W. Bush, *Decision Points* (New York, Crown, 2010), 243. In his later book, *41: A Portrait of My Father* (New York: Crown, 2014) Bush tried to reconcile differences in previous statements about whether he consulted with his father over the war; however, the same words of advice from his father are cited.

733 Franklin Roosevelt, "Message to Congress," in *God's New Israel*, ed. Conrad Cherry (Englewood Cliffs, NJ: Prentice Hall, 1971), 302.

734 Dwight Eisenhower, *Crusade in Europe* (New York: Heinemann, 1948).

735 Jim Wallis, *God's Politics* (San Francisco, CA: Harper San Francisco, 2005), 143.

Gabriel Moran

task. The subsequent tragedies of the Bush years followed inexorably from this attitude. That Bush learned little from his experience is shown by one of his many exit interviews, in which he pronounced, "Good and evil are present in the world, and between the two of them there can be no compromise." Dick Cheney, Bush's vice-president, said with less naïveté and more arrogance, "We do not negotiate with evil; we defeat it."[736]

During the 2008 presidential campaign, one of the few times that the two candidates met face-to-face was at Saddleback Church in Lake Forest, California.[737] Pastor Rick Warren asked the candidates what to do about evil.

McCain's answer to that question was forthright: "Defeat it. If I am the president of the United States, my friends, if I have to follow him to the gates of hell, I will get Osama bin Laden and bring him to justice ... Of course, evil must be defeated. My friends, we are facing the transcendent challenge of the 21st century – radical Islamic extremism ... we can face this challenge and we must totally defeat it."

Barack Obama's answer to the question of what to do about evil was "It has to be confronted squarely. And one of the things that I strongly believe is that we are not going to, as individuals, be able to erase evil from the world. That is God's task. But we can be soldiers in that process, and we can confront it when we see it. Now the one thing that I think is very important is for us to have some humility in how we approach the issue of confronting evil because a lot of evil has been perpetrated based on the claim that we were trying to confront evil."

In his answer, John McCain shows a frightening lack of humility and proportionality. He was supremely confident that he could kill evil, incarnated as Osama bin Laden. Barack Obama was more restrained. He admitted that we, as individuals, cannot erase evil. But the frightening line in his answer is that we can be soldiers in God's army for erasing evil. That idea is not a help to having the humility that he recommended.

One of Ronald Reagan's most famous and controversial speeches was delivered before the National Association of Evangelicals on March 8,

736 The comment did not help negotiations with North Korea or Iran. Warren Strobel, "U.S. Acting Tough with N. Korea," *Philadelphia Inquirer*, December 21, 2003.
737 "Showdown at Saddleback" *New York Times*, August 17, 2008.

308

1983.[738] Reagan caused an uproar by referring to the Soviet Union as an "evil empire." It is difficult to understand the liberal outrage at Reagan's phrase. If the word "evil" has any appropriate use, it would seem to apply to the Soviet empire. Reagan did not call Gorbachev or the Russian people evil. He was describing the corruption and inhumanity of a system that, having begun with great hopes, deteriorated until its collapse in the 1980s.

What was objectionable in Reagan's speech was the other half of it that received almost no comment. The opposite of the evil empire was the goodness of "America." A large part of why the Soviet empire could be described as evil was simply the fact that it was an empire. There is a built-in arrogance to the reality of empires. The United States, since World War II, has had one of the most powerful empires in history. Like all empires, the American empire has had its share of incompetence, greed, and corruption.

Allan Bloom, in *The Closing of the American Mind*, complained about the answer he got from college students to his question "What is evil?"[739] Bloom said that he always got the same one-word answer: Hitler. Whenever we are supposed to hate and destroy another evil person, the comparison to Hitler is inevitable. Saddam Hussein, Mahmoud Ahmadinejad, Muammar Qaddafi, Osama bin Laden, Kim Jong Un, or another authoritarian leader, as to who is the reincarnation of Hitler. If the person is a head of state, even an unelected head of state, the people of that nation are often included in the condemnation of the evil monster.

The fact that Bloom's students knew only Hitler as evil is not surprising. Hitler brought back the word "evil" after it had nearly disappeared. In the secularization of the West from the eighteenth century onward, evil was generally shunned. Its religious connotations made it an unnecessary and distracting idea. In religious history, the opposite of good is evil; in secular history, the opposite of good is bad. The origin of "evil" is the problem of trying to explain conflict, suffering and death. Some religions posit two gods—one that is good, one that is evil—and the humans in between them. However, the Jewish, Christian, and Muslim religions agreed that

---

738 The complete speech is in Ronald Reagan, *An American Life: The Autobiography* (New York: Simon and Schuster, 2011), 369-70.

739 Allan Bloom, *The Closing of the American Mind* (New York: Simon and Schuster, 1987), 67.

there is only one God who is good and is the source of all goodness. The three religions were then faced with the difficulty of explaining why the world is a mess.

Christianity developed an elaborate backstory of spiritual beings who revolted in heaven and established a counterforce in hell. Evil was personified in a character variously called the devil, a demon, Satan, Beelzebub, and Lucifer. He was not a co-god, but as the story developed, he became a worthy opponent for the good God, especially in tempting humans to share in his evil. As the Christian story lost its controlling power, Satan became a comical figure with red tights and a pitchfork. As the devil seemed no longer credible, and as human autonomy was celebrated, the idea of evil seemed outdated.

One event of the twentieth century, the Holocaust, occasioned the rediscovery of evil. Wars of the twentieth century killed up to 150 million people, but it was the killing of the six million Jews, the near elimination of European Jewry, that seemed truly demonic. That the Holocaust occurred in Germany, the seat of secular enlightenment, was inexplicable to both Jews and Gentiles. Was there some suprahuman force that caused the catastrophe?

At first there was silence. A change began with the publication of Hannah Arendt's *Origins of Totalitarianism*.[740] Her work can be seen as a reflection on evil or, more exactly, on totalitarian systems that breed evil results. The monstrous outcomes are not the doings of one evil person. A complex organization is needed to pull off the horrendous destruction produced by modern warfare. In the nineteenth century, Carl von Clausewitz's classic, *On War*, could describe war as "nothing but a duel on a larger scale." World War I changed that image of war by being a total war involving the whole population. In today's wars, as many as 90 percent of those killed are "noncombatants."

Arendt brilliantly analyzed the workings of bureaucracy, in which people obey the person at the next level. One might expect that authority would be at the top. The really frightening thing, argued Arendt, is that at the top "no man, neither the few nor the many, can be held responsible …

---

740 Hannah Arendt, *Origins of Totalitarianism* (New York: Harcourt Brace Jovanovich, 1973).

which could be properly called rule by Nobody."[741] The president or CEO of a large organization does not understand the system that, without anyone's evil intention, may be causing havoc in people's lives.

Shortly after he was elected president, Barack Obama had an opportunity to address the questions of evil and war. On the morning of October 9, 2009, Obama was notified that he had won the Nobel Peace Prize. It was the same day that he decided to send thirty thousand more troops into the Afghan war. Many people thought that giving Obama the prize was premature; it was for his intentions, not his achievements. In introducing Obama, the chairman of the Nobel Committee, Thorbjorn Jagland, said, "Mr. President, we are happy to see that through your presence here so much of Dr. King's dream has come true." Obama's acceptance speech must have shocked his audience, because he distanced himself from Martin Luther King Jr. and other advocates of nonviolence. Obama declared, "I face the world as it is, and cannot stand idle in the face of threats to the American people. For make no mistake, evil does exist in the world." [742]

Obama's implication was that the two wars that the United States were engaged in were necessary because of "threats to the American people." Obama made the same conflation of force and war that his predecessor had used. He did acknowledge "moral force" as an admirable ideal for an individual but indicated that it is not something relevant for nations. That distinction between individual morality and the realities of society is the standard way to marginalize the significance of nonviolent action.

Obama had referred to Reinhold Niebuhr as "one of [his] favorite philosophers." And George Packer accurately said that "the spirit of Niebuhr presided over the Nobel address."[743] In that world, violence by the government is necessary to protect nonviolent people. Obama said that "there will be times when nations – acting individually or in concert – will find the use of force not only necessary but morally justified." Obama cautioned against cynicism: "We can understand that there will be war and still strive for peace." It is safe to say that the Nobel Committee was not expecting to hear a line that could have been stated by any president

---

741 Hannah Arendt, *On Violence* (New York: Harvest Books, 1970), 38.
742 *New York Times*, December 10, 2009.
743 George Packer, "Peace and War," *New Yorker*, December 21, 2009, 46.

or prime minister at any time in history—that is, the statement that the way to peace is by means of war.

Obama had inherited two wars from his predecessor. He could conceivably have said that he was no longer waging war and therefore did not have to justify war. He could have said that he was just trying to withdraw the US military in the most responsible way possible. Obama on several occasions had said that he was not against all wars but was against only "dumb wars." He was against the war in Iraq, but he considered the war in Afghanistan to be a war of necessity. Whatever might have been necessary in 2001, the situation was certainly different in 2010 when, resisting only slightly what the military commanders wanted, Obama sent thirty thousand more soldiers into battle.

A troubling policy of Bush's wars, which was continued by Obama, was the use of drones—unmanned aircraft that target and kill suspected enemies. Obama claimed to have reined in the use of drones because he personally approved each use. But four hundred drone attacks during Obama's first term did not show a reining in of the program. And the use of drones not only in Afghanistan and Pakistan but also in Yemen, Somalia, and the Philippines raised further concerns. There was some outcry when several US citizens were killed by strikes from the sky, but there was not a widespread demand for reviewing a policy that pushes beyond the limits of international law and involves the United States in simple assassinations. No one was surprised by Donald Trump's enthusiasm for drones and his removing even the controls that Obama had put in place.

By leading in the use of this technology, the United States may eventually find it has opened a dangerous window. One can easily imagine not a few suicide bombers on hijacked planes hitting New York and Washington but hundreds of drones spewing destruction all over the United States.[744]

In some ways, drones are merely a continuation of the way the United States has fought wars since World War I. Rather than risk its soldiers in battle, the United States has preferred to bomb populations into submission. One "American life" is given more value than a dozen or a hundred lives of the enemy, even when those lives are mainly civilians who are not part

---

744 Peter W. Singer, *Wired for War: The Robotics Revolution in the 21ˢᵗ Century* (New York: Penguin Books, 2009).

of the war. The drone is the fulfillment of this policy. There is no risk at all to pilots during the bombing missions of the drones, manned as they are by computer operators in Colorado or Utah. The antiseptic separation from the killing is even more pronounced than for the pilot who opens the bomb doors of an aircraft thousands of feet above the ground. No one would ask that more US soldiers be put at risk. But the insanity of war becomes ever more manifest with computer technology.

American Religion

Religion may seem not to have played a big role in the chapters of this book. References have occasionally been made to Christianity, Judaism, Islam, and other religions. Protestant Christian religion has certainly been an important influence in United States history. In the nineteenth century, millions of Jewish and Roman Catholic immigrants entered the United States and, although first discriminated against, made themselves and their religious beliefs important factors in the life of the United States. Muslims have only recently experienced a similar struggle to be recognized as fully American.

The term "American religion" has two very different meanings. In the first meaning, America is a transformative influence on Christian, Jewish, Muslim, Buddhist, and other religions in the United States. On the plus side of this first meaning, the traditional religions have become more tolerant, more aware of the need for freedom of religion in the context of the American experience in the United States. For example, the Roman Catholic endorsement of religious freedom at the Second Vatican Council was directly attributed to the work of John Courtney Murray of the United States, who drew upon the experience of Catholics in US history.[745]

On the negative side of this transformative meaning, many commentators have complained that traditional religions have been trivialized by the influence of America. Religion in the United States tends to be an individual therapy with commercial possibilities. H. L. Mencken claimed that the United States was the only place in the world

---

745 John Courtney Murray, *We Hold These Truths: Catholic Reflections on the American Proposition* (New York: Sheed and Ward, 1960).

where people "get a religion"—that is, where religion is a "denomination" that can be, and often is, traded in for a new model.[746]

One of the most provocative books on American religion was *Protestant-Catholic-Jew* by Will Herberg. He proposed that there were three American faiths. "We might describe Protestantism, Catholicism and Judaism as three great branches or divisions of American religion."[747] Herberg acknowledged that his description left out some people. That inadequacy has become more obvious since the great influx of Asians after 1965 and the growing number of Muslim citizens. However, his scheme acknowledged the importance of religion in the United States and pointed out that most people have an "American faith" that is a variation on traditional religion.[748]

As Herberg argued, the "three American faiths" were a great help to millions of immigrants trying to find a home in the United States. Immigrants from Poland, Italy, and Ireland could find their way in their new home because they were "American Catholics."[749] It was not a smooth transition for the immigrants, but being an American Jew or an American Catholic was nonetheless a social glue. A mini ecumenical movement was intrinsic to the American religious experience in the United States.[750] Whether one thinks traditional religions have been improved or made worse by the influence of "America," their influence on US policies is fairly easy to track and, if necessary, to control.

---

746 H. L. Mencken, *The American Language* (New York: Knopf, 1984).

747 Will Herberg, *Protestant, Catholic, Jew* (Garden City, NY: Doubleday, 1955), 38.

748 "Religion and Culture in Present-Day America," in *Roman Catholicism and the American Way of Life*, ed. Thomas McAvoy (Notre Dame, IN: University of Notre Dame Press, 1960), 4-19. Herberg in later writings seemed to think the effect was mostly negative.

749 *Religious Change in America* (Cambridge, MA: Harvard University Press, 1996); *American Catholics: A Social Portrait* (New York: Basic books, 1978). Andrew Greeley's extensive sociological studies documented this role of the Catholic Church in the Americanization of immigrants. There is an extensive literature on the Jewish experience of Americanization. (See Irving Howe, *World of Our Fathers: The Journey of the East European Jews to America and the Life They Found and Made* [New York: Galahad Books, 2001].)

750 Herberg, *Protestant-Catholic-Jew*, 85.

There is a second meaning of American religion: America itself functioning as a religion unrestrained by the traditional religions. Without such restraint, America becomes the driving force of a mission to fix the world. From the moment of its coining, "America" was a religious or at least a quasireligious idea. Religions do not exist merely as ideas; religion is a set of practices, and religions are sociohistorical institutions. A new religion did not come into existence in 1507, but the idea of America did eventually become embodied in practices and institutions.

Throughout its entire five centuries "America" has never lost its religious character as a name for some ultimate good that provides a standard for living and a belief worth dying for. America seeks the good of all humanity so that any opposition to America is based on ignorance, envy, or evil.

Modern nationalisms have led to wars in which young men have been sacrificed for the national interest. Nations ask their soldiers to defend their families, communities, and people. Their motto is a line from the Latin poet Horace: "It is a sweet and honorable thing to die for one's *patria*, one's native land."[751] The United States asks for something similar but with an added twist. The United States asks its young men and women to go across the world to defend America as an idea worth dying for. The United States has repeatedly been involved in defending America even when there was no discernible threat to the *patria*. Did any US official think that if the US military did not intervene in Vietnam, an invasion of Hawaii or California was imminent?

Wars have always had religious overtones; ordinary human beings find it difficult to kill another human being simply because the other person is on a different team. The enemy in war has to be seen as embodying evil—a religious term. The United States does not do battle with another nation-state that is threatening US existence; America carries on a crusade against the enemies of liberty.

America as a stand alone religion is a threat to historical order because of the illusion that it holds the key to human history. When a US president announces what America wants, the rest of the world gets uneasy because the demands of America often float free from historical facts. US people find it easy to believe in America. But people in many other nations are

---

751 Horace, *Odes*, vol. 3, 2.13.

skeptical of this faith; they would like to see some facts on which to ground that faith.

In 1967, Robert Bellah published an essay entitled "Civil Religion in America."[752] It has had a strong and continuing influence on discussions of religion in the United States. There developed a cottage industry of writing on Bellah's notion of a "civil religion," He claimed that in addition to Catholic, Jewish, and Protestant religions, there is something that can be called civil religion that does not compete with those other religions so much as supplement them.

Bellah's attempt to describe American religion is prevented by the fact that he buried the answer in the question. Bellah looks for American religion inside of America instead of inside the United States. He asks about America's civil religion, but America does not have a civil religion; the United States has religions that are American. Bellah's essay uses "America/American" more than sixty times, while "United States" shows up only in quotations from George Washington and Lyndon Johnson.

Bellah took the idea of civil religion from Jean-Jacques Rousseau.[753] Rousseau claimed that since true Christianity is unconcerned with this world, there is needed in addition a "civil religion" that would inspire political action but would not be a nationalistic belief. Bellah's "dogmas of civil religion," borrowed from Rousseau, are a peculiar collection of beliefs that mostly originated with Christianity by way of modern Deism: a beneficent deity, rewards in heaven, punishment of the wicked, the sanctity of the social contract, and the exclusion of intolerance. When there are no longer any other religious creeds, intolerance will cease to exist. But Bellah, like Rousseau, could not show how such Deism inspires political action.

Bellah's essay ends with a section on the contemporary crises that were putting his civil religion on trial in the 1960s. He was understandably concerned with the racial problem at home and the Vietnam War abroad. Eighteenth-century Deism as the basis of an American religion will never inspire courageous stands against racial injustice or a militarized United

---

752 Robert Bellah, "Civil Religion in America," *Daedalus* 96 (winter 1967), 1-21.

753 Jean-Jacques Rousseau, *Social Contract* (New York: Washington Square Press, 1967). Rousseau's treatment of religion in *Emile* (New York: Basic Books, 1979) is more provocative and more influential than his view of religion in *Social Contract*.

States. In contrast, American Jewish, American Catholic, and American Protestant religions, while not having a shining record on such action for justice, have produced individuals who rose to the challenge. Sometimes even the religious institutions—especially when they have cooperated with each other—have shown some mettle.

The difference between a Deistic "civil religion" and an American religion with strong biblical roots can be seen by comparing the religions of Thomas Jefferson and Abraham Lincoln. Jefferson was a fairly typical eighteenth-century Deist. He managed to justify his ownership of slaves and a belief that black men were inferior to whites, despite his writing that "all men are created equal" and that "they are endowed by their Creator with certain unalienable rights." Historians have struggled to create a unity from these two pictures of Jefferson. The simple fact seems to be that Jefferson's Deistic dogmas had little influence on his racial prejudice.[754]

Bellah notes that Lincoln echoed many of Jefferson's phrases. But Lincoln was steeped in both the New Testament and the Old Testament. In his Second Inaugural Address, Lincoln warned his fellow citizens that slavery might bring down the United States. The wealth of the nation built upon slavery might be lost because slavery cannot be justified before the God of the Hebrew prophets.

In the meaning of "American religion" in which America is a transformative element of traditional religions, the path of American Muslims is not an easy one. The language, images, and symbols of the Bible continue to be central to American religiosity. The challenge for the United States and religious groups in the United States is to bring Islam into full partnership in a religious dialogue, which heretofore has been that of Christians and Jews.

It is impossible to eliminate the biblical overtones of "America." Fortunately, the Quran is not a contradiction of the Bible. In fact, Muhammad viewed the Torah, the Gospel, and the Quran as a single message.[755] On many points that are significant for the religion of the nation, Muslims can find agreement with Jews and Christians. Undeniably, there are some important differences between the Bible and the Quran,

---

754 Nicholas Guyatt, *Bind Us Apart: How Enlightened Americans Invented Racial Segregation* (New York: Basic Books, 2016).

755 Quran 42:13.

just as there are important differences between Jewish and Christian Bibles. "American Muslim" does not slip comfortably into the next slot for American religions. Instead, American Muslims raise a healthy challenge to Jewish-Christian dialogues to prove how ecumenical they really are. There is no intrinsic reason why Jews, Christians, and Muslims cannot cooperate in contributing to an American religion that can both inspire and restrain the United States.

Conclusion

In the twenty-first century, there has arisen a serious question as to whether a federation of fifty states is governable at all. People began running for the US Congress with the express purpose of opposing the government. They were interested in their state, and they fervently believed in America, but they showed little concern for the United States. The call for a smaller government was actually a movement for no national government, just a federal government that would provide a minimum of services. In today's complicated international system in which the United States is expected to be a responsible actor, the opponents of a United States government are content to try living in a mythical America.

Out of the vacuum of political problems that seemingly have no political solutions, there emerged Donald Trump. The rich man from Queens, New York, began with dreams of conquering the world of Manhattan real estate; subsequently he had bigger dreams of wealth and power. When he talked of running for president as early as 2000, the idea was treated as a joke. He achieved some success with his book *The Art of the Deal*.[756] The actual author, Tony Schwartz, said that Trump did not write a word of the book. But to this day he is famous for the art of the deal and regularly invokes his book as an indication that he knows how to win.

Trump found his ideal place for selling dreams of wealth in the world of television. He portrayed a master of the universe and proved to be very good at playing the role. He convinced millions of people that they, too, could be winners if they knew the right tricks. Every aspect of life is a contest that you either win or lose. He was clearly a winner because he was rich and famous.

---

756 Donald Trump and Tony Schwartz, *The Art of the Deal* (New York: Random House, 1987).

The mythical world of America had been waiting for a con artist who was clever enough and sufficiently lacking in scruples to exploit the dangerous underside of the American dream. He found an entry point to politics by becoming a leader in the birther movement, which challenged Barack Obama's legitimacy as president. Obama, like black men always and everywhere, was forced to show his papers. Even after Obama provided irrefutable proof of where he was born, his enemies refused to admit that they were wrong. When Trump ran for president, he grudgingly said where Obama was born, but as is always the case with Trump, he never said he was mistaken, let alone apologize. Instead he launched the preposterous charge that Hillary Clinton's campaign was the origin of the falsehood.

Trump adopted the slogan "Make America Great Again," which struck a chord with millions of disgruntled citizens. Their schoolbooks and the movies had taught them that they are living in America, the richest place on earth where opportunities are plentiful and success is all but guaranteed. These people could see that there are rich and successful people in some parts of the country; those people control the television networks, the universities, and the government in Washington. Since these "elites" look down on ordinary hardworking people, nothing they say, in the view of the aforementioned disgruntled citizens, can be trusted.

Donald Trump seemed an unlikely messenger of hope. He was a thrice-married rich New Yorker who had no history of concern with the masses. But he was a superb salesman who could make people believe that he could solve their problems easily. Trump surprised himself by how effective he was at rallies, where he said whatever popped into his mind. The speeches lacked any sentence structure and logical coherence. But that was part of his charm and believability. His supporters often said that he was not hiding behind big words and complicated arguments; he "told it like it is."

Trump probably did not expect to succeed very far—just far enough to advertise his brand and make a few hundred million dollars. On election night, he was among the most shocked people in the country. He had given little thought about how to actually govern. But he figured that the president sat at his desk, signed papers that told people what to do, and accepted the love and respect of the whole citizenry. After a few months in office, he complained that the job was much more difficult than he had expected. He had thought he was becoming the boss of America; he found himself president of the United States.

Although Trump had claimed thousands of times that he was going to make America great again, he was never pressed to answer an obvious question: When exactly was America great in the past? He suggested an answer to that question when he was talking about how easy it would be to wipe out America's enemies. He said that when he was a high school student, America used to win its wars. In the late 1950s, when Trump had begun high school, America represented goodness and the worldwide Communist conspiracy represented evil. The decade ended with John Kennedy's promise that America was ready to go wherever freedom and goodness were threatened.

Every schoolchild who was exposed to "American history" learned that America was the most peace-loving country on Earth. America went to war, reluctantly, only when free people were threatened by evil attackers. Americans did not like to fight, but once they were in a war, they were unstoppable. America never started a war, and America never lost a war. Perhaps all those things are true of America, but the history of the United States tells a different story. Even in the 1950s, it should have been obvious that the United States has been almost constantly at war for dubious reasons and has often not succeeded. Having set up the conditions that led to war on the Korean peninsula, the United States was unprepared when it found itself in a war. After three years of bloody stalemate, the fighting stopped, but the problem has continued to this day.

The United States tried to quickly forget its Korean disaster only to repeat an unwise intervention in an Asian land war in Vietnam—a war that Trump successfully avoided serving in. William Manchester, as noted earlier, said that "the American dream died in the jungles of Vietnam."[757] He underestimated the US capacity for forgetting its failures. In the twenty-first century, war seems to have become the permanent condition of the country. Trump's promise that America was going to start winning wars again is one of his many promises that proved to be more difficult to achieve than he had assumed.

---

757 William Manchester, *The Glory and the Dream* (Boston: Little, Crown and Company, 1974).

That the existence of a United States has become precarious was not caused by Donald Trump, but he fed the illusion that we live in America, which had a spotless past until the recent work of a conspiracy of people who hate America. He succeeded in creating a distraction of defending America – its flag, its military, its superiority to any nation – while the real problems of unifying the United States and fixing its malfunctioning government received little attention. The hope remains, as it has for more than a century, that the dream of America can hold together the United States, but today's media reveals the unfairness in the United States as to who comes out the winners and the losers.

In the 2016 presidential election, Hillary Clinton received almost three million more votes than Donald Trump. After every presidential election, some commentators (including, understandably, Hillary Clinton) ask, Why is there an electoral college? Why can't we get rid of this anachronism? The question shows a remarkable misconception of the country they live in. The electoral college is an embodiment of the federal union created in the eighteenth century. Have opponents of the electoral college not noticed that the United States Senate has two senators from each state regardless of the state's size? Because the electoral college is based on the number in each state's congressional delegation, it is biased toward the smaller states.[758] The smaller states would never vote to give up their disproportionate share of political power in the country. Even more crucial is the fact that the removal of the electoral college would shift most of the power that the states have to a national government.

The United States received its definition by the tenth amendment to the Constitution, which says that powers not delegated to "the United States" are reserved by the states or the people. The Constitutional Convention wished to create "a more perfect union," but the states did not want to give up their power. The slave states were most determined to keep their power over a federal government, but the electoral college is not entirely explained by that fact. The preamble of the US Constitution, which begins, "We the

758 Donald Trump endlessly repeats – and is seldom challenged – that the electoral college was almost impossible for a Republican to win. Since the Republican strength is in the small states, the electoral college is heavily biased toward Republicans. Trump won the election while losing the majority of votes only because of the electoral college's bias in his favor.

people of the United States," would have been more accurately rendered as "We the states of the United States."

It remains the case today that the presidential election is based not on the votes of the people but rather on the votes of the fifty states of the United States. In the twenty-first century, there is a need for a national unity with a national government, but there is no inclination of the states to give up their power. If one examines the rhetoric of recent presidential campaigns, there is a frightening tendency to replace debate about the policies of the United States government with sermons about a place called America.

The first step in trying to fix the United States would be to acknowledge its existence. When people constantly talk about "America" in referring to the United States, the severe problems of the existing country almost disappear. The blindness is worse on the political right, but the left responds in the same mythical language.

For a functioning government, it would be necessary to consider collapsing the fifty states into a dozen or fewer regions. The campaigns for president and congress should be shortened to twelve weeks, should be entirely funded by the government, and should consist mainly of real debates on television. Voting should be required for every citizen during a period of a week. A congress of about one-fourth the current size would consist of people who represent their respective regions but would be primarily dedicated to the good of the United States, its internal needs, and its place in the community of nations.

The American empire will eventually follow every other empire in moving off the stage of world history. How the United States copes with its no longer being able to claim "We're number one!" will bear careful watching by the rest of the world. It will not be an easy transition. America might still be an ideal toward which the United States moves, joined by other American nations and by nations that have amicable relations with the United States instead of having to choose to be either a client or an enemy of America. When the dominance of the United States ceases and the country becomes one of the many international players, the result may seem humiliating to some people, but for most US citizens, it would probably mean a less harried life with less violence in the national environment.

It was obvious at the time of the Marshall Plan that the United States had too much money and too many goods, not only for the world's welfare but also for the health of the United States' own economy and culture. In the 1950s, through the work of enlightened US officials and the leaders of European nations, a better balance was struck. The United States, however, continued to be the dominant economic and military force in the world.

In the course of the last half century, the hegemony of the United States has been in slow decline, but the claim to be America has hidden that fact and is dangerously covering up the need for drastic reforms. Instead of instituting political, economic, and social reforms, unscrupulous politicians can accuse groups, especially new immigrants, as being the reason why America is not as great as it once was. The idea of America functions either to help the acceptance of US diversity or to be a weapon against the most vulnerable of groups.

When health care became a topic of public debate, one could regularly hear it said that "America has the best health care in the world." The fact that by international standards the United States ranked way down the list of nations did not make any impression on defenders of America's greatness. The United States may indeed have some of the best medical technology in the world and can be proud of its ingenuity in this area. Nonetheless, the United States could get some practical help from studying Canada, Great Britain, or dozens of other countries for their health care policies. The political right wing resisted every attempt at health care reform until the Affordable Care Act, an imperfect instrument of reform, was passed. Ben Carson famously described "Obamacare" as "the worst thing in our country since slavery."[759] The Republicans set out to destroy the Affordable Care Act, despite having nothing better to offer.

A case of where the United States was once a world leader but is now far back is education. As in health care, a large part of the population lives in denial. They are not helped by the hundreds of books with "American Education" in the title. The books are actually about the schools of the United States, but the term "American" is everywhere present in this

---

759 Ben Carson, *One Nation: What We Can Do to Save America's Future* (New York: Sentinel, 2014), 12. When Carson was severely criticized for this statement, far from acknowledging that he had spoken badly, he complained that he was the victim of the "political correctness police."

literature. The purpose of state schools in the past was often said to be "Americanization." Late in the nineteenth century, and for the first part of the twentieth century, the state schools did a good job at this mission; they provided basic tools for surviving in the United States. The state schools were truly public schools.

The world has moved on, however, and the United States has badly neglected its primary and secondary schools, as well as the education of the public outside schools. A few of the country's universities are the best in the world, but that can obscure the fact that many of the country's other schools trail badly. An obsession with tests does not help. The most basic need is for the country to respect and support professional educators in their work. Money is one sign of respect, but school teaching also needs social recognition and appreciation by the general population. Parents and other adults have to be involved in the education of young people. The country also has to examine how the public is educated, especially by the new technological wizardry. The government should guarantee some form of postsecondary education for every citizen.

The theme of decline may seem not to apply in one area: military power. Since the United States has a larger military budget than the next ten countries combined, it can maintain an awesome military force. The constant pronouncement that America is the greatest military power in the history of the world is true if the measure is megatons of destructive firepower. (Three thousand nuclear warheads is an absurd amount of potential destructiveness.) But the world has moved on from the World War II strategy of war by massive ground assaults and saturation bombing.

Most of the wars now happen within, rather than between, countries. The people who fight the wars are often equipped with land mines that cost only a few dollars and the AK-47, a cheap and almost indestructible weapon. The United States has not often been successful since World War II in enforcing a military solution on any conflict. What is more often needed for "counterinsurgency" is people who speak the language of those who are fighting. United States education is not good at teaching languages. The United States needs people who understand complex cultural situations so that it can support groups who are fighting for their freedom. One thing that clearly is not helpful is a "war on terror." A war on an abstract noun is inevitably a thrashing in all directions with terrible consequences for anyone in the neighborhood.

The United States seems to have an excellent military, which is surprising because it is largely composed of young men and women who are poor, limited in academic credentials, and looking for work. It is not disrespectful of these soldiers to say that they deserve better and the country deserves better. There ought to be another way to defend the country than putting an insupportable burden on the shoulders of dedicated soldiers. The rates of suicide and mental sickness among soldiers returning from current wars are shocking. Representative Charles Rangel introduced a bill to install a universal draft of two years.[760] Rangel knew that there is no chance of a draft; the country is very comfortable with a volunteer army. Rangel was making the point that if there were a draft—it would now have to include women as well as men—then the rich and powerful in the country might pay attention to the wars being fought in their name. Leaders might be more careful about sending their own sons and daughters into wars half a world away.

The idea of a universal draft in the service of "America" is a good idea. If America stands for liberty, justice, and peace, then a draft for a year or two of service to the nation would be good experience for young people and a shining example of what America can provide to the world. The Peace Corps was a terrific idea, and many of its volunteers showed the world America at its best. It is unlikely that a universal program could ever be put in place, but the US government could give some money and attention to supporting programs in which the young get a taste of what it is like to do good work simply because it is good work. That kind of program could help to reform professions in this country while helping at "nation-building"—something soldiers are not trained to do.

The economic arena is a place where the United States was once dominant and no longer is. After the fall of the Soviet Union, many people hoped that the country could shift away from a war economy to promoting better living conditions for the hundreds of millions of people in the world who are destitute. Some of those millions live in the United States and do not have a share of the "American dream." The US economic system has

---

760 Charles Rangel, "Share the Burden, Ease the Pain," *New York Times*, March 20, 2012.

always had winners and losers; the split between rich and poor is part of the package. In the past, people accepted that fact and strove to get a share of the riches of the country. But in recent decades there has been a constantly widening gap between the rich and the poor.

The richest people in the country are obscenely rich. Some of them put their money to good use; others do nothing but stack their riches higher. Why would any human being want to have a billion dollars, let alone five, ten, or thirty billion dollars? Freud does have an explanation: A human being has unlimited desires that are buried in the unconscious; they are desires that one had as an infant. Money can be piled up without limit; it can create an illusion of infinity.[761] What the rich need to face is their own mortality.

The clamor for more and more money eventually has bad consequences. Early in the twenty-first century, the entire economy became trapped in a bubble of illusion. Real estate deals and new investment gimmicks led the way upward to fabulous wealth. Then the bubble burst, and everyone in the United States was affected. And because the US dollar is still a big deal, even if it is not what it used to be, the entire economy of the world was threatened. A few smart and courageous people, and a dose of good luck, saved the world from complete disaster. It is unclear what, if anything, was learned in a country that still speaks as if it were America.

The United States was too big to fail; the world's economy could not cope with a bankrupt United States. But "America" could not cover up bad banking practices and unemployment lines. Here again the United States might learn some caution from its neighbor to the north; it might also learn from mistakes in the structure of the European Union. And it might try to have a friendly competition instead of a deadly battle with China, India, or other countries that may pass the United States. It really would not be bad for the US or for the world if instead of America First, it becomes the case in the United States that we're proud to be number two.

Perhaps one area where the United States is not in obvious decline is in the spread of "American culture." Not everyone is happy at the popularity of this culture. France leads the way in distress at the invasion of American English, American food, American movies, American television, American

---

761 Sigmund Freud, "From the History of an Infantile Neurosis," *Standard Works of Sigmund Freud*, vol. 17 (New York: W. W. Norton, 1976), 1-122.

clothes, American music, and other cultural artifacts. "America" is an allure for young people around the world. Even in countries where there is political conflict with the United States, such as Iran, there is an appetite for the American way of doing things.

There is an obvious danger, as the French have seen, that local culture can suffer from American intrusions. For example, the movies that the United States launches into the world's theaters are most often expensive and violent. They are not necessarily of high quality, but they can overwhelm inexpensive and quiet films produced locally. The image of America that people have is mostly what movies and television convey. It is a violent America that people around the world know rather than the United States.

American culture nevertheless has positive possibilities. The cultural productions of the United States may often represent a dumbing down of the arts, but even art of questionable quality can be an opening to the world. If the United States and its government would put more trust in the artistic, scientific, athletic, and technological skill of its people and less in its military power, then "America" might regain some of its shine where it has been badly tarnished, and the United States could be a force for justice and peace in the world.

Appendix

The most difficult linguistic point in a philosophical essay on "America" is the absence of a proper name for the people who live between Canada and Mexico. US citizens are "Americans" insofar as they reside in (continental) America, but the problem is their assumed ownership of America. The constant and exclusive use of "American" for US people reinforces "America" as the name of the country. Most US people dismiss this issue as silly. Anyone who is bothered by the term "American" as the name for US citizens and *only* US citizens should just accept this usage as a simple fact. That is the way it has always been and always will be.

It is indeed a fact that "American" was used in the British American colonies. From the beginning of the United States, the people appropriated "American" as a self-description. As the United States gained in power within the American continent, it was able to teach most of the world to use "American" for the possessions and people of the United States. Other American nations may have disagreed, but they had difficulty in getting their voices heard.[762]

By the middle of the nineteenth century, Orestes Brownson could write, "The proper name of the country is America; that of the people is Americans. Speak of Americans simply and nobody understands you to mean the people of Canada, Mexico, Brazil, Chile, Paraguay but everybody understands you to mean the people of the United States. The fact is

---

762 Maya Jasanoff, in *Liberty's Exiles: American Loyalists in the Revolutionary World* (New York: Knopf, 2011), 332, quotes Canadian John Robinson, who complained in the early 1800s that a British friend "chose to twit me with the term Yankee, seeming to think it applied to all [North] Americans." Robinson uses the term "Yankee" for the people that Canadians "so detest and with whom they have so long been fighting." But Jasanoff undercuts the significance of Robinson's statement by inserting the term "North." Robinson is not saying that he is a North American; he is saying that as a Canadian, he is American.

significant and foretells for the people of the United States a continental destiny."[763] Brownson's final sentence connecting the use of "American" to a continental destiny was prescient; such a destiny was celebrated in the United States but not in other nations of the continent.

In nearly every country, the name for the people is directly derived from the country's name. The people of Canada are called Canadians, the people of France are French, and Greece has Greeks. "Israelis" was a successful invention for the people of Israel. Logically, the United States' people should be "Unitedstatesians," which does not exist in English and is unlikely to ever take hold. In the Spanish of the countries to the south, "*Estadounidense*" does exist but is of limited use. "*Norteamericano*" is used to describe US Americans, but it is not geographically accurate in equating the United States and North America. Mexicans may not be bothered, because the United States is, in fact, to its north. Canadians are understandably made uneasy by the equation. Especially during the last fifty years, Canadians have wished to maintain friendly relations with the United States but assert their own political and cultural differences.

In French-speaking Canada, the French term for the United States, "*Etats-Unis*," was used to create "*etats-unien*" for the people. In recent years, the editors of the newspaper *Le Monde* suggested that it might be time to try making general use of that term. The suggestion, when noticed at all, was met by derision in the United States.[764]

A popular southern American way to refer to US Americans is "Yankee," which became "*yanqui*" in Spanish. The word is older than the United States and has never died out. In Spanish it has had negative connotations, as in "Yankee imperialism" and "Yankee go home." The negative connotations increased as the United States grew in power and presumed a right to intervene in any American nation.

The origin of "Yankee" is unclear; it is likely derived from a native or a Dutch word. There was probably a note of derision associated with the term from its beginning. The term was especially applied to upper-class New Englanders. (In the New Hampshire town where I grew up, there were only three kinds of people: Irish Catholics, French Catholics, and

---

763 Orestes Brownson, *The American Republic* (New York: Hard Press, 2006).
764 Martine Rousseau and Olivier Houdart, "There's a Word for People Like You," *New York Times*, July 6, 2007.

Yankees.) During the nineteenth century, as New England led the drive for abolition, "Yankee" became a Southern US name for Northerners. That usage hardened with the US Civil War and remains in memories of the war that linger to the present. Any general use of "Yankee" for United States people as a whole can happen only after the US Civil War has faded from memory—something nowhere imminent in much of the southern United States.

An interesting twentieth-century development was the shortening of "Yankee" to "Yank." The term is used in other English speaking countries with neutral and sometimes positive meaning. The World Wars created a mostly affectionate image of the Yank in England, Ireland, Australia, and New Zealand (as reflected in the phrase "The Yanks are coming, the Yanks are coming!"). The use of "Yank" lived on after World War II, competing with less friendly phrases, such as "the ugly American." "*Yanqui*" has far more currency today than "Yankee" or "Yank." Any self-descriptive use of the term "Yankee" by US Americans is unlikely. Still, things could change. In a book entitled *Who Are We Now: The Changing Face of America in the Twenty-First Century,* author Sam Roberts writes, "The final decades of the American Century are transforming the nation into the least 'American' it has ever been by the conventional definition – or the *most* American if Central and South America count as Americans too."[765] As Spanish-speaking immigrants continue to come into the United States, legally or not, "Yankee" could still have a future. The United States is unlikely to become a bilingual country; English is too powerful and too well established for that to happen. Nevertheless, it is possible and likely that Hispanic ways of speaking will influence the English of the United States. US citizens in search of a name might someday rediscover "Yankee" by way of "*yanqui.*" Accepting the term would be a kind of apology for US policies in the past that drew strong opposition in southern parts of America.

---

765 Sam Roberts, *Who Are We Now?* (New York: Times Book, 2004), 71.

Bibliography

Adams, James Truslow. *The Epic of America*. Boston, MA: Little, Brown and Company, 1931

Adams, Michael. *Fire and Ice: The United States, Canada and the Myth of Converging Values*. Toronto, ON: Penguin Books, 2003.

Amar, Akhil Reed. *America's Unwritten Constitution*. New York: Basic Books, 2012.

Andersen, Kurt. *Fantasyland: How America Went Haywire: A 500-Year History*. New York: Random House, 2017.

Appiah, Kwame Anthony. "Battling with DuBois." *New York Review of Books*, December 22, 2011, 81-85.

Aptheker, Herbert. *One Continual Cry: David Walker's Appeal to the Colored People of the World: Its Setting and Its Appeal*. New York: Humanities, 1965.

———. *Nat Turner's Slave Rebellion: Including the 1831 Confessions*. New York: Grove Press, 2006.

Arber, Edwin and A. G. Bradley, eds. *Works of John Smith*. Chapel Hill, NC: University of North Carolina Press, 1986.

Arciniegas, Germán. "The Four Americas." In Louis Hanke, ed., *Do the Americas Have a Common History?* New York: Knopf, 1964.

Arendt, Hannah. *On Revolution*. New York: Viking Press, 1963.

———. *Eichmann in Jerusalem*. New York: Penguin Books, 2006.

Avery, Michael and Danielle McLaughlin. *The Federalist Society: How Conservatives Took the Law Back from Liberals*. Nashville, TN: Vanderbilt University Press, 2013.

Bailyn, Bernard. *Education in the Forming of American Society*. New York: Vintage Books, 1960.

———. *The Ideological Origins of the American Revolution*. Cambridge, MA: Harvard University Press, 1967.

———. *The Barbarous Years: The Peopling of British North America: The Conflict of Civilizations, 1600-1675*. New York: Knopf, 2012.

Baldwin, James. *The Fire Next Time*. New York: Dell, 1964.

Baudrillard, Jean. *America*. New York: Verso, 1986.

Beecher, Lyman. "A Plea for the West." In *God's New Israel*, ed. Conrad Cherry, 119-127. Englewood, NJ: Prentice Hall, 1971.

Bellah, Robert. "Civil Religion in America." *Daedalus* 96 (Winter 1967): 1-21.

———. *The Broken Covenant*. New York: Seabury Press, 1975.

Beeman, Richard. *Plain, Honest Men: The Making of the American Constitution*. New York: Random House, 2015.

Bender, Thomas. *A Nation among Nations: America's Place in World History*. New York: Hill and Wang, 2006.

Bercovitch, Sacvan. *American Jeremiad*. Madison, WI: University of Wisconsin Press, 1978.

Billington, James. *Fire in the Minds of Men: Origins of the Revolutionary Faith*. New York: Basic Books, 1980.

Billington, Rachel. *Glory: A Story of Gallipoli*. London: Orion Press, 2015.

Blair, Clay. *The Forgotten War: 1950-1953*. New York: Times Book, 1987.

Blassingame, John. *The Slave Community: Plantation Life in the Antebellum South*. New York: Oxford University Press, 1972.

———. *Slave Testimony: Two Centuries of Letters, Speeches, Interviews, and Biographies*. Baton Rouge, LA: Louisiana State University, 1977.

Blight, James and Janet Lang. *Virtual JFK: Vietnam if Kennedy Had Lived*. Lanham, MD: Rowman and Littlefield, 2010.

———. *The Armageddon Letters: Kennedy/Khrushchev/Castro in the Cuban Missile Crisis*. Lanham, MD: Rowan and Littlefield, 2012.

Bloom, Allan. *The Closing of the American Mind: How Higher Education Has Failed Democracy*. New York: Simon and Schuster, 1987.

Blum, William. *America's Deadliest Export: Democracy—The Truth about US Foreign Policy and Everything Else*. London: Zen Books, 2014.

Bolton, Herbert. *Wider Horizons of American History*. Notre Dame, IN: University of Notre Dame Press, 1967.

Boot, Max. "A War for Oil? Not This Time," *New York Times*, February 13, 2003.

Borgwardt, Elizabeth. *A New Deal for the World: America's Vision for Human Rights*. Cambridge, MA: Harvard University Press, 2007.

Bowers, Claude. *Beveridge and the Progressive Era*. Boston, MA: Houghton Mifflin, 1932.

Bradley, Omar. *A General's Life: An Autobiography*. New York: Touchstone, 1984.

Bradford, William. *Of Plymouth Plantation*. New York: Knopf, 1952.

Brandeis, Louis and Samuel Warren. "The Right to Privacy," *Harvard Law Review* 4 (1890): 193-200.

Brands, H. W. *American Colossus: The Triumph of Capitalism, 1865-1900*. New York: Doubleday, 2010.

Brownson, Orestes. *The American Republic: Its Constitution, Tendencies, and Destiny*. New York: P. O'Shea, 1866.

Burke, Edmund. *Works*. London: Bohn, 1854-59.

Burt, Robert. *Death Is That Man Taking Names: Intersections of American Medicine, Law, and Culture*. Berkeley, CA: University of California Press, 2012.

Buruma, Ian. *Taming the Gods: Religion and Democracy on Three Continents*. Princeton, NJ: Princeton University Press, 2010.

Bury, James. *A History of the Freedom of Thought*. New York: Henry Holt and Company, 1913.

Bush, George W. *Decision Points*. New York: Crown, 2010.

———. *41: A Portrait of My Father*. New York: Crown, 2014.

Carr, Edward H. *The Twenty Years' Crisis, 1919-1939*. London: Macmillan, 1940.

Carson, Ben. *One Nation: What We Can Do to Save America's Future*. New York: Sentinel, 2014.

Carstens, Patrick Richard. *Searching for the Forgotten War: 1812 Canada*. Indianapolis, IN: Xlibris, 2011.

Chace, James. *1912: Wilson, Roosevelt, Taft & Debs: The Election That Changed the Country*. New York: Simon and Schuster, 2004.

Chesterton, G. K. *What I Saw in America*. New York: Dodd, Mead and Company, 1922.

Chomsky, Noam. *American Power and the New Mandarins*. New York: The New Press, 2002.

Clarkson, Stephen. *Does North America Exist? Governing the Continent after NAFTA and 9/11*. Toronto, ON: University of Toronto Press, 2008.

Clarkson, Stephen and Matto Mildenberger. *Dependent America? How Canada and Mexico Construct U.S. Power*. Toronto, ON: University of Toronto Press, 2011.

Clausewitz, Carl von. *On War*. London: Wordsworth, 1997.

Clinton, Hillary. *Hard Choices*. New York: Simon and Schuster, 2014.

Cockburn, Andrew. "Washington Is Burning," *Harper's*, September 2014, 44-48.

Cohen, Adam. *Imbeciles: The Supreme Court, American Eugenics, and the Sterilization of Carrie Buck*. New York: Penguin Books, 2016.

Columbus, Christopher. *The Four Voyages of Christopher Columbus*. New York: Penguin Books, 1969.

Columbus, Ferdinand. *Life of the Admiral Christopher Columbus*. London: Folio Society, 1960.

Commager, Henry Steele. *The Empire of Reason*. New York: Phoenix Press, 2001.

Conrad, Peter. *Imagining America*. New York: Oxford University Press, 1980.

Constitution Project's Task Force, *Detainee Treatment*. Washington, DC: Constitutional Project, 2013.

Cooper, Jon Milton. *Breaking the Heart of the World: Woodrow Wilson and the Fight for the League of Nations*. Cambridge: Cambridge University Press, 2001.

Cornell, Paul. *Canada, Unity in Diversity*. Toronto, ON: Holt, Rinehart and Winston, 1967.

Cott, Nancy. *The Grounding of Modern Feminism*. New Haven, CT: Yale University Press.

Countryman, Edward. *What Did the Constitution Mean to Early Americans?* New York: St. Martin's Press, 1999.

Crevécoeur, J. Hector St. John. *Letters from an American Farmer*. New York: Dover Publications, 2005.

Croly, Herbert. *The Promise of American Life*. Cambridge, MA: Harvard University Press, 1965.

Cumings, Bruce. *The Korean War: A History*. New York: Modern Library, 2010.

Daniels, Roger. *Not Like Us: Immigrants and Minorities in America, 1890-1924*. Chicago, IL: Ivan Dee, 1997.

Degler, Carl. *In Search of Human Nature: The Decline and Revival of Darwinism in American Social Thought*. New York: Oxford University Press, 1992.

Delgado, Jaimé. *Introducción á la historia de América*. Madrid, 1957.

DeCaro, Louis. *Freedom's Dawn: The Last Days of John Brown in Virginia*. Lanham, MD: Rowman and Littlefield, 2015.

Deloria, Vine. *We Talk, You Listen*. New York: Dell, 1974.

Descartes, René. *The Philosophical Writings*. Cambridge: Cambridge University Press, 1985.

Dewey, John. "Force and Coercion." In *The Middle Works*, vol. 10, 246-52. Carbondale, IL: Southern Illinois University Press, 1980.

Dilke, Oswald and Margaret Dilke. "Ptolemy's Geography and the New World." In *Early Images of the Americas,* 238-86. Tucson, AZ: University of Arizona Press, 1993.

Douglas, Ann. *The Feminization of American Culture.* New York: Farrar, Straus and Giroux, 1977.

Dreisbach, Daniel. *Thomas Jefferson and the Wall of Separation between Church and State.* New York: New York University Press. 2003.

Du Bois, W. E. B. *The Souls of Black Folk.* New York: Dover Publications, 2012.

———. *Black Reconstruction in America: An Essay toward a History of the Part that Black Folk Played in Reconstructing Democracy, 1860-1880.* New York: Oxford University Press, 2014.

Frederick Douglass, "Oration in Memory of Abraham Lincoln," April, 14, 1876. In *Inaugural Ceremonies of the Memorial Monument to Abraham Lincoln.* St. Louis, MO, 1876, 16-26.

———. *Narrative of the Life of Frederick Douglass.* Cambridge, MA: Harvard University Press, 1967.

———. *Selected Speeches and Writings.* Edited by Philip Foner. Chicago, IL: Lawrence Hill Books, 1999.

D'Souza, Dinesh. *America: Imagine a World Without Her*. Chicago, IL: Regnery, 2014.

Edwards, Jonathan. "The Latter-Day Glory is Probably to Begin in America," in *God's New Israel: Religious Interpretations of American Destiny*, edited by Donald Cherry, 55-59. Englewood Cliffs, NJ: Prentice Hall, 1971.

Elkins, Stanley. *Slavery: A Problem in American Institutional and Intellectual Life*. New York: Universal Library, 1959.

Elliot, Emory. *Power and the Pulpit in Puritan New England*. Princeton, NJ: Princeton University Press, 1975.

Elliot, John. *Spain and its World, 1500-1700*. New Haven, CT: Yale University Press, 1990.

Ellis, Joseph. *The Quartet: Orchestrating the Second American Revolution, 1783-1789*. New York: Knopf, 2015.

Enriquez, Juan. *The Untied States of America*. New York: Crown, 2002.

Erikson, Kai. *Wayward Pilgrims: A Study in the Sociology of Deviance*. New York: Macmillan, 1966.

Eustace, Nicole. *1812: War and the Passions of Patriotism*. Philadelphia, PA: University of Pennsylvania Press, 2012.

Fallows, James. "Obama on Exceptionalism." *Atlantic Monthly*, April 4, 2009.

Fanning, Richard. *Peace and Disarmament: Naval Rivalry and Arms Control, 1922-1933*. Lexington, KY: University of Kentucky Press, 1995.

Faulks, Sebastian. *Birdsong: A Novel of Love and War*. New York: Vintage Books, 1997.

Fehrenbacher, Don. *The Dred Scott Case: Its Significance in American Law and Politics*. New York: Oxford University Press, 1978.

———. *Collected Works of Abraham Lincoln*. New York: Library of America, 1989.

Fernández-Armesto, Felipe. *Amerigo*. New York: Random House, 2007.

———. *The Americas: A Hemispheric History*. New York: Modern Library, 2009.

Foner, Eric. *A Short History of Reconstruction, 1863-1877*. New York: Harper, 1988.

———. *The Fiery Trial: Abraham Lincoln and American Slavery*. New York: W. W. Norton, 2011.

Foner, Philip Sheldon. *The Spanish-Cuban-American War and the Birth of American Imperialism, 1895-1902*. New York: Monthly Review, 1972.

Foote, Thelma Wills. *Black and White Manhattan: The History of Racial Formation in Colonial New York*. New York: Oxford University Press, 2004.

Francis, Diane. *Merger of the Century: Why Canada and America Should Become One Country*. New York: Harper Collins, 2013.

Frazier, E. Franklin. *The Negro Family in the United States*. Chicago, IL: University of Chicago Press, 1939.

Freidel, Frank. *The Splendid Little War*. Boston, MA: Little, Brown and Company, 1958.

Fund, John. "Is Canada Now More American than America?" *National Review*, September 5, 2014.

Fussell, Paul. *The Great War and Modern Memory.* New York: Oxford University Press, 1975.

Gallup, George and Jim Castelli. *The People's Religion: American Faith in the Nineties.* New York: Macmillan, 1989.

Genovese, Eugene. *Roll, Jordan, Roll: The World the Slaves Made.* New York: Vintage Books, 1970.

Gill, A. A. *To America with Love.* New York: Simon and Schuster, 2013.

Glendon, Mary Ann. *Rights Talk: The Impoverishment of Political Discourse.* New York: Free Press, 1993.

Gopnik, Alison. *The Philosophical Baby: What Children's Minds Tell Us about Truth, Love, and the Meaning of Life.* New York: Farrar, Straus and Giroux, 2009.

Grant, Madison. *The Passing of the Great Race; or, The Racial Basis of European History.* New York: C. Scribner's Sons, 1916.

Grant, Ulysses S. *Personal Memoirs of U. S. Grant.* New York: Library of America, 1990.

Grant, Susan Mary. *A Concise History of the United States of America.* Cambridge: Cambridge University Press, 2012.

Greenberg, Amy. *A Wicked War: Polk, Clay, Lincoln, and the 1846 Invasion of Mexico.* New York: Random House, 2012.

Guelzo, Allen. *Fateful Lightning: A New History of the Civil War and Reconstruction.* New York: Oxford University Press, 2012.

Gustafson, Thomas. *Representative Words: Politics, Literature, and the American Language, 1776-1865.* Cambridge: Cambridge University Press, 1992.

Gutman, Herbert. *The Black Family in Slavery and Freedom, 1750-1925.* New York: Pantheon Books, 1976.

Guyatt, Nicholas. *Bind Us Apart: How Enlightened Americans Invented Racial Segregation.* New York: Basic Books, 2016.

Hahn, Steven. *A Nation without Borders: The United States and its World in an Age of Civil Wars, 1830-1910.* New York: Viking Books, 2016.

Hamburger, Philip. *Separation of Church and State.* Cambridge, MA: Harvard University Press, 2004.

Hanke, Lewis. *The Spanish Struggle for Justice in the Conquest of America.* Philadelphia, PA: University of Pennsylvania Press, 1949.

Hanke, Lewis, ed. *Do the Americas Have a Common History?* New York: Knopf, 1964.

Harding, Vincent. *There Is a River: The Black Struggle for Freedom in America.* New York: Mariner, 1993.

Hatch, Nathan. *The Sacred Cause of Liberty.* New Haven, CT: Yale University Press, 1977.

Hathaway, Oona and Scott Shapiro. *The Internationalists: How a Radical Plan to Outlaw War Remade the World.* New York: Simon and Schuster, 2017.

Henderson, Timothy. *A Glorious Defeat: Mexico and its War with the United States.* New York: Hill and Wang, 2007.

Herberg, Will. *Protestant, Catholic, Jew: An Essay in American Religious Sociology.* Garden City, NY: Doubleday, 1955.

Hickey, Donald. *The War of 1812: A Forgotten Conflict.* Chicago, IL: University of Illinois Press, 1990.

Hobsbawm, Eric. *On Empire, America, War, and Global Supremacy*. New York: New Press, 2008.

Hodgson, Godfrey. *The Myth of American Exceptionalism*. New Haven, CT: Yale University Press, 2009.

Hoffman, Elizabeth Cobbs. *American Umpire*. Cambridge, MA: Harvard University Press, 2013,

Hofstadter, Richard. *The Age of Reform*. New York: Vintage Books, 1960

————. *Anti-Intellectualism in American Life*. New York: Knopf, 1963.

————. *The American Political Tradition and the Men Who Made It*. New York: Vintage Books, 1989.

Hoganson, Kristin. *Fighting for American Manhood: How Gender Politics Provoked the Spanish-American and Philippine-American Wars*. New Haven, CT: Yale University Press, 1998.

Hogeland, William. *Inventing American History*. Cambridge, MA: MIT Press, 2009.

Holter, Woody. *Unruly Americans and the Origin of the Constitution*. New York: Hill and Wang, 2007.

Honour, Hugh. *The European Vision of America*. Kent, OH: Kent State University Press, 1975.

Hoopes, Townsend and Douglas Brinkley. *FDR and the Creation of the U.N.* New Haven, CT: Yale University Press, 1997.

Hopkins, James and Mary Hargreaves. *Papers of Henry Clay*. Lexington, KY: University of Kentucky Press, 1959.

Horn, James. *A Kingdom Strange: The Brief and Tragic History of Roanoke*. New York: Basic Books, 2010.

Horne, Gerald. *The Counter-Revolution of 1776: Slave Resistance and the Origin of the U.S.A.* New York: New York University Press, 2014.

Humphrey, John. *The Inter-American System: A Canadian View.* Toronto, ON: Macmillan, 1942.

Hunt, Michael and Steven Levine. *Arc of Empire: America's Wars in Asia from the Philippines to Vietnam.* Charlotte, NC: University of North Carolina Press, 2012.

Huntington, Samuel. *Who Are We? The Challenge to America's Identity.* New York: Simon and Schuster, 2005.

Hutton, Will. *A Declaration of Interdependence: Why America Should Join the World.* New York: W. W. Norton, 2003.

Ignatieff, Michael. *Human Rights as Politics and Idolatry.* Princeton, NJ: Princeton University Press, 2001.

Jacobs, Jaap. *The Colony of New Netherland: A Dutch Settlement in Seventeenth-Century America.* Ithaca, NY: Cornell University Press, 2009.

James, Henry. *The American Scene.* Bloomington, IN: Indiana University Press, 1968.

Jasanoff, Maya. *Liberty's Exiles: American Loyalists in the Revolutionary World.* New York: Knopf, 2011.

Jefferson, Thomas. *Portable Thomas Jefferson.* New York: Penguin Books, 1977.

———. *Notes on the State of Virginia.* Charleston, SC: CreateSpace, 2011.

———. *Jefferson Bible: The Life and Morals of Jesus of Nazareth.* Charleston, SC: CreateSpace, 2014.

Jenkins, Philip. *The Great and Holy War: How World War I Became a Religious Crusade.* New York: HarperOne, 2014.

Jennings, Francis. *The Invasion of America: Indians, Colonialism, and the Cant of Conquest.* Charlotte, NC: University of North Carolina Press, 1975.

Jillson, Cal. *Pursuing the American Dream: Opportunity and Exclusion over Four Centuries.* Lawrence, KS: University of Kansas, 2004.

Jones, Gregg. *Honor in the Dust: Theodore Roosevelt, War in the Philippines, and the Rise and Fall of America's Imperial Dream.* New York: New American Library, 2012.

Jordan, Winthrop. "Familial Politics and the Killing of the King, 1776," *Journal of American History* 60 (September 1973): 294-308.

Josephy, Alvin. *Now that the Buffalo's Gone: A Study of the American Indian.* Norman, OK: University of Oklahoma Press, 1984.

Kael, Paul. *Reeling.* Boston, MA: Little, Brown and Company, 1977.

Kaplan, Benjamin. *Divided by Faith: Religious Conflict and the Practice of Tolerance in Early Modern Europe.* Cambridge, MA: Harvard University Press, 2007.

Kaplan, Robert. *An Empire Wilderness: Travels into America's Future.* New York: Random House, 1998.

Kaplan, Sidney and Emma Nogrady Kaplan. *The Black Presence in the Era of the American Revolution.* Amherst, MA: University of Massachusetts Press, 1989.

Karier, Clarence. *Roots of Crisis.* New York: Macmillan, 1973.

Karp, Walter. *Politics of War: The Story of Two World Wars which Altered Forever the Political Life of the American Republic.* New York: Harper and Row, 1979.

Kendi, Ibram. *Stamped from the Beginning: The Definitive History of Racist Ideas in America.* New York: Perseus, 2016.

Keegan, John. *A History of Warfare.* New York: Knopf, 1993.

———. *The First World War.* New York: Vintage Books, 2000.

———. *The Second World War.* New York: Penguin Books, 2005.

Kennan, George. "The Sources of Soviet Conduct," *Foreign Affairs* 25(July 1947): 566-82.

———. *American Diplomacy, 1900-1950.* Chicago, IL: University of Chicago Press, 1951.

———. *The Nuclear Delusion: Soviet-American Relations in the Atomic Age.* New York: Pantheon Books, 1982.

———. "Morality and Foreign Policy," *Foreign Affairs* 64(Winter 1985): 205-18.

Kesler, Charles. *I Am the Change: Barack Obama and the Future of Liberalism.* New York: Harper Collins, 2012.

King, Martin Luther Jr. *Strength to Love.* New York: Harper and Row, 1963.

Kinzer, Stephen. *Overthrow: America's Century of Regime Change from Hawaii to Iraq.* New York: Henry Holt and Company, 2006.

Kolodny, Annette. *The Land before Her: Fantasy and Experience of the American Frontier, 1630-1860.* Chapel Hill, NC: University of North Carolina Press, 1984.

Konig, Hans. *Columbus: His Enterprise*. New York: Monthly Press, 1976.

Kouwenhoven, Atlee. *The Beer Can by the Highway: Essays in What's American about America*. Baltimore, MD: Johns Hopkins University Press, 1988.

Krushchev, Sergei. "The Thwarted Promise of the 13 Days," *New York Times*, February 4, 2001.

Kupperman, Karen Ordah. *The Jamestown Project*. Cambridge, MA: Harvard University Press, 2007.

Kuznick, Peter and Oliver Stone. *The Untold History of the United States*. New York: Gallery Books, 2012.

Langley, Lester. *America in the Americas: The United States in the Western Hemisphere*. Athens, GA: University of Georgia Press, 1989.

———. "The Two Americas." In *Whose America?*, edited by Virginia Bouvier, 23-33. Westport, CT: Praeger, 2001.

Larson, Edward. *Summer for the Gods: The Scopes Trial and America's Continuing Debate over Science and Religion*. New York: Basic Books, 2006.

Las Casas, Bartolomé de. *The Log of Christopher Columbus: First Voyage to America in 1492*. New York: Linnet Book, 1989.

———. *The Devastation of the Indies*. Baltimore, MD: Johns Hopkins University Press, 1992.

———. *Witness: Writings of Bartolomé de Las Casas*. New York: Orbis Books, 1992.

Latimer, Jon. *1812: War with America*. Cambridge, MA: Harvard University Press, 2007.

Lawrence, William. "The Relation of Wealth to Morals." In *God's New Israel*, ed. Conrad Cherry, 244-54. Englewood Cliffs, NJ: Prentice Hall, 1971

Lester, Toby. *The Fourth Part of the World: The Race to the Ends of the Earth and the Epic Story of the Map That Gave America Its Name*. New York: Free Press, 2009.

Leuchtenberg, William. "Progressivism and Imperialism: the Progressive Movement and American Foreign Policy, 1898-1916." *Mississippi Valley Historical Review* 39 (1952): 483-504.

Levine, Steve and Michael Hunt. *Arc of Empire: America's Wars in Asia from the Philippines to Vietnam*. Chapel Hill, NC: North Carolina Press, 2012.

Lewis, Bernard. *Cultures in Conflict: Christians, Muslims, and Jews in the Age of Discovery*. New York: Oxford University Press, 1996.

Lewis, Martin and Kären Wigen. *The Myth of Continents*. Berkeley, CA: University of California Press, 1997.

Lilla, Mark. "The Tea Party Jacobins," *New York Review of Books* 57(May 27, 2010).

Limbaugh, Rush. *Rush Revere and the First Patriots: Time Travel Adventures with Exceptional Americans*. New York: Simon and Schuster, 2014.

Limerick, Patricia. "The Adventures of the Frontier in the Twentieth Century." In *The Frontier in American Culture*, 67-102. Berkeley, CA: University of California Press, 1994.

Lincoln, Abraham. *Collected Works of Abraham Lincoln*. Edited by Roy Basler. New Brunswick, NJ: Rutgers University Press, 1953.

———. *Abraham Lincoln: His Speeches and Writings*, ed. Roy Basler. Boston, MA: Da Capo Press, 2001.

Lind, Michael. *The Next American Nation: The New Nationalism and the Fourth American Revolution*. New York: Free Press, 1995.

Lippmann, Walter. *Drift and Mastery*. Madison, WI: University of Wisconsin Press, 1914.

———. *U.S. Foreign Policy: Shield of the Republic*. Boston, MA: Little, Brown and Company, 1943.

———. *The Cold War*. New York: Harper and Brothers, 1947.

Lipset, Seymour. *Continental Divide: The Values and Institutions of the U.S. and Canada*. New York: Routledge, 1990.

———. *American Exceptionalism: A Double-Edged Sword*. New York: W. W. Norton, 1997.

Locke, John. *The Second Treatise on Civil Government*. Buffalo, NY: Prometheus Books, 1986.

Logevall, Frederick. *Choosing War: The Lost Chance for Peace in the Escalation of War in Vietnam*. Berkeley, CA: University of California Press, 1999.

Luce, Henry. "The American Century," *Life*, February 17, 1941.

Luker, Ralph. "Garry Wills and the New Debate over the Declaration of Independence," *The Virginia Quarterly Review* 46 (Spring 1980): 244-61.

Lundestad, Geir. *The Rise and Decline of the American "Empire"*. New York: Oxford University Press, 2012.

Luther Standing Bear. *My Indian Boyhood*. Lincoln, NE: Bison Books, 2006.

McArthur, John. *Second Front: Censorship and Propaganda in the 1991 Gulf War*. Berkeley, CA: University of California Press, 2004.

Macdonald, Dwight. *The Responsibility of Peoples and Other Essays in Political Criticism*. New York: Gollancz, 1957.

McGerr, Michael. *A Fierce Discontent: Rise and Fall of the Progressive Movement in America, 1870-1920*. New York: Free Press, 2003.

McPherson, James. *Battle Cry of Freedom*. New York: Oxford University Press, 2013.

Madison, James. *The Papers of James Madison*. Charlottesville, VA: University of Virginia, 1984-92.

Mahan, Alfred Thayer. *The Influence of Sea Power upon History*. Boston, MA: Little, Brown and Company, 1890.

Maier, Pauline. *American Scripture: Making the Declaration of Independence*. New York: Knopf, 1997.

Malcolm X and George Breitman. *Malcolm X Speaks: Selected Speeches and Statements*. New York: Random House, 1988.

Martí, José. *Our America: Writings on Latin America and the Struggle for Cuban Independence*, edited by Philip Foner. New York: Monthly Press Review, 1977.

Masur, Louis. *The Civil War: A Concise History*. New York: Oxford University Press, 2011.

Mayhew, Jonathan. *A Sermon Preached in the Audience of his Excellency William Shirley*. Ithaca, NY: Cornell University Press, 2009.

Mead, Walter Russell and Richard Leone, *Special Providence: American Foreign Policy and How It Changed the World*. New York: Routledge, 2002

Midgley, Mary. *Beast and Man: The Roots of Human Nature*. Ithaca, NY: Cornell University Press, 1978.

Middlebrooks, Martin. *The First Day on the Somme*. New York: Penguin Books, 1971.

Mill, John Stuart. "A Few Words on Non-Intervention." In *Foreign Policy Perceptions* 8. London: Libertarian Alliance, 1859.

Miller, Stuart. *Benevolent Assimilation: The American Conquest of the Philippines, 1899-1903*. New Haven, CT: Yale University Press, 1984.

Millis, Walter. *Road to War: America, 1914-1917*. New York: Houghton Mifflin, 1935.

Moran, Gabriel. *Education toward Adulthood*. New York: Paulist Press, 1979.

More, Thomas. *Utopia*. New York: Harmony Books, 1978.

Morgan, Edmund. *The Puritan Family*. New York: Harper Torch, 1966.

Morgenthau, Hans. "Human Rights and Foreign Policy," in *Moral Dimensions of American Foreign Policy*. Edited by K. W. Thompson, 341-48. New York: Transaction Publishers, 1994.

————. *Politics among Nations*. New York: McGraw Hill, 2005.

Morrison, Samuel Eliot. *Admiral of the Ocean Sea: A Life of Christopher Columbus*. Boston, MA: Little, Brown and Company, 1942.

Mourton, George. *Mourt's Relation*. Boston: Wiggin, 1865.

Moynihan, Daniel Patrick. *The Negro Family: The Case for National Action*. Cambridge, MA: MIT Press, 1970.

Myrdal, Gunnar. "A Worried America," *Christian Century*, December 14, 1977, 1161-66.

Newman, Louise Michelle. *White Women's Rights: The Racial Origins of Feminism in the United States*. New York: Oxford University Press, 1999.

Niebuhr, Reinhold. *Moral Man and Immoral Society: A Study in Ethics and Politics*. New York: Charles Scribner's Sons, 1932.

———. *Man's Nature and His Communities*. New York: Charles Scribner's Sons, 1965.

Noonan, John. *A Church That Can Change and Cannot Change*. Notre Dame, IN: University of Notre Dame Press, 2005.

Norman, Michael and Elizabeth Norman. *Tears in the Darkness: The Story of the Bataan Death March and its Aftermath*. New York: Farrar, Straus and Giroux, 2009.

Offe, Claus. *Reflections on America: Tocqueville, Weber & Adorno in the United States*. Cambridge, MA: Polity Press, 2005.

O'Gorman, Edmundo. *The Invention of America*. Bloomington, IN: Indiana University Press, 1961.

One Nation, Many Peoples. Albany: New York State Social Studies Committee, 1991.

O'Sullivan, John. "The True Title." In *God's New Israel*. Edited by Donald Cherry, 128-30. Englewood Cliffs, NJ: Prentice Hall, 1971.

Oviedo, Gonzales Fernandez de. "General and Natural History of the Indies." In *Four Voyages of Christopher Columbus*. 27-36. New York: Penguin Books, 1963.

Packer, George. "Peace and War," *New Yorker*, December 2009: 45-46.

Paz, Octavio. "América en plural y singular," *Vuelta* 194 (January 1993): 11.

Perez, Louis. *Cuba under the Platt Amendment.* Pittsburgh, PA: University of Pittsburg Press, 1986.

————. *Cuba and the United States Ties of Singular Intimacy.* Athens, GA: University of Georgia Press, 1997.

Perlstein, Rick. *The Invisible Bridge: The Fall of Nixon and the Rise of Reagan.* New York: Simon and Schuster, 2014.

Philbrick, Nathaniel. *Mayflower: A Story of Courage, Community, and War.* New York: Viking Books, 2006.

Philipott, William. *Bloody Victory: The Sacrifice on the Somme and the Making of the Twentieth Century.* Boston, MA: Little, Brown and Company, 2009.

Pius XII. "Destiny of Humanity in US Hands," *Colliers Magazine,* December 29, 1945.

Potter, Andrew. "Introduction." In *Lament for a Nation: The Defeat of Canadian Nationalism.* By George Grant, 1-lxviii. Montrea, Q: McGill-Queen's University Press, 2005.

Pratt, Julius. *American Business and the Spanish-American War.* New York, Quadrangle, 1934.

————. *Expansionists of 1898: The Acquisition of Hawaii and the Spanish Islands.* New York: Quadrangle, 1936.

Putin, Vladimir. "A Plea for Caution from Russia," *New York Times,* September 11, 2013.

Qutb, Sayyid. "The America I Have Seen." In *The Sayyid Qutb Reader.* New York: Routledge, 2008.

Raboteau, Albert. *The "Invisible Institution" in the Antebellum South.* New York: Oxford University Press, 2004.

Rakove, Jack. "The Perils of Originalism." In *What Did the Constitution Mean for Early Americans.* Edited by Edward Countryman, 141-63. Boston, MA: Bedford, 1999.

————. *Revolutionaries: A New History of the Invention of America.* Boston: Houghton Mifflin Harcourt, 2010.

Records of the Federal Convention of 1787. New Haven, CT: Yale University Press, 1937.

Reichlin, Lucrezia. "The Marshall Plan Reconsidered," In *Europe's Postwar Recovery.* Edited by Barry Eichingreen, 29-67. Cambridge: Cambridge University Press, 1995.

Reid, T. R. *The United States of Europe: The New Superpower and the End of American Supremacy.* New York: Penguin Books, 2004.

"Responsibility to Protect:" *The Report of the International Commission on Intervention and State Sovereignty.* New York: IDRC Books, 2002.

Reynolds, David. *America, Empire of Liberty.* New York: Basic Books, 2009.

Richardson, James, ed. *A Compilation of the Messages and Papers of the Presidents, 1789-1902.* Washington, DC: Bureau of National Literature, 1903.

Rodgers, Daniel. *Atlantic Crossings: Social Politics in a Progressive Age.* Cambridge, MA: Harvard University Press, 1998.

Rolfe, John. *A True Relation of the State of Virginia.* New Haven, CT: Yale University Press, 1951.

Ross, Edward. *The Old World in the New.* New York: The Century Company, 1914.

Roosevelt, Theodore. *Campaigns and Controversies,* edited by Herman Hagedorn. New York: Charles Scribner's Sons, 1926.

————. *American Ideals, the Strenuous Life, Realizable Ideals.* In *The Works of Theodore Roosevelt.* Edited by Herman Hagedorn. New York: Charles Scribner's Sons, 1926.

Rousseau, Jean-Jacques. *The Social Contract.* New York: Washington Square Press, 1967.

————. *Emile; or, On Education.* New York: Basic Books, 1962.

Rubin, Barry and Judith Cole Rubin. *Hating America: A History.* New York: Oxford University Press, 2004.

Russ, William Adam. *The Hawaiian Republic(1894-1898) and its Struggle to Win Annexation.* Selinsgrove, PA: Susquehanna University Press, 1961.

Russell, Jeffrey Burton. *Inventing the Flat Earth: Columbus and Modern Historians.* New York: Praeger, 1991.

Sahagun, *General History of the Things of New Spain.* Edited by Arthur Anderson and Charles Dibble. Salt Lake City, UT: University of Utah Press, 1950-82.

Sánchez, Luis-Alberto. "A New Interpretation of the History of America," *Hispanic American Historical Review* 23 (1943): 441-56.

Schaff, Philip. *America: A Sketch of its Political, Social, and Religious Character.* Cambridge, MA: Harvard University Press, 1961 (1855).

Scheman, L. Ronald. *Greater America: A New Partnership for the Americas.* New York: New York University Press, 2003.

Schlesinger, Stephen. *Act of Creation: The Founding of the United Nations.* New York: Basic Books, 2003.

Schroeder, John. *Mr. Polk's War: American Opposition and Dissent, 1846-1848.* Madison, WI: University of Wisconsin Press, 1973.

Schwarz, Benjamin. "The Real Cuban Missile Crisis," *Atlantic Monthly,* January/February, 2013: 73-81.

Schweikart, Larry and Michael Allen. *A Patriot's History of the United States: From Columbus's Great Discovery to the War on Terrorism.* New York: Penguin Books, 2004.

Scott, F. R. *Canada and the United States.* Boston, MA: World Peace Foundation, 1941.

Seelye, John. *The River in Early American Life and Literature.* New York: Oxford University Press, 1971.

Segal, Charles. *Puritans, Indians & Manifest Destiny.* New York: Putnam, 1977.

Seidman, Louis Michael. *On Constitutional Disobedience.* New York: Oxford University Press, 2013.

Shirer, William. *Berlin Diary: The Journal of a Foreign Correspondent, 1934-1941.* New York: Knopf, 1941.

Shorto, Russell. *The Island at the Center of the World: The Epic Story of Dutch Missionaries and the Forgotten Colony that Shaped America.* New York: Vintage Books, 2005.

———. "Founding Fathers," *New York Times Magazine,* February 14, 2010: 32-47.

Singletary, Otis. *The Mexican War.* Chicago, IL: University of Chicago Press, 1960.

Smith, John, *History of Virginia: A Selection*. Edited by David Freeman Hawke. Indianapolis, IN: Bobbs-Merrill, 1970.

———. *A True Relation of Virginia*. Ann Arbor, MI: ProQuest, 2010.

Smith, Michael Joseph. *Realist Thought from Weber to Kissinger*. Baton Rouge, LA: Louisiana State University Press, 1990.

Smith, Tony. *America's Mission: The United States and the Worldwide Struggle for Democracy in the Twentieth Century*. Princeton, NJ: Princeton University Press, 1994.

Smith-Rosenberg, Carroll. *This Violent Empire: The Birth of American National Identity*. Chapel Hill, NC: University of North Carolina Press, 2010.

Sosa, Lionel. *The Americano Dream: How Latinos Can Achieve Success in Business and in Life*. New York: Dutton, 1998.

Stack, Carol. *All Our Kin: Strategy for Survival in a Black Community*. New York: Harper, 1975.

Stangneth, Bettina. *Eichmann Before Jerusalem: The Unexamined Life of a Mass Murderer*. New York: Knopf, 2014.

Stavans, Ilan. *A Most Imperfect Union*. New York: Basic Books, 2014.

Stephens, Alexander. "Cornerstone Address, March 21, 1861." In *The Rebellion Record*, vol. 1. edited by Frank Moore, 44-46. New York: Putnam, 1862.

Stern, Sheldon. *The Cuban Missile Crisis in American Memory: Myths versus Reality*. Stanford, CA: Stanford University Press, 2012.

Stern, Philip Van Doren. *The Pocket Book of America*. New York: Pocket Books, 1942.

Stiglitz, Joseph. *The Euro: How a Common Currency Threatens the Future of Europe.* New York: W. W. Norton, 2016 (1992).

Stone, I. F. *The Hidden History of the Korean War.* New York: Monthly Press, 1952.

Strong, Josiah. *Our Country: Its Possible Future and Its Present Crisis.* New York: American Home Mission Society, 1885.

———. *The Twentieth-Century City.* New York: Forgotten Books, 2012.

Stowe, Harriet. *The Annotated Uncle Tom's Cabin.* Edited by Henry Lewis Gates. New York: W. W. Norton, 2007.

Taft, William Howard. *The United States and Peace.* New York: Forgotten Books, 2012.

Taylor, Alan. *The Civil War of 1812: American Citizens, British Subjects, Irish Rebels, & Indian Allies.* New York: Knopf, 2010.

———. *The Internal Enemy: Slavery and War in Virginia, 1772-1832.* New York: W. W. Norton, 2014.

Taylor, Telford. *The Nuremberg Trials.* New York: Knopf, 1992.

TePaske, John, ed. *Three American Empires.* New York: Harper and Row, 1967.

Terkel, Studs. *"The Good War:" An Oral History of World War II.* New York: New Press, 1997.

Thomas, Evan. *The War Lovers: Roosevelt, Lodge, Hearst, and the Rush to Empire.* Boston, MA: Little, Brown and Company, 2010.

———. *Ike's Bluff: President Eisenhower's Secret Battle to Save the World.* Boston, MA: Little, Brown and Company, 2012.

Thompson, Charles. *Is the United States Worth Saving: For a More Perfect Union*. Indianapolis, IN: Xlibris, 2013.

Thompson, James, Peter Stanley, and John Curtis Perry. *Sentimental Imperialists: The American Experience in East Asia*. New York: Harper and Row, 1981.

Thompson, Nicholas. *The Hawk and the Dove: Paul Nitze, George Kennan, and the History of the Cold War*. New York: Picador, 2010.

Thucydides. *The Peloponnesian War*. New York: Cassell, 1962.

Tocqueville, Alexis de. *Democracy in America*. Edited by Henry Reeve. New York: Bantam, 2000.

Todorov, Tzvetan. *The Conquest of America*. New York: Harper and Row, 1984.

———. *The Morals of History*. Minneapolis, MN: University of Minnesota Press, 1995.

Toulmin, Stephen. *Cosmopolis: The Hidden Agenda of Modernity*. Chicago, IL: University of Chicago Press, 1990.

Trollope, Frances. *Domestic Manners of the Americans*. New York: Knopf, 1949 (1832).

Trump, Donald and Tony Schwarz. *The Art of the Deal*. New York: Random House, 1987.

Turner, Frederick Jackson. *The Frontier in American History*. New York: Holt, Rinehart and Winston, 1962.

Twain, Mark. "To the Person Sitting in Darkness." *North American Review* 172 (February 1901): 109-117.

Twomey, Steve. *Countdown to Pearl Harbor.* New York: Simon and Schuster, 2016.

Ugarte, Manuel. *The Destiny of a Continent.* New York: AMS Press, 1925.

Vespucci, Amerigo. *Mundus Novus.* Princeton, NJ: Princeton University Press, 1916.

Waldman, Michael. *The Second Amendment: A Biography.* New York: Simon and Schuster, 2014.

Walker, David. *One Continental Cry: David Walker's Appeal to the Colored Citizens of the World, 1829-1830.* Edited by Herbert Apthecker. New York: Humanities Press, 1965.

Warren, Joseph. *Oration Delivered at the Request of the Town of Boston to Commemorate the Evening of the Fifth of March, 1770.* Boston, MA: W.T. Clap, 1807.

Washington, George. *The Papers of George Washington.* Edited by W. W. Abbot and others. Charlottesville, VA: University Press of Virginia, 1987.

Webber, Thomas. *Deep Like the Rivers.* New York: W. W. Norton, 1980.

Weber, Max. *The Protestant Ethic and the Spirit of Capitalism.* New York: Penguin Books, 2002.

Webster, Noah. *On Being an American: Selected Writings, 1783-1828.* Edited by Homer Babbidge Jr. New York: Praeger, 1967.

Wheelan, Joseph. *Invading Mexico: America's Continental Dream and the Mexican War, 1846-1848.* New York: Public Affairs, 2007.

Whitaker, Arthur. *The Western Hemisphere Idea: Its Rise and Decline.* Ithaca, NY: Cornell University Press, 1954.

White, E. B. "The Wild Flag." Editorial from the *New Yorker* on federal world government. Boston, MA: Houghton Mifflin, 1946.

White, Richard and Patricia Limerick. *The Frontier in American Culture.* Berkeley, CA: University of California Press, 1994.

White, Richard. *The Republic for Which It Stands: The United States during Reconstruction and the Gilded Age.* New York: Oxford University Press, 2017.

Whitman, James. *Hitler's American Model: The United States and the Making of Nazi Race Law.* Princeton, NJ: Princeton University Press, 2017.

Wills, Garry. *Inventing America: Jefferson's Declaration of Independence.* New York: Warner Books, 2002.

———. *Lincoln at Gettysburg: The Words that Remade America.* New York: Simon and Schuster, 2006.

Wilson, Woodrow. *Public Papers of Woodrow Wilson.* New York: Harper Brothers, 1925.

Wittgenstein, Ludwig. *Philosophical Investigations.* New York: Macmillan, 1953.

Wollstonecraft, Mary. *A Vindication of the Rights of Woman.* Edited by Charles Hagelman, Jr. New York: W. W. Norton, 1967.

Wood, Michael. *America in the Movies.* New York: Dell, 1975

Wood, Gordon. *The Creation of the American Republic.* New York: W. W. Norton, 1972.

———. *Empire of Liberty: A History of the Early Republic, 1789-1815.* New York: Oxford University Press, 2009.

———. *The Idea of America.* New York: Penguin Books, 2011.

Woodard, Colin. *American Nations: A History of the Eleven Regional Cultures of North America.* New York: Viking, 2011.

Wright, James. *Those Who Have Bourne the Battle: America's Wars and Those Who Have Fought Them.* New York: Public Affairs, 2012.

Zimmerman, Jonathan. *Whose America? Culture Wars in the Public Schools.* Cambridge, MA: Harvard University Press, 2002.

Zimring, Franklin. *The City That Became Safe: New York's Lessons for Urban Crime and Its Control.* New York: Oxford University Press, 2012.

Zinn, Howard. *A People's History of the United States.* New York: Harper, 2001.

Index

Jagland, Thorbjorn, 311
James, D. Clayton, 270
James, William, 229
Jamestown, 70–74
Jay Treaty (1794), 122–123
Jefferson, Thomas, 21, 72, 85, 91,
    93–94, 96, 102, 105, 113, 123,
    131, 140, 141, 161, 317
Jewish, 208, 309, 313, 316, 318
Jewish-Christian misunderstanding,
    6–7
Jim Crow laws, 174
Joachim of Fiore, 47n86
Johnson, Andrew, 171
Johnson, Lyndon, 148, 282–284, 285,
    286, 316
Jujia Ou, 201

K

Kael, Pauline, 289
Kearny, Stephen, 152
Keegan, John, 216
Kellogg, Frank, 224n543
Kennan, George, 220, 232, 239, 259–
    262, 263, 264, 265–266
Kennedy, John, 275, 276–277, 280,
    282, 321
Kennedy, Joseph, 237
Kent, Clark (fictional character), 234
Khrushchev, Nikita, 277, 278, 282
Kim Il Sung, 268
Kim Jong Un, 309
King, Martin Luther, Jr., 144, 280–
    281, 311
Kirkpatrick, Jeanne, 252
Kissinger, Henry, 263, 286, 287
Know Nothings (American Party),
    156–157
Korean War, 266–274, 321
Koretsky, Victor, 251
Kuznick, Peter, 3n3

L

La America (Lastarria), 17
labor unions, 182–183, 204, 208
LaFollette, Robert, 218
language
artistic speech, 9–10
meaning and context, 3–7
meaning and exclusion, 10–12
meaning and form, 8
offensive, 7
philosophical question of, 3
political speech, 8–9
US language, 12–16
Las Casas, Bartolomé de, 40, 48, 58,
    59–60, 61, 62
Lastarria, José Victorino, 17
Latimer, Jon, 121, 122
Latin America, 55–57
Le Monde, 295, 297n704, 330
League of Nations, 221, 222, 223,
    229, 249
Lee, Robert E., 168
Lemay, Curtis, 242, 249
Leo XIII (pope), 208
Lester, Toby, 54
Letter to Philomen (Paul), 142
Lexington, 88
Leyte, battle in gulf of, 243
liberty
as central concept of Protestant
    Christianity, 83
as distinguished from freedom, 66–69
and revolution, 83–90
Library of Congress, 51, 52
Liebling, A. J., 114
*Life and Voyages of Christopher
    Columbus* (Irving), 35
Liliuokalani (queen), 186
Limerick, Patricia, 184
Lincoln, Abraham, 68, 146, 156,
    158, 159, 160, 161, 162–163,